Insurance Administration
Fourth Edition

ONLINE COURSE PORTAL

The LOMA 301 Course Portal, available online at www.LOMANET.org via your "My Learning" page, includes numerous multi-media features designed to reinforce and enhance your learning experience and help you prepare for the exam. Among these features are numerous "Learning Aids" that illustrate key concepts presented in the assigned course materials, the Test Preparation Guide's popular interactive Practice Questions and Sample Exam with answer feedback, and the "Top 10 Tough Topics" review of the most challenging topics in this course. If you are not already using the online Course Portal but would like access to the many additional study resources for this course, please follow the log-in instructions provided in your Enrollment Confirmation e-mail, or call 1-800-ASK-LOMA or e-mail education@loma.org for assistance.

LOMA (Life Office Management Association, Inc.)—an LL Global, Inc. company—is an international association founded in 1924. LOMA is committed to a business partnership with the worldwide members in the insurance and financial services industry to improve their management and operations through quality employee development, research, information sharing, and related products and services. Among LOMA's activities is the sponsorship of several self-study education programs leading to professional designations. These programs include the Fellow, Life Management Institute (FLMI) program and the Fellow, Financial Services Institute (FFSI) program. For more information on all of LOMA's education programs, please visit www.loma.org.

Statement of Purpose: LOMA Educational Programs Testing and Designations.

Examinations described in the LOMA Education and Training Catalog are designed solely to measure whether students have successfully completed the relevant assigned curriculum, and the attainment of the FLMI and other LOMA designations indicates only that all examinations in the given curriculum have been successfully completed. In no way shall a student's completion of a given LOMA course or attainment of the FLMI or other LOMA designation be construed to mean that LOMA in any way certifies that student's competence, training, or ability to perform any given task. LOMA's examinations are to be used solely for general educational purposes, and no other use of the examinations or programs is authorized or intended by LOMA. Furthermore, it is in no way the intention of the LOMA Curriculum and Examinations staff to describe the standard of appropriate conduct in any field of the insurance and financial services industry, and LOMA expressly repudiates any attempt to so use the curriculum and examinations. Any such assessment of student competence or industry standards of conduct should instead be based on independent professional inquiry and the advice of competent professional counsel.

Insurance Administration
Fourth Edition

Mary C. Bickley, J.D., FLMI, FFSI, CLU, AIRC, ACS, AIAA, PAHM, AAPA, ARA
Kristen L. Falk, FLMI, AAPA, ACS, AIAA, AIRC, ARA
Elizabeth A. Mulligan, FLMI, FLHC, PCS, PAHM, AAPA, AIRC, ARA, AIAA
Miriam A. Orsina, FLMI, PCS, AAPA, ARA, PAHM

LOMA Education and Training
Atlanta, Georgia
www.loma.org

Information in this text may have changed or been updated since its publication date. For current updates visit www.loma.org.

PROJECT TEAM:

Authors:	Mary C. Bickley, J.D., FLMI, FFSI, CLU, AIRC, ACS, AIAA, PAHM, AAPA, ARA
	Kristen L. Falk, FLMI, AAPA, ACS, AIAA, AIRC, ARA
	Elizabeth A. Mulligan, FLMI, FLHC, PCS, PAHM, AAPA, AIRC, ARA, AIAA
	Miriam A. Orsina, FLMI, PCS, AAPA, ARA, PAHM
Manuscript Editors:	Jo Ann Appleton, FLMI, PCS, ALHC, HIA, CEBS
	Harriett E. Jones, J.D., FLMI, ACS, AIRC
	Miriam A. Orsina, FLMI, PCS, AAPA, ARA, PAHM
Examinations Editor:	Jo Ann Appleton, FLMI, PCS, ALHC, HIA, CEBS
Project Manager:	Julia K. Wooley, FLMI, ACS, ALHC, HIA, MHP
Indexer:	Robert D. Land, FLMI, ACS
AVP, Marketing:	Paul Wilson
Lead Graphic Designer:	Marlene McAuley
Typesetters:	Allison Ayers-Molette
	Amy Stailey
Production Coordinator:	Amy Stailey
Product Sourcing Manager:	Carol A. Wiessner, ACS
Administrative Support:	Mamunah Carter

ISBN 978-1-57974-354-3

www.loma.org

Contents

Module 2: Underwriting

Module 3: Claim Administration

Module 4: Reinsurance

Chapter 11: Reinsurance Administration 229

Module 5: Customer Service

Chapter 12: Effective Customer Service......................... 255

Preface

Insurance Administration, Fourth Edition describes the principles and practices of individual and group life insurance administration. The text is divided into five modules:

- Module 1: Introduction to Insurance Administration (Chapters 1–3)

- Module 2: Underwriting (Chapters 4–7)

- Module 3: Claim Administration (Chapters 8–9)

- Module 4: Reinsurance (Chapters 10–11)

- Module 5: Customer Service (Chapters 12–13)

Although the text focuses primarily on the United States and Canada, the principles and practices described in this text are instructive of the principles and practices found worldwide.

Acknowledgments

LOMA texts are the result of a joint effort between industry experts and LOMA's own staff. Both groups make invaluable contributions to the success of LOMA's texts, and *Insurance Administration*, Fourth Edition is no exception.

Textbook Review Panel

Insurance Administration, Fourth Edition benefited from a large textbook review panel of industry experts who reviewed the Third Edition of this text prior to its publication in 2008. The textbook review panel for the Third Edition made many substantive comments on the outline and chapters, provided suggestions for content, submitted relevant research materials, and answered numerous questions. The reviewers cared enough about the educational needs of current and future industry employees to volunteer their time and expertise to this project. They improved the accuracy and clarity of the text, although the authors claim responsibility for any errors. The following individuals devoted countless hours to the Third Edition's review, for which we are most grateful:

- David K. Anderson, FALU, CLU, FLMI, Corporate Vice President, Atlanta Underwriting Center, New York Life Insurance Company

- Suzanne L. Bathke, ARA, ACS, AIRC, CPIW, Vice President, Business Administration, Hannover Life Reassurance Company of America

- Carole Bellm, HIA, FLMI, GBA, Director, Group Underwriting, RGA Life Reinsurance Company of Canada

- Glenn Beuschel, ACS, Director, Treaties, Optimum Reassurance Inc.

- Linda J. Brissette, ALHC, Lead Disability Benefits Specialist, Unum Group

- Nazir Damji, FLMI, FALU, Vice President and Chief Underwriter, Max New York Life Insurance Co. LTD

- Shaun Downey, FLMI, ARA, ACS, AVP–Market and Project Research, Manulife Reinsurance

- Jill Y. Dupuis, ARA, ACS, Manager, Operations Analysis, Reinsurance Division, Manulife Financial

- Brian Eichhold, ACS, Assistant Vice President and Director, New Business, Western & Southern Financial Group

- Susan C. Fletcher, FLMI, FLHC, ACS, AIAA, AIRC, Retired Vice President of Compliance, Harleysville Life Insurance Company

- Robert Frank, CLU, FLMI, ACS, Chief Underwriter, AXA–Equitable

- Dean Franzen, RHU, HIA, MHP, DIA, DHP, HCSA, LTCP, EHBA, Senior Underwriting Consultant, Wisconsin Underwriting Associates

- Nicolle G. Galipeau, J.D., FLMI, LTCP, HCAFA, Associate Counsel, Transamerica Life Insurance Company

- Kevin C. Glasgow, ACS, FLMI, FLHC, Senior Vice President, Claims and Liability Management, Swiss Re Life and Health America, Inc.

- James B. Hiers, III, FLMI, ALHC, HIA, ACS, Assistant Vice President, Munich American Reassurance Company

- Pamela F. Hilton, FLMI, ACS, AIRC, Senior Underwriter, Munich American Reassurance Company

- Sue Jacobson, ACS, FLMI, Contact Center Manager, CUNA Mutual Group

- David Kanney, AALU, CLU, FLMI, Officer, Life Underwriting, Nationwide Financial

- Jerry A. Kapitz, FLHC, CLU, ChFC, AIRC, AALU, ACS, FLMI/M, Manager: Policyowner Services, Northwestern Mutual

- Carol G. King, FLMI, ACS, AIAA, AIRC, FLHC, HIA, MHP, Supervisor, Group Life Underwriting, HCC Life Insurance Company

- Irene Klatt, CFP, Vice President, Health Insurance, Canadian Life and Health Insurance Association Inc.

- Tim Kuraszek, FLMI, ACS, AIRC, HIA, AHLC, Independent Reviewer

- Josée Malboeuf, FLMI, ALHC, Vice President, Underwriting & Claims, RGA Life Reinsurance Company of Canada

- Paula L. Mango, CIPP, CLU, FLMI, ALHC, ACS, Assistant Vice President, AML and Privacy Officer, Lincoln Financial Group

- Anthony O'Neale Mayers, FLMI, FLHC, AIAA, ACS, Chief Claims Consultant, North American Company for Life and Health Insurance

- Jon P. McElhaney, FLHC, ACS, Manager, Specialty Support Unit, Claims Operations, FSO, Thrivent Financial for Lutherans

- Luke C. McLaren, J.D., FFSI, FLMI, AAPA, ACS, AIAA, AIRC, ARA, Associate General Counsel, Genworth Financial

- Julio E. Payés O., FLMI, ACS, Reinsurance Manager, HSBC Seguros Salvadoreno, S.A.

- Nina Rhines, FLMI, AFSI, ACS, ARA, Investment Accountant, Securian Financial Group

- David M. Rose, ChFC, FLMI/M, ACS, ARP, Assistant Vice President—Information Technology, Lincoln Financial Group

- Carol A. Rubsam, ALHC, HIA, Six Sigma Green Belt, Life Reinsurance Claims Audit Director, Employers Reassurance Corporation

- Jonathan Sager, J.D., FLMI, Vice President and General Counsel, MIB Group, Inc.

- Maureen Shippy, FLMI, ARA, ACS, Vice President, Global Technical Accounting & Services, Swiss Re Life and Health America, Inc.

- Michele D. Smith, FLMI, PCS, AIAA, AVP, Customer Service, The Baltimore Life Companies

- Sharon B. Smith, FALU, FLMI, ALHC, ACS, President, Amalfi Consulting, Inc.

- Patricia E. Stevenson, FLMI, ACS, AIAA, AIRC, AAPA, ARA, Compliance and Tax Specialist, The Baltimore Life Insurance Company

- Gerry T. Stewart, ASA, MAAA, FFSI, FLMI, AIRC, ARA, AAPA, AIAA, ACS, Assistant Vice President and Assistant Actuary, Protective Life Insurance Company

- Nancy L. Sulkers, FLMI, FALU, RHU, Director Living Benefits Administration, Great-West Life/Canada Life

- Laurie Szabo, CEBS, ACS, HIAA, Chief Underwriter, The Hartford

- Deborah Taylor, Director of Life and Disability Claims, HCC Life Insurance Company

- William W. Wade, Jr., FLMI, ACS, FLHC, HIA, Director, Insurance Services Division, Combined Insurance Company

- Sandi Weinberg, FLMI, ACS, AIAA, AIRC, HIA, Administrative Assistant, Physicians Mutual Insurance Company

- Cynthia K. Weurdig, ACS, ALHC, Manager, Claims Consumer Affairs, Transamerica Life Insurance Company

- Frank Zinatelli, LL.B., FLMI, Vice President and Associate General Counsel, Canadian Life and Health Insurance Association Inc.

Because of the thorough work of this textbook review panel, a complete external review of the Fourth Edition was not needed. However, a major revision of reinsurance content required that these chapters be submitted to external review. A dedicated review panel conducted a thorough review of the reinsurance content for the Fourth Edition. The following reviewers, whose efforts resulted in improved reinsurance content for industry students, are greatly appreciated:

- Shaun Downey, FLMI, ARA, ACS, AVP–Reinsurance, John Hancock

- Jill Y. Dupuis, ARA, ACS, Manager, Operations Analysis, Reinsurance Division, Manulife Financial

- Mark W. Yokley, FLMI/M, FFSI, ACS, AIAA, AIAF, ARP, AIRC, ARA, AAPA, PCS, CLU, Director, Group Reinsurance and Outsourcing, Horace Mann Life Insurance Company

LOMA Staff/Consultants

We also wish to thank talented LOMA staff members who contributed in many ways to the success of *Insurance Administration*, Fourth Edition. Deserving of special thanks are Jane Lightcap Brown, Ph.D., FLMI, ACS, ALHC, Senior Associate, who wrote this text's first edition and Kristen L. Falk, FLMI, AAPA, ACS, AIAA, AIRC, ARA, Senior Associate, who wrote the text's second edition. A huge debt of gratitude goes to the authors of *Insurance Administration*, Third Edition: Mary C. Bickley, J.D., FLMI, FFSI, CLU, AIRC, ACS, AIAA, PAHM, AAPA, ARA; Jane Lightcap Brown, Ph.D., FLMI, ACS, ALHC; Kristen L. Falk, FLMI, AAPA, ACS, AIAA, AIRC, ARA; Miriam A. Orsina, FLMI, PCS, AAPA, ARA, PAHM; and Dorinda Paige, ACS.

Insurance Administration, Fourth Edition also benefited from the expertise of many talented LOMA staff members. Jo Ann Appleton, FLMI, PCS, ALHC, HIA, CEBS, Senior Associate, Designation Programs, served as both manuscript editor and examination editor for this edition. Harriett E. Jones, J.D., FLMI, ACS, AIRC, Senior Associate, Designation Programs, edited the first seven chapters of the text and Miriam A. Orsina, FLMI, PCS, AAPA, ARA, PAHM, Senior Associate, Learning & Development Services, edited the reinsurance chapters. Steven R. Silver, J.D., FLMI, AFSI, ACS, AIAA, AIRC, Associate, Designation Programs, secured the necessary permissions for this edition. Also deserving of thanks are the individuals in LOMA's Information Center who provided valuable research services: Olivia Blakemore, ACS, Technical Administrator; and Mallory Eldridge, Research Analyst.

Thanks go to all of the people at LOMA and LIMRA who contributed to the design and development of the Course Portal for the LOMA 301 text. LOMA staff contributors included Kelly Neeley, FLMI, ALHC, ACS, AIAA, PAHM, Senior Associate, Training Programs; Kristen L. Falk, FLMI, FFSI, AAPA, ACS, AIAA, AIRC, ARA, Senior Associate, Training Programs; David A. Lewis, FLMI, ACS, Senior Associate, Learning & Development Services; Brad Kimmel, Associate, Learning & Development Services; Stephen Hill, Manager, Learning & Development Services; Marlene McCauley, Lead Graphic Designer, Production and Graphics; Kathryn H. Brown, PCS, Marketing Associate, LOMA Society Support Team; Nick Desoutter, FLMI, AAPA, PCS, Senior Associate, Training Programs; Gene Stone, FLMI, ACS, CLU, Senior Associate, Training Programs; Tonya Vaughan,

Learning Coordinator, Training Programs; and Carie Crane, FLMI, ACS, AIAA, ARA, Assistant Vice President, Education & Training Division. LIMRA staff contributors included Bill Maura, Assistant Vice President, Marketing; Anthony Leathers, Multi-Media Assistant; Frank Robinson, Jr., Multi-Media Technical Specialist; and John Rocchetti, Multi-Media Technical Specialist Assistant.

Additional thanks go to the LOMA staff members who were responsible for examinations and related study materials for the course. These included Jo Ann Appleton, FLMI, PCS, ALHC, HIA, CEBS, Senior Associate, Designation Programs; Melanie R. Green, FLMI, ACS, AIAA, Senior Associate, Designation Programs; and Vivian Heeden, FFSI, FLMI, CLU, FLHC, AAPA, AIAA, ARA, AIRC, PCS, Senior Associate, Designation Programs. Thanks also to Mamunah Carter, Administrative Assistant III, Education & Training Division, who provided administrative support.

Thanks also go to Carol A. Wiessner, ACS, Product Sourcing Manager, who coordinated the printing of the text and associated study materials; and to Amy Stailey, Production Coordinator II/Scheduling Coordinator and Allison Ayers-Molette, Production Coordinator II, who typeset the text. In addition, we thank Robert D. Land, FLMI, ACS, a consultant, who created the index for the text.

We extend a very special thank you to Julia K. Wooley, FLMI, ACS, ALHC, HIA, MHP, Assistant Vice President, Designation Programs, who served as Project Manager and provided guidance and support throughout the project and Katherine C. Milligan, FLMI, ACS, ALHC, Vice President, Education & Training Division, who provided leadership, guidance, resources, support, and encouragement for this project.

Elizabeth A. Mulligan, FLMI, FLHC, PCS,
PAHM, AAPA, AIRC, ARA, AIAA
Atlanta, Georga
2010

The purpose of *Insurance Administration*, Fourth Edition is to provide an overview of the principles and practices of individual and group life insurance administration. To enhance your learning experience, LOMA has developed a Course Portal for this course that is accessible upon course enrollment in LOMANET.

A LOMA Course Portal is an online resource from which learners access everything they need to study and prepare for the course examination. The Course Portal organizes the assigned text material into convenient Modules—chapter clusters that help to focus the learning process by breaking up the course content into meaningful sections. In addition to the assigned study materials, the Course Portal provides access to an array of blended learning resources, including some multimedia features designed to enhance the learning experience. The LOMA 301 Course Portal provides access to

- An introductory course video

- Protected PDFs of the assigned text and Test Preparation Guide, which can be printed or read online

- The interactive version of the Test Preparation Guide's Practice Questions and Sample Exam

- Review tools, including Learning Aids—animations of important concepts— and a "Top Ten Tough Topics" tutorial

- Recommended study plans to help you set goals and manage your learning experience

- Related links which help you apply the course instruction to the real world

LOMA 301—Insurance Administration—is part of the Associate, Life Management Institute (ALMI) and Fellow, Life Management Institute (FLMI) programs. Students preparing to take the examination for LOMA 301 will find that the assigned study materials—the protected PDFs of the text and Test Preparation Guide—include many features designed to help learners more easily understand the course content, organize their study, and prepare for the examination. These features include lists of Learning Aid topics available on the Course Portal, chapter outlines, chapter learning objectives, key terms, figures containing real-world examples of course content, and a comprehensive glossary. As we describe each of these features, we give you suggestions for studying the material.

- **Learning Aids and Top Ten Tough Topics.** A list of Learning Aids is provided in the protected PDF for the entire text as well as for each Module. Review this list to become familiar with topics for which an animated learning aid is available on the Course Portal. Viewing these Learning Aids allows you to see topics in action or to view topics from a different perspective than from simply reading about them in the text. Also included is a Top Ten Tough Topics tutorial. This tutorial contains animations and study tips for topics that learners often find difficult when answering questions on the examination. Both the Learning Aids and the Top Ten Tough Topics tutorial enhance the learning experience, appeal to a variety of learning styles, and offer a great way for learners to advance their understanding and retention of course content.

- **Learning Objectives.** The first page of each chapter contains a list of learning objectives to help you focus your studies. Before reading each chapter, review these learning objectives. Then, as you read the chapter, look for material that will help you meet the learning objectives. The interactive version of the Test Preparation Guide's Practice Questions and Sample Exam questions (accessible from the Course Portal) are linked to the learning objectives to give you an idea of how the learning objective might be measured on an examination, as well as to help you assess your mastery of the learning objectives.

- **Chapter Outline.** Each chapter contains an outline of the chapter. Review this outline to gain an overview of the major topics that will be covered; then scan through the chapter to become familiar with how the information is presented. By looking at the headings, you can gain a preview of how various subjects in each chapter relate to each other.

- **Key Terms.** This text explains key terms that apply to the text material and, where appropriate, reviews key terms previously presented in LOMA courses. Each key term is highlighted with ***bold italic type*** when the term is defined and is included in a list of key terms at the end of each chapter. All key terms also appear in a comprehensive glossary at the end of the protected PDF of the text. As you read each chapter, pay special attention to the key terms.

- **Figures.** We include figures throughout the text to illustrate and bring a real-world perspective to the text's discussion of selected topics. Information contained in figures may be tested on the examination for the course.

- **Glossary.** A comprehensive glossary that contains definitions of all key terms appears at the end of the protected PDF of the text. Following each glossary entry is a number in brackets that indicates the chapter in which the key term is defined. The glossary also references important equivalent terms, acronyms, and contrasting terms.

LOMA may periodically revise the assigned study materials for this course. To ensure that you are studying from the correct materials, check the current LOMA *Education and Training Catalog* available at www.loma.org or on the Course Portal. Also be sure to visit the Announcements page on the Course Portal to learn about important updates or corrections to the assigned study materials.

Using the Test Preparation Guide

LOMA's *Test Preparation Guide for LOMA 301* (TPG) is assigned reading for students preparing for the LOMA 301 examination. It contains Practice Questions organized by chapter and a full-scale Sample Exam. The TPG is available in two versions, both accessible from the Course Portal: (1) a printable, protected PDF that includes answer keys for all questions, and (2) an interactive version that can be used online or downloaded for offline use. The interactive version has the added advantage of answer-choice explanations for all Practice Questions and Sample Exam questions. The TPG is designed to help you learn the course content and prepare for the examination. Used along with the assigned text, the TPG will help you master the course material. **Studies indicate that students who use LOMA TPGs consistently perform significantly better on LOMA examinations than students who do not use TPGs.**

The LOMA 301 Course Portal, available online at www. LOMANET.org, includes several Learning Aids designed to reinforce concepts covered in the assigned text. If you are not already using the online Course Portal but would like access to the Learning Aids for this course, please follow the log-in instructions provided in your enrollment confirmation email, or call 1-800-ASK-LOMA or email education@loma.org for assistance. **PLEASE NOTE:** Examination questions will be based only on content presented in the assigned text.

Module 1

✓ Insurance Administration Functions

✓ Technologies That Enhance Insurance Administration

✓ Security Risks and Technological Tools

✓ Risk Classes

✓ Organizing the Underwriting Workflow

✓ Premium Receipts

✓ Insurable Interest

Module 2

✓ MIB as a Source of Underwriting Information

✓ Personal Risk Factors

✓ Assessing Financial Factors

✓ Charging for Substandard Risks

✓ Underwriting Niche Policies

✓ Solvency, Liquidity, Profitability

✓ Contributory and Noncontributory Plans

✓ Risk Factors for Group Prospects

✓ Rating Methods for Group Classes

Module 3

- ✓ Claim Evaluation Process
- ✓ Insurance Fraud
- ✓ Proof of Death
- ✓ Policy Proceeds and Beneficiaries

Module 4

- ✓ Reinsurance Cession Arrangements
- ✓ Proportional Reinsurance Arrangements
- ✓ Plans of Reinsurance
- ✓ Reinsurance Reports for In-Force Business

Module 5

- ✓ Customer Service Organizations
- ✓ Customer Service Quality Control
- ✓ Customer Service Transactions

Chapter 1

Overview of Insurance Administration

Objectives:

After studying this chapter, you should be able to

- Explain how an insurer fulfills its ethical duties pertaining to insurance administration

- Identify the primary purpose of the following insurance administration functions: underwriting, claim administration, reinsurance, and customer service

- Describe how the following insurance functions—marketing, actuarial, accounting, treasury operations, legal, compliance, human resources, and information technology—coordinate their work with staff in insurance administration

- Identify the four major technology components of an insurance administration system

- Describe how a database management system, data mining, predictive modeling, a business rules engine, a document management system, and an automated workflow system enhance insurance administration processes

- Identify security risks related to information management and technological tools insurers use to combat such risks

- Define quality control and distinguish between performance measurement and performance standards

Outline

Insurers' Ethical Duties to Customers
- Equity in Risk Acceptance
- Prompt and Equitable Claim Handling
- Honest, Objective, and Fair Customer Service
- Privacy and Confidentiality of Customer Information
- Adequate Financial Resources

Insurance Administration Functions
- Underwriting
- Claim Administration
- Reinsurance
- Customer Service

Other Insurance Functions
- Marketing
- Actuarial
- Accounting and Treasury Operations
- Legal and Compliance
- Human Resources
- Information Technology

Administration Systems
- Technology Components
- Technologies that Enhance Insurance Administration Processes
- Systems Integration
- Security

Quality Control

Life insurance companies are complex organizations that engage in many diverse activities. In this text, we refer to those insurance company activities specifically associated with administering insurance policies—such as underwriting, reinsurance, claims, and customer service—as *insurance administration*. The purpose of this text is to give an overview of these functions as they apply to individual and group life insurance. The text sets out those company practices, policies, and procedures typically found in the life insurance industry. Nevertheless, individual company practices, policies, and procedures vary widely.

Before proceeding, we need to clarify the terminology used throughout this text to describe the people and entities involved in the creation and administration of an insurance policy. In this text, the term *producer* refers to any person or entity that (1) sells insurance, including agents, brokers, financial advisors, and bank personnel or (2) is involved in insurance sales made through direct marketing or the Internet.

The *applicant* is the person or entity that submits an application for individual insurance and seeks to purchase the insurance coverage. The *insured*, also known as the *assured* in some countries, is the person whose life, health, property, or income is covered by an insurance policy. During the underwriting process, this person often is referred to as the *proposed insured*. The *policyowner* is the person or entity that owns an individual insurance policy. The applicant, insured, and policyowner of an individual insurance policy may be, and often are, the same person. If, for example, you apply for and are issued an insurance policy on your life, then you are the applicant, the insured, and the policyowner. If, however, your spouse applies for a policy on your life, then your spouse is the applicant and you are the insured. When the policy is issued, your spouse—the applicant—becomes the policyowner. When one person purchases an individual insurance policy on the life of another person, the policy is known as a *third-party policy*.

In group insurance, the *master group insurance contract*, also known as a *group insurance policy*, is an insurance contract that insures a number of people. The *policyholder* is the employer or other organization that decides what kind of coverage to purchase for the group and negotiates the terms of and enters into the master group insurance contract with the insurer. The policyholder usually helps administer and pays for part or all of the group coverage. During the underwriting process, a group that has applied, but has not yet been approved, for group coverage from an insurance company may be referred to as the ***group prospect*** or *proposed group*.

In the United States and Canada, the individuals covered by a master group insurance contract are referred to as the ***group insureds*** or *covered persons*. These individuals sometimes are referred to as *certificate holders* because they receive a document called a ***certificate of insurance*** that describes (1) the coverage that the master group insurance contract provides and (2) the group insured's rights under the contract.

If the event insured against occurs while an insurance policy is in force, the insurer pays the benefits provided under the terms of the policy. Life insurance policy proceeds are paid to the ***beneficiary***—the person or party that the owner of an individual policy or the group insured named to receive the policy benefit.

Insurers' Ethical Duties to Customers

Ethics is a system of accepted standards of conduct and moral judgment that combines the elements of honesty, integrity, and fair treatment. Acting in an ethical manner involves behaving in accordance with accepted legal and moral principles of right and wrong. Every area of an insurance company, including insurance administration, is responsible for behaving ethically. Figure 1.1 sets forth some of an insurer's ethical duties pertaining to insurance administration functions.

Equity in Risk Acceptance

Equity in risk acceptance is maintained when the insurer evaluates every application for insurance consistently in accordance with the insurer's established underwriting guidelines and charges each policyowner a premium rate that is based solely on factors that affect the degree of risk the insurer is accepting by issuing a policy. For example, individual life insurance premium rates generally differ

Figure 1.1. Ethical Duties for Insurance Administration

- Maintain equity in risk acceptance among all insureds
- Provide prompt and equitable claim handling
- Provide honest, objective, and fair customer service
- Preserve customers' privacy and confidentiality
- Maintain adequate financial resources

among insureds on the basis of factors such as the age, sex, health, occupation, and avocations of the insured because such factors affect the degree of risk the insurer is accepting. Note that the term *risk* can refer to not only the possibility of loss to an insurer, but also the actual person or persons being insured.

Prompt and Equitable Claim Handling

Insurers have an ethical and legal duty to process claims in a timely and equitable manner. Equitable claim handling includes assessing every claim in accordance with the terms of the policy and paying only covered claims. States will impose fines if forms aren't provided or claims aren't processed in a timely manner.

Honest, Objective, and Fair Customer Service

When a customer applies for new coverage, changes existing coverage, requests information, or interacts with the insurer in any other way, the customer deserves honesty, objectivity, and fairness from the insurer. The customer also expects prompt, accurate, and empathetic responses. Producers conducting business with the insurer also deserve such treatment.

Privacy and Confidentiality of Customer Information

Insurers have an ethical and sometimes legal duty to

- Use only lawful, reasonable, and ethical means of obtaining information

- Obtain authorization to collect information when required

- Use only accurate information

- Restrict access to personal information to only those people who have a lawful and business-specific need for it

- Establish written guidelines for information handling so that employees will know exactly how to safeguard confidential information

Adequate Financial Resources

An insurer must have adequate financial resources to pay contractual benefits when covered events occur. Therefore, insurers must conduct business in a manner that allows them to remain financially stable and profitable. To strengthen their financial positions, insurers focus on using resources wisely, managing expenses, and becoming more efficient in serving their customers.

Insurance Administration Functions

Figure 1.2 introduces the insurance administration functions that we discuss in this text—underwriting, reinsurance, claim administration, and customer service.

Figure 1.2. Insurance Administration Functions

UNDERWRITING

- Investigates, assesses, and classifies degree of risk
- Accepts or declines risk

REINSURANCE

- Transfers a portion of the risk to another insurer

CLAIM ADMINISTRATION

- Evaluates claims
- Pays eligible claims
- Denies ineligible claims

CUSTOMER SERVICE

- Answers customers' questions
- Provides requested information to customers
- Processes customers' policy changes and transactions
- Solves customers' problems

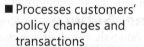

Underwriting

Underwriting is the process of (1) assessing and classifying the degree of risk represented by a proposed insured or group with respect to a specific insurance product and (2) making a decision to accept or decline that risk. An *underwriter* is an individual who (1) assesses and classifies the degree of risk represented by a proposed insured or group with respect to a specific insurance product and (2) makes a decision to accept or decline that risk. Note that producers in the United States historically have been known as *field underwriters*. In this text, however, the term *underwriter* refers to an insurance company home office or regional office employee who performs the risk assessment, classification, and selection process.

Sound underwriting decisions help insurance companies remain financially strong and competitive. If an insurer accepts too many improperly assessed risks at premium rates that are not adequate for the true risks, the insurer will pay more in claims than it can afford. If an insurer fails to accept enough appropriate risks at appropriate rates, the insurer will lose potentially profitable business to competitors.

Underwriting is one of the primary functions that make up the group of activities known as new business. The term *new business* can have a variety of meanings, including the policies an insurer underwrites and issues. In addition, producers may think of new business as potential clients, as all the activities they engage in to sell insurance, or as applications submitted. In this text, we use the term *new business* to refer to the activities an insurer undertakes in receiving applications, underwriting applications, and issuing policies.

Claim Administration

An insurer has a legal and an ethical obligation to pay all eligible claims promptly and to deny liability for all others. *Claim administration* is the process of evaluating each submitted claim, deciding whether or not the claim is eligible, informing the person who submitted the claim of the decision, and authorizing the payment of each eligible claim according to the terms of the policy.

Reinsurance

Reinsurance is insurance that one insurance company obtains from another insurance company on risks associated with insurance policies issued by the first company. In this context, risk refers to the possibility of financial loss. Briefly, reinsurance is insurance for an insurer. In a reinsurance arrangement, one insurer transfers a portion of a risk to a second insurer, which agrees to pay part of the claims of the first insurer in exchange for a reinsurance premium.

Customer Service

A company has many customers, including policyowners, insureds, beneficiaries, and producers. Maintaining positive relationships with all its customers is essential for an insurance company. *Customer service* refers to the broad range of activities that a company and its employees perform to keep customers satisfied so they will continue doing business with the company and speak positively about it to other potential customers. *Policyowner service* is a specific type of customer service that includes all the service activities performed for people or entities that own individual insurance policies. *Member service* is a specific type of customer service that includes all the service activities performed for group insureds.

Because customer service staff members typically have direct contact with customers, these employees often can provide feedback to other areas of the company about customer needs, wants, and problems. Such feedback assists the company in the design of products and processes that better meet the needs of customers.

Other Insurance Functions

Insurance administration staff members typically coordinate many aspects of their work with other insurance company staff working in such functional areas as marketing, actuarial, accounting and treasury operations, legal and compliance, human resources, and information technology.

Marketing

Marketing is the functional area of an insurer that has primary responsibility for identifying the insurer's prospective customers and what they want, as well as planning the promotion and distribution of the insurer's products. Marketing also seeks to improve the insurer's competitive position by (1) gathering information about the insurer's business environment, including data about its competitors; (2) assessing the insurer's sales performance in the marketplace; and (3) assisting in the development of competitive, profitable insurance products. Marketing typically has several units, one of which is devoted to providing support to producers.

Actuarial

Actuarial is the functional area composed of *actuaries*—technical experts in insurance, annuities, and financial instruments who apply mathematical knowledge to industry and company statistics to calculate various financial values. Among other activities, members of an insurer's actuarial staff

- Use statistics to predict the rates of death among life insureds

- Calculate premium rates for insurance products

- Determine legal reserve liabilities

- Conduct research on trends in mortality rates, policy lapses, policy loans, company expenses, and interest rates

- Engage in financial reporting activities

An insurer uses actuarial information to develop assumptions used in pricing new products and in selecting risks. Members of the actuarial staff also may be involved in developing new products and making reinsurance decisions.

Accounting and Treasury Operations

Accounting is the functional area of an insurance company that collects, records, summarizes, analyzes, and reports data about a company's financial condition. Members of the accounting staff develop financial information that is used throughout the company to make decisions, measure financial performance, and satisfy internal and regulatory financial reporting requirements.

Treasury operations is the functional area of an insurance company that manages cash as it flows through the company. This function's responsibilities include setting up bank accounts, managing lockboxes for the collection of premium payments, and disbursing policy proceeds via checks or automatic deposits. In some companies, a separate unit in the customer service area handles premium billings.

Legal and Compliance

The *legal department* of an insurance company— also known as the *law department*—handles all legal matters for the company. Company lawyers may be called on to advise life insurance claim personnel when claims are disputed; represent the company or supervise outside attorneys in any litigation involving the company; and develop or review policy forms, agency contracts, business contracts, and other legal documents.

The *compliance department* is the functional area of an insurance company that is responsible for ensuring that the insurer adheres to all applicable laws and regulations in each jurisdiction in which the company does business. Some companies combine the legal and compliance functions into one department, while other companies have separate departments.

Human Resources

Human resources is the functional area of an insurance company that recruits and screens job applicants; helps select qualified employees; plans and presents appropriate orientation, training, and development for each employee; administers employee benefit programs; and maintains employee records. Human resources staff members also guide an insurer's management in conducting performance appraisals of employees and in determining compensation levels for various jobs. Finally, human resources personnel assist with employee separations resulting from resignation, layoff, retirement, or discharge.

Some companies have a separate training and development (T&D) area that helps employees plan their career paths and access education and training resources. As part of their T&D activities, some companies offer their employees tuition assistance for the completion of educational programs relevant to their jobs.

Information Technology

Information technology (IT) is the functional area of an insurance company that develops and maintains the company's information systems and oversees information management throughout the company. An ***information system*** is an interactive combination of technology, people, and processes that collects, manipulates, and disseminates information. ***Information management*** is the use of information systems to provide a company's information users with the information they need to carry out their job responsibilities. These responsibilities include administering products, maintaining records, formulating strategy, and providing information to customers.

Administration Systems

Information systems are essential to the efficient and effective operation of insurance administration functions in today's insurance company. An information system that an insurer uses to manage information about insurance policies is referred to as an ***administration system***. Insurers typically have more than one administration system.[1]

Technology Components

The technology components of a computer-based administration system include a technology platform, application software, databases, and communications technology, as illustrated in Figure 1.3.

Technology Platform

A ***technology platform*** is the combination of hardware and operating system software on which an administration system runs. Whereas the broad definition of hardware is the equipment and mechanical devices included in a computer-based information system, in the context of a technology platform, ***hardware*** refers to the types of computers the insurer uses. ***Software*** consists of computer programs that provide the sequences of instructions for a computer and that govern its operation. One type of software, known as ***operating system software***, controls the basic operations of a computer. Among other functions, the operating system software performs common computer tasks, such as saving data to different storage mediums or devices. The most commonly used operating system for personal computers is Microsoft Windows®.

Figure 1.3 The Technology Components of an Administration System

TECHNOLOGY PLATFORM

■ Hardware, e.g., mainframes, servers, and/or personal computers

   AND

■ Operating system software, e.g., Windows®*, UNIX, or Mac

APPLICATION SOFTWARE

■ Software that performs specific, business-related tasks

DATABASES

■ Organized collections of data and information

COMMUNICATIONS TECHNOLOGY

■ Use of telecommunications to communicate and transfer data electronically

*****Windows**® is a registered trademark of Microsoft Corporation.

Source: Adapted from Mark Adel and Nicolas L. Desoutter, *Annuity Systems and Administration*, 2nd Ed. [Atlanta: LOMA (Life Office Management Association, Inc.), © 2004], p. 177. Used with permission; all rights reserved.

Application Software

Application software, also known as a *software application* or simply an *application*, is software used to perform specific tasks or solve particular types of problems. Word processing software that creates text documents and spreadsheet software that creates data tables and performs calculations are types of application software. Insurers use many specialized types of application software to perform insurance-specific tasks. Examples include software that can

■ Prepare quotes for insurance policies

■ Process the issuance of policies

■ Administer policy loans and policy dividends

■ Prepare policy value statements

■ Calculate correct benefit payments

■ Print benefit payment checks

Such software applications form one component of a ***transaction processing system***, which is an organized collection of procedures, software, databases, and devices used to perform high-volume, routine, and repetitive business transactions. A ***transaction*** is any business-related exchange—such as a death benefit paid in exchange for proof of death received or payment of a renewal premium for the continuation of coverage. Various transaction processing systems work together to perform the different processes involved in insurance administration.

Vendors offer many different types of software applications and many different varieties of each type. Insurers also can develop their own applications. Often, application software is purchased from a vendor and then customized by the insurer or vendor to better support the insurer's products and processes.

An insurer's choice of application software depends on its specific administration processes. An insurer seeks the application software that can best accomplish the tasks it performs. Although administration processes are much the same from one company to the next, each insurer's processes are to some extent unique. An insurer's history, culture, business philosophy, corporate strategy, corporate structure, target markets, products, distribution channels, business policies, and business practices all shape its administration processes. Therefore, the ideal application software performs certain core administration processes and also meets an insurer's distinctive needs.

Databases

A ***database*** is an organized collection of data and information. The term ***data*** refers to unprocessed facts. A policyowner's name, address, and policy number are pieces of data. Data are combined, manipulated, and analyzed to create ***information***, which is a collection of data that has been converted into a form that is meaningful or useful for the accomplishment of some objective, such as performing a transaction, drawing a conclusion, or solving a problem.

Databases are vitally important for insurers because of the vast amounts of data that insurers collect, store, access, and process relating to policyowners, insureds, claimants, producers, and policies. In addition to the internal databases insurers create for their own uses, insurers also use external databases developed and maintained by government agencies, industry associations, business partners, and other information providers.

Communications Technology

Communications technology makes use of ***telecommunications***, which is the electronic transmission of communication signals. Telecommunications enables organizations to link computer systems into networks. A ***network*** is a group of interconnected computers and computer devices, including the telecommunications equipment and software that connect them. The Internet is an example of a worldwide network among unrelated users. An ***intranet*** is an organization's internal computer network that uses Internet technology but is accessible only to people within the organization. An ***extranet*** is a portion of an organization's intranet that is accessible to people within the organization and to selected external parties. Insurers often establish extranets to allow home office employees and producers to communicate electronically.

Examples of how telecommunications and networks are useful to businesses are the commonly-known electronic mail, electronic data interchange, and electronic commerce.

■ *Electronic mail (e-mail)* is a form of telecommunication that allows a user to type a message into a computer and then send the message to other computers connected to a network.

■ *Electronic data interchange (EDI)* is the computer-to-computer exchange of data between organizations using a data format agreed upon by the sending and receiving parties. Organizations that exchange data through EDI are called *trading partners* and are said to be part of an EDI network. The primary purpose of an EDI network is to allow an organization to transmit data directly from its computers to the computers of other organizations on the network. In the life insurance industry, EDI networks are used for many purposes, such as transferring medical laboratory results to underwriting departments, depositing policy benefits into a policyowner's bank account, and exchanging data with reinsurers.

■ *Electronic commerce (e-commerce)* is the use of the Internet and other networks to deliver commercial information and to facilitate business transactions and the delivery of products and services. The sale of products over the Internet is the classic example of e-commerce. Other examples include electronic applications for insurance and electronic claims submittals.

Technologies that Enhance Insurance Administration Processes

Business process management (BPM) is a strategy for optimizing business processes or adapting them to meet changing needs. The functions of underwriting, reinsurance, and claims in particular are very process oriented. Business process management seeks to combine proven management practices with technology to automate and improve these processes. Some software vendors sell BPM suites (BPMSs), which are collections of software tools that support and manage the design, modeling, construction, deployment, monitoring, and refinement of business processes.

The goal of many insurers that focus on business process management is *straight through processing (STP)*, which is the electronic processing of every step of a transaction without manual intervention. For example, STP can enable complete electronic processing of certain types of new business from the submission of the application for insurance to the actual issuing of the policy. An applicant and a producer can complete and submit an application electronically, and then the insurer's administration system can do everything else necessary to produce a policy, including underwriting and printing the policy. Pure STP would result in a paperless environment in which all forms and records are maintained electronically. Straight through processing provides the following advantages for insurers:

■ Increased efficiency and, thus, reduced expenses

■ Decreased error rate because of the decreased need for data entry and other human input

- Improved consistency and quality

- Increased employee productivity

- Faster service to customers and producers

STP is not yet a single product that an insurer can buy off the shelf. It is composed of many available applications that can interface with one another to produce a straight through process. Critical components of STP include database management systems, data mining, predictive modeling, business rules engines, document management systems, and automated workflow systems.

Database Management Systems and Data Mining

Many functional areas of an insurer must have access to customer and policy data. Rather than replicating this data in separate database files for each separate function, the insurer typically uses a *centralized data repository*, a database that houses all the relevant data contained in the insurer's separate administration systems. To access the centralized data repository or other databases, insurance company employees typically use a *database management system (DBMS)*, which is a group of computer programs that organizes data in a database and allows users to obtain the information they need. A DBMS manipulates the data in response to queries from users in different functional areas of the company and allows them to access and share the data in the centralized data repository. For example, underwriters can obtain data on policy applications, claims staff can access data on benefits and policy terms, and customer service representatives can retrieve information necessary to answer customers' questions.

A *data warehouse* is a type of DBMS that collects data from the company's existing databases and possibly from sources outside the company, screens and edits the data, puts the data in a standard format, and then stores the data in the centralized data repository. An insurer can analyze the data in its data warehouse, as well as data from other sources, through *data mining*, which is the analysis of large amounts of data to discover previously unknown trends, patterns, and relationships. As an example, data mining technology might bring together payment history data and claims experience on all of an insurer's covered insureds to reveal relationships that profile a potentially profitable segment of people who then could be targeted for marketing. These characteristics also could be incorporated into an insurer's underwriting guidelines.

Data mining systems can analyze data from internal and external sources. For example, information on other policies owned by a proposed insured would come from the insurer's internal records; additional data, such as the current financial status of the proposed insured, could come from external sources, such as credit bureaus. Data mining systems are often Internet-based, allowing information gathering to be automatic and instantaneous.

Predictive Modeling

The results of data mining can generate especially useful information when they are used as the input in *predictive modeling*, which is an automated technique for predicting future behavior or events. The predictive modeling process involves collecting the patterns and relationships unearthed by data mining, formulating a statistical model, and generating predictions based on the model.[2] For example, using predictive modeling, insurers can develop company-specific models that take into account the company's policy, underwriting, and claim data, as well as data from outside sources. Such models can forecast mortality rates by predicting the development of medical conditions and the onset of illnesses, as well as the likelihood of losses due to risky professions and avocations. Thus, predictive modeling improves risk evaluation and selection, as well as premium rating.

As new data become available, predictive models are validated or revised.[3] For example, scientific progress in the field of genetic testing will lead to improvements in disease prevention. These improvements become new data inputs into the models and thus lead to improved predictions.

Business Rules Engines

A **business rules engine (BRE)** is application software that automates the decision-making process by creating and applying rules to all available information. Any decision-making process that can be stated in an "if…then…" format can be automated. For example, a business rules engine would be able to make the decision that if a proposed insured has a certain number of medical conditions, then she should be declined coverage.

Business rules engines are particularly useful in the underwriting decision-making process, which is characterized by the application of certain rules to data and combinations of data. In fact, hard copy underwriting manuals are nothing more than business rules books. However, whereas an underwriter using an underwriting manual can evaluate quite a few variables, business rules engines—supported by data mining and predictive modeling—can consider hundreds of variables. In addition, BREs can ensure the consistent processing of these variables, leading to more equitable underwriting decisions.

By using BREs, insurers can engage in exception-based underwriting in which rules are applied to process all applications electronically, except the most difficult ones that require an underwriter to apply human judgment in the decision-making process. Business rules engines also can identify missing pieces of information necessary to make the underwriting decision and can order this information from people and systems both inside and outside of the company. For example, the software can request data, such as payment history and claims, on other policies owned by the applicant. It also can request data over the Internet from third parties.

Increasingly, insurers are using BREs in functional areas. They frequently are used in the processing of routine claims, and they can be used to guide employees through the benefit enrollment process, assist in ordering supplies, evaluate investment alternatives, and help a policyowner make an address change via the Internet.

Document Management Systems

A **document management system** is a type of technology that stores, organizes, and retrieves documents that have been converted to digital images. Insurers can enter documents into a document management system either by creating documents electronically and converting them to digital images or by converting paper documents to digital images through imaging. **Document imaging**, also known as *scanning*, is a process of converting printed characters or graphics into digital images on a computer by inserting paper documents in a type of hardware called a *scanner*. The scanner "reads" the documents and "translates" them into electronic files, which are then converted to digital images, indexed, and stored in the insurer's document management system. Employees can use a document management system to search for, view, print, and share the digitized documents when processing applications and other customer transactions.

Document management systems provide staff members with computer access to a variety of company-specific forms and documents, such as completed applications. In addition, these systems can provide computer access to correspondence and other documents—such as credit scores—from outside the company. The advantages of document management systems include

- Eliminating the expense of storing thousands—if not millions—of paper documents that can instead be stored electronically

- Avoiding the complicated logistics of storing paper documents

- Increasing efficiency, as processors never have to wait for a paper document to be pulled from a paper file or passed from processor to processor

- Reducing frustration, delays, and wasted time that result from lost and misfiled documents

- Facilitating document sharing because several employees in different locations can view the same document at the same time on their computer screen

Automated Workflow Systems

Document management systems often are used in conjunction with automated workflow systems. An **automated workflow system**, also called a *workflow application*, is a technology used to create computer-based records pertaining to the status and processing of specific transactions. Basically, an automated workflow system can be thought of as a tracking sheet that accompanies a transaction through the entire workflow process from initial receipt through completion and filing. The automated workflow system shows the type of transaction, the employee to whom it was assigned, when it was received, questions that arose, actions taken, documents created, completion dates and times, and so on. Rather than include this information in a paper file, an automated workflow system stores it electronically.

An automated workflow system can route documents automatically to staff members for processing, placing the jobs in a work queue so that the jobs are available when staff members are ready to work on them. After a staff member has finished working on a case, the workflow system then routes the job to the next staff member who needs to work on the case. Automated workflow systems can use business rules engines for purposes such as (1) gauging the priority of a work item and placing high priority items in the front of queues and (2) determining what skill set is needed for a particular work item and then routing the work to an employee with those particular skills.

Automated workflow systems can increase accuracy by creating an **audit log**, which is a record of the work that has been completed on a case. The insurer can use the audit log to make sure that all the proper procedures are followed on each case.

Systems Integration

Many insurers maintain more than one administration system, using different systems to administer different portions of their business. For example, an insurer may have a life insurance administration system and a disability income insurance administration system. In addition, individual business and group business typically are administered on separate systems. Furthermore, an insurer that has acquired or merged with another insurer may maintain two sets of systems—one from each insurer.

If an insurer administers different portions of its business on different systems, the different systems may not work well together or they might not work together at all. In these situations, the insurer takes steps to integrate the otherwise incompatible systems. One way insurers integrate incompatible systems is by using *middleware*, which is a type of software used to enable two or more systems to work together.

Another way to integrate systems involves a centralized data repository that houses all the relevant data contained in the insurer's separate administration systems. On a regular basis—usually daily—the various administrative systems update the centralized database. The centralized database then can provide the systems with updated data as required for processes or transactions. This process allows each of the various administration systems to retain data in a format that works best for them, while providing a centralized, holistic view of data from all of the systems. The downside of this method of integrating systems is the expense of maintaining multiple copies of the same data, along with the complexity of keeping multiple copies in sync. Once an insurer establishes a centralized database, the insurer can begin modifying its administration systems to use data directly from the centralized database, as opposed to the database unique to the administration system. However, this can prove to be a long and expensive project.

As an example of how middleware and a centralized data repository operate, consider the information a customer service representative (CSR) might view on his computer monitor when he receives a telephone call. The insurer might use middleware to search all the systems, retrieve the relevant information, and present it to the CSR. Alternatively, if the insurer's customer information resides on several systems, the CSR might actually see data contained in a centralized data repository made up of data from all of the insurer's administrative systems.

Security

One of the challenges insurers face when they maintain and exchange data and information electronically is providing adequate security. *Security* refers to the physical, technical, and procedural steps a company takes to prevent the loss, wrongful disclosure (accidental or intentional), or theft of data or information. Security is to be distinguished from *privacy* of data and information. Figure 1.4 lists the major types of security risks that insurers face and the technological tools they use to combat such risks.

Figure 1.4. Security Risks and Technological Tools

Security Risk: Unauthorized persons might intercept data traveling over the Internet or a private network.

Technological Tools:

Encryption. Technology that encodes data so that only an authorized person, who possesses the required hardware and/or software that contains the decryption key, can decode the data.

Virtual private network (VPN). An organization's network that uses public telecommunications infrastructure such as the Internet to provide authorized individual users or remote offices with secure access.

Security Risk: Hackers might gain access to company databases and view, manipulate, or steal data.

Technological Tools:

Firewall. A combination of hardware and software that creates an electronic barrier between the public and private areas of a company's systems. Only those individuals who know the appropriate security procedures can access the areas behind the firewall.

Intrusion detection software. Software that monitors system traffic and identifies sequences of commands that indicate an unauthorized user is attempting to access the organization's systems or databases.

Security Risk: Unauthorized persons might gain access to private customer information by impersonating authorized persons.

Technological Tools:

Authentication. A combination of technology and procedures designed to verify a user's identity before giving the user access to a system or database. The typical authentication procedure calls for someone trying to access the system or database to provide a user name and password.

Cookie. A file that the server—a computer that contains shared resources—places on a user's personal computer that enables the server to recognize the personal computer. The user can access the protected file only from a computer containing the cookie.

Biometric authentication. Technology that identifies users by "reading" a physical trait that is unique to each user, such as the user's fingerprint or retina.

Security Risk: A virus or worm might destroy data and/or programs or disable computers.

Technological Tools:

Antivirus software. A software application that detects viruses and prevents them from infecting a computer and/or helps an infected computer recover.

Security Risk: A natural or manmade disaster might destroy data or the system's ability to function.

Technological Tools:

Data backup software. Companies use systems to back up data to the Internet or intranets while the data is being created and then store the back-up copies off site.

Disaster recovery software. Software applications are available that can aid insurers in developing disaster recovery plans. Insurers regularly conduct disaster recovery tests to practice the recovery of key systems and data.

Quality Control

Quality control is the process of ensuring that an organization accomplishes its objectives and follows its standards. Organizations set objectives both to measure their own current performance and to guide future activities. Periodically, organizations evaluate their activities to see how well their performance meets their objectives. If an organization is not meeting its objectives, then the organization can determine the causes and can implement changes to improve its performance.

Most insurers evaluate the quality of their administrative activities by measuring results and then comparing actual performance to set standards. *Performance measurement* is a process through which a company (1) decides what activities are key to the achievement of the company's goals and objectives, how to measure the performance of those activities, and what performance standards it hopes to achieve; (2) gathers the information; and (3) communicates the results. A *performance standard* is an established level of performance against which a company or an individual compares actual performance. *Benchmarks* are performance standards, often based on standards achieved by leading companies, that represent a company's goals for performance.

As part of a company's quality control program, the company creates written documentation of its policies, processes, and procedures. These written documents define how the processes work and give employees clear guidance on how they should accomplish administrative tasks. The documents also provide a basis for monitoring compliance with the established procedures.

Key Terms

insurance administration	member service
producer	marketing
applicant	actuary
insured	accounting
proposed insured	treasury operations
policyowner	legal department
third-party policy	compliance department
master group insurance contract	human resources
policyholder	information technology (IT)
group prospect	information system
group insured	information management
certificate of insurance	administration system
beneficiary	technology platform
ethics	hardware
underwriting	software
underwriter	operating system software
new business	application software
claim administration	transaction processing system
reinsurance	transaction
customer service	database
policyowner service	data

information
telecommunications
network
intranet
extranet
electronic mail (e-mail)
electronic data interchange (EDI)
electronic commerce (e-commerce)
business process management (BPM)
straight through processing (STP)
centralized data repository
database management system (DBMS)
data warehouse
data mining
predictive modeling
business rules engine (BRE)
document management system
document imaging

automated workflow system
audit log
middleware
security
encryption
virtual private network (VPN)
firewall
intrusion detection software
authentication
cookie
biometric authentication
antivirus software
data backup software
disaster recovery software
quality control
performance measurement
performance standard
benchmark

Endnotes

1. This section is adapted from Miriam Orsina and Gene Stone, *Insurance Company Operations*, 2nd Ed. [Atlanta: LOMA (Life Office Management Association, Inc.), © 2005], 309–324; Mary C. Bickley, Barbara Foxenberger Brown, Jane Lightcap Brown, and Harriett E. Jones, *Life and Health Insurance Underwriting*, 2nd Ed. [Atlanta: LOMA (Life Office Management Association, Inc.), © 2007], 95–100; and Mark Adel and Nicholas L. Desoutter, *Annuity Systems and Administration*, 2nd ed. [Atlanta: LOMA (Life Office Management Association, Inc.), © 2004], 177–187. All sources used with permission; all rights reserved.
2. LOMA, *Predictive Modeling: Life and Health Insurance Underwriting and Risk Analysis*, LOMA Information Center Brief, August 2003, 1. Used with permission; all rights reserved.
3. Ibid.

New Business Processing and Underwriting Principles

Objectives:

After studying this chapter, you should be able to

- Describe the new business process
- Explain common quality control methods used in the new business/ underwriting area
- Explain the importance of risk assessment and risk classification and describe the factors that insurers consider when they evaluate a risk
- Distinguish among the preferred, standard, substandard, and declined risk classes
- Explain how an insurer ensures that it approves and issues coverage that is equitable to the insureds, equitable to the insurer, and deliverable by the producer
- List typical underwriting job positions and authority levels and define the different approaches that insurers use to organize the work within underwriting units and list examples of each approach

Outline

New Business Process
- Field Underwriting
- Teleunderwriting
- Data Entry and Review
- Underwriting
- Policy Issue

New Business/Underwriting Quality Control

Underwriting Principles
- Risk Assessment
- Risk Classification
- Underwriting Philosophy and Underwriting Guidelines

Underwriting Organization
- Job Positions
- Authority Levels
- Organizational Systems

The new business process includes all activities an insurer undertakes in receiving applications, underwriting applications, and issuing policies. In some companies, underwriting and new business are part of the same unit; in other companies, they are separate units. In this chapter, we describe the new business process and some basic principles of underwriting.

New Business Process

Individual and group insurance applications go through basically the same new business process before a policy is issued. In general, (1) data is gathered and entered into an administration system; (2) additional data is acquired, if necessary; (3) data is assessed; (4) the decision is made whether to accept the risk; and, (5) if the decision is favorable, a policy is issued. However, the processes for underwriting individual and group coverages differ in many respects. In this section, we describe the individual life insurance new business process.

Figure 2.1 illustrates the steps an individual application goes through from field underwriting to policy issue. Although field underwriting is not technically a part of new business, it is included because of its importance in the underwriting process.

Field Underwriting

Underwriting an application for insurance often begins well before the application reaches the insurer's home office underwriters. *Field underwriting* is the practice of gathering initial information about applicants and proposed insureds and screening proposed insureds to determine if they are likely to be approved for a specific type of coverage. Effective field underwriting

- Reduces the insurer's costs by eliminating the need for home office processing and underwriting of clearly unacceptable applications

- Helps ensure that underwriters have the information they need to assess each proposed risk

- Assures that applicants are applying for an appropriate amount and type of coverage at an appropriate premium rate, which fosters better relations with applicants because false expectations are not created

Figure 2.1. Processing of an Application

1 Field underwriting
  - ✓ Gather data
  - ✓ Screen applicant and proposed insured (if different from applicant)

2 Teleunderwriting
  - ✓ Gather data

3 Data entry and review
  - ✓ Create case file
  - ✓ Enter data
  - ✓ Conduct good order check
  - ✓ Conduct suitability check
  - ✓ Search records for existing information on applicant and proposed insured (if different from applicant)

4 Underwriting
  - ✓ Assess risk
  - ✓ Classify risk
  - ✓ Make underwriting decision

5 Policy issue
  - ✓ Enter data
  - ✓ Assemble policy
  - ✓ Facilitate policy delivery
  - ✓ Collect post-issue requirements

Sometimes producers submit informal applications to several insurers to determine which company offers the best terms and rates for a specific proposed insured. Producers expect insurers to respond very quickly with a rate quote. Such informal applications typically are shorter than the formal application and do not require the applicant or proposed insured to authorize the collection of additional information, although some companies do require such authorization. When the producer finds the offer that is best for the client, he will submit a formal application to the insurer that made that offer. The application then is fully underwritten.

Traditionally, formal applications for individual life insurance have consisted of two sections—Part I and Part II. Some insurers no longer divide the application into two parts, but every application requests essentially the same types of information. Part I seeks nonmedical information and Part II requests medical information. For organizational purposes, we still refer to the two-part application.

Part I of an application contains questions designed to identify the applicant and proposed insured (if different from the applicant), specify the amount and type of coverage requested, and provide the insurer with basic information about the proposed beneficiary and proposed insured. Figure 2.2 lists the types of information typically sought in Part I of an application for individual life insurance.

Most individual life insurance applications include a section called the ***agent's statement***, in which the producer can comment on any factors relevant to the case and the risk it involves. When an underwriter knows that a producer tends to submit quality business, the agent's statement can be particularly valuable in explaining circumstances that may otherwise cause delays in underwriting when it appears that more information is needed to ensure a sound decision. Unlike the rest of the application, the agent's statement is not made a part of the insurance contract. The insurer keeps the agent's statement confidential so that producers will feel free to comment honestly on elements that affect the risk represented by each proposed insured. A typical agent's statement includes the following questions:

- How long has the producer known the applicant/proposed insured?

- How well does the producer know the applicant/proposed insured?

- What is the producer's impression of the applicant's/proposed insured's financial worth and annual income?

- Does the producer have any additional information about the proposed insured that could affect the proposed insured's insurability?

- Did the producer actually see the proposed insured when the application was completed? If so, did the proposed insured appear to be in good health and free from any defect, deformity or abnormality that might affect the underwriting decision?

- Did the producer solicit the business or did the applicant initiate the purchase?

- What is the applicant's reason for buying the requested coverage?

- Is the producer a full-time representative of another insurance company?

- Has the producer submitted an application on the proposed insured to any other insurer within the past six months?

- Does the policy replace another policy?

- Are the proposed insured and a family member applying for insurance at the same time?

- Is the proposed insured applying for two policies (for example, life and disability income) at the same time?

Figure 2.2. Information Sought in Part I of an Individual Life Insurance Application

- The proposed insured's name, government identification number (for example, Social Security number in the United States and social insurance number in Canada), date of birth, place of birth, age, sex, address, telephone number, length of time at the current residence, marital status, driver's license number, occupation, current employer, income, and length of time with the current employer

- The applicant's name (if the policy is applied for by someone other than the proposed insured), government identification number, address, and relationship to the proposed insured

- The policyowner's name (if the policy is to be owned by someone other than the applicant or proposed insured), government identification number, address, and relationship to the proposed insured

- The plan of insurance, face amount, and premium payment mode requested

- Dividend options and special features or riders desired

- Name of the beneficiary and relationship to the proposed insured

- The proposed insured's
  - Avocations and aviation activities, including hazardous activities such as sky diving, hang-gliding, and scuba diving
  - International residence and travel
  - Driving history
  - Tobacco use
  - Criminal convictions

- Insurance history, including
  - The total amount of insurance already in force on the life of the proposed insured with any insurance company and the purpose of such coverage
  - Whether any applied-for insurance is pending at the time of this application
  - Whether any in-force insurance coverage will be replaced by the coverage applied for
  - Whether the proposed insured ever has been declined for insurance coverage, been offered coverage with restricted benefits or other than standard rates, or applied for or received insurance benefits because of ill health or injury

Source: Adapted from Mary C. Bickley et al, *Life and Health Insurance Underwriting*, 2nd ed. [Atlanta: LOMA (Life Office Management Association, Inc.), © 2007], 82. Used with permission; all rights reserved.

To help producers perform field underwriting, most insurers maintain a *field underwriting manual*, which is a document that (1) presents specific guidance for a producer's assessment of the risk represented by a proposed insured and (2) guides the producer in assembling and submitting the application and any other information needed for the underwriter to evaluate the risk. Although printed manuals are still used, more and more companies provide their producers with online access to field underwriting manuals. A field underwriting manual typically contains for each product an *age and amount requirements chart*, also known as *table of underwriting requirements*, that specifies the kinds of information the underwriter must obtain and review in assessing the insurability of a proposed insured. Producers are responsible for ordering the appropriate underwriting requirements listed in this chart. The typical contents of a field underwriting manual are listed in Figure 2.3.

Another resource commonly included in a field underwriting manual is an *impairment guide*, which is a list of common impairments and the probable underwriting decision for proposed insureds who have each type of impairment. An *impairment* is a physical or psychological abnormality or loss of function. By using the impairment guide, a producer can inform a proposed insured about coverage types and amounts for which she is most likely to be approved.

Figure 2.3. Typical Contents of a Field Underwriting Manual

- The insurer's **underwriting philosophy**, also known as an *underwriting objective*, which is a set of objectives that guides all of an insurer's underwriting actions, generally reflects the insurer's strategic business goals, and includes its pricing assumptions for products

- An outline of the producer's responsibilities, including compliance issues

- Specific guidance on completing applications and on submitting changes and reinstatements

- Brief definitions of common medical terms and common impairments to help the producer describe impairments revealed by a proposed insured

- Lists of questions related to common impairments so that the producer can obtain sufficiently detailed information about them

- Age and amount requirements charts

- Impairment guide

- Criteria for a preferred rating

- Criteria for qualifying as a tobacco nonuser

Traditionally, the producer helps the applicant complete a paper application and mails or faxes it to the home office. Some companies encourage producers to use document imaging for the submission of applications. Using a document imaging system, the producer scans the application so it can be stored in and retrieved from the insurer's document management system. When a producer submits an application by mail, fax, or imaging, a new business case analyst must enter the information from the application into the insurer's new business administration system.[1] This double-entry process means that, in effect, two different people—the producer and a new business case analyst—each perform the same function, which creates additional work, adds to processing time, and increases the likelihood of errors.

To reduce the amount of time insurers spend on new business processing and improve accuracy, some companies use an ***electronic application system***, which is a technology that allows producers or applicants to enter application information into a computer, rather than on paper, and transmit the information to the insurer over a computer network. Some insurers that use electronic applications have built business rules engines into their systems. Such rules engines can determine if the information submitted is incomplete or inaccurate and will require the producer and applicant to correct the problem before they can proceed with filling out the application. When the electronic application is complete, the system transfers the information directly into the insurer's new business administration system. Electronic application systems, thus, can form part of a straight through processing system.

Applicants and proposed insureds are required to sign applications, as well as authorizations for the release, collection, use, and disclosure of information. Obviously, with an electronic application system, signatures cannot be in ink on paper. Some insurers obtain "wet" signatures after the electronic application has been submitted. Others accept an ***electronic signature***, which is a unique personal identifier that makes a legally binding contract using electronic communications media like the Internet. Often, the signature consists of the applicant clicking on an "I agree" or "I accept" icon.

Teleunderwriting

Teleunderwriting is a method by which someone other than a producer takes responsibility for gathering most of the information needed for underwriting an insurance application. When teleunderwriting is used, the producer and the applicant complete an abbreviated application that includes only basic information about the proposed insured and the coverage applied for. After receiving the abbreviated application, an insurer's underwriter, a specially-trained employee of the insurer, or an employee of a company that provides underwriting services to the insurer, gathers the additional information required for underwriting.

Typically, teleunderwriting is conducted by telephone, but some insurers conduct such interviews online via their Internet sites. The interviewer may use a software application that presents him with a prepared script of questions similar to those that appear on the application and that are customized for the product being underwritten. The software incorporates a business rules engine (BRE) that guides the interviewer through the questions in the interview. Based on the proposed insured's answer to a question, the BRE determines the follow-up questions the interviewer should ask. Voice signatures in which an applicant simply voices his agreement that he has honestly and fully answered the questions often are acceptable for teleapplications.

Data Entry and Review

A case file is created for each application received in the home office. The case file includes a number or code for identification and tracking purposes. The application then goes through a manual or an automated *good order check* process to verify that the

- Application form is the proper one for the issuing jurisdiction

- Other forms required by the insurer or regulatory authority have been completed and received

- Producer and the insurer are licensed to sell the type of coverage requested in the applicable jurisdiction

- Application is complete

If an application does not pass the good order check, a new business case analyst or an underwriter attempts to rectify the problem.

Applications for some products also must undergo a *suitability check* to determine whether the amount and type of coverage applied for are appropriate, considering the age and circumstances of the proposed insured. Producers are expected to submit only suitable applications, but the new business unit typically is responsible for confirming suitability.

Next, a new business case analyst or an automated system searches the insurer's records for information about the applicant and proposed insured, such as previous life and/or health insurance applications or claims.

Some companies assign applications to case managers, who are responsible for overseeing the entire new business process from receipt of application to policy issuance for those cases assigned to them. Typically, however, new business case analysts are assigned to certain tasks such as data entry, and policy issue analysts are responsible for assembling policies.

Some companies tier their new business service so that the highest producers receive the highest level of service from the most experienced new business personnel. Other companies provide the highest level of service to new producers to entice them to perform well and to help in their training.

Underwriting

The goal of underwriting is to accept the greatest number of qualified proposed insureds while keeping the insurer financially stable and profitable. After evaluating the degree of risk represented by a proposed insured, the underwriter decides whether to

- Issue the policy as applied for.

- Rate the policy. If a proposed insured is insurable but has risk factors that make him uninsurable at standard premium rates, the underwriter rates the policy. *Rating* is the process of increasing the premium rate or modifying the type or amount of coverage in order to approve the risk. For example, assume that a proposed insured presents a higher than average risk because he flies experimental aircraft. The underwriter might decide to approve the policy at a higher premium rate or for a lower amount of coverage than applied for. Or, the underwriter might decide to approve the policy at an average premium rate, and for the amount of coverage requested, as long as the policy excludes payment of the policy benefit should the proposed insured die while involved in experimental aviation activities. This last option involves the use of an *exclusion*, which is an insurance policy provision that describes circumstances under which the insurer will not pay the policy benefit following an otherwise covered loss. An exclusion is often attached to an insurance policy by means of a *policy rider*, an amendment to an insurance policy that becomes part of the insurance contract and either expands or limits the benefits payable under the contract.

■ Decline to issue a policy.

■ Postpone offering coverage for a specified period of time (usually 6, 12, or 24 months) until the level of risk is reduced to one that the underwriter can evaluate on a reasonable basis. For example, an underwriter might postpone offering coverage on a proposed insured with pending cardiac surgery until the surgery has been completed and the level of risk can be determined.

Policy Issue

When an underwriter has made a decision to approve a case, he forwards the file—electronically or manually—to the policy issue unit of new business. *Policy issue* is the insurance company unit that prepares the insurance contract and facilitates the delivery of the policy to the customer. A policy issue analyst enters the policy's rating and other necessary information into the administration system. Although some insurers allow some producers to print and bind policies, most insurers rely on policy issue analysts to print and bind the correct policy with any required forms, which may include a copy of the application and amended illustrations. Some insurers rely on their compliance department to maintain an updated list of all forms required for each product in each jurisdiction.

Most insurers use automated systems to produce policy documents promptly and accurately. In addition, an insurer's administration system typically verifies that the initial premium payment has been received and that all policy requirements have been met. The policy issue analyst typically then mails the policy to the producer for deliver to the policyowner. If no producer was involved in the sale, the policy issue department sends the policy documents directly to the applicant.

Most companies inform a producer of the underwriting decision *in advance* of the producer's receipt of the policy, especially if the policy is issued other than as applied for. The new business case manager, the underwriter, or a member of the underwriting staff may communicate the underwriting decision to the producer. In some companies, producers may learn the fate of applications through online status reports that the insurer uses to advise producers of activity on all cases they have handled.

Some jurisdictions also require that the insurer inform the applicant in writing of the reason the coverage was rated, modified or declined; even when not required to do so by law, insurers typically send such a letter to the applicant and the proposed insured. Because of privacy concerns, the applicant's letter will contain generic information, such as "The application was declined due to medical reasons." The proposed insured's letter will contain more specific information, such as "The application was declined due to cardiac test results."

Typically, if an underwriter rates a policy, the policy is still issued and delivered to the producer, who then attempts to deliver it to the policyowner. A skillful producer who can explain the inherent value of a rated policy to the policyowner can often obtain a successful delivery. In such a situation, the policyowner usually must sign a document saying that he understands that the policy was not issued as applied for.

The policy issue unit verifies that all delivery requirements are met.

New Business/Underwriting Quality Control

Insurers measure performance of the new business/underwriting area on a regular basis to ensure that applications are evaluated fairly and promptly, and that every step in the underwriting process is documented accurately. For example, insurers often measure turnaround times for the number of days between the receipt of an application and the approval of that application. Comparing this measurement to a company standard allows the insurer to monitor the promptness of its underwriting processes and make necessary changes when the desired goal is not met.

Audits are another frequently used quality control tool in the underwriting area. An *audit* is an evaluation of a company's records and operations to ensure the accuracy of the records and the effectiveness of operational policies and procedures. The underlying purpose of underwriting audits is to strengthen risk assessment, classification, and acceptance. Underwriting audits reveal whether underwriters are

- Making appropriate and consistent decisions

- Complying with applicable laws and regulations

- Documenting cases clearly and completely

Audits can be internal or external. An *internal audit* is an audit conducted by a company's own staff. Typically, insurers conduct internal audits of their underwriting operations not only to ensure the accuracy of their records and the effectiveness of their procedures and policies, but also to judge the quality of their underwriters' work.

An *external audit* is an audit conducted by a third party who is not employed by the company being audited. Insurers are subject to regular external audits by regulatory authorities. One of the most important quality control tools for insurers, though, is the external audit conducted by its reinsurance partners. Reinsurers periodically conduct external audits of most insurers with which they do business, and insurers are subject to separate audits by each reinsurer with which they do business. Reinsurers audit not only an insurer's reinsurance operations, but also an insurer's underwriting and claim operations.

Underwriting Principles

Risk assessment and risk classification are the foundations of underwriting individual and group insurance. These activities also are an important component of the pricing of an insurer's products.

Risk Assessment

Risk assessment is the process of determining the degree of risk represented by each proposed insured using a number of factors established when the insurance product was designed and priced. Risk assessment for life insurance is particularly concerned with mortality. *Mortality* is the incidence of death among a specified group of people. A *mortality rate* is the rate at which death occurs among a specified group of people during a specified period, typically one year.

Underwriters assess proposed insureds for coverage and evaluate the level of risk by reviewing proposed insureds' risk factors. For individual insurance underwriting purposes, a *risk factor* is any aspect of a proposed insured's present health, medical history, family history, health habits (such as tobacco use), financial condition, reputation, driving record, criminal record, occupation, or activities that increases the likelihood that the person will suffer a covered loss. In third-party policy situations, the underwriter also takes into account the applicant's financial condition to determine whether the applicant has the ability to pay for the coverage. Individual insurance risk factors typically are categorized as medical risk factors, personal risk factors, and financial risk factors, which are explained in Figure 2.4.

Figure 2.4. Individual Insurance Risk Factors

- A *medical risk factor* is a physical or psychological characteristic that may increase the likelihood of loss. For example, a history of emphysema is a medical risk factor because a person who has this disease is more likely to die prematurely or incur increased medical expenses than is a person of the same age and sex who does not have a history of emphysema.

- A *personal risk factor* is a lifestyle choice that can significantly affect a person's health or longevity. For example, a proposed insured with a record for reckless driving poses a greater risk than does a proposed insured with a clean driving record.

- A *financial risk factor* is financial information that an underwriter considers to determine whether a person is applying for more insurance than he reasonably needs or can afford. For example, if a person is seeking life insurance to replace his income so that his dependents will continue to have financial support after his death, the amount of insurance applied for must bear a reasonable relationship to the amount of income to be replaced. Furthermore, proposed insureds who buy more insurance than they can afford tend to let their policies lapse.

Source: Adapted from Mary C. Bickley et al., *Life and Health Insurance Underwriting*, 2nd ed. [Atlanta: LOMA (Life Office Management Association, Inc.), © 2007], 12. Used with permission; all rights reserved.

In assessing the degree of risk represented by a proposed insured, an underwriter also considers the possibility of antiselection, which produces a high degree of risk. *Antiselection* is the tendency of people who believe they have a greater-than-average likelihood of loss to seek insurance protection to a greater extent than do those who believe they have an average or a less-than-average likelihood of loss. For example, a person who believes she has a serious illness may be more likely to purchase insurance than a person who believes he is in good health.

Another risk factor that underwriters must be aware of is moral hazard. *Moral hazard* is a characteristic that exists when the reputation, financial position, or criminal record of an applicant or proposed insured indicates that the person may act dishonestly in the insurance transaction. Moral hazard exists, for example, when a person applies for coverage with the intention of seeking a financial gain rather than as protection against a financial loss. If an underwriter suspects that an applicant or proposed insured presents a moral hazard to the insurer, the underwriter may have reason to believe that the applicant or proposed insured has not answered questions on the insurance application honestly. Therefore, the underwriter verifies as much information as possible.

Risk Classification

After assessing the degree of risk a proposed insured represents, an underwriter classifies the proposed insured into one of several specific risk classes. A *risk class* is a group of insureds who represent a similar level of risk to an insurance company. Insureds in the same risk class are charged the same premium rate. A person who represents a higher degree of risk is charged a proportionately greater premium rate for coverage than a person who represents a lesser degree of risk.

Each insurer defines the parameters of its own risk classes. The terms insurers use for these classes may differ; however, most insurers identify risk classes as preferred, standard, substandard, and declined.

- *Preferred classes* designate proposed insureds whose anticipated mortality rates are lower than average and who represent the lowest degree of mortality risk. Proposed insureds who fall in the preferred classes typically are the healthiest and are charged lower-than-average premium rates.

- *Standard classes* designate proposed insureds whose anticipated mortality rates are average. The mortality risk of people in standard classes is higher than the mortality risk for people in preferred classes, but lower than the mortality risk for people in substandard classes. Traditionally, most proposed insureds fell within standard classes; today in some companies, most proposed insureds for individual life insurance fall within preferred classes.

- *Substandard classes*, also called *special classes*, designate proposed insureds whose anticipated mortality rates are higher than average, but who are still considered to be insurable. Many insurers assign to substandard classes those proposed insureds who are recovering from serious illnesses or accidents, whose occupations or avocations produce a significant risk of illness or accident, or who have permanent significant medical conditions. Thus, insurers charge higher premium rates to people in the substandard classes than they charge to people in standard classes.

- The ***declined class*** designates proposed insureds whose anticipated mortality rates are so great that the insurer cannot provide coverage at an affordable cost or whose mortality risk cannot be predicted because of recent or unusual medical conditions or other risk factors.

An insurer's risk classes are defined when a product is designed; actuaries design the product's premium rate structure so that the premium rate charged to each insured is based on the amount of risk that the insured represents relative to others insured by the same product.

When setting premium rates, actuaries also predict and factor into the calculation the probable rate of loss—the *loss rate*—that a given group of insureds will experience. To predict the loss rate for a given group of insureds, actuaries must predict the number and timing of covered losses that are likely to occur in that group of insureds.

Underwriters bear the responsibility of assessing and classifying risks appropriately to ensure that (1) each insured is placed in the appropriate risk class and (2) the insurer's claim experience is as close as possible to the assumed loss rate used to establish premium rates. Underwriters obtain guidance for risk assessment and risk classification from an insurer's underwriting philosophy and underwriting guidelines.

Underwriting Philosophy and Underwriting Guidelines

An insurer's underwriting philosophy is a set of objectives that guides all of an insurer's underwriting actions, generally reflects the insurer's strategic business goals, and includes its pricing assumptions for products. An insurer's underwriting philosophy describes in general terms the types of risks that the company will and will not accept. And that philosophy strongly influences the insurer's underwriting guidelines.

Underwriting guidelines are general standards that underwriters follow as they establish the level of risk presented by a proposed insured or group. For individual life insurance, an insurer's underwriting guidelines specify the parameters within which an applicant may be assigned to one of the risk classes established for each insurance product. Figure 2.5 sets forth the most common factors considered in individual and group life insurance underwriting guidelines.

In establishing its underwriting philosophy and underwriting guidelines, an insurer may consider ***industry experience***, which is the collective data about insurance claim experience generated by industry-wide studies. For instance, studies on mortality rates, policy lapse rates, impairments, and demographics contribute to industry experience. These studies generally are conducted by large insurers, reinsurance companies, and industry associations. An insurer also uses the experience data from its own insurance products. Industry experience and an insurer's own experience are useful guides for the insurer's future actions and decisions, especially for establishing underwriting requirements, risk classes, and premiums rates for new coverages.

As an insurer's experience changes over time, the insurer may modify its underwriting philosophy and underwriting guidelines. Despite changes to the insurer's underwriting philosophy and underwriting guidelines, underwriters always must focus on approving and issuing coverage that is equitable to the insureds, equitable to the insurer, and deliverable by the producer.

Figure 2.5. Factors Typically Considered in Underwriting Guidelines

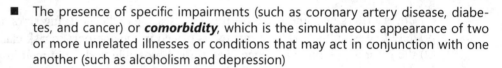

Individual life insurance underwriting guidelines typically focus on factors relating to the proposed insured such as

- Age

- Height and weight

- Blood pressure

- Cholesterol levels

- The presence of specific impairments (such as coronary artery disease, diabetes, and cancer) or *comorbidity*, which is the simultaneous appearance of two or more unrelated illnesses or conditions that may act in conjunction with one another (such as alcoholism and depression)

- Medical history

- Family medical history

- Financial circumstances

- Occupation

- Indications of specific behaviors (such as tobacco use, substance abuse, poor driving record, and participation in certain avocations)

- The type and amount of coverage applied for

- The purpose of the insurance

Group life insurance underwriting guidelines typically focus on factors relating to the group such as the

- Size of the group

- Nature of the group's business

- Employee occupational classes

- Type and amount of coverage requested

Source: Adapted from Mary C. Bickley et al., *Life and Health Insurance Underwriting*, 2nd ed. [Atlanta: LOMA (Life Office Management Association, Inc.), © 2007], 15. Used with permission; all rights reserved.

Equitable to the Insureds

Risk classification maintains equity among insureds by ensuring that each insured pays a premium rate that reflects the degree of risk that the insured represents. By charging higher rates for higher risks and by declining risks it cannot afford to cover, an insurer is better able to protect its long-term financial well-being, thus enabling it to provide coverage for all the risks it does accept.

To maintain equity among insureds, risk assessment and risk classification must be as objective as possible—that is, the risks must be evaluated fairly, without bias or prejudice. Being objective in underwriting is sometimes difficult, however, because an underwriter makes decisions under considerable pressure from producers, actuaries, and company management:

- Producers want underwriters to issue coverage quickly and assign proposed insureds to preferred or standard classes.

- Actuaries want underwriters to use risk classification methods that keep actual mortality rates very close to those on which the pricing assumptions for the insurance product are based.

- The insurer's management wants underwriters to accomplish both these objectives—fast issue and favorable mortality results—while keeping underwriting costs as low as possible.

Equitable to the Insurer

An insurer's underwriting guidelines and premium rates help ensure that the underwritten coverage will be equitable to the insurer. If an insurer's underwriting guidelines are too strict or its premium rates are not competitive with other companies, insurance producers are less likely to submit applications to the company. Therefore, the insurer will lose potential premium income. If an insurer's underwriting guidelines are too lax or its premium rates are too low in relation to the level of the risks accepted, over time the insurer might not have sufficient funds to pay all legitimate claims. Eventually, the insurer could become financially impaired or insolvent, which would be inequitable to the insurer, as well as the insureds, policyowners, and shareholders.

Deliverable by the Producer

An individual insurance applicant makes the final decision whether to accept an insurance policy when it is delivered. If an applicant chooses not to accept a policy when a producer attempts to deliver it, the policy is said to be **undeliverable**. A policy may be undeliverable because the underwriter has rated the policy.

For group coverage, the policy is not prepared and delivered until after the sale is finalized, except perhaps for small groups. Thus, although an undeliverable group policy is rare, the same principle applies: a group prospect may refuse to purchase a policy offered with a premium rate greater than or coverage less than anticipated.

One of the greatest challenges facing the underwriter is explaining tactfully and persuasively to a producer the reasons for rating or declining an application for insurance so that the producer will be satisfied that the underwriting decision was equitable and in turn will be able to explain the decision to the applicant and place the policy. A successful underwriter not only makes equitable decisions, but also earns the confidence and respect of producers in doing so. Underwriters form a productive relationship with producers by

- Completing work on each application in a timely manner

- Assessing each application in a consistent manner

- Keeping producers informed of progress in cases that are delayed because of requirements for additional information

- Communicating with producers about rating, modifying, or declining an application without disclosing confidential information

- Making use of opportunities to educate producers and their staffs about the insurer's underwriting philosophy and guidelines

Underwriting Organization

The underwriting departments of life insurance companies may have variations, but they all are composed of different ranks of underwriters who have different authority levels and are organized in certain ways.

Job Positions

The typical underwriting job positions include underwriting trainee, junior underwriter, intermediate underwriter, senior underwriter and chief underwriter. An individual is promoted from one rank to another as his knowledge, skills, and abilities improve. The chief underwriter is the highest ranking underwriter in an insurance company. This individual is an expert in risk selection and also is quite knowledgeable about claim administration, reinsurance, and customer service.

The chief underwriter's typical responsibilities include

- Establishing the insurer's underwriting philosophy and guidelines

- Monitoring the cost and quality of underwriting

- Assisting with underwriting large or unusually difficult cases

- Deciding which products, services, and vendors to use

- Overseeing the training of all underwriters

- Reviewing contestable claims

- Serving as a liaison with the insurer's other functional areas

Examples of serving in this last capacity might involve working with the company's legal staff to create contract wording, the information technology staff to develop underwriting systems, and the actuarial staff to establish preferred risk criteria and other product characteristics. The chief underwriter typically also is involved with the negotiation and administration of reinsurance agreements. Note that in some companies, underwriting managers—rather than the chief underwriter—may have responsibility for workflow and personnel issues. In addition, in some companies, the chief underwriter is the highest-level technical underwriter; the vice president of underwriting has responsibility for managerial and executive duties.

Most insurers also use physicians as underwriting medical experts who consult with underwriters on cases with unusual or difficult medical histories and may be responsible for developing and updating the insurer's medical underwriting guidelines. Large insurers usually appoint a medical director to lead a medical underwriting staff composed of physicians and other medical personnel.

Authority Levels

In general, an underwriter's authority to approve, rate, or decline applications increases as the underwriter's level of experience increases and as her demonstrated ability and quality of judgment improve. An underwriter's level of authority is specified by (1) the maximum coverage amount that the underwriter can approve and (2) the degree to which the underwriter may rate or decline a policy without approval or review by a more experienced underwriter.

Authority to Approve Specified Coverage Limits

Most individual life insurers develop charts or schedules of underwriting authority to specify the highest amount of coverage that can be approved by each level of underwriter. Figure 2.6 provides an example of authority levels to approve specified coverage limits for individual life insurance.

Authority to Rate or Decline Cases

As Figure 2.6 indicates, some insurers require underwriting decisions to rate a policy, add an exclusion rider, or decline a case to be reviewed and approved by a higher-level underwriter. In other words, the underwriter's authority to approve a case as applied for does not also permit the underwriter to rate, modify or decline the case without review by a higher-level underwriter.

In some insurance companies, all rated and declined cases are reviewed by an underwriter one level higher than the original underwriter. Other insurers require the chief underwriter to perform this kind of review. The review is performed to

■ Ensure the appropriateness of the original underwriting decision

■ Ensure the consistency of underwriting actions

■ Evaluate the underwriter's job performance

■ Train the underwriter

■ Enhance producers' confidence in the insurer's underwriting practices

Organizational Systems

Some insurers establish separate underwriting units to handle applications for various types of coverage. For individual coverages, insurers may organize the work within these units according to a case assignment system, a work division system, or a combination of the two systems. Group insurers may organize their underwriting departments by case size, geographic location, or producer. Typically, senior group underwriters will work on larger, more complex groups. Some group underwriting departments prefer to assign groups randomly to give their group underwriters a wide variety of experience.

Figure 2.6. Example of Case Authority Levels

Underwriter Level	Approve Standard Cases up to	Approve Substandard Cases or Cases with Exclusions up to	Decline Cases up to
Junior Underwriter with less than 1 year of experience at this level	$100,000	Not authorized without review	Not authorized without review
Junior Underwriter with 1 year or more of experience at this level	$400,000	$100,000	Not authorized without review
Intermediate Underwriter with less than 1 year of experience at this level	$500,000	$200,000	Not authorized without review
Intermediate Underwriter with 1 year or more of experience at this level	$750,000	$500,000	Not authorized without review
Senior Underwriter with less than 1 year of experience at this level	$1,000,000	$500,000	$200,000
Senior Underwriter with 1 year or more of experience at this level	$1,500,000	$1,000,000	$500,000
Chief Underwriter	All amounts	All amounts	All amounts

Note: The dollar amounts stated in the figure are used for illustration only. Specific amounts and the number of levels of coverage approval authority vary from one insurer to another.

Case Assignment System

A *case assignment system* is a method of assigning cases to underwriters based on the characteristics of the case. The benefit of this system is that it enables an underwriter to specialize in certain types of cases. The basis used to assign case files to underwriters varies depending on the size of the insurer, the number of applications usually received, and the difficulty of the cases to be underwritten.

An advantage of the case assignment system is that the underwriters may become more productive and effective through specialization. A drawback of this system is that underwriters can become well informed about only their own areas of specialization. As a result, employees' vacations and absences may cause other underwriters to work temporarily—and probably less productively—with "unfamiliar" cases. Insurers control this problem, however, by periodic rotation of assignments and cross-training so that several underwriters become familiar with the characteristics of other types of cases.

■ **Type of Application or Policy Change.** When cases are based on the type of application or policy change requested—usually an increase in the coverage amount or the addition of a rider—one life insurance underwriter may be assigned only nonmedical applications that don't require medical proof of insurability, a second underwriter may handle only applications requiring a medical examination report, and a third underwriter may be responsible only for requests for accidental death benefit coverage.

■ **Geographic Origin.** If the geographic origin of the application is the basis of an insurer's case assignment system, the underwriting department is divided into regional sections, with each section handling all business submitted from a specific geographic area. Case assignment on the basis of geographic origin enables underwriters to become more knowledgeable about legislative and regulatory requirements within specific jurisdictions, learn more about impairments or occupations that may be peculiar to a certain geographic region, and operate in the same time zones as their customers.

■ **Producer Submitting Application.** Alternatively, some insurers assign specific producers to each underwriter, regardless of the producers' geographic locations. This case assignment method enables an underwriter to become familiar with the quality of the producers' business and develop effective working relationships with the producers.

Work Division System

A *work division system* is a method of assigning cases to underwriters that divides cases according to the person or group that underwrites them. In many insurance companies, applications are assigned according to a work division system known as *independent underwriting* in which underwriters work alone to assess each risk. Some insurers assign only cases requiring extensive research to independent underwriters.

Team underwriting is a work division system in which underwriters are divided into small groups. The team usually includes one or more senior underwriters who handle large-amount or complex cases, and one or more lower-level underwriters who handle simpler cases. Team underwriting usually enables team members to exercise considerable autonomy in making underwriting decisions. Members of the team are responsible for setting work assignments and establishing priorities for themselves. Team members make recommendations to the supervisor or chief underwriter on such issues as team training and development, work and vacation schedules, solutions to production problems, and conflict resolution. Compared to other underwriting methods, team underwriting can be more cost effective and can provide producers with faster service because if one team member is out of the office, another team member can handle the case.

Designed to underwrite simple cases quickly, ***jet unit underwriting*** is a work division approach in which a separate group of employees are authorized to approve certain types of individual insurance applications for immediate policy issue. For example, individual life insurance applications with the following characteristics are typically eligible for consideration by a jet unit:

- Proposed insured's age, height, and weight are within specified ranges

- Proposed insured has no significant health problems

- Proposed insured has an acceptable occupation

- Application is being made for an amount of insurance below a specified limit, depending on the proposed insured's age and the insurer's requirements

- Applicant has not made an unusual beneficiary designation

- Applicant has answered all questions on the application

- Insurer's records contain no adverse underwriting information on the proposed insured

The jet issue process can take only days when completed manually and even less when done electronically by a jet issue system that uses business rules engines (BREs). A jet issue electronic system is an example of how BREs are used in the underwriting process. A ***jet issue electronic system*** uses business rules engines to determine that certain criteria are met and the application is approved for issue; or the rule engine determines that the criteria are not met, and the application is either declined or sent to an underwriter. Thus, BREs free underwriters from the more routine cases, leaving them to handle those cases that are particularly complex or call for a particular expertise.

A jet unit usually is not authorized to request further information or to rate or decline an application. All applications that are not approved for immediate coverage are sent from the jet unit to other underwriters, who gather additional information and make the final decisions on the cases. Some insurers are able to underwrite policies in only minutes by engaging in real-time underwriting. ***Real-time underwriting***, or *instant-issue underwriting*, is a straight through processing system that evaluates insurance applications that are typically submitted over the Internet, and almost instantly provides the applicant or producer with an underwriting decision.

Cases involving large coverage amounts or special problems, such as unusual occupations, may require committee evaluation. ***Committee underwriting*** is a work division approach in which a committee of highly qualified people from inside and outside the underwriting function is called together for case assessment. Usually the committee is composed of the chief underwriter, the medical director, and representatives from the legal and actuarial functions. By pooling their technical expertise, the committee members can reach an appropriate decision on cases that otherwise might have to be passed from person to person in a less efficient manner.

Some insurers combine a case assignment system with a work division system. For example, a jet unit may handle only nonmedical applications that don't require medical proof of insurability, or an underwriting team may handle only term life insurance applications from a specific geographic area or certain producer.

Key Terms

field underwriting

agent's statement

field underwriting manual

age and amount requirements chart

impairment guide

impairment

underwriting philosophy

electronic application system

electronic signature

teleunderwriting

rating

exclusion

policy rider

policy issue

audit

internal audit

external audit

risk assessment

mortality

mortality rate

risk factor

medical risk factor

personal risk factor

financial risk factor

antiselection

moral hazard

risk class

preferred class

standard class

substandard class

declined class

underwriting guidelines

industry experience

comorbidity

undeliverable

case assignment system

work division system

independent underwriting

team underwriting

jet unit underwriting

jet issue electronic system

real-time underwriting

committee underwriting

Endnote

1. The section on application completion and electronic application systems was adapted from Mark Adel and Nicholas L. Desoutter, *Annuity Systems and Administration*, Second Edition [Atlanta: LOMA (Life Office Management Association, Inc.), © 2004], 197–198. Used with permission; all rights reserved.

Chapter 3

Legal Aspects of Underwriting

Objectives:

After studying this chapter, you should be able to

- Describe temporary insurance agreements and distinguish among the basic types of premium receipts that include a temporary insurance agreement

- Define insurable interest and identify when insurable interest must exist in order for an insurance contract to be valid

- Describe how governments in the United States and Canada regulate privacy

- Describe how governments in the United States and Canada regulate discrimination, medical testing, replacements, money laundering, and financing terrorists during the individual life insurance underwriting process

- Describe how governments in the United States and Canada regulate group life insurance policies during the underwriting process

- Recognize the responsibilities of an underwriter when reviewing applications, acting promptly on applications, and documenting underwriting

Outline

Premium Receipts

Insurable Interest

Regulatory Compliance Issues Affecting Individual Insurance Underwriting
- Privacy Protection
- Nondiscrimination
- Medical Testing
- Replacements
- Money Laundering and Financing Terrorists

Regulatory Compliance Issues Affecting Group Insurance Underwriting
- U.S. State Regulatory Requirements
- U.S. Federal Regulatory Requirements
- Canadian Regulatory Requirements

Underwriting Standards
- Reviewing Applications for Proper Completion
- Processing Applications Promptly
- Documenting Underwriting

During most of the underwriting process, underwriters focus on evaluating the insurability of the proposed insured—who typically is the applicant for insurance—or on the characteristics of the proposed group. However, in reviewing applications, underwriters also must be knowledgeable about a range of legal and regulatory requirements so that as they perform their jobs, they help the insurer meet its legal duties to applicants, policyowners, beneficiaries, and others.[1]

Premium Receipts

Underwriting some life insurance coverages can take weeks or even months. The applicant for life insurance typically pays the initial premium at the time he completes the application, and in exchange the insurer often provides some type of temporary insurance coverage during the underwriting period. How much coverage the insurer provides and when the coverage takes effect is dependent upon the *premium receipt*, which the insurer uses to acknowledge receipt of the payment.

The premium receipt often includes a ***temporary insurance agreement (TIA)***, which is a contract between the insurer and the applicant that provides temporary coverage on the proposed insured before a policy is issued and delivered; such coverage may be subject to certain conditions. A premium receipt that provides temporary insurance coverage typically states when the coverage becomes effective, the conditions that must be met for the coverage to become effective, and when the coverage will end.

Premium receipts also usually state that the temporary insurance coverage is provided subject to the terms of the insurance policy for which the applicant applied. For example, if the policy applied for contains a suicide exclusion provision, then the TIA also contains that suicide exclusion provision, even if the premium receipt is silent concerning suicide. However, if the terms of a premium receipt conflict with the terms of the policy applied for, then the terms of the premium receipt control. For example, premium receipts often limit the amount of life insurance benefits available to a stated dollar amount, which is often less than the amount of insurance that the applicant applied for. If the proposed insured dies while insured under a TIA, the amount of the death benefit payable is limited to the amount specified in the premium receipt.

Figure 3.1 describes the basic types of premium receipts with temporary insurance agreements issued in the United States: binding premium receipts and two types of conditional premium receipts: (1) approval premium receipts and (2) insurability premium receipts. Underwriters must be aware of the type of premium receipt issued with a given application and the amount of coverage provided by such a receipt. Some insurers use the same type of premium receipt for all types of policy applications, and other companies use specific premium receipts with specific policy applications. To protect the insurer against liability for a risk it otherwise would not have accepted, the underwriter must make an underwriting decision quickly on a proposed insured covered under the terms of a premium receipt. If the underwriter's decision is to decline an application, the insurer returns the initial premium paid and coverage under the premium receipt terminates.

Figure 3.1. Types of Premium Receipts

A **binding premium receipt** provides temporary insurance coverage that becomes effective on the date specified in the receipt. Temporary coverage under a TIA generally remains effective until the earliest of the following occurrences:

- The insurer issues the applicant a policy

- The insurer declines the application

- The insurer terminates or suspends coverage under the receipt

- A specified time—usually 45 to 60 days—expires

Conditional premium receipts, which include approval premium receipts and insurability premium receipts, specify certain conditions that must be met before the temporary insurance coverage provided by the receipt becomes effective.

- An **approval premium receipt** is a conditional premium receipt that provides temporary insurance coverage only when the insurer approves the proposed insured as a standard or better-than-average risk. If the insurer approves the risk, the insurance coverage is effective on the date of the insurer's approval. If the proposed insured dies before the application is approved, the receipt provides no coverage. U.S. life insurers rarely issue approval premium receipts.

- An **insurability premium receipt** is a conditional premium receipt that provides temporary insurance coverage on condition that the insurer finds that the proposed insured was insurable at least as a standard risk on a certain date specified in the premium receipt. The date is typically that of the premium receipt, application, or medical examination. Should a proposed insured die before the application is approved, the insurer completes the underwriting process as if the proposed insured were still alive. If the underwriter determines that the proposed insured was insurable on the date specified in the receipt, then a death benefit is payable.

Source: Adapted from Harriett E. Jones, *Business Law for Financial Services Professionals* [Atlanta, GA: LOMA (Life Office Management Association, Inc.), © 2004], 206–209. Used with permission; all rights reserved.

Insurable Interest

If an agreement's purpose is illegal or against public policy, the agreement is void (not valid) and cannot be legally enforced. Laws in each jurisdiction define the agreements that are illegal; in most jurisdictions, wagering agreements are illegal. A *wagering agreement* is an agreement under which either party may gain or lose depending on the outcome of an uncertain event, such as the timing of an individual's death.

To guard against the purchase of insurance contracts as wagering agreements that allow a person to profit from another person's death, laws in many jurisdictions impose an insurable interest requirement on the issuance of individual insurance. An *insurable interest* exists when a person is likely to suffer a genuine financial loss or detriment should the event insured against occur. Underwriters must make sure that any insurable interest requirement is met before they issue an insurance policy.

For an individual insurance contract to be valid, or enforceable at law, an insurable interest must exist at the time of contracting. If an insurer issues an individual insurance policy and the policyowner—and in some cases, the beneficiary—did not in fact have an insurable interest in the insured when the contract was created, then the agreement is void. Most jurisdictions do not require an insurable interest to continue throughout the life of the policy. For example, if spouses purchase life insurance policies on each other's lives and then the spouses later divorce, the policies are not voided at the time of the divorce because of lack of insurable interest.

Group insurance contracts are not required to meet the insurable interest requirement because the group policyholder's interest in the contract does not induce wagering as does a policyowner's interest in an individual insurance contract. The lawful purpose requirement for a group insurance contract is met if the group policyholder purchases the coverage to provide a benefit to covered group members. In other respects, the requirements for the formation of a valid group insurance contract are the same as the requirements to form a valid individual insurance contract.

Regulatory Compliance Issues Affecting Individual Insurance Underwriting

Laws in many countries impose requirements that affect the individual life insurance underwriting process. In the United States and Canada, federal, state, and provincial laws and regulations govern some aspects of individual insurance underwriting.

Privacy Protection

To conduct business, insurers need to acquire, store, and use a great deal of personal information about their customers. Such personal information can include facts about a person's health, medical history, financial situation, credit history, occupation, and avocations. To protect the privacy of customers and the confidentiality of personal information, most jurisdictions have passed laws regulating the use and disclosure of that information. Insurance underwriting is subject to such laws in the United States and Canada.

U.S. Federal Fair Credit Reporting Act

When assessing the risk represented by a proposed insured, an underwriter often obtains a consumer report. The U.S. federal *Fair Credit Reporting Act (FCRA)* regulates the reporting and use of consumer information and seeks to ensure that consumer reports contain only accurate, relevant, and recent information.[2] Under the FCRA, only individuals are considered to be consumers; corporations and other types of businesses are not protected by the act. For purposes of the FCRA, a *consumer report* is any communication of information by a consumer reporting agency that (1) bears on an individual consumer's creditworthiness, credit standing, credit capacity, character, general reputation, personal characteristics, or mode of living and (2) is used or collected as a factor in establishing a consumer's eligibility for insurance or credit. A *consumer reporting agency* is a private business that assembles or evaluates information on consumers and furnishes consumer reports to third parties in exchange for a fee.

The FCRA regulates not only consumer reporting agencies, but also third parties, such as insurance companies and banks, that (1) obtain investigative consumer reports and (2) take adverse actions based on the information in such reports. An *investigative consumer report* is a consumer report that contains information obtained through personal interviews with an individual's neighbors, friends, associates, or others who may have information about the individual. For insurance purposes, an *adverse action* means a denial or revocation of insurance coverage, a change in the terms of existing insurance coverage, or a refusal to grant insurance in substantially the amount or on substantially the terms requested.

To comply with FCRA requirements regarding investigative consumer reports, underwriters must notify an applicant and the proposed insured that this type of report may be ordered. The insurer must mail or deliver the disclosure to the applicant no later than three days after the insurer requests the investigative consumer report. As a matter of practice, insurers routinely include the disclosure notice in the application for insurance. The disclosure must also inform the applicant that she has the right to make a written request to the insurer for information about the nature, scope, and results of the investigation. The insurer must respond no later than five days after receiving a request from the applicant regarding the nature and scope of the investigation.

When an insurer takes an adverse action based on information contained in any consumer report, the insurer has a duty to contact the applicant and the insured and notify them of

- The name, address, and telephone number of the consumer reporting agency that provided the report to the insurer

- Their right to obtain a free copy of the report from the consumer reporting agency

- Their right to dispute with the consumer reporting agency the accuracy or completeness of any information contained in the report

- The fact that the consumer reporting agency did not make the adverse decision and is unable to inform the consumer why the adverse decision was made

In addition, insurers must allow customers an opportunity to opt out of the sharing of information in any consumer reports with the insurer's affiliates. Insurers also must safeguard consumer information when it is being disposed of to help prevent identity theft.

U.S. Federal Gramm-Leach-Bliley Act

The *Gramm-Leach-Bliley (GLB) Act* is a U.S. federal law that removed many of the barriers to affiliations among institutions in the various segments of the financial services industry.[3] A purported benefit of the GLB Act is the ability of various industry segments to share customer information. However, the GLB Act requires financial institutions, including insurance companies, to respect customers' privacy and to protect the security and confidentiality of those customers' nonpublic personal information. Under the GLB Act, *nonpublic personal information* is personally identifiable information about a consumer that is not publicly available. Subject to certain exceptions, the GLB requires insurers to

- Disclose their policies for obtaining and sharing customers' nonpublic personal information at the beginning of the relationship and at least annually thereafter

- Provide the customer with an opportunity to opt out of information sharing with nonaffiliated third parties

- Explain to the customer how to opt out of the information sharing

- Maintain policies to protect the security and confidentiality of nonpublic information

The GLB Act does not restrict insurers from sharing information with affiliated parties that are related to the insurer by common ownership or control.

U.S. State Laws and Regulations

Insurance privacy laws in many states are based on the National Association of Insurance Commissioners' (NAIC's) *Insurance Information and Privacy Protection Model Act (Model Privacy Act)*, which is a model law that establishes standards for the collection, use, and disclosure of information gathered in connection with insurance transactions. The Model Privacy Act applies only to personal insurance and not to insurance for business or professional needs, and the act primarily governs underwriting and claim evaluation. Figure 3.2 sets forth the requirements that the Model Privacy Act imposes on insurers.

The privacy provisions of the GLB Act preempt—or supersede—state privacy laws unless a state's laws provide for stricter protections of the privacy of consumer information than does the GLB Act. In response to the GLB Act, some states amended their privacy laws by including additional provisions consistent with the GLB Act. Other states responded by adopting new regulations based on the NAIC's *Privacy of Consumer Financial and Health Information Regulation* (Model Privacy Regulation), which includes requirements similar to those contained in the GLB Act, including limits on an insurer's right to disclose nonpublic personal information about a consumer without the consumer's consent.

Figure 3.2. Model Privacy Act's Privacy Requirements

An insurer must provide a consumer with a written notice of the insurer's information practices when the insurer (1) intends to collect information about a consumer who has applied for insurance, policy renewal, or policy reinstatement and (2) will collect that information from sources other than the consumer or public records.

- With a few exceptions, an insurer may disclose personal or privileged information only if it first obtains the individual's written authorization. For purposes of the Model Privacy Act, *personal information* is information gathered about an individual in connection with an insurance transaction and from which judgments can be made about the individual's personal characteristics, such as character, habits, finances, credit, and health. *Privileged information* is information that relates to either an insurance claim or a court proceeding.

- Insurers may use investigative consumer reports in connection with insurance transactions, but they must inform the individual who is the subject of the report that he may request to be interviewed in connection with the investigative consumer report and may obtain a copy of the report.

- With one exception, insurers are prohibited from conducting pretext interviews in connection with insurance transactions. A *pretext interview* is an interview in which one person attempts to gain information from another person by (1) pretending to be someone he is not, (2) pretending to represent someone he does not represent, (3) refusing to identify himself, or (4) misrepresenting the purpose of the interview. The exception is that, within stated limits, an insurer may conduct pretext interviews during the investigation of a claim only if the insurer has a reasonable basis to suspect criminal activity, fraud, or material misrepresentation in connection with the claim.

- Individuals have the right to access recorded personal information that an insurer has collected about them by submitting a written request to the insurer. An insurer that receives such a written request has 30 days in which to (1) provide the information to the individual, (2) identify the persons to whom the information has been disclosed, and (3) inform the individual how to request that the information be corrected, amended, or deleted.

Canadian Federal and Provincial Laws

In Canada, the federal *Personal Information Protection and Electronics Document Act (PIPEDA)* governs the collection, use, and disclosure of personal information by organizations in the private sector.[4] Figure 3.3 sets forth the principles of PIPEDA.

Like other commercial organizations, insurance companies are governed by PIPEDA, except in Quebec, British Columbia, and Alberta, where substantially similar provincial privacy laws apply. On the provincial level, the Canadian Life and Health Insurance Association has issued Right to Privacy Guidelines. Insurers may either adopt these guidelines or develop their own stricter guidelines.

Figure 3.3. PIPEDA Privacy Principles

Organizations subject to Canada's Personal Information Protection and Electronics Document Act (PIPEDA) are responsible for complying with the following 10 principles:

Be accountable. Develop policies and procedures for the safeguarding of personal information and appoint an individual responsible for assuring compliance.

Identify purpose. Before or at the time of collecting personal information, identify the purpose for doing so.

Obtain consent. Inform the individual from whom personal information is collected of the purpose of the collection and obtain the individual's consent for the collection, use, or disclosure of the information.

Limit collection. Limit the collection of information to the purpose for which it was intended.

Limit use, disclosure, and retention. Use or disclose information only for the purpose for which it was collected, unless the individual consents or the law provides for broader use or disclosure. Establish policies and procedures for retention and destruction of information.

Be accurate. Ascertain that information is accurate, complete, and up to date as is necessary for the purpose for which it is to be used.

Establish and use appropriate safeguards. Protect information against loss and theft, as well as unauthorized access, disclosure, copying, use, or modification.

Be open. Make policies and procedures easily understandable and available to customers and employees.

Give individuals access. Give individuals access to their information at minimal or no cost, subject to certain exceptions.

Provide recourse. Develop and inform customers of simple-to-use and easily accessible complaint procedures.

Source: Adapted from Mary C. Bickley, *Canadian Supplement to Business Law for Financial Services Professionals* [Atlanta: LOMA (Life Office Management Association, Inc.), © 2006], 70. Used with permission; all rights reserved.

Nondiscrimination

An underwriter's responsibility is to distinguish risks that are acceptable from risks that are unacceptable by carefully examining the facts about proposed insureds. Such discrimination among risks is usually lawful when it is based upon

(1) recognized actuarial principles or (2) actual or reasonably anticipated experience. However, many U.S. jurisdictions have enacted laws that prohibit insurers from using the following factors as underwriting criteria:

- Sex

- Marital status

- Sexual orientation

- Blindness or partial blindness

- Status as a victim of physical abuse

- Race

Underwriters in Canada generally may not discriminate among proposed insureds for life insurance coverage on the basis of whether a person is male or female. In addition, some provinces specifically prohibit discrimination on the basis of physical and mental impairments, marital status, and sexual orientation.

Medical Testing

Acquired immune deficiency syndrome (AIDS) and genetic testing present insurers with unique underwriting challenges.

HIV Testing

Proposed insureds with the human immunodeficiency virus (HIV) or AIDS have an increased mortality risk. Thus, insurers typically include questions about those physical conditions on applications for individual life insurance.

A variety of issues about the collection and use of medical testing information in the underwriting process have been raised because (1) certain segments of the population—homosexual and bisexual men and intravenous drug users—have been most affected by HIV and AIDS, (2) AIDS can be a fatal disease, and (3) maintaining confidentiality is essential. Many states have adopted the following regulatory guidelines that insurers must abide by when they request and use information about AIDS-related conditions in the underwriting process. In accordance with these guidelines, insurers must

- Conduct testing for AIDS-related conditions on a nondiscriminatory basis; an insurer must not single out certain segments of the population or specific applicants for such testing.

- Notify the proposed insured that an AIDS-related blood test will be performed and obtain the proposed insured's written consent.

- Base an adverse underwriting decision on an HIV blood test that is positive—that is, a test that indicates that HIV is present—or indeterminate only if the test was conducted in accordance with an established test protocol. Such a test protocol involves repeated testing to ensure that a positive test result is accurate.

- Maintain the confidentiality of medical information.

In Canada, according to the CLHIA *Guidelines with Respect to AIDS for the Sale and Underwriting of Life and Health Insurance*, a proposed insured must give written consent before his blood or other bodily fluid is taken to test for the presence of HIV. If a proposed insured refuses to consent to such a test, then the insurer may decline the application for insurance. Questions contained in applications for insurance should not be directed toward determining the proposed insured's sexual orientation. Questions may relate to past instances of sexually transmitted diseases and past testing for HIV or AIDS; however, the proposed insured must be given the opportunity to explain any affirmative answers to these questions. An insurer cannot base an adverse underwriting decision on (1) the proposed insured's sexual orientation, (2) previous testing for HIV if the result of such a test was negative or is unknown, or (3) an unconfirmed positive test result.

Tests for HIV must follow a current standard protocol, which involves a screening test and a confirmatory test. For an insurer to consider a test result as proof of the presence of the virus, (1) two screening tests must indicate the presence of HIV and (2) the positive results then must be confirmed by a more refined test.

Genetic Testing

Although the term is defined in numerous ways, basically a ***genetic test*** is a test of human DNA used to indicate a person's predisposition to a certain illness or disease. Researchers have developed genetic tests for a variety of life-threatening diseases, and the information gained from such testing obviously would be useful to life insurers in their underwriting process.

Nevertheless, many jurisdictions have enacted laws that limit insurers' ability to use genetic testing results. These restrictions exist for a number of reasons: (1) regulators have made policy decisions that genetic material is personal and confidential, (2) genetic testing is still new and its results are not always reliable, (3) regulators fear that insurance decisions made on the basis of genetic information will be unfairly discriminatory, and (4) regulators do not want to force individuals to learn that they have a predisposition to a certain disease or illness if the person does not want to have such testing. State laws vary widely, however. Figure 3.4 provides examples of state laws concerning genetic testing.

Reflecting a policy promulgated by the Canadian Life and Health Insurance Association, life and health insurers in Canada do not require applicants to undergo genetic testing. Furthermore, no laws in Canada specifically address the issue of genetic testing for insurance underwriting purposes.[5]

Replacements

A ***replacement*** is the purchase of one life insurance policy or annuity contract to take the place of another. Although replacement of an existing life insurance policy is not illegal, the replacement may not be in a policyowner's best interest. Because most producers earn high first-year commissions on new sales, producers sometimes are tempted to place their own financial interests above the interests of their clients and of the insurers they represent by recommending replacements that are adverse to the client's interests.

Figure 3.4. Regulation of Genetic Testing

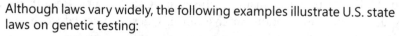

Although laws vary widely, the following examples illustrate U.S. state laws on genetic testing:

- Only a few states permit insurers to require a proposed insured to undergo genetic testing and to deny coverage to proposed insureds who refuse to undergo such testing.

- Most states that have enacted genetic testing laws permit insurers to use the results of genetic testing for purposes of underwriting life insurance and disability income insurance, but they prohibit insurers from using such information in underwriting medical expense insurance. Some states prohibit the use of genetic testing results in underwriting life insurance, disability income insurance, and medical expense insurance.

- Some states permit insurers to use the results of genetic testing only if those results are actuarially significant.

- Laws in some states focus on consumers' privacy rights and impose restrictions on the ability of insurers to access genetic information that consumers have obtained for themselves.

Source: Adapted from Mary C. Bickley et al., *Life and Health Insurance Underwriting*, 2nd ed. [Atlanta: LOMA (Life Office Management Association, Inc.), © 2007], 69. Used with permission; all rights reserved.

When an application involves a replacement, an underwriter must be alert to evidence that producers are engaged in twisting or churning. *Twisting* occurs when a producer misrepresents the features of a policy to induce a client to purchase a policy. *Churning* occurs when a producer induces a customer to replace one policy after another so that the producer can earn a series of first-year commissions on the replacements.

To help prevent unethical replacement, most states have adopted some version of the NAIC's ***Replacement of Life Insurance and Annuities Model Regulation***, which states that replacement of policies is generally permissible if the replacing insurer provides full and fair disclosure and no deceptive practices are involved. State replacement regulations usually do not govern certain types of policies, including group policies, conversion policies, and temporary coverage issued under a premium receipt.

Producers have certain duties under these replacement regulations, and underwriters may be required to verify that producers have fulfilled these duties, which are set forth in Figure 3.5.

Figure 3.5. U.S. State Replacement Requirements

U.S. state regulations typically provide that in the issuance of any new policy, the producer must submit to the insurer a replacement statement signed by the applicant and producer indicating whether an in-force policy will be replaced. If no policy is to be replaced, the producer's duties are fulfilled. If a policy will be replaced, the producer has the following additional duties:

- Provide the applicant with a Notice to Applicants Regarding Replacement, which contains general information about the potential effects of a replacement and advises the applicant to receive all the relevant facts before making a replacement.

- Obtain a list of all existing life insurance policies that will be replaced and ensure those policies are listed on the notice regarding replacement. For each such policy, the notice must identify the name of the insurer, the name of the insured, and the policy number or other identifying number.

- Submit to the insurer the completed and signed notice regarding replacement and provide the applicant a copy of the completed notice.

- Leave with the applicant copies of all sales materials that the producer showed the applicant and provide the insurer with a list of all such materials.

When another insurer's policy will be replaced, most states require the replacing insurer to send a written notification to the insurer that issued the policy that may be replaced. Along with such notification, the replacing insurer must provide the original insurer with certain information about the new policy for which the applicant has applied. The original insurer then may contact its policyowner to offer additional information about the existing policy and to attempt to conserve its existing business. Underwriters may bear the responsibility of contacting the original insurers, but in most companies, a new business case analyst handles this task.

In Canada, provincial regulations govern replacements. These regulations call for full and accurate disclosure and mandate that certain disclosure forms be used.

Money Laundering and Financing Terrorists

The *USA Patriot Act of 2001* was designed to strengthen the federal government's ability to investigate, prosecute, and seize the assets of terrorists.[6] This act extended anti-money laundering requirements to all financial institutions, including insurers, and prohibited doing business with known terrorists. *Money laundering* is the practice of engaging in financial transactions to hide the identity, source, and/or destination of money associated with criminal activity.

While criminals traditionally have used accounts in banks and other depository institutions to launder money, they now sometimes use products issued by insurance companies. As a result, many jurisdictions have enacted laws requiring insurers to establish anti-money laundering programs if they issue products with features that allow them to be used to launder money, such as cash value life insurance policies.

Underwriters must be alert to cases that could involve money laundering activities, such as when a customer

- Applies for an insurance product that seems inconsistent with the customer's needs

- Indicates a desire to use an unusual method of paying premiums, such as paying in cash

- Shows little concern for the financial performance of a product but a great deal of concern about the product's early termination features

- Is reluctant to provide identifying information when purchasing a product or provides minimal or seemingly fictitious information

The U.S. Treasury's Office of Foreign Assets Control (OFAC) maintains a list of countries, individuals, and organizations that participate in or sponsor terrorism and other illegal acts. Insurers must monitor OFAC's list constantly to guard against doing business with prohibited entities or people. New business staff or underwriters typically bear responsibility for making sure that applicants, policyowners, proposed insureds, and beneficiaries are not on the list. Policyowner service staff must not approve any kind of policy changes, such as a change of beneficiary or assignment of ownership, if the change involves any entity or person on the list. Claim staff must be certain that no payments are made to anyone on the list. Insurers typically comply with OFAC's requirements by using software designed to automatically check transactions for the involvement of any prohibited entity or individual.

In Canada, the *Proceeds of Crime (Money Laundering) and Terrorist Financing Act* requires companies, including life insurers, to report every financial transaction that occurs for which there are reasonable grounds to suspect that the transaction is related to money laundering or financing terrorists.[7]

Regulatory Compliance Issues Affecting Group Insurance Underwriting

In the United States and Canada, group insurance underwriters must comply with many of the same laws that affect individual insurance underwriting, as well as laws that specifically affect group insurance underwriting.

U.S. State Regulatory Requirements

The NAIC's *Group Life Insurance Definition and Group Life Insurance Standard Provisions Model Act (Group Life Insurance Model Act)* defines the types of groups eligible for group life insurance and sets forth provisions that group policies must contain. Most states have adopted laws based on the Group Life Insurance Model Act and, thus, group life insurance regulation is relatively uniform in the United States.

Underwriters must ensure that groups applying for coverage are eligible to do so under the applicable state laws. Group underwriters also must be familiar with policy provisions that are required in those jurisdictions in which the insurer does business.

Group life insurance policies must include specified policy provisions according to the Group Life Insurance Model Act. For example, most states require group life insurance policies to contain a ***conversion provision*** that gives a group insured who meets specific conditions the right to obtain an individual life insurance policy without providing evidence of insurability. The conversion provision applies in the following situations:

■ If a group insured's coverage terminates because the insured's employment terminates or the insured is no longer a member of a class eligible for coverage, then the insured must be given the right to purchase any type of individual policy the insurer is then issuing at the insurer's customary premium rate for that policy based on the insured's age. The exception is that the group policy may exclude the option of purchasing term life insurance. The amount of insurance provided by the individual policy is limited to the amount of group life insurance that terminated, less any amount of group life insurance for which the insured becomes eligible within 31 days after termination of the group life coverage.

■ If a covered dependent of a group insured no longer qualifies for group coverage, then the dependent must have the right to obtain an individual life insurance policy on the same terms described in the previous bullet point.

■ If an individual insured under a group life policy dies, then the insured's surviving dependents who were covered under the group plan at the insured's death must have the right to obtain an individual life insurance policy on the same terms we described in the first bullet point.

■ If a group policy terminates or is amended so as to terminate the coverage of any class of group insureds, then each group insured—including dependents— whose coverage terminates is entitled to obtain an individual life insurance policy provided the group insured has been insured under the group policy for at least five years. The amount of insurance that must be provided by the individual policy is limited to the smaller of (1) $10,000 or (2) the amount of group life insurance that terminated less the amount of group life insurance for which the group insured becomes eligible within 31 days after termination of the group policy.

To convert group coverage to an individual policy, the group insured must complete an application for the individual policy and pay the premium to the insurer within 31 days after becoming ineligible for group coverage. If a person applies for coverage in accordance with the conversion provision, the insurer's policyowner service or customer service department verifies the applicant's eligibility and the benefit amount that can be approved, and then issues an individual life insurance policy. However, if an applicant requests coverage of a different type or amount than what was provided under the group policy, then the application usually is forwarded to an underwriter who specializes in underwriting individual life insurance coverage and who evaluates the application in accordance with the insurer's usual underwriting guidelines for the requested policy.

U.S. Federal Regulatory Requirements

In this section, we describe some of the U.S. federal laws that affect the design and operation of group life insurance policies.

Employee Retirement Income Security Act

The *Employee Retirement Income Security Act (ERISA)* regulates employee retirement plans and specifies minimum requirements that employee welfare benefit plans must meet.[8] For purposes of ERISA, group life insurance plans established by employers are welfare benefit plans that must meet ERISA requirements, which include

- Establishing and maintaining the plan in accordance with a written plan document

- Meeting reporting and disclosure requirements

- Providing a summary plan description to each plan participant

Federal Employment Laws

U.S. federal employment laws have been enacted to ensure that all employees are treated fairly in the workplace. Employment laws prohibit discrimination regarding hiring, advancement, wages, and other terms and conditions of employment. Employer-sponsored plans that provide employee benefits, such as group life insurance plans, must comply with all applicable federal employment laws. The following federal laws impose nondiscrimination requirements on most employers and, thus, affect the design of employee benefit plans:

- The *Civil Rights Act of 1964* prohibits employment discrimination on the basis of race, color, sex, religion, or national origin.[9] The act applies to employers that are engaged in interstate commerce and have 15 or more employees.

- The *Pregnancy Discrimination Act* is a part of the Civil Rights Act and requires employers to treat pregnancy, childbirth, and related medical conditions the same as any other medical condition.[10]

- The *Americans with Disabilities Act (ADA)* protects disabled individuals against all types of discrimination, including employment discrimination.[11] The ADA applies to all employers with 15 or more employees.

- The *Age Discrimination in Employment Act (ADEA)* protects workers who are age 40 and older from being discriminated against because of their age.[12] The ADEA, which applies to employers with 20 or more employees, permits an employer to reduce the level of group life insurance benefits provided to older employees if the employer's premium contributions for those benefits is at least equal to its contributions provided to fund the benefits provided to younger workers.

Canadian Regulatory Requirements

Group life insurance is governed in most provinces by legislation based on the Uniform Life Insurance Act and the Uniform Accident and Sickness Insurance Act. Quebec has its own insurance regulations to cover group life insurance. In addition, CLHIA's Guideline G-3: Group Life and Group Health Insurance (Group Guidelines) provides important details about group life insurance regulation, such as required policy provisions in regard to policy termination and conversion, as well as the contents of group certificates.

The *Canada Pension Plan (CPP)* is a federal program that provides a pension for wage earners who have contributed money into the plan during their working years. The CPP covers workers in all provinces except Quebec, which has elected to establish its own provincial plan. The *Quebec Pension Plan (QPP)* functions in the same manner as the CPP except that the QPP applies only to wage earners in Quebec. The CPP and QPP are coordinated closely and tend to operate as one plan. In addition to pension benefits, the CPP and QPP provide survivorship benefits, lump-sum death benefits, benefits for orphans, and long-term disability benefits. To know what supplemental benefits can be offered to prospective customers, underwriters become familiar with the provisions of relevant laws.

Underwriting Standards

Insurers establish certain standards to ensure that applications are processed properly and risks are evaluated fairly, without bias or prejudice. By adhering to these standards, underwriters protect the insurer should the policy become the subject of a legal action.

Reviewing Applications for Proper Completion

Applicants and proposed insureds have a duty to answer completely and honestly any questions contained in the application for insurance, asked during a medical examination, or furnished to the insurer by any other means as evidence of insurability. Thus, in addition to ascertaining whether the requirements for a valid contract have been met, an underwriter must evaluate an application to ensure that it provides complete, accurate, and consistent information and is signed. If an insurer allows an application with missing or incomplete information to proceed to policy issue, the insurer may lose its right to contest the policy based on the missing or incomplete information.

Courts typically will permit an application as evidence in a lawsuit only if it is the original, unaltered document signed by the applicant. Thus, no one can alter an application after the applicant submits it to the insurer unless the applicant affirms the change in writing. Most insurers use an amendment, signed by the applicant, to modify or complete the answer to a question on the application. Such an amendment then becomes part of the application.

Sometimes an application contains an untrue statement of a fact, known as a *misrepresentation*. Some misrepresentations do not affect the underwriter's decision, but others do. A *material misrepresentation* is a misrepresentation that induces the other party—in this case, the insurer—to enter into a contract that it would not have entered into had it known the truth. In general, a misrepresentation is material to the formation of an insurance contract if an insurer that knew the true facts would have either

- Declined to issue the policy

- Increased the premium rate charged for the policy

- Excluded coverage for certain risks

Figure 3.6 lists some potential warning signs that might indicate material misrepresentation in an application for insurance.

If the insurer finds material misrepresentation, the insurer may rescind—or avoid—the policy, subject to certain limitations. *Rescission* is a remedy provided by law to an insurer that discovers that it has issued a policy based on material misrepresentation. If a contract is rescinded, it is void from the beginning. In the United States, the parties are returned to the positions they would have been in had no contract ever been created. Thus, rescission obligates the insurer to return the premiums paid for the policy. In Canada, whether the insurer repays the premiums depends on the terms of the contract.

Insurers are limited in their right to rescind policies by a policy's incontestability provision, which in individual insurance policies denies the insurer the right to avoid the contract on the grounds of a material misrepresentation in the application after the contract has been in force for a stated period during the life of the insured. In the United States, this *contestable period*—the time period within which the insurer has the right to avoid a life insurance policy on the grounds of a material misrepresentation in the application—typically is two years from the date the policy was issued. In Canada, an insurer loses the right to contest the validity of a contract after the contract has been in force for two years during the lifetime

---

Figure 3.6. Material Misrepresentation Warning Signs

- The applicant requested an amount of coverage that is slightly less than the amount of coverage that would require the proposed insured to undergo a physical examination.

- The applicant's signature on the application does not match the applicant's signature on other documents, such as a physical examination report.

- Answers to questions on the application have been changed or covered by correction fluid.

- The applicant requested an unusually large amount of coverage for her occupation and income.

Source: Adapted from Mary C. Bickley et al., *Life and Health Insurance Underwriting*, 2nd ed. [Atlanta: LOMA (Life Office Management Association, Inc.), © 2007], 58. Used with permission; all rights reserved.

of the insured unless the misrepresentation was fraudulent. In some U.S. states, an insurer still can contest the validity of a contract after the contestable period if the misrepresentation was fraudulent.

Processing Applications Promptly

Underwriters process applications promptly not only to assure that the applicant does not change his mind, but also to avoid a court ruling that the insurer is liable for paying benefits if the event insured against occurs before the underwriting decision is made. If the insurer is held liable for not acting with reasonable promptness in processing an application, the insurer will have to pay benefits under the policy regardless of the proposed insured's insurability. The courts have been especially strict in holding an insurer liable when an applicant submits a premium with the application. Consequently, insurers typically issue premium receipts, which we discussed earlier, to set forth their own terms of liability before the court does so for them.

Documenting Underwriting

Insurers create a case file for each application, and underwriters working on the case must be careful to note in the file all communications and actions concerning the application. Each notation must be specific and should include the date and time, the exact action taken or requested, and the underwriter's full signature. The file must be precise and thorough because it may become evidence in a court proceeding.

In addition, all comments included in a case file must be relevant to the risk assessment and classification process and must not indicate personal bias against an applicant or proposed insured. Thus, underwriters must avoid writing unsubstantiated or personal comments in a case file such as "Applicant probably drinks more than he indicated on his application," which could be interpreted as showing an underwriter's bias against an applicant. Underwriters must be able to demonstrate effectively that their decisions were based on objective criteria and not on personal judgments.

Most insurers require underwriters to use a worksheet to keep track of the information requested and received, as well as to record the final decision on each case. An *underwriting worksheet* is a document that contains records of telephone calls, letters, and other communications; documentation of requests for reinsurance; lists of reports and other information requested; and other notations that will explain clearly the manner in which the underwriter has handled the case beginning with the submission of the application to the insurer. Electronic versions of the underwriting worksheet have greatly simplified the underwriter's task of tracking and maintaining this information. If the underwriter responsible for the case is out of the office, another underwriter usually will be able to answer inquiries on the case by reviewing the underwriting worksheet. The worksheet also explains to the insurer's internal auditors unusual or exceptional handling of a case.

Key Terms

temporary insurance agreement (TIA)

wagering agreement

insurable interest

binding premium receipt

conditional premium receipt

approval premium receipt

insurability premium receipt

Fair Credit Reporting Act (FCRA)

consumer report

consumer reporting agency

investigative consumer report

adverse action

Gramm-Leach-Bliley (GLB) Act

nonpublic personal information

Insurance Information and Privacy Protection Model Act (Model Privacy Act)

personal information

privileged information

pretext interview

Privacy of Consumer Financial and Health Information Regulation (Model Privacy Regulation)

Personal Information Protection and Electronics Document Act (PIPEDA)

genetic test

replacement

twisting

churning

Replacement of Life Insurance and Annuities Model Regulation

USA Patriot Act of 2001

money laundering

Proceeds of Crime (Money Laundering) and Terrorist Financing Act

Group Life Insurance Definition and Group Life Insurance Standard Provisions Model Act (Group Life Insurance Model Act)

conversion provision

Employee Retirement Income Security Act (ERISA)

Civil Rights Act of 1964

Pregnancy Discrimination Act

Americans with Disabilities Act (ADA)

Age Discrimination in Employment Act (ADEA)

Canada Pension Plan (CPP)

Quebec Pension Plan (QPP)

misrepresentation

material misrepresentation

rescission

contestable period

underwriting worksheet

Endnote

1. Portions of this chapter are adapted from Mary C. Bickley et al., *Life and Health Insurance Underwriting*, 2nd ed. [Atlanta: LOMA (Life Office Management Association, Inc.), © 2007], 49–75 and 237–256. Used with permission; all rights reserved.

2. 15 U.S.C. § § 1681 *et seq.* (2001).

3. 15 U.S.C. § 6801(a) (2001).

4. S.C. 2000, c. 5.

5. HumGen International, "Genetic Testing and Screening," www.humgen.umontreal.ca/int/faq.cfm?Idcat=7 (6 December 2006).

6. Public Law 107–56.

7. S.C. 2000, c. 17.

8. 29 U.S.C. § § 1001 *et seq.* (2000).

9. 42 U.S.C. § § 2000 *et seq.* (1999).

10. 42 U.S.C. § § 2000e(k) *et seq.* (1999).

11. 42 U.S.C. § § 12101–213 (1999).

12. 29 U.S.C. § § 621–634 (2000).

Chapter 4

Underwriting Individual Life Insurance: Assessing Mortality Risk

Objectives:

After studying this chapter, you should be able to

- Describe the sources of information that individual life insurance underwriters use to assess medical risk factors

- Distinguish among a nonmedical supplement, a paramedical report, and a medical report

- Describe the underwriting information obtained from MIB Group, Inc. and the process underwriters use to obtain and use this information

- Discuss the importance of the following factors for underwriting individual life insurance: impairments, age, sex, and build

- Describe the sources of information that individual life insurance underwriters use to assess personal risk factors

- List the personal risk factors used in underwriting and describe how individual life insurance underwriters assess a proposed insured's personal risk factors

Outline

Medical Risk Factors	**Personal Risk Factors**
■ Sources of Medical Information	■ Sources of Personal Information
■ Assessing Medical Factors	■ Assessing Personal Factors

Risk assessment is the process of determining the degree of risk represented by each proposed insured person or group using a number of criteria established when the insurance product was designed and priced. Risk assessment for life insurance is particularly concerned with mortality, which is the incidence of death among a specified group of people. An individual life insurance underwriter assesses a proposed insured's mortality risk by evaluating the proposed insured's medical risk factors and personal risk factors.

Medical Risk Factors

To accurately assess a proposed insured's mortality risk, an underwriter needs information about the person's medical history. In this section, we describe the sources of medical information that an individual life underwriter reviews in evaluating a proposed insured's mortality risk and how the underwriter assesses medical risk factors.

Sources of Medical Information

An underwriter's goal in gathering information about a proposed insured's health status is to have enough data to assess the risk fairly without accumulating unnecessary data, incurring excessive costs, or taking too much time. The most common sources of medical information used by an individual life underwriter are

■ The application for insurance

■ MIB Group, Inc.

■ Physicians

■ Medical tests

■ Personal history interviews

■ Inspection reports

■ Pharmaceutical databases

Application for Insurance

The application for individual life insurance is one of the underwriter's most important risk assessment tools. As described in Chapter 2, Part I of the application contains questions designed to identify the applicant and the proposed insured, specify the amount and type of coverage requested, and provide the insurer with basic information about the proposed beneficiary and the insurability of the proposed insured.

Part II of the application asks for the proposed insured's medical information and may take one of three forms: (1) a nonmedical supplement, (2) a paramedical report, or (3) a medical report. The type of Part II application required in any given case is specified in the insurer's age and amount requirements chart for the product; that chart specifies the kinds of information the producer must submit and the underwriter must review in assessing the insurability of a proposed insured. Generally, applications that represent a greater degree of risk—for example, large amounts of coverage or insurance for older people—require greater amounts of information about insurability than do applications representing less risk. Information about insurability is also known as *evidence of insurability.*

Figure 4.1 shows a portion of an age and amount requirements chart developed by one insurer for a specific individual life insurance product. As the amount of insurance applied for increases within each age group, the amount of underwriting information required also increases.

Figure 4.1. Portion of an Age and Amount Requirements Chart for Individual LIfe Insurance

Age at Last Birthday	Amount of Coverage Applied For	Underwriting Requirements
31–40	Up to $99,999	Nonmedical
	$100,000 to $300,000	Nonmedical, blood profile
	$300,001 to $1,000,000	Paramedical, blood profile
	$1,000,001 to $2,000,000	Paramedical, blood profile, ECG
	$2,000,001 and up	Medical, blood profile, ECG
41–45	Up to $99,999	Nonmedical
	$100,000 to $500,000	Paramedical, blood profile
	$500,001 to $1,500,000	Paramedical, blood profile, ECG
	$1,500,001 to $3,000,000	Medical, blood profile, ECG
	$3,000,001 and up	Medical, blood profile, ECG, X-ray, inspection report
46–50	Up to $49,999	Nonmedical
	$50,000 to $100,000	Paramedical
	$100,001 to $200,000	Paramedical, blood profile
	$200,001 to $1,000,000	Paramedical, blood profile, ECG
	$1,000,001 to $3,000,000	Medical, blood profile, ECG
	$3,000,001 and up	Medical, blood profile, ECG, X-ray, inspection report
51–60	Up to $99,999	Paramedical
	$100,000 to $750,000	Paramedical, blood profile, ECG
	$750,001 to $2,000,000	Medical, blood profile, ECG
	$2,000,001 and up	Medical, blood profile, ECG, X-ray, inspection report

The proposed insured answers questions about her medical history in all three types of Part II applications. Such questions ask about her current and past medical conditions, diseases, and injuries; the extent of her drug, tobacco, and alcohol use; her family's history of medical impairments; the ages of her parents and any siblings; and, if a parent or sibling is deceased, the cause of death. The proposed insured signs the medical history portion to verify that the information was recorded correctly. If a policy is issued, the application including this medical history portion becomes part of the insurance contract.

Life insurance often is issued on a *nonmedical basis*, which means that the proposed insured is not required to provide medical proof of insurability by undergoing any type of physical examination. In such cases, the type of Part II application the insurer uses is known as a *nonmedical supplement* that contains the proposed insured's answers to medical history questions recorded by a producer or teleunderwriter.

Typically, insurers require a physical exam when the face amount applied for exceeds a set limit. An insurer's *nonmedical limit* is the total amount of insurance that the insurer will permit to be issued on a proposed insured without requiring the proposed insured to undergo a physical examination. For example, an insurer may specify the following nonmedical limits for a specific insurance product:

Age	Limit of Nonmedical Coverage
0–30	$250,000
31–40	200,000
41–45	100,000
46–50	75,000
51–60	50,000

Nonmedical limits usually apply to the total of (1) insurance being applied for and (2) insurance already in force. That is, if a proposed insured already has a certain amount of life insurance coverage in force and applies for an additional amount of life coverage, the total amount of in-force and applied-for coverage cannot exceed the insurer's nonmedical limits if the applicant wants to apply on a nonmedical basis. For example, if a 43-year-old applicant already has $50,000 of life insurance coverage in force and is applying for an additional $100,000 of coverage, the total of $150,000 would exceed the nonmedical limits specified in the preceding table. In such a case, the proposed insured typically would undergo a medical examination to apply for the $100,000 additional coverage.

Note that some insurers consider only in-force coverage that has been issued in the last 6 to 12 months when determining whether total coverage exceeds the nonmedical limit. Furthermore, some insurers consider only in-force coverage issued by their own company, while other insurers take into account coverage issued by other companies.

Based on the information provided in the nonmedical supplement, the underwriter may need to confirm information or investigate further. Thus, the underwriter may request a paramedical exam, a medical exam, or an attending physician's statement, which we discuss later in this chapter.

Another type of Part II application is the *paramedical report*, which contains the proposed insured's answers to medical history questions recorded by a paramedical examiner and the results of an examination conducted by a paramedical examiner. This examination typically includes measuring and recording height, weight, blood pressure, pulse, and chest and waist measurements (for men only). Sometimes the paramedical examiner also collects a blood or urine sample.

The proposed insured signs the section of the paramedical report that contains answers to medical history questions, and that section of the report becomes a part of the insurance contract. However, the portion of the paramedical report containing the paramedical examination results is not signed by the proposed insured and does not become a part of the insurance contract.

A paramedical examination generally is used when the face amount of coverage is too high for the insurer to rely on a nonmedical supplement alone. If the information on a paramedical report indicates a possible medical impairment, an underwriter can request a medical examination of the proposed insured by a physician. Many insurers use paramedical examinations instead of medical examinations because paramedical exams are less expensive and faster for the insurer and more convenient for the proposed insured. Furthermore, in many cases, paramedical exams provide all the information needed for accurate underwriting.

The third type of Part II application is a ***medical report***, which contains the proposed insured's answers to medical history questions recorded by a physician and the results of a medical examination conducted by a physician. Unlike the answers to the medical history questions, the results of the medical examination do not become part of the contract.

During a medical examination, the physician collects the same medical information as obtained in a paramedical examination, plus the physician examines the proposed insured, including her heart, lungs, liver, eyes, ears, nose, and throat. The main differences between a medical report and a paramedical report are (1) the medical exam is more extensive, (2) the physician may comment on any symptoms noted, and (3) the medical report is completed and signed by a physician. Figure 4.2 presents an example of a medical report.

MIB Group, Inc.

An underwriter in the United States or Canada may be able to request information about a proposed insured from ***MIB Group, Inc. (MIB)***, a not-for-profit membership corporation established to provide coded information to insurers about impairments that applicants have disclosed or other insurance companies have detected in connection with previous applications for insurance. MIB maintains information about people applying for coverage with MIB-member life and health insurance companies. MIB members may request information to find out whether proposed insureds have significant impairments or avocational risks that they did not disclose on their current applications for insurance. Such information is provided as an alert to initiate further investigation, not to use as the sole basis for denying coverage. MIB strictly prohibits its member companies from using MIB information as the sole basis of an unfavorable underwriting decision or action.

MIB operates to protect life and health insurance companies—and, ultimately, life and health insurance purchasers—from proposed insureds who knowingly or unknowingly omit information about their insurability. If underwriters had no means of detecting and investigating these unadmitted impairments, some people with uninsurable medical conditions might obtain insurance coverage, and other people might purchase insurance at insufficient premium rates.

Figure 4.2. Example of a Medical Report

Questions to be Answered by the Proposed Insured and Recorded by a Physician

Proposed Insured _____ | Birth Date _____
First Name   Middle Initial   Last Name | Day   Month   Year

1. a. Name and address of your personal physician _____
   (If none, so state)

   b. Date and reason last consulted? _____

   c. What treatment was given or medication prescribed? _____

2. Have you ever had medical treatment for: YES   NO
   a. Disorder of eyes, ears, nose, or throat?   ☐   ☐
   b. Dizziness, fainting, convulsions, headache; speech defect, paralysis or stroke; mental or nervous disorder?   ☐   ☐
   c. Shortness or breath, persistent hoarseness or cough, blood spitting; bronchitis, pleurisy, asthma, emphysema, tuberculosis or chronic respiratory disorder?   ☐   ☐
   d. Chest pain, palpitation, high blood pressure, rheumatic fever, heart murmur, heart attack or other disorder of the heart or blood vessels?   ☐   ☐
   e. Jaundice, intestinal bleeding; ulcer, hernia, appendicitis, colitis, diverticulitis, hemorrhoids, recurrent indigestion, or other disorder of the stomach, intestines, liver, or gall bladder?   ☐   ☐
   f. Sugar, albumin, blood or pus in urine; veneral disease; stone or other disorder of kidney, bladder, prostate, male or female reproductive organs, breasts?   ☐   ☐
   g. Diabetes; thyroid or other endocrine disorders?   ☐   ☐
   h. Neuritis, scintica, rheumatism, arthritis, gout, or disorder of the muscles or bones, including the spine, back, or joints?   ☐   ☐
   i. Deformity, lameness or amputation?   ☐   ☐
   j. Disorder of skin, lymph glands, cyst, tumor, or cancer?   ☐   ☐
   k. Allergies; anemia or other disorder of the blood?   ☐   ☐
   l. Excessive use of alcohol, tobacco, or any habit-forming drugs?   ☐   ☐
   m. Any mental or physical discorder not listed abvoe?   ☐   ☐

3. Are you now under observation or taking treatment?   ☐   ☐

4. Have you had any change in weight in the past year?   ☐   ☐

5. *Other than the foregoing*, have you within the past 5 years:
   a. Had a checkup, consultation, illness, injury, surgery?   ☐   ☐
   b. Been a patient in a hospital, clinic, sanatorium, or other medical facility?   ☐   ☐
   c. Had electrocardiogram, X-ray, other diagnostic test?   ☐   ☐
   d. Been advised to have any diagnostic test, hospitalization or surgery which was not completed?   ☐   ☐

6. Have you ever had military service deferment, rejection or discharge because of a physical or mental condition?   ☐   ☐

7. Have you ever requested or received a pension, benefits or payment because of an injury, sickness, or disability?   ☐   ☐

8. Family History: Tuberculosis, diabetes, cancer, high blood pressure, heart or kidney disease, mental illness or suicide   ☐   ☐

	Age if Living?	Cause of Death	Age at Death?
Father			
Mother			
Brothers and Sisters			
No. Living _____			
No. Dead _____			

9. Have you been diagnosed by a member of the medical profession for:
   a. AIDS (Acquired Immune Deficiency Syndrome), ARC (AIDS Related Complex) or any other immunological disorder?   ☐   ☐
   b. Enlargement of lymph nodes (glands), chronic diarrhea, unusual or persistent skin lesions or unexplained infections?   ☐   ☐

Please give details of all "Yes" answers. Include diagnoses, dates, duration, and names and addresses of all attending physicians and medical facilities. _____
_____

It is hereby represented that the statements and answers in all parts of this application are true, complete, and correctly recorded, to the best of my knowledge and belief.

I hereby authorize ANY PHYSICIAN, HOSPITAL, CLINIC, INSURANCE COMPANY OR OTHER ORGANIZATION, INSTITUTION OR PERSON, that has any records or knowledge of me or my health, to give to the Company any and all information about me with reference to my health and medical history and any hospitalization, advice, diagnosis, treatment, disease or ailment. A photographic copy of this authorization shall be as valid as the original.

Date _____ Witness _____ M.D. _____
Medical Examiner   Signature of Proposed Insured

continued on next page...

Figure 4.2. Example of a Medical Report *continued*

To be completed by a Physician

1.HEIGHT (IN SHOES)	WEIGHT (CLOTHED)	CHEST (FULL INSPIRATION)	CHEST (FORCED EXPIRATION)	ABDOMEN AT UMBILICUS RELAXED	Details of "Yes" answers. (Identify Item.)

FT. _____ IN.   _____LBS.   _____IN.   _____IN.   _____IN.

Did you weigh? ❑ Yes   ❑ No   Did you measure? ❑ Yes ❑ No
Weight change in past year?_____lbs. ❑ Gain ❑ Loss – Cause?
Is appearance unhealthy or older than stated age? ❑ Yes ❑ No

2. Blood Pressure (Take three readings at rest—3 minutes apart)

	1st	2nd	3rd
Systolic			
Diastolic			

3. Pulse:

	BEFORE EXERCISE	AFTER EXERCISE	AFTER REST
Rate			
Irregularities			

4. Heart:
   a. Is there any cyanosis, dyspnea, edema, arteriosclerosis, peripheral
      vascular or other cardiovascular disorder? ❑ Yes ❑ No
   b. Is heart enlarged?   ❑ Yes   ❑ No (If yes, describe)
   c. Is murmur present?   ❑ Yes   ❑ No (If yes, complete 4d)
   d. Murmur is:
      Timing: ❑ Stystolic   ❑ Prestyolic   ❑ Diastolic
      Intensity: ❑ Faint   ❑ Moderate   ❑ Loud
      Quality: ❑ Soft   ❑ Blowing   ❑ Rough
      Location: ❑ Apex   ❑ Base
   e. How is murmur affected by:
      Respiration? _____
      Exercise? _____
      Recumbency?_____
   f. Is murmur transmitted? .... Yes ❑ No ❑
      If yes, where_____
   g. Degree of hypertrophy:
      ❑ None ❑ Slight ❑ Moderate ❑ Marked
   h. Is there evidence of decompensation?...........................Yes ❑ No ❑
   i. Is there a thrill?..Yes ❑ No ❑
   j. Is murmur: ❑ Organic ❑ Functional ❑ Unsure

   Show location of

   Apex by   X

   Area of murmur by   ⊙

   Point of greatest intensity by   ◯

   Transmission by   ⟶

   Your impression?

5. Do you FIND any evidence of past or present abnormalities or disease of:
   (Check applicable items and give details.)   YES NO
   a. Eyes, ears, nose, or throat?... ❑   ❑
      (If vision or hearing markedly impaired, indicate degree and correction.)
   b. Brain or nervous system (Test pupillary and patellar reflexes.
      Note gait. Any paralysis?).. ❑   ❑
   c. Glands? (thyroid, lymph, endocrine)..................................
   d. Lungs or other respiratory organs?.................................. ❑   ❑
   e. Heart or blood vessels?.. ❑   ❑
   f. Stomach or other abdominal organs?................................ ❑   ❑
   g. Genito-urinary system? (including prostate)...................... ❑   ❑
   h. Bones, joints, or skin?.. ❑   ❑

continued on next page...

Figure 4.2. Example of a Medical Report *continued*

6. IS THERE		YES	NO
a. Hernia		☐	☐
If "Yes" is it reducible?		☐	☐
b. Evidence of varicose veins or ulcers?		☐	☐
c. Deformity, loss of limb or lameness?		☐	☐

7. GENERAL
a. How well do you know examinee? .... ☐ ☐
b. Have you ever treated the examinee or been consulted by him/her?   ☐   ☐
c. Do you find that the examinee has any physical or mental defect, or is in ill health? .... ☐ ☐
d. Do you believe the examinee is older than the age given? .... ☐ ☐
e. Have you reason to suspect that the examinee is or has been an intemperate user of alcohol or a user or narcotics? ...... ☐ ☐

8. URINALYSIS	Specific Gravity	Albumin	Sugar

9. Have you any pertinent information not brought out above? .... ☐ ☐

Dated this____day of_____, 20_____ Signature of Examiner _____ M.D.

_____
(Please Print or Stamp Name)

_____
Address

_____

In interacting with MIB, underwriters of MIB-member companies engage in two primary activities: reporting and requesting impairment information. MIB has established procedures for each of these two activities, as well as requirements for underwriting on the basis of MIB information and for ensuring confidentiality.

Reporting Information to MIB. MIB furnishes its members with a confidential list of factors that are considered important to risk selection and a code that identifies each factor. Member companies are required to report these codes to MIB when they find evidence of these factors in the course of underwriting. The codes are brief summaries of medical and avocational information that may have a bearing on health or longevity. These reports are encoded to protect confidentiality. Codes that have been reported already should not be reported again unless some new, intervening factor has been disclosed or has developed.

Member companies are required to notify MIB if they have reason to believe that an MIB report contains inaccurate or incomplete information. For example, if a proposed insured has been rated in the past but tests conducted during a more recent application process show that the rating is no longer justified, the member company reports this information to MIB to benefit the proposed insured. Member companies do *not* send MIB any actual medical reports or information about (1) specific amounts of insurance applied for or issued, (2) underwriting decisions, or (3) claim decisions.

Requesting Information from MIB. Before an underwriter at a member company can ask MIB to search its files for coded information about a proposed insured, the company must

- Obtain the proposed insured's written authorization to release medical information to the member company on a form expressly naming MIB as an authorized source of such information.

- Furnish the proposed insured for individual life or health insurance with a written pre-notice specifying that a report regarding the person's insurability may be made to MIB and further, that if he later applies for life or health insurance (or files a claim for benefits) with an MIB member company, then MIB may supply such company with an MIB report. The notice also indicates that the person has a right to contact MIB for a copy of his MIB file under the procedures specified in the Fair Credit Reporting Act (FCRA).

Note that authorization forms are subject to various state and federal laws and regulations, including the NAIC Insurance Information and Privacy Protection Model Act, the Gramm-Leach-Bliley Act, and the Health Insurance Portability and Accountability Act (HIPAA). Among other things, the authorization should cover nonmedical as well as medical sources. The authorization should not imply to the consumer that MIB information may be given to another consumer reporting agency. Further, no authorization can permit any organization other than an MIB member to obtain MIB record information.

Some MIB members use a single document that combines the MIB authorization together with the MIB pre-notice, the Fair Credit Reporting Act pre-notice, and the NAIC Insurance Information and Privacy Protection Model Act "Notice of Information Practices." The combined document may be incorporated into the company's application form or put into a separate form.

If the search of the MIB files shows that an insurer previously reported coded information as a result of underwriting an application on the proposed insured, the codes are sent to the inquiring insurer. Any coded information received from MIB may be used only to alert members to the possible need for further investigation of a proposed insured's insurability. In the interest of sound underwriting and to avoid unfair competitive practices in the underwriting of risks, MIB-coded information cannot be used as the basis for establishing a proposed insured's eligibility for insurance.

Adverse actions (for example, declined or rated coverages or postponed applications) must not be based solely on an unverified MIB report without an independent investigation. MIB deems it inappropriate for a member to make an underwriting decision based on an MIB report where the identities of the proposed insured and the person about whom the MIB report relates have not been clearly matched and where the coded information has not been verified by independent investigation. Furthermore, state laws based on the NAIC Insurance Information and Privacy Protection Model Act prevent insurance companies from making an adverse underwriting decision on the sole basis of information received from an "insurance support organization."

If the underwriter is unable to find medical information consistent with the reported codes for the proposed insured in the application or in other documents submitted by the applicant or producer, then the underwriter typically will make an effort to obtain more comprehensive medical information from a variety of sources.

If an underwriter's investigation does not verify coded information from MIB and if the underwriter has met specific MIB requirements, the underwriter can ask MIB to provide details about the coded information, and MIB then asks the reporting insurer for further information. The reporting insurer is encouraged but not obligated to furnish such information, which typically consists of the documents (or document summaries) that were the basis of the reporting insurer's report to MIB, such as an attending physician's statement or medical test result. The underwriter then can use this information as the basis of her own decision.

According to current MIB rules, all MIB information must be kept absolutely confidential. Only authorized medical, underwriting, and claim personnel of member companies are allowed access to MIB information. Member companies also must establish and maintain internal security procedures that will prevent unauthorized people and entities from seeing or using MIB information. To ensure confidentiality, an insurer's MIB code books are locked in desks or cabinets when not in use, and underwriters do not discuss information about MIB codes with other employees, producers, or other unauthorized people or entities. Among the people and entities considered unauthorized in this sense are companies that are not members of the MIB, brokers, nonmember corporate affiliates of member companies, and consumer reporting agencies.

Physicians

A physician, whether he is a primary care physician or a specialist, who has provided medical care for a proposed insured usually is called an *attending physician*. A physician who performs an examination of a proposed insured at the request of the insurance company usually is called an *examining physician*. When an underwriter reviews an application on which the health information requires clarification or amplification, the underwriter can (1) request an attending physician's statement, (2) ask the attending or examining physician to complete a specialized medical questionnaire, or (3) talk to the attending or examining physician. Although the proposed insured signs a HIPAA-compliant authorization for the physician's release of health care information to the insurer at the time of application, some doctors now require their own HIPAA-compliant authorization to be signed.

The *attending physician's statement (APS)* is a report by a physician who has treated or is currently treating the proposed insured. The APS contains a proposed insured's medical records. Although an APS can be a valuable source of underwriting information, the increased costs of and the time involved in obtaining an APS, have resulted in a decline in its usage. Underwriters typically order an APS when

- The insurer's age and amount requirements specify that an APS is required for the proposed insured.

- The application mentions a specific illness or medical history. For example, histories of coronary artery disease and cancer usually require at least one APS from the primary physician and perhaps additional APSs from specialists, such as the cardiologist or oncologist.

- The application reports a recent visit to a doctor and the underwriter wants to confirm the absence of antiselection.

- Information on the application isn't consistent with information from MIB.

An underwriter also might gather more detailed information about certain conditions such as coronary artery disease, chest pain, or diabetes by using a *specialized medical questionnaire*, which is a document that requests detailed information about a specific illness or condition from a proposed insured's attending physician or examining physician. Figure 4.3 is an example of a specialized medical questionnaire requesting detailed information about a neuropsychiatric condition.

Figure 4.3. Specialized Medical Questionnaire for a Neuropsychiatric Condition

NEUROPSYCHIATRIC QUESTIONNAIRE

Please complete from patient's existing medical records. A current medical exam is NOT required.

Patient's Name _____

Application Number _____

1. Please classify the disorder

   ____ Affective Disorder   ____ Personality Disorder

   ____ Anxiety Disorder   ____ Psychotic Disorder

   ____ Organic Brain Disorder

2. What is the appropriate DSM IV American Psychiatric Diagnostic Code? _____

3. Date of onset?_____

4. Please classify the degree of impairment

   ____ Mild   ____ Moderate   ____ Severe

5. Please indicate if any of the following have occurred

   ____ Substance Abuse   ____ Suicide Ideation

   ____ Suicide Attempt

6. Indicate dates of psychiatric care

   In-patient (hospitalization)_____

   Out-patient_____

7. Please specify the type of treatment prescribed

   ____ Individual Counseling

   ____ Electroconvulsive Therapy

   ____ Medication (include name and dosage of drug)

   ____ Group Counseling

   ____ Other (please specify) _____

8. Is the condition under effective control?

   ____ Yes   If yes, for how long? _____

   ____ No

9. Date of full recovery and return to work or school _____

10. Is there any reason to believe that psychiatric care may be necessary in the future? _____

Date _____

Physician's Name (signature not required)_____

An underwriter sometimes contacts an attending or examining physician or the physician's staff to gather additional information on a proposed insured's specific disorder, verify dates and details of treatment, or clarify the reasons for certain diagnoses and medications. In addition, sometimes an underwriter finds that information obtained from a source such as an APS or an MIB report discloses a medical impairment or condition that was not reported on the application for insurance. Because the third-party information may be incorrect, the underwriter is careful not to reach a conclusion before contacting the physician. Underwriters may telephone the physician, but written communication may be required to properly document the file. Sometimes the underwriter finds it more efficient for a doctor on the insurer's staff to call the physician on behalf of the underwriter.

Medical Tests

Usually producers are the ones to order medical tests in accordance with the insurer's published age and amount requirements. However, an underwriter also may order medical tests in addition to those ordered by the producer. Insurers keep medical test results confidential and only disclose the results to those with a legitimate need to know them. Figure 4.4 provides a brief description of four common tests. Note that a urinalysis, a blood chemistry profile, and an oral specimen (saliva) test commonly are referred to as *laboratory tests*.

Personal History Interviews

The insurer also may require a *personal history interview (PHI)*, which is a conversation between an underwriter or another insurance company employee and the proposed insured in which the underwriter verifies the accuracy of information already received about the proposed insured and obtains any additional information needed for underwriting. The personal history interview is conducted by telephone or in person and is sometimes used in teleunderwriting. Some companies have a special PHI unit that conducts PHIs. If the underwriter has additional questions, she may ask the PHI unit to follow up with the applicant or proposed insured.

Inspection Reports

An *inspection report* is a type of investigative consumer report that a consumer reporting agency prepares about a proposed insured. The consumer reporting agency's inspector gathers the information for an inspection report from public records, including court records, bankruptcy records, motor vehicle records, credit reports, documents verifying business ownership, and interviews with the proposed insured, as well as some of his friends, neighbors, and business associates.

Generally, an inspection report gathers more personal and financial information than it does medical information. The medical information collected on an inspection report includes

■ The proposed insured's height and weight

■ The proposed insured's health history

Figure 4.4. Four Medical Tests Commonly Ordered for Underwriting

Electrocardiogram. An *electrocardiogram (ECG)* is a graphic record of the electrical forces produced by the heart and is a diagnostic tool for detecting a disease or an abnormality of the heart.

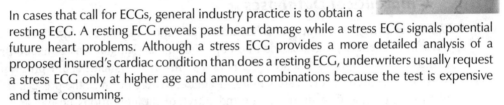

- A *resting ECG* is taken when a proposed insured is at rest and the heart is beating at its normal rate.

- A *stress ECG*, also known as an *exercise ECG*, is the same test taken during and after a proposed insured has engaged in a strictly defined amount of exercise.

In cases that call for ECGs, general industry practice is to obtain a resting ECG. A resting ECG reveals past heart damage while a stress ECG signals potential future heart problems. Although a stress ECG provides a more detailed analysis of a proposed insured's cardiac condition than does a resting ECG, underwriters usually request a stress ECG only at higher age and amount combinations because the test is expensive and time consuming.

Urinalysis. *Urinalysis* is the analysis of a urine specimen. A urinalysis is frequently required because it can detect the presence of protein, sugar, blood cells, and hypertension, as well as prescription medication and certain other drugs. Because urinalysis also can detect cotinine (a byproduct of nicotine that stays in the body far longer than nicotine) in urine, insurers use this test to verify whether a declared nonuser of tobacco is qualified for nonuser rates. A urinalysis also may test for human immunodeficiency virus (HIV). A required urine specimen typically is collected during the paramedical or medical examination, and insurance industry laboratories produce detailed reports of the findings. Urinalysis is performed in a laboratory chosen by the insurer.

Blood chemistry profile. A *blood chemistry profile* is a group of laboratory tests that analyze a sample of blood to identify factors that point to possible chronic and acute

diseases. The standard blood profile has 15 to 18 components related to liver function, kidney function, glucose/diabetes, blood lipids, and serum proteins. In addition, as we mentioned in Chapter 3, some insurers require genetic and/or HIV testing. Blood also can be tested for cotinine. Blood specimens typically are collected during paramedical or medical examinations and are analyzed in insurance industry laboratories.

Oral specimen (saliva) test. An *oral specimen (saliva) test* is a means of screening proposed insureds for habitual use of nicotine or cocaine and the presence of HIV antibodies by testing a specimen of the proposed insured's saliva. The specimen typically is collected by the producer at the time of application and sent to a laboratory to be tested. Oral specimen testing is usually more convenient and less expensive and invasive than blood or urine testing. However, oral specimen tests cannot be used to test for as many substances as blood or urine tests can.

- The names and addresses of the proposed insured's attending physicians and other medical caregivers

- The date and cause of death of the proposed insured's parents if either is deceased

This information is the same as that requested on the application. If the information provided on the application conflicts with information in the inspection report, the underwriter will be alerted to the need for further investigation.

Insurers typically establish age and amount limits above which underwriters routinely order inspection reports. Below such limits, the underwriter may use a PHI instead. When ordering inspection reports, insurers must abide by the provisions of the Fair Credit Reporting Act.

Pharmaceutical Databases

Pharmacy benefit managers (PBMs) are clearinghouses that manage health care prescription benefit programs and maintain pharmaceutical databases that contain records of prescriptions filled by the persons enrolled in such benefit programs. These prescription histories are valuable to underwriters because the prescriptions taken by a proposed insured may be indicative of the conditions he has and the treatment he is receiving.

Insurers contract with vendors known as *prescription drug profiling services* that access these databases. Some insurers obtain prescription histories rather than APSs because obtaining a prescription history can be less expensive and time consuming than getting an APS. However, note that these histories are not available if the proposed insured is not enrolled in a health care prescription benefit program. If the proposed insured is enrolled in such a program, the underwriter must obtain his written consent to access this information. As with MIB information, information in a pharmaceutical database cannot be the sole basis for an underwriting decision.

Assessing Medical Factors

Individual life underwriters must have a high degree of medical knowledge because of the importance of medical factors in the assessment of mortality risk. While a detailed discussion of impairments is beyond the scope of this text, in this section we briefly mention the most common impairments that affect mortality risk. We also discuss age, sex, and build. While age and sex are not medical factors, per se, we discuss age here because of its correlation with impairments and importance in the individual life insurance underwriting decision; we discuss sex because of its correlation with mortality rating and impact on pricing.

Impairments

To accurately assess a proposed insured's mortality risk, an individual life insurance underwriter needs to know about the human body's systems, possible impairments of those systems, treatments of those impairments, and interactions of multiple impairments. Impairments that typically are of particular concern to underwriters include heart disease, lung disease, kidney disease, liver disease, cerebrovascular disease, gastrointestinal disorders, congenital heart defects, neurological impairments, diabetes, cancer, psychiatric impairments, alcohol and drug abuse, and AIDS.

Age

Current age is the most important factor indicating a proposed insured's expected longevity because, as people age, the chance that they have an impairment increases. With young proposed insureds—generally ages 15 through 39—underwriters are more concerned about accidental death than they are with impairments. The situation changes if the proposed insured is middle-aged, which traditionally has been defined as ages 40 through 60, but which some companies now define as ages 50 to 70. At these ages, many proposed insureds develop health problems. At ages above 60 or 70, the chance that a proposed insured has or soon will develop an impairment is fairly high. A 72-year-old woman who does not admit to having seen any doctors during the previous five years or who lists only minor or very few injuries or illnesses is not typical. An underwriter probably would conduct a very thorough review of such a case, and some companies would require that the woman undergo a full medical examination.

Age also can be an indication of antiselection. For example, a 60-year-old man purchasing life insurance for the first time is statistically a greater risk for possible antiselection than is a 60-year-old man who has purchased insurance throughout his adult life. The fact that the first man has decided to purchase coverage only at an older age, perhaps as a result of sudden concern for his declining health, indicates the possibility of antiselection.

The underwriter may approve first-time coverage for a proposed insured of an advanced age if the underwriter determines that the reason for the insurance purchase is legitimate. For example, the proposed insured may have come to the realization belatedly that his family lacks adequate means of support upon his death. In addition, some older people who previously felt they lacked the financial means to purchase life insurance may apply for it to pay their final expenses.

Nearly all life insurers establish maximum age limits beyond which they will not issue coverage. The maximum age limits usually vary according to the insurance product applied for and are generally lower for term insurance (about 75) and higher for whole life insurance (about 80). Some insurers now issue policies to proposed insureds up to age 85, and a few insurers issue policies up to at least age 90.

Sex

Individual life insurance underwriters typically disregard the sex of the proposed insured in determining the amounts and types of coverage issued because of laws and competitive pressure. However, many insurers do use sex-based actuarial tables to determine premiums rates because, statistically, females live longer than males.

Build

Build is the shape or form of the body, including the relationships among height, weight, and distribution of the weight. To evaluate build, underwriters typically use a ***build chart***, which is a chart that indicates average weights for various heights, along with the mortality debits associated with increases in weight. (We discuss mortality debits and credits in Chapter 5.) Some companies now rate the policy if the proposed insured is underweight, which is a particular concern when underwriting proposed insureds who are suffering from anorexia or are elderly. Underwriters also consider whether the proposed insured has gained or lost weight recently, because substantial or rapid gains or losses in weight may indicate medical impairments. Underwriters typically use separate male and female build charts, as well as separate adult, child, and infant build charts.

Some underwriters now use body mass index (BMI) instead of build charts to evaluate build. BMI measures body fat and is based on height and weight. The BMI formula for male and female adults, teens, and children is

$$\text{Weight (lb)} \div \text{Height (in)}^2 \times 703$$

For example, if an adult male is 5'10" tall and weighs 170 pounds, his BMI is $170 \div 70^2 \times 703 = .035 \times 703 = 24.6$. According to the adult BMI chart set forth below, this adult male's weight is normal for his height.

BMI	Weight Status
Below 18.5	Underweight
18.5–24.9	Normal
25.0–29.9	Overweight
30.0 and above	Obese

BMI charts that categorize weight status differ for adults, teens, and children.

Personal Risk Factors

Individual life underwriters have a wide variety of sources of information about a proposed insured's personal risk factors. In this section, we discuss these sources and how an underwriter assesses personal risk factors, which are listed in Figure 4.5.

Sources of Personal Information

To assess a proposed insured's personal risk factors, an underwriter may consult many sources of information, including the application for insurance, the producer, the proposed insured's motor vehicle record (MVR), the inspection report, and personal questionnaires.

Figure 4.5. Personal Risk Factors Considered in Underwriting

Occupation

Driving history

Avocations

Tobacco use

Alcohol use

Drug abuse

Subject of physical abuse

Criminal history

Civilian and military aviation

Military status

International residence and travel

Foreign citizenship

Source: Adapted from Mary C. Bickley et al., *Life and Health Insurance Underwriting*, 2nd ed. [Atlanta: LOMA (Life Office Management Association, Inc.), © 2007], 161. Used with permission; all rights reserved.

The Application for Insurance

Some of the questions on the application for insurance are so personal that they could not be asked in other situations. For example, during a job interview, a prospective employer cannot make direct queries about marital status, weight, physical handicaps or defects, past illnesses, number and ages of children, net worth, and outstanding loans. However, such personal information helps an underwriter not only make an accurate assessment of the risk, but also view the proposed insured as an individual rather than just as another request for coverage.

The insurance application typically requests such information as the proposed insured's

■ Date and place of birth

■ Marital status

■ Length of time at current residence

- Occupation

- Driving history, including driver's license suspension or revocation, driving convictions, pending charges, or more than a specified number (usually two or three) of moving traffic violations during a specified time period

- Participation in hazardous avocations that could result in physical injury (including motor vehicle racing, scuba or sky diving, hang gliding, parachuting, mountain climbing, and participating in rodeos)

- Tobacco use

- Alcohol use

- Drug abuse

- Criminal history information, including arrests and convictions for any criminal offenses

- Aviation activities other than as a passenger on scheduled commercial airline flights

- Residence or travel outside the country in which coverage is being sought

If any of the information provided on the application indicates the possibility of an increased risk—for example, if the proposed insured participates in a dangerous avocation, uses tobacco, or has a criminal history—the underwriter gathers sufficient information to decide whether to issue, rate, modify, or decline the requested coverage.

Also, if information on the application appears contradictory—for instance, if business travel seems inconsistent with the proposed insured's occupation—the underwriter seeks additional information to clarify the apparent inconsistencies. An underwriter also might seek additional information if the application indicates that the proposed insured has unexplained gaps in her employment history.

Producer

Because the producer may interact with and know the proposed insured personally, the producer is often in a unique position to provide first-hand knowledge about the proposed insured to the life underwriter. Thus, the underwriter carefully examines the agent's statement and any letter the producer may have submitted with the application.

Motor Vehicle Record

A *motor vehicle record (MVR)* is a report that contains information about a person's driving history, including information about traffic violations, arrests, and convictions. The underwriter uses information in the MVR to assess the degree of risk represented by a proposed insured's driving habits. Note that the MVR may not be available to underwriters in all jurisdictions, as some jurisdictions will not release the MVR to insurers due to privacy regulations and some jurisdictions have increased fees to obtain a MVR to a prohibitive level.

Inspection Report

An inspection report may include some or all of the following information concerning personal risk factors:

- The type and frequency of the proposed insured's tobacco, alcohol, and drug use

- The proposed insured's avocations, driving history, and police record, including arrests and convictions

- The type of business in which the proposed insured has been employed, the length of time employed, and typical work duties

Personal Questionnaires

Personal questionnaires typically ask for information about the proposed insured's participation in a specified activity that is known to increase the risk of injury or death. Examples include personal questionnaires about avocations, alcohol usage, and drug usage. Avocation questionnaires ask if the proposed insured is licensed or certified to take part in the specified activity and by whom. Figure 4.6 is an example of a personal questionnaire requesting information about a proposed insured's participation in scuba diving.

The questions in a personal questionnaire are based on statistical information about the relationship of specific activities to injury and death. Many insurers rely on standard questionnaires that have been used in the industry for years and have been proven to be helpful in gathering information needed for underwriting.

Insurers verify the quality of specialized personal questionnaires in two ways. First, insurance regulatory authorities must approve questionnaire forms that are to be signed by proposed insureds and will become part of the application for insurance. Second, insurance companies doing business with reinsurers usually ask the reinsuring companies to review and revise the questionnaires to assure that the questionnaires ask the questions necessary to assess each risk correctly.

Note that if the insurer discovers that the proposed insured made a material misrepresentation of fact in a questionnaire that is considered to be part of the policy, then the insurer has the right to rescind the policy during the policy's contestable period.

Assessing Personal Factors

In this section, we consider how each of the personal risk factors listed in Figure 4.5 affects the underwriting of individual life insurance.

Occupation

A proposed insured's occupation usually is not a factor in underwriting individual life insurance unless the insurer considers the occupation to be hazardous. An underwriter typically assesses two kinds of occupational hazards: *accident hazards* (such as working on high-rise construction) and *health hazards* (such as exposure to toxic chemicals). Accident hazards are more common among some workers, such as lumber workers and demolition experts, while health hazards are

Figure 4.6. Scuba Diving Questionnaire

SCUBA DIVING QUESTIONNAIRE

Purpose of diving____ Business ____ Pleasure

Type of diving (if applicable) __ Instruction ___ Construction ___ Salvage
___ Research ____ Night diving

Where do you dive? ____ Inland waters __ Ocean or sea

Diving History

Depth (in ft.)	Last 12 months		Next 12 months	
	No. of Dives	Average Duration of Dives	No. of Dives	Average Duration of Dives
<50				
50–100				
>100				

Maximum depth obtained_____

Are you a member of a diving organization?   Yes ____ No

Are you a certified diver? __ Yes __ No

If yes, please list certification(s) and level(s):

_____

Have you ever had a diving-related accident? __ Yes __ No

If yes, please give details:

_____

I declare that the above information is true and complete and shall form part of my application to ABC Assurance Company.

Signature _____

Date _____

more common among other workers, such as those involved in radium analysis. Moreover, some workers—coal miners, for example—are subject to both types of hazards. Figure 4.7 lists and describes some occupations that many insurers consider hazardous.

Within certain categories of occupations, some policies generally are issued as standard and others generally are rated, depending on the proposed insured's actual job duties. For example, a coal miner who is an above-ground machinist might be issued a standard policy, while an underground worker typically would be issued a rated policy.

Figure 4.7. Occupations that Many Insurers Consider Hazardous

Occupation	Description of Risk
Building demolition	**Accident hazards**: collapse of unsound structures, explosions, blasting
Open mining and quarrying	**Accident hazards**: rock falls, cave-ins, quarrying fire, explosions **Health hazards**: asphyxiation, poisonous gases
Stunts in films	**Accident hazards**: high-speed driving, leaps and dives, fire, explosions
Radium analysis	**Health hazards**: radioactive poisoning, potential carcinogenic effects

Source: Adapted from Mary C. Bickley et al., *Life and Health Insurance Underwriting*, 2nd ed. [Atlanta: LOMA (Life Office Management Association, Inc.), © 2007], 165. Used with permission; all rights reserved.

A rating for occupation may be reduced or removed when the insured's occupation changes. Generally, insurers require that an insured person who has previously been in a hazardous occupation must work for at least one year in a less hazardous occupation and must not be likely to return to the former, more hazardous occupation for the rating to be reduced or removed. Some ratings also may be removed automatically when the insured reaches a certain age, such as age 65.

Driving History

Because accidental deaths frequently result from motor vehicle accidents, underwriters pay considerable attention to a proposed insured's driving history. Underwriters consider the number, type, and timing of traffic violations, as well as whether alcohol or drugs were involved in any of the violations. Proposed insureds who have many traffic violations generally pose greater risks for fatal motor vehicle accidents.

Most insurers attempt to identify poor drivers by including in the application a question asking if the proposed insured has been convicted of a moving traffic violation or been charged with driving under the influence (DUI) within a certain period of time. To obtain additional information about a proposed insured's driving record, an underwriter may request a motor vehicle record (MVR).

For people who have unfavorable driving histories, most insurers rate the policy, modify the benefit amounts to compensate for the extra risk, postpone making a decision, or decline the application. For example, a proposed insured who has had two DUIs within the last five years probably would be denied coverage.

Avocations

Underwriters usually distinguish between people who pursue activities as an occupation (professional) and those who do it as an avocation (amateur). As examples, automobile racing, boxing, wrestling, and rodeo riding can be either avocations or occupations. To gather information about an applicant's avocations, or leisure activities, underwriters use specialized personal questionnaires such as the one shown in Figure 4.6. Such a questionnaire may focus on just one activity or may gather information on several avocations. In underwriting avocations, underwriters consider the proposed insured's age, training, and type and quality of equipment to determine whether the policy should be rated for participation in a potentially risky avocation.

Tobacco Use

People who use tobacco in any form show greater mortality at every age than people who do not. As a result, life insurers generally charge higher premium rates for tobacco users than for nonusers. Insurers accomplish this premium rate differential in a number of ways, including

- Developing separate premium rate schedules for tobacco users and nonusers.

- Assigning higher ratings for impairments that are sensitive to tobacco use, such as coronary artery disease, cancer, and lung disease, than the impairments would be assigned if the proposed insured did not smoke.

- Placing tobacco users in a standard classification and nonusers in a preferred classification.

- Adjusting premium rates for tobacco users and nonusers. Under this approach, tobacco use and nonuse are considered risk factors that have a negative or positive impact, respectively, on mortality risk.

- Offering discounted premiums for tobacco nonusers.

Answers to tobacco-use questions are some of the most frequently misrepresented answers on applications for insurance because most proposed insureds who use tobacco know that answering truthfully about their use will increase their premium rates. Therefore, when a proposed insured undergoes a physical examination, underwriters usually ask the paramedical or medical examiner to test a sample of the proposed insured's blood, urine, or saliva for the presence of cotinine. Underwriters also can require a tobacco questionnaire or an inspection report that includes comments on the proposed insured's use of tobacco.

Alcohol Use

Underwriters investigate a proposed insured's use of alcohol to ascertain the potential for alcohol abuse or alcoholism, both of which can increase a proposed insured's mortality risk. An underwriter decides whether to rate or decline a policy for alcohol use depending on the degree of use.

Obtaining information about a proposed insured's use of alcohol can be very difficult. Underwriters usually gather information from inspection reports, alcohol usage questionnaires, MVRs, APSs, and liver function tests. In addition, underwriters can order two specific laboratory tests that can indicate heavy drinking—HAA and CDT, which are known as "alcohol markers."

An alcohol usage questionnaire asks a proposed insured to provide information on his consumption of alcoholic beverages, as well as details about the effects of alcohol use on his health, driving, and occupation.

Drug Abuse

Drug abuse generally refers to the excessive or inappropriate use of prescription drugs or the use of illegal drugs. Drugs subject to abuse include marijuana, narcotics, hallucinogens, stimulants, and sedatives. People who abuse these drugs may have or may develop psychological impairments, physical dependence, or personality disorders that can constitute additional risk.

When investigating the possibility of drug abuse, underwriters try to ascertain what drugs are being used and to what extent. Life insurers typically decline coverage for any proposed insured who currently engages in drug abuse, although some companies will offer coverage to proposed insureds who admit to moderate marijuana use.

A distinct difference between alcohol abuse and the abuse of some drugs is that alcohol is legal and, if used in moderation, acceptable in our society; whereas the use of some drugs is illegal. As a result, gathering information about a proposed insured's drug abuse often is difficult, especially because positive answers to questions concerning a person's use of illegal drugs can be incriminating. Additionally, the fact that a proposed insured uses illegal drugs raises the question of moral hazard.

When drug abuse is suspected and the amount of insurance applied for is sufficient to warrant such an extensive investigation, the underwriter may order an APS, a urine test, a drug usage questionnaire, and an inspection report focused on drug abuse. The underwriter verifies that any tests for the presence of illegal drugs are conducted properly and that the test results are kept confidential.

Subject of Physical Abuse

The risk that results from the physical abuse of a proposed insured by a spouse, partner, or other family member is a sensitive issue for underwriters. Several U.S. jurisdictions have enacted legislation that prohibits insurers from requesting or using information about whether a proposed insured is abused in making an underwriting decision. However, in states where the law permits insurers to consider abuse status when making an underwriting decision, assessing the risk posed by potential abuse requires the underwriter to evaluate impartially the level of risk that the abuse represents and to determine the degree to which the risk is acceptable or unacceptable to the insurer. Insurers typically try to insure subjects of abuse unless the abuse constitutes a grave risk of serious injury or death.

To investigate abuse, an underwriter may focus on hospital emergency room records that indicate treatment for traumatic injuries. Also, because physical abuse often is accompanied by alcohol and/or drug abuse, as well as severe depression, the underwriter checks medical records, inspection reports, producer's comments, and other sources for evidence of such conditions.

Criminal History

Underwriters carefully investigate proposed insureds who have a history of criminal or illegal activities. Although an underwriter cannot predict that criminal activity will recur, such a case requires a thorough review of the facts, an extensive inspection report, and detailed interviews with people who are likely to know the current activities and character of the proposed insured.

Generally, an underwriter considers the following factors in evaluating a proposed insured's criminal activity:

■ The length of time the proposed insured was involved in crime

■ The length of time that has elapsed since the proposed insured was involved in crime

■ The proposed insured's history in relation to police, courts, and correctional institutions

■ The nature of the offense or offenses committed

Recent criminal activity in the history of a proposed insured usually causes underwriters to rate or decline the case. Proposed insureds who have been arrested for multiple or violent crimes, have been involved in criminal activity over a period of time, or have a history of criminal activity coupled with alcohol abuse, drug abuse, compulsive gambling, extreme aggression, or severe psychological problems are rarely, if ever, accepted for coverage. Insurers generally give more lenient consideration to proposed insureds who have no history of violent crime and have noncriminal family members, consistent work records, and associates and friends who are not involved in criminal activity. In addition, insurers may be more lenient when the crime was in the distant past and the proposed insured appears to be rehabilitated.

Civilian and Military Aviation

Although civilian and military aviation are underwritten somewhat differently, the primary sources of information for both include the application for insurance, aviation questionnaire, inspection report, and personal history interview. Typically, if a proposed insured indicates on the application that he is involved in aviation activities, the insurer requires the proposed insured to complete an aviation questionnaire.

Civilian aviation includes air ambulance, ballooning, commercial aviation, crop dusting, fire fighting, power line and pipe inspecting, mail service, mapping, policing, racing, sightseeing, and weather or traffic control. Civilian aviation also includes flying for pleasure.

For most civilian aviation, the proposed insured's total hours of flying experience and the number of hours that the person plans to fly annually are important information. Another factor that an underwriter considers is the aviation certificate or ratings that the proposed insured holds. Studies show that proposed insureds with high levels of flying certification or ratings, as well as extensive flying experience, have a greater degree of skill and are less likely to be involved in aviation accidents than proposed insureds with lower levels of certification or ratings or less experience.

An underwriter also considers the medical certificate held by a proposed insured. The medical certificate is the only proof required for a pilot to be medically certified to fly. However, underwriters also are aware that, even if a person is denied a medical certificate, numerous appeal mechanisms enable a person with even severe medical impairments, such as alcoholism or a history of coronary bypass surgery, to obtain medical certification. In short, a proposed insured who holds an aviation medical certificate is not necessarily a standard risk for insurance.

Insurers typically issue individual life insurance coverage at standard rates to most civilian pilots who apply for coverage. However, the underwriter may rate a policy for the aviation hazard if she determines that the pilot represents a greater-than-standard risk. Another approach to insuring a greater-than-standard risk is to issue the policy with an aviation exclusion rider, although some jurisdictions limit or prohibit such riders. Generally, aviation exclusion riders are used only in cases in which (1) the aviation hazard is greater than the insurer is willing to accept, (2) the aviation hazard cannot be measured, or (3) the pilot has a history of certain medical impairments, such as depression, stroke, or heart disease.

In assessing risk for pilots flying employer-owned aircraft, an underwriter ascertains whether the pilot has either an airline transport certificate or a commercial certificate with an instrument flight rating, indicating that the pilot is qualified to fly in all weather conditions. Insurers typically rate policies issued to pilots who do not hold one of these certificates.

When underwriting military aviation, underwriters consider many of the same factors evaluated in underwriting civilian aviation. In addition, underwriters look carefully at the duty area of all proposed insureds who are military aviators, as well as the type of aircraft in which they fly.

Life insurers typically rate policies for proposed insureds engaged in military aviation. Generally, the extra charges for military aviation are higher for people under the age of 30 than for people age 30 and older. Also, the extra amounts charged for military pilots are usually higher than the extra amounts charged for aviation crew members. Usually, proposed insureds who are serving in a hazardous place are not acceptable risks; underwriters typically will not issue coverage until a proposed insured returns from such a dangerous assignment and has no pending hazardous assignments.

Military Status

If a country is not at war or involved in a military conflict, most insurers approve most military personnel for coverage at standard rates. Underwriters generally consider most career military personnel as good risks and underwrite them as if they were civilians. However, many insurers do not issue coverage to noncareer military personnel from the lower pay grades because those people have statistically higher-than-average lapse rates and accidental death rates.

If an armed conflict occurs, most insurers will refuse an application from military personnel for as long as the conflict lasts or will attach a rider to the policy excluding losses as a result of war. Some insurance companies, however, issue individual life insurance coverage at standard rates to all military personnel who do not exhibit extraordinary risk other than that associated with military service.

International Residence and Travel

Many insurers in the United States and Canada do not approve coverage for proposed insureds who reside abroad for extended periods because of the difficulty of gathering complete underwriting information and, if coverage is issued and death occurs, of conducting an adequate, cost-effective claim investigation. Insurers that conduct considerable business in foreign countries and have established foreign offices, however, typically do issue insurance to people residing there either temporarily or permanently. The rates for such coverage are generally higher than for similar people not living abroad.

Vacation trips of three to six weeks duration are usually of no concern to the underwriter unless a proposed insured plans to travel to an area with great political unrest, military activity, or known, widespread deadly disease. If the proposed insured plans to travel to such a high-risk area, the underwriter may approve coverage at a higher premium or decline to issue the coverage. Recently, the U.S. Congress considered prohibiting life insurance underwriters from rating or declining coverage based on a proposed insured's foreign travel plans. In addition, similar legislation has passed or is pending in several states.

Because of the uncertainty surrounding the legality of asking about foreign travel, some companies do not ask about foreign travel. Other companies keep track of legislation in each jurisdiction and underwrite accordingly. Alternatively, the underwriter may postpone the decision to issue coverage until the proposed insured returns to her home country. Most U.S. and Canadian insurers remove extra premiums after an insured has been home for a period of one to two years.

One of the most important factors in all applications that involve foreign residence and travel is the type of insurance requested. In general, when a proposed insured requests the lowest premium term insurance and wishes to make monthly payments for it, the underwriter considers the coverage to be "trip insurance" which the applicant probably has no intention of maintaining after the trip is completed. Therefore, the underwriter usually declines the risk.

Foreign Citizenship

Underwriting life insurance for recent immigrants and residents who are citizens of foreign countries is based on individual consideration of the class of risk presented, the reason for the insurance purchase, the reputation of the submitting producer, and the quality of the producer's previously submitted business. Generally, insurers give favorable consideration to foreign citizens who

- Intend to become permanent residents of the country in which the insurer does business

- Possess a permanent resident visa

- Own property or have bank accounts in the country in which the insurer does business

If a proposed insured is a foreign citizen who has lived in the new country for less than one year, most insurers require a medical examination and a complete blood profile for any amount of life insurance coverage. Certain factors in developing countries can contribute to higher morbidity and mortality in people who leave those countries and establish residence elsewhere. These factors include

- Scarcity of medical resources

- Malnutrition

- Unsafe water and provisions for sanitation

- Inadequate education about healthful practices

Most North American insurers do not issue coverage to foreign nationals who are only visiting or temporarily living in North America because such a person has little apparent reason to own a policy issued outside the native country. Insurers are concerned that the policy may lapse upon the person's departure and that claims may be difficult to investigate should the insured die in his native country.

Key Terms

nonmedical basis	personal history interview (PHI)
nonmedical supplement	inspection report
nonmedical limit	electrocardiogram (ECG)
paramedical report	urinalysis
medical report	blood chemistry profile
MIB Group, Inc. (MIB)	oral specimen (saliva) test
attending physician	pharmacy benefit manager (PBM)
examining physician	build
attending physician's statement (APS)	build chart
specialized medical questionnaire	motor vehicle record (MVR)

Chapter 5

Underwriting Individual Life Insurance: Financial Underwriting and Risk Classification

Objectives:

After studying this chapter, you should be able to

- Describe the risks deterred by financial underwriting
- List and describe the sources of financial information used in underwriting individual life insurance
- Identify three generally accepted needs for purchasing personal life insurance
- Describe the financial factors an underwriter assesses to determine whether the amount of individual life insurance coverage requested is appropriate
- Use a factor table and the percentage-of-income rule to calculate the maximum amount of coverage a proposed insured with a specified income could qualify for
- Explain how underwriters use the numerical rating system to classify individual life insurance risks and calculate the total risk represented by a proposed insured
- Describe three methods of charging for substandard individual life insurance risks and identify which method is most appropriate based on whether a risk is expected to increase, decrease, or remain constant over time

Outline

Financial Underwriting
- Risks Deterred by Financial Underwriting
- Sources of Financial Information
- Assessing Life Insurance Needs and Financial Factors
- Tools to Determine the Appropriate Amount of Insurance

Risk Classification
- Numerical Rating System
- Charging for Substandard Risks

When an individual applies for insurance on his own life, the underwriter assesses the individual's financial condition. In this chapter, we focus on personal insurance, which is insurance that fulfills the needs of an individual rather than a business. The term *personal insurance* includes property and liability coverages that meet the needs of an individual, but we limit our discussion to individual life insurance that meets such needs.

Financial Underwriting

An individual life insurance underwriter assesses the proposed insured's financial condition to determine whether (1) the proposed insured needs the coverage, (2) a reasonable relationship exists between the need for the coverage and the amount of coverage applied for, and (3) the premiums are affordable. This assessment of the proposed risk based on financial factors is known as *financial underwriting*. Note that when we refer to the proposed insured's financial condition, we assume that the proposed insured, applicant, and policyowner are the same person. If the proposed insured is not the policyowner, who typically is the person responsible for paying premiums, the underwriter also will assess the policyowner's financial condition to evaluate his ability to afford the premium payments.

Risks Deterred by Financial Underwriting

By engaging in financial underwriting, an underwriter can detect and protect against the risks of lapse, antiselection, speculation, and money laundering.

Lapse

Insurers know from experience that proposed insureds who buy more insurance than they can afford tend to let their policies lapse, and lapses negatively affect an insurer's financial statements. Underwriters are concerned with maintaining an excellent *persistency rate*, which is the percentage of a specified group of contracts that remain in force during a specified period, such as a year. Thus, underwriters engage in financial underwriting to ensure that the proposed insured can afford the premiums and that the policy does not lapse. However, when the application is for relatively inexpensive term insurance, underwriters do not examine the proposed insured's ability to pay premiums but they do evaluate the person's need for the amount of coverage applied for.

Antiselection

Underwriters ensure that the proposed insured needs the coverage because they know that people who buy more life insurance than they appear to need may be engaging in antiselection. For example, if a person who has never applied for life insurance does so at an advanced age and the application indicates that the person has no impairments, the underwriter may suspect antiselection and investigate for undisclosed impairments. The underwriter's investigation may reveal facts that will prompt her to decline the coverage. However, if the underwriter determines that the proposed insured never had any dependents and thus had no need for insurance to support them upon his death but that he now needs the insurance proceeds to pay the estate taxes on his large estate, the underwriter is less likely to suspect antiselection.

Note that insurers' experience has shown that the possibility of antiselection tends to be greater when applicants seek policies with large face amounts. In underwriting an application for a substantial amount of coverage, the underwriter needs to know considerably more about the proposed insured's financial background than is necessary for smaller amount cases.

Speculation

In terms of insurance, **speculation** is the unethical purchase of insurance to make a profit on the proceeds rather than to protect against the risk of financial loss. The possibility of speculation may arise when the amount of insurance applied for exceeds the potential financial loss that a beneficiary might suffer if a proposed insured were to die. Thus, underwriters engage in financial underwriting to ensure that the amount of coverage applied for is consistent with the potential financial loss.

For example, an application made by an adult child for insurance on an aged, dependent parent requires special examination, because such an application may present an element of speculation. Upon the death of the proposed insured, the adult child not only would receive the death benefit, but also would be relieved of the expenses of supporting the parent. The underwriter might, however, approve coverage on the life of an elderly parent who provides a service, such as babysitting for grandchildren for which the adult child would have to pay. Note that in the case of a third-party policy, the policyowner's lack of an insurable interest in the proposed insured can indicate speculation. Without an insurable interest, the policyowner, who is usually the beneficiary, would benefit rather than suffer a loss from the proposed insured's death.

Some believe that a life settlement is another example of speculation. A **life settlement** is the sale of a life insurance policy to a third party for a discount from the policy's face amount. While some see them as a viable way of funding end of life costs, others feel they are speculative because the company purchasing the policy (generally known as a *life settlement provider*) expects to earn a profit by receiving the full death benefit from a life insurance policy for which it paid a discounted amount.

Money Laundering

Money laundering is a crime involving hiding the identity, source, and/or destination of money associated with criminal activity. If a proposed insured applies for more cash value coverage than she needs or if she is hesitant to provide financial information, an underwriter may suspect money laundering. However, the large amount applied for may be the result of an exaggerated financial needs analysis.

Figure 5.1 illustrates how an underwriter would analyze a case for lapse, antiselection, speculation, and money laundering from a financial underwriting point of view.

Sources of Financial Information

An underwriter relies on three main sources of information to assess a proposed insured's financial situation: (1) the application for insurance, (2) the producer, and (3) the inspection report. If additional information is needed, an underwriter may

---

Figure 5.1. Analysis of Lapse, Antiselection, Speculation, and Money Laundering

Caroline Bender's aunt, Teresa, had lived with Caroline and her two children for three years. During that time, Teresa was in good health and volunteered at Caroline's antique shop three days a week. Caroline paid Teresa's living expenses. After Teresa suffered a fall that broke her arm, Caroline applied for a $50,000 life insurance policy on her aunt naming herself as the beneficiary.

In reviewing this case, the underwriter engaged in the following analysis to detect the possibility of lapse and the presence of antiselection, speculation, and money laundering:

■ **Lapse.** The underwriter analyzed Caroline's financial condition to determine if she could afford the premiums.

■ **Antiselection.** Although Teresa had never been insured, the underwriter recognized that this was the first time that her death would result in a financial loss to anyone. Teresa was healthy at the time of the application, as the broken arm was a minor injury from which she was expected to fully recover. Thus, antiselection was probably not a factor.

■ **Speculation.** Even though, upon Teresa's death, Caroline would be relieved of paying Teresa's living expenses, the death benefit Caroline would receive would serve to offset the salary she would have to pay an employee to replace Teresa's volunteer services. Thus, Caroline was protecting against the risk of a financial loss rather than trying to make a profit.

■ **Money Laundering.** The amount of coverage requested in relation to the loss suffered was not great enough for suspicions of money laundering to arise.

---

consult tax documents, financial questionnaires, and financial statements. The amount and type of financial information gathered generally are determined by the amount of coverage requested. To manage and organize financial information, an underwriter may use a *financial worksheet*, which is a document that enables an underwriter to organize financial information and develop a clear picture of a person's financial situation.

The Application for Insurance

The application for insurance provides the underwriter with an initial picture of the proposed insured's financial status. A person's *financial status* includes his (1) current income expressed in terms of amount, sources, and permanency and (2) *net worth*, which is the difference between the person's assets and liabilities. In examining the application information, the underwriter determines whether an insurable interest exists and whether the amount of insurance requested is appropriate. Figure 5.2 summarizes and gives examples of the significant financial information an underwriter can obtain from the insurance application.

Figure 5.2. Information on the Insurance Application of Significance to Financial Underwriting

Information	Underwriting Significance
Age of proposed insured	Years of future employment
Occupation	Future potential income
Income	Current income
Insurance in force and amount of requested coverage	Current and requested coverage compared to total needed coverage
Relationship between proposed insured and policyowner, if not the same person	Presence of insurable interest
Relationship between proposed insured and beneficiary	Presence of insurable interest Justification of amount of coverage
Net worth	Determination of appropriate amount of coverage needed to preserve a proposed insured's estate

Source: Adapted from Mary C. Bickley et al., *Life and Health Insurance Underwriting*, 2nd ed. [Atlanta: LOMA (Life Office Management Association, Inc.), © 2007], 136. Used with permission; all rights reserved.

Producer

A producer who has established a strong relationship with an insurer and who generally requests coverage only for qualified proposed insureds is likely to be considered a reliable source of financial information during underwriting. If the underwriter has questions or doubts about the justification for requested insurance, the underwriter typically communicates with the producer to clarify the submitted information. For underwriting large-amount cases, the underwriter might request a letter from the producer explaining the proposed insured's need for a large amount of insurance. If doubts persist, the underwriter may request more information from the producer, the proposed insured, or a consumer reporting agency.

Inspection Report

The information in an inspection report can be useful in verifying information from the application and the producer and in gathering further information. For example, the underwriter may ask the consumer reporting agency to check for any liens—which are claims on the proposed insured's property in connection with outstanding debts—bankruptcies, poor credit history, outstanding lawsuits, and other significant debts in the proposed insured's financial history. The underwriter also may ask the consumer reporting agency to interview the proposed insured's attorney, tax adviser, and/or accountant to verify or gather further details about financial information on the application.

Tax Documents

An underwriter can gather valuable information from a proposed insured's W-2 form (in the United States) or T4 form (in Canada), which provides the underwriter with information about the amount of money paid to the proposed insured by an employer. For example, when a proposed insured has listed alimony paid or large amounts of business expenses, the underwriter may question whether the proposed insured has sufficient funds to pay for insurance. Moreover, if the proposed insured lists a considerable deduction for medical or dental expenses, the underwriter may seek further information about the proposed insured's health.

For large-amount applications, some insurers use statements from a proposed insured's banker or certified public accountant instead of or in addition to information from tax documents. The statements typically cover several years and report gross income, net income, net worth, and financial losses.

Financial Questionnaire

For a large-amount application, the insurer may require the proposed insured to complete and sign a financial questionnaire. Each insurance company typically designs its own financial questionnaire to gather detailed information about proposed insureds. In handling financial questionnaires, the underwriter is especially careful to adhere to the insurance company's rules of confidentiality.

If a proposed insured is requesting personal life insurance as a means of paying a future estate tax liability, the underwriter may use a financial questionnaire to gather such information as the value of the proposed insured's estate, the composition of the estate (for instance, property, investments, and other sources of assets), the estimated value and the dates of all gifts made from the estate, the estimated amount of estate tax payable, and the name of the person who is liable for paying the estate tax after the proposed insured's death.

Financial Statements

When a proposed insured who owns a business wishes to purchase a considerable amount of life insurance, the underwriter usually requests financial statements—that is, standardized reports summarizing the business's finances—to determine the stability of the business. In assessing financial statements, an underwriter usually considers the following information:

■ The historic trend of profit or loss in the business, typically for a period of at least the three to five years prior to the date of application for insurance

■ Financial obligations to which the business is or will be committed

■ Evidence of plans to expand, restructure, or sell the business

The debt of a business can rise and fall substantially during the year. Therefore, in analyzing the amount of debt a company carries, underwriters typically use annual financial statements, rather than recent quarterly reports, which could present a distorted view of the company's financial strength or weakness. Figure 5.3 describes the types of financial statements an underwriter may examine.

Figure 5.3. Financial Statements Used by Underwriters

Statement of owners' equity (also known as a *statement of changes in owners' equity*). A financial statement that shows the changes in owners' equity during a specified period. In the context of valuing a business, **equity** is the amount of the business owned—and not financed—by the owners. The underwriter uses the statement of owners' equity to determine the dollar amount of the owners' shares in a business.

Balance sheet. A financial statement that shows the business's financial position on a certain date. The balance sheet includes information on the business's *assets*, which are all things of value owned by the business; the business's *liabilities*, which are the business's debts and future obligations; and the *equity* of the owners of the business, which represents the value of the business as determined by deducting liabilities from assets.

Income statement. A financial document, (also known as a *profit and loss statement*), that reports the business's revenues and expenses during a specified period and indicates whether the business experienced net income or a net loss during the period. The income statement attempts to match the revenues—or income—for the specified period with the expenses—or costs of doing business—during that period.

Statement of cash flows. A financial statement that indicates the amounts of cash received and paid in the operating, investing, and financing activities associated with the business. A statement of cash flows helps an underwriter to assess a firm's ability to produce adequate future cash flows. This statement also helps the underwriter determine the reason for any gaps that exist between a company's net income and the amount of cash received. A company that shows increasing deficiencies in cash flow from year to year may be in financial difficulty.

Some businesses—typically those that sell stock to the public—produce annual reports that may be helpful to an underwriter. An ***annual report*** is a financial document that a corporation issues to its stockholders to report the business's activities and financial status for a specified period, which is usually the preceding year. The annual report includes independently audited financial statements, along with information from the business's management team concerning the organization's current and future business position and performance.

Assessing Life Insurance Needs and Financial Factors

An underwriter evaluates a proposed insured's financial situation in part to assess that person's need for insurance. An underwriter must determine that the need for the coverage is legitimate and the amount of insurance requested to cover this need is reasonable and affordable. In other words, the amount of insurance applied for and in force must make sense and not create a situation in which the proposed insured is worth more dead than alive. Some generally accepted financial needs for purchasing personal life insurance include:

■ **Family income protection.** Funds needed to pay the ordinary living expenses of a family that were formerly paid by the income of a deceased person. Underwriters generally approve coverage for family income protection if the need for the amount requested is shown clearly.

■ **Estate settlement.** The process of paying debts after a person's death. Estate settlement typically requires funds to pay taxes, medical expenses not covered by insurance, funeral costs, attorneys' fees and other expenses incurred to settle the estate, as well as funds to repay debts owed by the deceased person. Life insurance can provide the funds needed to pay these expenses. Underwriters usually approve coverage intended to pay such expenses when evidence of the obligations is clear.

■ **Charitable contributions.** The naming of a charitable institution as the beneficiary in an application for life insurance. A person who has made regular contributions to a charitable organization may wish to continue to support that organization after her death. Life insurance proceeds can be used to replace the future contributions she would have made. Even if a person has made no previous contributions, using life insurance proceeds to benefit a charity is a legitimate and widely recognized way of making charitable gifts.

Life insurance is designed to meet the needs of insureds by providing policy proceeds that compensate for a financial loss but do not represent a profit to the beneficiary. Most proposed insureds demonstrate a clear need for the requested coverage and can afford the premiums, especially in these days of low-cost term insurance. However, determining whether the amount of coverage is appropriate—in other words, whether the coverage will compensate for a loss but will not be so great as to represent a profit to the beneficiary—may be a challenge to underwriters.

Financial Status

To determine whether the proposed amount of coverage is appropriate, an underwriter assesses the proposed insured's financial status, which includes his current income, potential income, and net worth. In addition, bankruptcies can affect the proposed insured's financial status.

- **Current Income.** *Current income*, also referred to as annual income, is one of the elements used to determine the appropriate amount of coverage to issue. Current income may be earned or unearned. *Earned income* is income that will not continue after the insured dies—such as salary from a full- or part-time job, regular bonuses and commissions, and stock options—and is a measure of the financial loss that family members would suffer in the event of the person's death. *Unearned income*, sometimes called *passive income*, is income that may continue after the person dies, such as interest income, dividends, and capital gains. Many insurance companies will consider only the proposed insured's earned income when determining the need for insurance, but will consider both the earned and unearned income when determining ability to pay for the coverage.

- **Potential Income.** Besides looking at current income, the underwriter considers the *potential income* of a proposed insured. The person may be in the process of establishing a career and may not yet have reached her full potential for earning income. If a proposed insured has an irregular or unstable income—for instance, if a person has little business experience and is starting a new company—the underwriter may have difficulty estimating the person's potential income. Consultation with the chief underwriter and research into the performance of similar business enterprises can help the underwriter develop the information needed to make a sound decision on the case.

- **Net Worth.** Underwriters use net worth—the difference between the person's assets and liabilities—to determine the appropriate amount of coverage needed to preserve a proposed insured's estate. Keep in mind that while the amount of life insurance in force is not considered as part of a person's net worth, the cash value of any cash value life insurance policy in force is considered as an asset when calculating the person's net worth.

- **Bankruptcy.** An underwriter who discovers that a proposed insured has been or is involved in a bankruptcy must assess the increased risks of antiselection and lapse. An underwriter also must investigate whether a proposed insured who has been involved in a bankruptcy still has the legal ability to enter into an insurance contract involving the payment of premiums. For a proposed insured who has been or is involved in a bankruptcy, the producer submitting the application should provide the underwriter with a letter explaining what caused the bankruptcy, how the proposed insured has settled or is settling the bankruptcy, and how the proposed insured is managing his current finances. If a proposed insured is involved in an ongoing bankruptcy proceeding, many insurers postpone making an underwriting decision until the proposed insured has been discharged from bankruptcy for a certain period of time, usually one to seven years.

Insurance in Force

To rule out the risks of antiselection, speculation, and money laundering, the underwriter makes certain that the proposed insured is not overinsured. ***Overinsurance*** refers to an amount of applied-for insurance that, together with in-force insurance, is excessive in relation to the need for which coverage is being purchased. Therefore, the underwriter evaluates the amount of insurance that a proposed insured currently has in force with all insurers and the amount of insurance for which the person is applying. Typically, the various purposes of coverage also are considered. If the proposed insured is replacing one policy with another, the underwriter subtracts the amount of the policy being replaced from the proposed insured's total amount of coverage. Each insurer sets its own limits for the total acceptable amount of in-force coverage.

In some insurance companies, the calculation of the amount of insurance in force includes any accidental death benefit (ADB), which provides a death benefit above the face amount of the policy if the insured dies in an accident as defined in the policy. Some insurers establish separate limits for face amount coverage and for ADB coverages.

When reviewing an application for personal insurance, an underwriter typically does not consider as in-force coverage any business life insurance coverage paid for by the proposed insured's employer to the extent the employer is the beneficiary. In addition, the death benefits of pensions and Social Security are usually small and generally are not included in the calculation of in-force coverage. Group life insurance generally is not considered, either because the amount is small or because coverage terminates when employment does.

Tools to Determine the Appropriate Amount of Insurance

To determine a proposed insured's need for coverage and ability to pay for the coverage, underwriters use factor tables and/or the percentage-of-income rule. Underwriters use these tools as guidelines, not as rigid decision-making rules, and they may consider other factors in determining an appropriate amount of insurance for a specific case.

Factor Tables

A *factor table* is a chart that shows the maximum amount of insurance—expressed in multiples of a person's salary or current gross earned income—that an insurer typically will approve in each of several age ranges. Because each insurer develops its own factor tables, the amount of insurance a person can buy may vary from one insurer to another. Figure 5.4 shows a typical factor table for life insurance; the table specifies the amount of insurance, figured as a multiple of a proposed insured's current gross earned income that may be purchased at specified ages.

An underwriter usually is not bound absolutely by the numbers in a factor table. Higher amounts of coverage can be approved for proposed insureds whose current income is low, but who can be expected to have higher earnings in later years. For example, young doctors, attorneys, financial consultants, and sales people generally can be expected to earn considerably more money as they gain experience and

Figure 5.4. A Typical Factor Table for Whole Life Insurance

Age	Multiple of Current Gross Earned Income
20–40	20
41–50	15
51–60	10
61–64	5
65 and older	4

develop larger practices and more clients. For such proposed insureds, an underwriter often requests documentation indicating the proposed insured's potential future earnings.

Percentage-of-Income Rule

To determine a person's ability to pay premiums, some insurers use a ***percentage-of-income rule***, which stipulates the amount of money a proposed insured can afford to spend on insurance annually according to a specified percentage of the proposed insured's current gross earned and unearned annual income. The percentage generally varies between 6 percent and 20 percent, depending on the level of the person's current gross earned and unearned annual income and the type and amount of coverage requested. Each insurer establishes its own percentages for each insurance product.

As an example, one insurer's percentage-of-income rule specifies that a proposed insured for a certain life insurance product can afford premiums no greater than 7 percent of the first $10,000 of her current gross earned and unearned annual income, 11 percent of the next $15,000, and 18 percent of the remainder. According to this insurer's percentage-of-income rule, a proposed insured whose current gross earned and unearned annual income is $100,000 a year can afford to pay a maximum premium of $15,850 annually for life insurance coverage, computed as follows:

$$
\begin{array}{ll}
\$700 & [0.07 \times \$10,000] \\
+\ 1,650 & [0.11 \times \$15,000] \\
\underline{+13,500} & \underline{[0.18 \times \$75,000]} \\
\$15,850 &
\end{array}
$$

Because $15,850 a year is the maximum amount of premiums that the proposed insured can afford to pay, the underwriter may not approve more coverage than that amount will purchase.

Underwriters typically do not consider a proposed insured's liabilities as a separate factor when determining the amount of coverage to issue. Underwriters generally feel that the large multiples used in factor tables and under the percentage-of-income rule already take into account certain liabilities, such as mortgages.

Risk Classification

In making an underwriting decision for individual life insurance, an underwriter assesses the risk presented by a proposed insured by examining medical, personal, and financial information concerning the proposed insured. The underwriter then classifies the proposed insured as a preferred, standard, or substandard risk or declines to approve coverage. In this section, we discuss how an underwriter determines a proposed insured's appropriate risk class. We also explain different approaches to charging premiums for substandard risks. Note that typically financial risk factors are not rated. Rather, unfavorable financial information may cause the underwriter to lower the amount of coverage offered or decline to issue the policy.

Numerical Rating System

Most individual life insurance underwriters use the numerical rating system to place the proposed insured in the appropriate risk class. The *numerical rating system* is a risk classification method in which an underwriter calculates a numerical value for the degree of risk a proposed insured presents to the insurer; the underwriter then places the proposed insured in a risk class according to the numerical value. The higher the numerical value, the higher the degree of risk presented by the proposed insured.

Insurers set the numerical value of the average, or standard, mortality risk accepted for coverage at 100 percent. The underwriter then assigns a positive or negative number to each medical and personal factor that has been determined statistically to have a positive or negative impact on the mortality risk presented by a proposed insured.

A proposed insured's medical and personal risk factors that have an unfavorable effect on mortality are assigned "plus" values (such as +25) and are called *debits*. Debits increase the numerical value indicating an applicant's predicted percentage of standard mortality. In contrast, a proposed insured's medical and personal risk factors that have a favorable effect on mortality are assigned "minus" values (such as –25) and are called *credits*. Credits lower the numerical value indicating an applicant's predicted percentage of standard mortality. Combining debits and credits with the basic standard value of 100 produces the total numerical value of the risk represented by an individual proposed insured.

For example, suppose Van Ellsworth's medical records indicate that he has a slightly enlarged heart. The insurer from which Mr. Ellsworth is requesting coverage typically assigns a debit of +50 to such an impairment, indicating that this type of impairment represents 150 percent of the mortality rate for standard risks. On the other hand, the insurer may assign a credit of –10 if both Mr. Ellsworth's parents are alive, healthy, and in their 80s. If Mr. Ellsworth has no other impairments or personal factors that decrease or increase his predicted mortality, then the total numerical value of the risk Mr. Ellsworth represents is equal to 140 (100 points representing standard mortality, plus 50 points representing the additional risk of his enlarged heart, minus 10 points representing the better than average risk posed by the health status of his parents).

Figure 5.5 presents a typical life underwriting worksheet showing debits and credits assigned. Note that the debits and credits and the extra ratings that insurers assign to mortality risks vary from one insurer to another because of differences in assumptions about expected mortality.

Figure 5.5. Underwriting Worksheet

Life Underwriting Worksheet

Life App $ ELR $	**250,000**		
☑WP	☑AD	☐GB	☐VB	☐PUA

Personal	☑Male ☑Non-Smoker ☐Female ☐Smoker	+/-	Request	Requirements	Receive	Clear	Waive
Age: **47**			✓	Para	✓	✓	
Height **5'11"** Weight **190**				Med			
Family History *both parents in 80s and in*		–10	✓	Ecg	✓	✓	
MB ☐Yes ☐No	*good health*			X-Ray			
General				Spec ☐1 ☐2			
Enlarged heart		**+50**	✓	Blood Profile	✓	✓	
		———		Insp. ☐ MVR 47 ☐			
		+40	✓	Aps/Dr *Smith*	✓		
				Aps/Dr			
				EP ☐1 18 ☐2			
				23 ☐ 25 ☐ 29 ☐ F37 ☐			
				Smoking Q F170			
				Fin. Ques. 17			
				Reinsurance 45			
				Branch Reply 02			
				Replacement 29			
☐ELR/CTB ☐Male ☐Non-Smoker ☐Female ☐Smoker							
Age:							
Height Weight							
Family History							
MB ☐Yes ☐No							
General							
			Financial Calculation		Life		A.D.
			In Force (all Co's)				
			New (all Co's)				
			Total				
			Income:		Required Income		
			Factor:		$		

Note: The total of the debits and credits equals 40, but the number representing the proposed insured's mortality risk is 140, representing the standard mortality of 100 plus the total of the debits and credits.

The information an insurer uses to assign numerical values—that is, debits and credits—to a proposed insured's medical and personal risks is contained in a document known as an ***underwriting manual***, which also typically provides descriptive information on impairments and serves as a guide to underwriting action. Whereas in the past underwriting manuals were provided in paper form, now they typically are located on the insurer's intranet.

Each underwriting manual includes an index listing synonyms and derivative terms for characteristics, with page references. Most manuals also include a laboratory section that lists basic laboratory test data and a "normal" range of values for the most commonly used laboratory tests. To help underwriters interpret medical information, many manuals contain a glossary of symptoms and medical terms, as well as a list of medical abbreviations. Most insurers emphasize that the suggested actions and ratings listed in their underwriting manuals are intended to be flexible and may be modified by an underwriter according to individual circumstances.

In addition to descriptions of various impairments associated with each organ and system of the body, the underwriting manual may include

- A list of debits or credits, or both, for specific impairments and personal factors

- Extra-percentage tables to be used for table ratings, which we discuss in the next section

- A statement of the amount of flat extra premium to be charged for certain impairments and personal factors

Note that in today's highly technical environment, most companies have the extra percentage tables automated within their policy issue systems. In such cases, an underwriter would indicate the case is rated at 150 percent and the policy issue system would calculate the premium based on actuarially derived extra percentage tables.

Charging for Substandard Risks

For individual life insurance, insurers compensate for the extra mortality represented by a substandard risk by charging a premium based on a table rating, a flat extra premium, or a combination of the two. The approach to charging for a particular substandard risk depends on whether the mortality risk of a given medical or personal factor is assumed to remain constant, increase with age, or decrease with age.

Table Rating Method

The **table rating method** is a method for adjusting individual life insurance premium rates to compensate for extra mortality that divides substandard risks into broad groups—or tables—according to their numerical value. The extra mortality for each substandard group is expressed as a percentage added to standard mortality as has been shown by the insurer's actual mortality experience. The total mortality for each substandard group is presented in an **extra-percentage table,** which is a document that lists all the tables used in the table rating method. Each table is labeled by either a number or a letter of the alphabet. Underwriters calculate a proposed insured's numerical rating and determine which table the rating falls within. Typically the table rating is then entered into the administration system, which automatically calculates the appropriate premium rate.

The table rating method is appropriate when extra mortality increases with age, as is found in diabetic and overweight people. Underwriters use table ratings for the majority of substandard risks, and the table ratings are generally the same from one insurer to another. Typically, underwriters classify numerical total mortality values of up to approximately 125 as preferred or standard, and the numerical values above that number are classified as substandard or declined. Figure 5.6 shows an example of an extra-percentage table.

According to Figure 5.6, the total mortality for each class is figured as 100 (representing standard mortality) plus the total of debits (representing extra mortality) and credits (representing favorable mortality). For example, Table 1's (or A's) total mortality of 125 equals 100 debits for standard mortality *plus* 25 debits for the extra mortality. The 25 debits for extra mortality actually could be composed of 50 debits for extra mortality offset by 25 credits for favorable mortality.

Each table represents an increase in extra mortality of 25 debits. Therefore, a case rated Table 1 has a mortality rating of 125, or 1.25 times the standard mortality; a case rated Table 2 has a mortality rating of 150, or 1.5 times standard mortality; and so on.

Another way to calculate the amount of extra mortality represented by each table is to multiply the table number by 25, then add 100 (which represents standard mortality). For instance, a case rated Table 4 has a mortality rating of 200 [(4 × 25) + 100] or two times the standard mortality, and a case rated Table 5 has a mortality rating of 225 [(5 × 25) + 100] or 2.25 times the standard mortality.

Figure 5.6. Typical Extra-Percentage Table

Table (or Substandard Class)	Total Mortality (Standard Mortality + Extra Mortality)
1 or A	125
2 or B	150
3 or C	175
4 or D	200
5 or E	225
6 or F	250
8 or H	300
10 or J	350
12 or L	400
16 or P	500

Note: Tables 7, 9, 11, 13, 14, and 15 do exist and each increases by 25 debits over the prior table, but underwriters rarely use these tables.

Flat Extra Premium Method

The *flat extra premium method* is a method of charging for substandard individual life insurance in which the insurer adds to the standard premium a specified extra dollar amount for every $1,000 of insurance. The flat extra premium method is used mainly in cases involving extra mortality that is considered to be either constant or decreasing with age.

The amount of extra premium charged under this method varies according to the amount of risk represented by the medical impairment or personal factor, but does not vary from year to year during the time the extra premium is charged. For example, an insurer may charge $2 per $1,000 for a mild impairment, but $7 or $15 per $1,000 for a more serious impairment. Whatever the amount charged, it will remain the same ($2 or $7 or $15) throughout the period that the flat extra premium is charged.

An insurer may charge either a temporary or a permanent flat extra premium. A *temporary flat extra premium* is an amount added to the premium for a risk factor for which the extra mortality risk is expected to decrease and eventually disappear over a limited time period. A temporary flat extra premium is charged for such impairments as cancers in remission and heart conditions from which the proposed insured is recovering. Most insurers program their administration systems to remove this type of premium automatically at the appropriate time. When insurers do impose a flat extra premium for a medical impairment, the extra premium is almost always temporary.

A *permanent flat extra premium* is an amount added to the premium for cases in which a personal risk factor is expected to remain constant throughout the life of the policy. This type of rating is most commonly used for hazardous occupations, dangerous avocations, or unfavorable driving records.

Combining Methods

Insurers often use a combination of a flat extra premium and a table rating when the risk of death is expected to increase during a certain period and to decrease after that period. For example, experience has shown that a person who has been treated for certain cancers has the greatest risk of recurrence during the first 10 years following the initial treatment. After 10 years, the risk of recurrence is much lower, although it still exists. Thus, a proposed insured who was treated for cancer six years before applying for life insurance might be accepted with a Table 4 rating (200 percent), plus a $15 flat extra premium per $1,000 of coverage for each of the next four years. After four years, the $15 flat extra premium would be removed automatically, but the table rating would continue.

Key Terms

financial underwriting

persistency rate

speculation

life settlement

financial worksheet

financial status

net worth

statement of owners' equity

equity

balance sheet

income statement

statement of cash flows

annual report

overinsurance

factor table

percentage-of-income rule

numerical rating system

debits

credits

underwriting manual

table rating method

extra-percentage table

flat extra premium method

temporary flat extra premium

permanent flat extra premium

Chapter 6

Niche Policies, Business Life Insurance, Replacements, and Supplemental Benefits

Objectives:

After studying this chapter, you should be able to

- List the basic features of multi-life policies, juvenile insurance policies, and direct response policies and explain how each type of coverage is typically underwritten

- List the basic features of a buy-sell agreement, key-person life insurance, split-dollar life insurance, and creditor insurance and explain how each type of coverage is typically underwritten

- Identify the warning signs that indicate a business is in financial difficulty or may be engaging in commercial fraud

- Describe three methods an underwriter can use to estimate the value of a business

- Calculate a debt-to-equity ratio, current ratio, quick ratio, and return-on-equity (ROE) ratio and explain how an underwriter uses these ratios to assess the financial condition of a business's solvency, liquidity, and profitability

- Describe underwriting considerations for policy replacements

- Identify five different types of supplemental benefits that life insurance policies may provide and describe typical underwriting considerations for each type of benefit

Outline

Underwriting Niche Policies
- Multi-Life Policies
- Juvenile Insurance Policies
- Direct Response Policies

Underwriting Business Life Insurance
- Financial Assessment of a Business
- Underwriting Considerations for Various Types of Business Life Insurance

Underwriting Policy Replacements

Underwriting Supplemental Benefits
- Waiver of Premium for Disability Benefit
- Accidental Death Benefit
- Family Benefit
- Guaranteed Insurability Benefit
- Accelerated Death Benefits

Chapters 4 and 5 of this text deal with the underwriting of basic individual life insurance policies designed to be sold by producers to individuals to meet traditional personal needs. We begin this chapter by discussing the underwriting of individual life insurance policies designed to meet other personal needs. We then explore how underwriters analyze individual life insurance policies that meet business needs. We conclude with sections on underwriting replacement policies and *supplemental benefits*, which are benefits added to the coverage specified in the basic insurance policy.

Underwriting Niche Policies

Niche personal life insurance policies are life insurance policies that an insurer designs to fulfill the needs of a specific marketing segment. Niche policies, which serve personal insurance needs, include multi-life policies, juvenile insurance policies, and direct response policies. Underwriters of niche policies assess many of the same factors assessed in underwriting traditional individual life policies that meet personal needs.

Multi-Life Policies

A life insurance contract that is written on two or more lives is a *multi-life policy*. Some insurers write policies on as many as 10 to 20 lives. Although some multi-life policies pay a portion of the benefits when each of the insured persons dies, the two most common types of multi-life policies are the

- *Joint life insurance policy*, also known as a *first-to-die life insurance policy*, which provides that proceeds will be paid when the first of two (or more) insureds covered by the policy dies

- *Last survivor life insurance policy*, also known as a *second-to-die life insurance policy*, which provides that proceeds will be paid when the second (or last) of two (or more) insureds covered by the policy dies

An underwriter makes a separate evaluation of each life to be covered under a multi-life policy. If an underwriter determines that one of the proposed insureds represents a ratable risk, the policy typically can be issued at an increased premium rate. Some insurers allow a multi-life policy to be issued even if one of the proposed insureds is uninsurable.

Juvenile Insurance Policies

A *juvenile insurance policy* is an insurance policy issued on the life of a child but owned and paid for by an adult—usually the child's parent, grandparent, or legal guardian—who typically is also the beneficiary. Most insurers will approve coverage after a full-term, newborn child has been released from a hospital. Infants born prematurely typically are declined coverage. However, most insurers will consider coverage again when the infant has reached a certain weight or age, depending on the insurer's underwriting requirements. Insurers cover adopted children in the same manner as biological children, but insurers do not issue coverage until an adoption is final. Note that some jurisdictions limit the amount of coverage that can be issued on a juvenile.

Underwriters use most of the same information sources to assess a juvenile proposed insured as those used to assess an adult. Some insurers offer a special, nonmedical juvenile application that is similar to an adult nonmedical application and is completed by the adult applying for coverage on the child's life.

In assessing an application for juvenile insurance, underwriters consider many of the same factors considered for risk appraisal of an adult. These factors include the age and medical history of the child, as well as the financial status of the policyowner. However, underwriters regard the policy face amount and policy ownership differently when evaluating an application for juvenile insurance than when evaluating an application for an adult.

In evaluating the appropriateness of the face amount requested, an underwriter considers the insurance in force or applied for on the parents or guardian. Typically, the amounts for the "breadwinners" must be at least equal to or, in some companies, twice that of the amount applied for on the child.

An underwriter also looks at whether other children in the family are similarly insured. If only one child of several is insured, or if one child is being insured for a larger amount of coverage than are the other children, the underwriter investigates the reason for such unusual treatment of one child. Singling out one child for life insurance coverage may be justified if that child brings in an income, for example, as a child star. However, disparate treatment of children when applying for life insurance coverage may indicate the presence of antiselection. Insuring only one child also could indicate the presence of speculation because the death of a seriously ill child who requires expensive medical treatments would relieve the family of a financial burden rather than create a need for compensation for a financial loss.

Underwriters also consider who will be the owner and the beneficiary of a juvenile policy. Usually, only parents, grandparents, or legal guardians are considered to have an insurable interest in the life of a child. Therefore, insurers usually require that one of these parties be either the owner or the beneficiary of the policy, or both. When grandparents purchase a juvenile policy, an underwriter also considers insurance in force and applied for on all other grandchildren for the same reasons mentioned above.

When parents are not the owners of a policy covering a child, the underwriter typically obtains the parents' written consent to the issuance of the coverage and requires them to attest to the accuracy of responses to medical questions because they should have first-hand knowledge of the child's current state of health. The parental consent is kept on file with the application or is made a part of the policy.

Insurers typically do not require a physical examination for juvenile insurance for two reasons: (1) after the first year of life, the mortality rate for children is very low; and (2) most juvenile insurance applications do not involve large sums of money and therefore do not justify the expense of a physical examination. If the information provided on the juvenile application indicates that the child has a health problem or if the parent or legal guardian cannot complete the nonmedical portion of the application, then the underwriter usually requests an APS.

Some juvenile policies include a ***waiver of premium for payor benefit,*** which is a supplemental benefit that provides that the insurer will waive payment of the policy's premiums if the payor—the person paying the policy premium—becomes disabled or dies prior to the insured child's attainment of a specified age, usually 21. Insurers usually require modest evidence of insurability from the payor before approving this benefit. Typically, the payor's age, occupation, height and weight, and a brief medical history are sufficient evidence of the payor's insurability. The payor usually provides this information as part of the regular application for juvenile coverage. Insurers seldom require a medical examination of the payor unless the payor's medical history indicates that an examination is warranted. Insurers normally issue the waiver of premium for payor benefit only if the payor is rated a preferred, standard, or slightly substandard risk.

Direct Response Policies

Some insurers sell some or all of their products through a ***direct response distribution system***, which is a type of distribution channel in which customers purchase products directly from a company by responding to advertisements, Internet Web sites, or telephone solicitations. Policies distributed through a direct response system, known as ***direct response policies***, may be underwritten on a guaranteed-issue basis, underwritten on a nonmedical basis, or fully underwritten.

When products are offered on a ***guaranteed-issue basis***, no individual underwriting takes place; every eligible proposed insured who applies and meets specified conditions is automatically issued a policy. The term *guaranteed-issue* does not imply that everyone who applies is approved but that if the proposed insured meets the eligibility requirements for applying for the policy, he will be approved. The eligibility requirements are relatively liberal and typically concern the insured's age or the amount of coverage already in force with the insurer.[1] For example, direct response products offered on a guaranteed issue basis usually limit coverage only to people within a certain age range such as between the ages of 40 and 60. Also, such products typically impose maximum limits on the face amounts of coverage that will be issued to one person. The maximum amount of coverage allowed usually decreases as the proposed insured's age increases.

If a direct response policy is underwritten on a nonmedical basis, the direct response policy application asks a proposed insured to respond to certain medical history inquiries, such as

- Within the past five years, have you consulted a doctor or received medical treatment for any of the following conditions? (A list follows, containing impairments such as heart trouble, stroke, cancer, lung disease, diabetes, chest pains, cancer, tumors, convulsions, and diabetes.)

- Within the last five years, have you tested positive for the human immunodeficiency virus (HIV) or been told you have acquired immune deficiency syndrome (AIDS)?

- Within the last three years, have you consulted a doctor, been hospitalized, or taken prescription medication?

Most insurers that use such direct response policy applications either accept or reject the application solely on the basis of the answers to these questions. However, after reviewing the answers to these medical questions, some insurers will go on to request additional medical information before accepting or rejecting the application for the direct response policy. In some companies, if the underwriter determines that the proposed insured falls outside the parameters of the direct response policy applied for, the underwriter may suggest another product to the proposed insured. In such a case, the underwriter would request additional medical information and underwrite in accordance with that product's guidelines.

Underwriting Business Life Insurance

Business insurance is insurance that serves the needs of a business organization rather than those of a person. Note that whereas the term business insurance includes property and liability coverages that meet the needs of a business organization, the scope of our discussion is limited to life insurance that meets the needs of a business. Figure 6.1 describes some of the needs met by business life insurance.

Unlike most personal life insurance, business life insurance is usually third-party insurance. Thus, the proposed insured is not the applicant and will not be the policyowner if a policy is issued. An exception is a policy issued to the sole owner of a business under which the proposed insured, applicant, and policyowner are the same individual.

For business life insurance purposes, an insurable interest is present if the premature death of the insured party in a business relationship would result in a financial loss to the surviving parties or to the business. For example, insurable interest generally is considered to exist when partners in a partnership wish to insure each other's lives or a business wishes to insure the lives of certain key employees who are essential to the continued success of the company.

When underwriting individual life insurance that serves business needs, underwriters examine the same risk factors pertaining to the proposed insured—medical, personal, and financial—as they do when underwriting individual life insurance that serves personal needs. However, if an applicant is purchasing life insurance for business reasons, the underwriter will focus more closely on the business's finances than she would if evaluating the risk represented by an applicant who owns a business and is buying insurance for personal reasons.

Figure 6.1. Needs Met by Business Life Insurance

BUSINESS CONTINUATION NEEDS

A business owner may need a means of assuring that the business will continue to operate after her death. Thus, she may establish a **business continuation insurance plan**, which is an insurance plan designed to enable a business to continue operations upon the death or disability of an owner or other person important to the business. A business continuation insurance plan may include a buy-sell agreement or key person life insurance.

- A **buy-sell agreement** is an agreement in which one party agrees to purchase a second party's financial interest in a business following the second party's death, and the second party agrees to direct his estate to sell his interest in the business to the purchasing party. If an individual life insurance policy is used to fund the buy-sell agreement, the first party takes out a life insurance policy on the second party's life; and upon the death of the second party, the first party uses the life insurance proceeds to purchase the business interest from the estate of the second party.

- **Key-person life insurance** is individual life insurance that a business purchases on the life of a **key person**, who is a person whose continued participation in the business is necessary to its success and whose death would cause substantial financial loss to the business. A key person can be almost anyone important to the business who possesses special skills, knowledge, business contacts, or other abilities including an owner, a top salesperson, or an employee.

EMPLOYEE BENEFITS NEEDS

To attract and retain quality employees, an employer often provides an **employee benefit plan**, which is a program under which an employer provides its employees with various benefits in addition to their wages. Group life and group health insurance are popular employee benefits. Another employee benefit is a **split-dollar life insurance plan**, which is "any arrangement between an owner of a life insurance contract and a non-owner of the contract under which either party to the arrangement pays all or part of the premiums, and one of the parties paying the premiums is entitled to recover (either conditionally or unconditionally) all or any portion of those premiums and such recovery is to be made from, or is secured by, the proceeds of the contract."[2]

For example, a business might provide individual cash value life insurance policies for certain employees, who share in paying the cost of the policies. The employer pays the portion of each annual premium that is equal to the amount by which the policy's cash value will increase that year, and the employee pays the remainder of the annual premium. The policy can be owned by the employer or the employee. If the employee dies while still an employee and while the policy is in force, the employer receives proceeds equal to the policy's cash value, and the beneficiary named by the employee receives the rest of the proceeds. If the employee retires or leaves the company, the employee typically is given ownership of the policy but must reimburse the employer for the premiums it paid on the employee's behalf.

CREDITOR PROTECTION NEEDS

Sometimes creditors need assurance that they will be repaid if a key person of a business borrower dies. **Creditor insurance**, also known as *loan coverage* or *debt coverage*, is coverage designed to pay for the economic loss suffered by a creditor when a key person of a debtor business dies before the debt is paid. To maintain the principle of insurable interest, the proceeds of creditor insurance cannot be greater than the unpaid debt.

Source: Adapted from Mary C. Bickley et al., *Life and Health Insurance Underwriting*, 2nd ed. [Atlanta: LOMA (Life Office Management Association, Inc.), © 2007], 182–183. Used with permission; all rights reserved.

Financial Assessment of a Business

When underwriting business life insurance, underwriters assess the value and financial well-being of a business to ensure (1) a legitimate need for the insurance exists, (2) the amount of coverage requested is appropriate, and (3) the business will be able to pay the premiums.

Many of the sources of financial information used in underwriting business life insurance are the same as those used in underwriting personal life insurance. These sources of financial information include the application for insurance, the agent's statement, an inspection report, the business's income tax returns, and the business's financial statements. In addition, if a business's creditor has required the proposed insured to be covered by a specific amount of insurance, the underwriter usually asks the producer to obtain copies of relevant loan documents.

A business life insurance underwriter also may use a specialized questionnaire called a ***business financial supplement***, which is a document that requests information about the type of business, the current financial condition of the business, and the purpose for which the insurance is being requested. This type of supplement also is used occasionally for underwriting personal life insurance when the value of a proposed insured's business is important in assessing that person's financial worth. Figure 6.2 illustrates a typical business financial supplement.

An underwriter assesses financial documents for business life insurance in much the same way as for personal coverage applications. However, one special consideration for business coverages is that a business's audited financial statements sometimes require investigation because of variations in acceptable methods of valuing assets and liabilities and of reporting profits and earnings. An underwriter also can have difficulty assessing the financial strength of nondomestic corporations whose accounting practices differ considerably from those generally applied to domestic organizations. Underwriters may ask the insurer's accounting area for help with investigating and understanding business-related financial documents.

Underwriters who specialize in business life insurance look for indications that a business is in financial difficulty. Such indications include

- Negative cash flow from operations and inadequate financing

- Excessive debt that probably cannot be paid within a reasonable time or without reducing the funds that the business needs for maintenance and expansion

- Unusual financing arrangements, such as loans from family members, subsidiaries, or clients

- Dependence on only a few projects or clients instead of a wide variety of projects or clients

- A trend of declining sales or revenues

- A history of defaults on loans or debts, denial of credit by lenders, or recent financial restructuring

- Unexplained or illogical sale of substantial assets

- Bankruptcy

Figure 6.2. Business Financial Supplement

BUSINESS FINANCIAL SUPPLEMENT

I.   NAME OF COMPANY _____

II. TYPE OF ORGANIZATION ❐ Corporation   ❐ Partnership   ❐ Sole Proprietorship

III. Please attach a copy of your company's latest audited financial statements.
If not available, please provide the requested information.

A. CURRENT COMPANY BOOK VALUE

Assets	$_____
Liabilities	$_____
Net Worth	$_____

B. CURRENT COMPANY MARKET VALUE

Market Value	$_____
Insured's % Ownership	_____%
Market Value of Insured's Ownership	$_____

C. COMPANY NET PROFIT—Past Three Years
(before taxes and bonuses)

20____	$_____
20____	$_____
20____	$_____
This year (est.)	$_____

D. What other stockholders, partners, or key persons also are being insured in favor of the company? (Please name.)

_____
_____
_____
_____

IV. (Check at least one box and provide details.)

❐ **KEY PERSON**

A. Why is the person to be insured important to the company? What special skills, knowledge, or abilities does he/she possess that make insurance necessary?_____

_____
_____

B. How is it expected that the proceeds will be utilized? _____

_____

❐ **BUY AND SELL**

A. Is there a written agreement: In effect? ❐ Yes ❐ No (If in effect, attach signed copy.)
Contemplated? ❐ Yes ❐ No
(If contemplated, give expected finalization date.) _____

B. How is the business being valued in the agreement? _____

_____

❐ **BUSINESS LOAN**

A. Name and address of the lender _____

B. Amount of loan $_____   **C.** Date of loan _____

D. The repayment terms are_____

E. The purpose of the loan is_____

F. Is lender requiring the insurance? ❐ Yes   ❐ No

I understand that ABC Life Insurance Company will rely on the above statements in determining the need and justification for the insurance applied for, and I represent that all answers are true and accurate statements to the best of my knowledge and belief as of the date of application for life insurance. A photographic copy of this statement may be attached to and made part of any insurance contract issued.

Signature of Proposed Insured _____   Date _____

Signature of Owner_____   Date _____

Witnessed by _____   Date _____

- Labor strife

- Recent or substantial litigation

- Large losses that were not covered by insurance

Because a large percentage of new businesses fail within the first two to three years of existence, underwriting coverage for a new company that will own the business life insurance policy is more conservative than for businesses with a longer history of operation. The insurer is concerned that a new business might fail before the insurer has collected enough premiums to cover the expenses of underwriting, issuing, and administering the policy.

An underwriter also is trained to look for signs of commercial fraud. Figure 6.3 lists some of the warning signs of commercial fraud.

Business Valuation

Sometimes a certified public accountant (CPA) who supplies a business's financial statements also submits an assessment of a business's value to the underwriter. If no valuation is provided, the underwriter assesses the value of the business himself. Underwriters typically employ one or more of the following approaches to valuing a business:

- **Asset-based approach.** The underwriter places a value on the business by calculating the book value of the business, which is the excess of the business's assets over its liabilities.

Figure 6.3. Warning Signs of Commercial Fraud

- Evidence that the ownership of a company is being concealed

- A partner or other key person has worked for a number of companies that are no longer in business

- A partner or other key person is unable to provide information concerning her business history and past associations

- An overly complex organizational or partnership structure, or a confusing web of subsidiaries and conglomerates

- Trade, bank, or business references that appear fraudulent or unbelievably positive

- Financial statements that have been issued at irregular intervals, list assets that cannot be confirmed by other sources, use round figures instead of specific amounts, or list accounts receivable that are inconsistent with other figures such as inventory and purchasing records

---

■ **Income-based approach.** The underwriter places a value on the business by focusing on the earning capacity of the business.

■ **Market approach.** The underwriter places a value on the business by researching the selling prices of comparable businesses. General guidelines have been established to aid an underwriter in the valuation of businesses using a market approach. For example, on average, dental practices sell for 70 percent of annual gross sales.

When using one of these three approaches to valuing a business, an underwriter may consider one or more of the following factors:

■ Tangible assets (such as buildings, equipment, and inventory)

■ Intangible assets (such as goodwill, an established customer base, favorable industry reputation, market presence, franchise value, name recognition, a desirable location of the business, logos, copyrights, trademarks, and patents)

■ Historic trend of profit or loss, especially the average earning capacity over a period of at least three to five years prior to the date of application for insurance

■ Performance of the business relative to its industry during the same three- to five-year period

■ Current economic conditions and the future outlook of the business sector in which the business operates and of the economy as a whole

■ Availability of qualified employees and customers so that the business may maintain its present position and/or continue to grow and strengthen itself

■ Current price and recent sales of the company's stock, if any, and the dividend-paying capacity of the business

■ Financial obligations to which the business is or will be committed

■ Evidence of plans to expand, restructure, or sell the business

Solvency, Liquidity, and Profitability

An underwriter also may assess a business's financial condition by examining the business's solvency, liquidity, and profitability. Such an evaluation may employ financial ratios. A *ratio* is a comparison of two numeric values that results in a measurement expressed as a percentage or fraction. *Financial ratio analysis* consists of calculating the relationships between various pairs of financial values for the purpose of assessing a company's financial condition.

Considered in isolation, the ratios concerning solvency, liquidity, and profitability mean little, if anything. Underwriters typically compare these ratios for a business to the range of acceptable values established for other businesses in the same or similar industries.

Solvency is an entity's ability to meet its financial obligations on time. A business that is unable to maintain sufficient funds to pay its debts not only may be unable to pay insurance premiums, but also may be likely to suffer financial failure. In either situation, such a company is not a sound candidate for business coverage.

Generally, solvency analysis compares the amount of an entity's financial obligations with its resources available to meet those obligations. One measure of solvency is a ***debt-to-equity ratio***, also known as a *debt ratio*, which is calculated by dividing a company's total debt by its owners' equity. The formula for the debt-to-equity ratio is

$$\text{Debt-to-Equity Ratio} = \frac{\text{Total Debt}}{\text{Owners' Equity}}$$

The greater the owners' equity in relation to total debt, the more resources the company has to pay its debts. A financially sound company should have more owners' equity than debt. In other words, the value of a company's debt-to-equity ratio should certainly be less than 1. An underwriter's comfort with any given level of debt depends on many factors; in general, the greater the margin of equity over debt, the more confident an underwriter should be with a company's financial position.

For example, suppose owners' equity is $4,750,000 and total debt is $4,500,000. When we divide the total debt by owners' equity, the result is 0.947, as shown:

$$\text{Debt-to-Equity Ratio} = \frac{\$4,500,000}{\$4,750,000} = 0.947$$

In this example, the value of the debt-to-equity ratio is less than 1, so the company is technically solvent.

If the total debt were increased to $4,900,000 and owner's equity remained $4,750,000, the value of the ratio would be greater than 1, indicating a lack of solvency, as shown:

$$\text{Debt-to-Equity Ratio} = \frac{\$4,900,000}{\$4,750,000} = 1.03$$

Liquidity is a company's ability to readily convert its assets to cash for an approximation of their true value. To determine a company's liquidity, many insurers calculate a ***current ratio*** by dividing current assets by current liabilities as shown:

$$\text{Current Ratio} = \frac{\text{Current Assets}}{\text{Current Liabilities}}$$

Current assets usually are items that the company presently has or owns that can be readily converted to cash at a close approximation of their true value. Examples include cash, cash equivalents such as money market accounts, and inventory. If a current appraisal of asset values is available, the underwriter uses it. If such information is not available, the underwriter estimates the market values of the assets. **Current liabilities** are all the debts and obligations due and payable within the next accounting period. Current liabilities include salaries payable and interest payable.

Although the minimum acceptable value for the current ratio varies greatly among industries, underwriters generally require at least $2 in current assets for every $1 in current liabilities. That is, current assets should be at least two times as great as current liabilities.

Underwriters also sometimes assess a company's liquidity by examining its ability to pay its debts immediately. Immediate debt payment requires cash or its equivalent rather than proceeds from selling such assets as inventory, which may sell slowly, at a lower-than-expected price, or not at all. A company's ability to liquidate debt immediately can be measured using a **quick ratio**, also called a *quick liquidity ratio* or an *acid-test ratio*. The quick ratio is calculated by dividing a company's most liquid current assets—consisting of cash, liquid investments, and accounts receivable, which are also known as quick assets—by the company's current liabilities, as shown:

$$\text{Quick Ratio} = \frac{\text{Liquid Assets}}{\text{Current Liabilities}}$$

The range of acceptable values for the quick ratio varies greatly by industry; but in general, the greater the excess of liquid assets over current liabilities, the more liquid a company would be. Compared to the current ratio, the quick ratio provides a more realistic view of a company's debt-paying ability because the quick ratio eliminates any reliance on noncash assets that are not immediately available to meet emergency needs for cash.

A company's **profitability** is the degree to which it is successful in consistently generating returns to its owners and measures the productivity of the company's assets and its return on the owners' investment in the company. One ratio for evaluating profitability is the **return-on-equity (ROE) ratio**, which is determined by dividing net income by owners' equity as shown:

$$\text{Return-on-Equity (ROE) Ratio} = \frac{\text{Net Income}}{\text{Owners' Equity}}$$

Acceptable return on equity varies with the risk involved in a business. Underwriters expect companies operating in higher risk businesses to produce a higher ROE ratio, whereas underwriters expect companies operating in lower risk businesses to produce a comparatively lower ROE ratio. Note that the general state of the economy also influences acceptable values for return on equity.

Underwriting Considerations for Various Types of Business Life Insurance

The approaches used to assess risks are basically the same for every type of business life insurance. However, each type of business life insurance coverage has slightly different underwriting considerations.

Buy-Sell Agreements

When the applied-for insurance is intended to fund a buy-sell agreement, an underwriter evaluates the proposed insured's medical, personal, and financial factors and makes an estimation of the business's value and the proposed insured's financial interest in the business. The underwriter also confirms that the insurance is being purchased to continue the business and verifies the ability of the prospective purchaser to run the business. Life insurance can be used to fund buy-sell agreements for sole proprietorships, partnerships, and small corporations.

A *sole proprietorship* is a business owned by one person (or, in some jurisdictions, by a husband and wife). The owner of a sole proprietorship may enter into a buy-sell agreement with another person, typically an employee. This other person then may purchase life insurance coverage on the sole proprietor's life and may use the proceeds to purchase the business from the sole proprietor's estate. The underwriter typically determines the amount of insurance to issue based on the value of the business. An individual has an insurable interest in the owner of a sole proprietorship if the individual has entered into a buy-sell agreement with the sole proprietor and the insurance is intended to fund the buy-sell agreement.

Although a partnership dissolves by law in most jurisdictions upon the death of a partner, partners often plan for the funding of the business's continuation after the death of a partner by entering into a buy-sell agreement that sets out the terms under which a deceased partner's interest in the partnership will be purchased. Surviving partners then may continue the business as a new partnership; or, if only one partner remains, he may continue as a sole proprietor. Two kinds of buy-sell agreements can accomplish this purpose—a cross-purchase agreement and an entity agreement.

A *cross-purchase agreement* is a type of buy-sell agreement in which each partner agrees to purchase a share of a deceased partner's interest in the partnership. Each partner funds the buy-sell agreement by purchasing an insurance policy on the life of each of the other partners. Thus, each partner owns, pays the premiums on, and is the named beneficiary of a policy on the life of each of the other partners. If one partner dies, each surviving partner will receive the proceeds of a life insurance policy and can use those proceeds to purchase a share of the deceased partner's ownership interest in the partnership.

An *entity agreement* is a type of buy-sell agreement under which the partnership—rather than the individual partners—agrees to purchase the share of any partner who dies. The partnership also agrees to distribute a share of that ownership interest to each of the surviving partners. The partnership purchases an insurance policy on the life of each of the partners, pays the premiums, and is the named beneficiary of each policy. If a partner dies, the partnership uses the life insurance policy proceeds to purchase the deceased partner's share in the business from the deceased's estate.

With either the cross-purchase or the entity method of funding a buy-sell agreement, all partners' lives should be insured unless a strong reason exists not to do so. Each partner is considered to have an insurable interest in the lives of the other partners.

To determine the amount of insurance to approve, the underwriter needs to know the value of the partnership and the value of the proposed insured's interest in the partnership. An underwriter uses a financial questionnaire that focuses on the partnership to obtain initial figures on these values, as well as other information about the partnership and partners. Figure 6.4 illustrates such a partnership questionnaire.

Stockholders of a small corporation may enter into a buy-sell agreement using either funding method described in the preceding section on partnerships. However, in a corporate setting, the entity method of funding a buy-sell agreement is known as a *stock redemption agreement*; the corporation redeems, or retires, the deceased's stock rather than redistributing the shares to the surviving shareholders.

Stockholders of a small corporation each have an insurable interest in the lives of the other stockholders, and a small corporation has an insurable interest in its stockholders. To guard against antiselection, the underwriter makes sure that the lives of all major stockholders are covered by insurance.

In deciding the appropriate amount of insurance coverage to issue in connection with a buy-sell agreement involving a small corporation, an underwriter determines the present and projected value of the stock and the business's net worth. Another underwriting concern for stock repurchase insurance is the proportion of the total amount of stock owned by a proposed insured. If the proposed insured's stock holdings represent a significant portion of the company's equity, a need for the coverage exists. However, no real need for the coverage may exist if the proposed insured's stock holdings represent an insignificant portion of the company's equity.

Key-Person Life Insurance

Although the insurable interest that a business has in the life of a key person is usually obvious, certain situations may prompt the underwriter to look more closely for insurable interest. If the proposed insured is nearing retirement age and has not been insured by that business previously, the underwriter questions why that person has become important to the company. If a company applies for a large amount of coverage on a proposed insured who holds what appears to be only a moderately important position in the company, the underwriter may investigate further to determine insurable interest.

The size of a business is important for underwriting key-person coverage. Generally, the more people a business employs, the less likely the loss of one person is to produce a significant loss to the business. If a business appears to have other equally valuable employees who are not being proposed for key-person coverage, the underwriter usually questions why the business is singling out the proposed insured.

In evaluating the amount of coverage requested on a key person, the underwriter determines the monetary value of the proposed insured to the company, which generally is based on the amount of her compensation multiplied by a factor that represents the cost to recruit and train a replacement and to recover from the loss of her skills, special knowledge, and other benefits to the business. This monetary value of the proposed insured usually is set at 5 to 10 times the proposed

Figure 6.4. Partnership Questionnaire

1. Name of applicant _____

2. Name of proposed insured _____

3. How many partners are there?_____

   3a. What are the partners' names and what percentage of the business
      do they each own?

      _____ _____ %

      _____ _____ %

      _____ _____ %

4. What is the nature of business transacted? _____

5. How long has the partnership been in existence? _____

6. What has been the profit/loss of the partnership over each of the last three years?
   20 _____ $ _____
   20 _____ $ _____
   20 _____ $ _____
   This year (est.)$ _____

7. What has been the proposed insured's salary/share of profits over each of the last three years?
   20 _____ $ _____
   20 _____ $ _____
   20 _____ $ _____
   This year (est.)$ _____

8. What is the current value of the partnership? $ _____

   8a. How was the value established? _____

9. What is the proposed insured's percentage share of the partnership?_____%

10. Does a buy-sell agreement exist?_____

   10a.If not, is one to be executed in the near future? _____

11. Are policies to be purchased on the lives of all other partners?_____

   11a.If not, please give reasons _____

Signature _____

Date_____

insured's current annual salary, but the underwriter also may include the monetary value of other compensation, whether in cash (such as bonuses) or in fringe benefits (such as employer-provided health insurance or use of a company car).

Underwriters pay particular attention to applications for insurance for key persons in multinational companies—those that operate in two or more countries. The financial documents may be written in another language, may be abridged or unaudited, and/or may use accounting terms with different meanings from those in the underwriter's country.

Figure 6.5 illustrates a typical questionnaire used to gather information necessary to assess the risk for key-person life insurance.

Split-Dollar Life Insurance Plans

The individual life insurance policies that are part of split-dollar plans are underwritten in basically the same manner as individual life insurance policies purchased to fulfill personal insurance needs. The underwriter takes into account medical, personal, and financial factors in assessing the risk presented by the proposed insured. Also, the underwriter analyzes the employer's financial condition, but the extent of the analysis depends on the employer's ownership interest in the policy and the amount of coverage requested.

Creditor Insurance

In underwriting creditor insurance, an underwriter determines whether a borrower has means other than insurance to repay the debt. An underwriter investigates whether money from the loan is being used to purchase something that can serve as collateral for the loan, and, if so, whether the collateral will continue to produce income to pay off the loan. If it seems likely that the borrower will have to rely on the life insurance proceeds to pay off the loan, then the underwriter declines the case.

An underwriter also may want to see the loan repayment schedule. Generally, issuing creditor insurance for short-term loans is not in an insurer's best interest because a short-term creditor policy may lapse before the insurer can recover the costs of underwriting, issuing, and administering the policy.

If a company applies for creditor insurance a significant amount of time after a loan was granted, an underwriter guards against antiselection by investigating whether a debtor's financial situation or the health of the proposed insured has deteriorated since the loan was granted. Therefore, the underwriter verifies that loan payments have been made in a timely fashion, the debtor's financial condition is sound, and the proposed insured is healthy.

A potential overlap exists between creditor insurance and key-person insurance. In a creditor insurance situation, the creditor typically has inserted a clause in a loan agreement requiring immediate payment upon the death of the key person. The death of such a person could present a loss so severe that the debtor business may not survive without sufficient life insurance on the key person to pay off the loan. In a key-person insurance situation, the business may purchase life insurance on the key person in an amount sufficient to pay off the loan upon the key person's death, plus an amount to compensate the business in other ways

Figure 6.5. Key-Person Life Insurance Questionnaire

1. Name of applicant _____

2. Name of proposed insured (key person) _____

3. What is the key person's precise occupation and nature of duties?_____

   _____

4. What is the nature of the business transacted by the key person's employer? _____

   _____

5. How long has the employer been in business? _____

6. How many other employees are there?_____

7. How long has the key person been employed by the employer? _____

8. What has been the key person's gross salary over each of the last three years? This figure
   should include bonuses and commissions.
   20_____ $ _____
   20_____ $ _____
   20_____ $ _____
   This year (est.) $ _____

9. What has been the net profit/loss of the employer over each of the last three years?
   20_____ $ _____
   20_____ $ _____
   20_____ $ _____
   This year (est.) $ _____

10. Is the key person a shareholder in the employer's business? _____
    10a. If so, what percentage of shares does the key person hold? _____ %

11. What special abilities does the key person possess to justify classification as a key person?

    _____

12. What existing coverage is in force on the key person's life? _____

    _____

    _____

13. Why has the amount of insurance applied for been chosen? _____

    _____

14. What is the nature of the risk that is subject to loss?
    • Future earnings or sales jeopardized _____
    • Investment jeopardized _____
    • Forced liquidation of assets _____
    • Working capital jeopardized _____
    • Loss of management expertise _____
    • Other_____

15. Will the employer insure the lives of other employees as key persons? If so, how many lives
    and what amounts of coverage are proposed? Include lives already insured under key-person
    coverage. _____

    _____

Signature _____

Date_____

for the key person's death. This example illustrates the potential overlap between creditor insurance, which only pays off the loan, and key-person insurance, which does more than pay off the loan.

In analyzing the application for a business insurance policy on a person who is already insured under another business insurance policy, the underwriter must be sure that the total amount of coverage does not exceed the total need. For example, if a key person is insured under a creditor insurance policy and the debtor business applies for a key-person policy on the person, the underwriter must be sure that the key person policy is not intended to provide funds for payment of the outstanding amount of the loan.

Underwriting Policy Replacements

Policyowners can replace personal and business life insurance policies, and those replacements can be internal or external. In an *internal replacement*, the new policy is purchased from the same insurer that issued the original policy. In an *external replacement*, the new policy is purchased from an insurer other than the insurer that issued the original policy. Most replacing insurers underwrite internal and external replacements in accordance with their current underwriting requirements, but sometimes insurers will offer special programs with reduced underwriting requirements that allow replacements—typically internal only—of policies issued fairly recently.

In evaluating an application for a policy replacement, an underwriter considers the possibility that antiselection has motivated the request for the replacement, particularly when the proposed insured is of an advanced age. The underwriter also must be wary of twisting and churning when a policy is being replaced, especially when the producer does a high volume of replacement business.

In the United States, an underwriter also must be aware of whether a policy replacement involves a 1035 exchange. Named after Section 1035a of the United States Internal Revenue Code, a *Section 1035 exchange* is a tax-free replacement of an insurance policy for another policy insuring the same person and meeting conditions specified in the tax code.

Many policyowners in the United States use a 1035 exchange to avoid paying income tax on any gain realized from surrendering a policy and receiving its cash surrender value. Any portion of the cash surrender value that exceeds the cost basis for the policy is considered a gain and is taxable as ordinary income to the policyowner. Usually, the cost basis of an insurance policy is equal to the total premiums paid minus the total accumulated policy dividends. In a 1035 exchange, the policyowner receives no financial gain on the transaction because the cash surrender value of the original policy is used to pay premiums on the new policy. Because the policyowner experiences no gain, no tax is due.

Generally, a policy issued as part of a 1035 exchange is underwritten in the same manner as any other individual life insurance policy. However, if the new policy—whether or not a 1035 exchange is involved—must be issued with a less desirable rating than the original policy, the underwriter obtains from the applicant a letter stating that the applicant understands that a higher premium will be required if the face amount of the new policy remains the same as that of the original policy. Alternatively, the applicant may elect to receive a lower face amount of coverage rather than pay a higher premium than he was paying for the original policy.

Underwriting Supplemental Benefits

Insurers can provide most or all of the various supplemental benefits through standard policy provisions in their life insurance policies. However, insurers usually provide supplemental benefits by adding riders—or policy amendments—to the policies. By using riders, the insurer can customize a basic life insurance policy prior to policy issue or adapt an existing policy to meet the policyowner's changing needs. Insurers typically charge a premium for these supplemental benefits.

If an applicant desires supplemental coverage, the request is considered during underwriting. If a current policyowner asks for supplemental coverage, the insurer's policyowner service staff usually considers the request first. When such a request involves no increase or only a slight increase in the insurer's risk, policyowner service staff can approve the request. However, if the supplemental benefit may cause the insurer to bear a greater degree of risk, the policyowner service staff forwards the request to underwriting for more detailed consideration.

Waiver of Premium for Disability Benefit

A *waiver of premium for disability (WP) benefit* is a supplemental insurance benefit that provides that, in the event an insured is totally disabled as defined in the WP benefit, the insurance company will waive the payment of all premiums that become due during the period of disability. Note that the WP benefit is designed for policies issued to a policyowner who also is the policy's insured. The WP benefit reduces the possibility of the policyowner/insured canceling her policy when she experiences a loss of income from disability. The insurer pays the premiums waived by the WP benefit.

When underwriting the WP benefit, an underwriter considers medical and personal factors, but rarely financial factors. Because the risk of disability increases with age, issuance of the benefit is normally limited to proposed insureds below age 55 or 60, and the WP benefit usually covers only disabilities that begin before the insured reaches a specified age, such as age 65.

If a proposed insured's mortality rating is standard according to health history and physical condition, an underwriter usually will approve the WP benefit. In some situations, however, even if the policy was issued as a standard mortality risk, the insured's avocation or occupation may present enough of a disability hazard that a higher-than-usual premium will be required for the WP benefit or the underwriter may decline to approve it.

Accidental Death Benefit

An *accidental death benefit (ADB)* is a supplemental benefit that provides a death benefit above the face amount of the basic policy if an insured's death occurs as the result of an accident. This additional amount can be a multiple of the amount of the basic life coverage or an unrelated amount. The amount of ADB coverage approved usually depends on the amount of life insurance in force and the amount of coverage requested.

In underwriting ADB coverage, the underwriter usually adheres to the same principles used in underwriting basic personal life insurance. In certain business life insurance cases, the ADB may not be justified. For example, if a business needs $100,000 to fund a buy-sell agreement, the amount is fixed and specific.

The business has no reason to receive a multiple of that amount simply because the insured's death is accidental. However, personal insurance needs—as well as some business insurance needs, such as key-person coverage—are not fixed and specific and are not as easily measured. Accidental death benefit coverage may be an appropriate supplement to life insurance to cover the beneficiary's increased economic loss that results from an accidental death.

Age is an important factor considered in underwriting ADB coverage because as people age, they are prone to more accidents. Insurers rarely issue such coverage to insureds over age 55 or 60, and most ADB riders expire when the insured reaches age 65 or 70.

Rather than trying to assess each case individually, most insurers establish underwriting guidelines that specify a mortality rating range in which the underwriter can accept proposed insureds for coverage. For example, underwriting guidelines may state that the accidental death benefit may be issued at standard rates to proposed insureds rated at 200 percent mortality or below, but will be rated or denied for those who exceed 200 percent mortality.

ADB riders usually are not available to proposed insureds rated for alcohol or substance abuse. In addition, proposed insureds with certain hazardous occupations or avocations may have to pay an extra premium for ADB coverage, or the underwriter may deny them the ADB coverage.

Family Benefit

A *family benefit* is a supplemental benefit that insures the lives of the insured's spouse and children. After a policy with such a benefit is issued, children who are born or adopted into the family, or who become part of the family by marriage, usually are covered when they reach the age of at least 15 days (or whatever minimum age the benefit provision or rider specifies). A family benefit usually covers a child from a previous relationship but generally does not cover foster children.

To underwrite family benefit coverage, the underwriter requires insurability information for all family members, but usually the basic information on the application fills this need. An underwriter generally accepts a spouse and children, including those with slight impairments, as standard risks if the mortality rating of each family member is no higher than 200 percent. Underwriters usually decline to issue family benefits for mortality risks higher than 200 percent.

Some insurers establish age requirements for family benefit coverage. For example, an insurer might require that a spouse be at least 17 years old and no more than 10 to 15 years younger than the proposed insured. The insurer also might establish an upper age limit for a spouse. To be accepted for coverage, children typically must be under 18 years old at the time of policy issue. Furthermore, unless a child has a physical disability and is a dependent, coverage on the child ends when the child reaches age 21 or 25.

Guaranteed Insurability Benefit

A *guaranteed insurability (GI) benefit* is a supplemental benefit that gives the policyowner the right to purchase additional insurance of the same type as the basic life insurance policy—for an additional premium amount—on specified option dates during the life of the policy without supplying evidence of the insured's insurability. If the policyowner does not exercise the option under the GI benefit to buy additional insurance at the time specified, that opportunity is lost; the policyowner cannot purchase the amount of insurance available under those circumstances at a subsequent option date. The purpose of the requirement to exercise options promptly is to avoid antiselection.

If a GI benefit is not included in the basic policy when the policy is issued, a policyowner usually may add a GI benefit up to 60 days after issue. The underwriter's main concern is to determine the probability of a change in insurability during the 60-day post-issue period. Some insurers allow the addition of the GI rider more than 60 days after issue if the insured presents acceptable evidence of insurability.

An important underwriting factor for the GI benefit is age. Usually, the maximum age for issuing a GI benefit is 40 or 45. Aside from age, the risk selection factors involved in underwriting a GI benefit are typically the same as those considered in underwriting the basic policy. The additional coverage provided by the GI benefit has the same risk class rating as the policy. Note that insurers typically do not add a GI benefit to a basic policy that was issued on a substandard basis.

Accelerated Death Benefits

Some life insurance policies offer policyowner-insureds the option of taking an **accelerated death benefit**, also known as a *living benefit* in the United States, which is a supplemental benefit that gives a policyowner-insured the right to receive all or part of the policy's death benefit before her death if certain conditions are met.[3] When the policyowner-insured dies, the amount of the death benefit payable under the policy to the named beneficiary is reduced by the amount of the accelerated death benefit that was paid out to the policyowner-insured.

The three most common types of accelerated death benefits are the terminal illness benefit, the dread disease benefit, and the long-term care insurance benefit.

Terminal Illness Benefit

A **terminal illness (TI) benefit** is an accelerated death benefit under which the insurer pays a portion of the policy's death benefit to a policyowner-insured if he suffers from a terminal illness and has a physician-certified life expectancy of 12 months or less. The underwriter obtains a statement from an attending physician that establishes evidence of the terminal condition and certifies that the insured is likely to die within the time period specified by the benefit.

Dread Disease Benefit

A **dread disease (DD) benefit**, also known as a *critical illness* benefit, is an accelerated death benefit under which the insurer agrees to pay a portion of the policy's death benefit to a policyowner-insured if he suffers from one of a number of specified diseases. The specified diseases usually include

■ Life-threatening cancer

■ AIDS

■ End-stage renal (kidney) failure

■ Myocardial infarction (heart attack)

■ Stroke

■ Coronary bypass surgery

Most insurers provide DD coverage only to insureds who are under the age of 70 and who have no serious health problems.

Long-Term Care Insurance Benefit

A *long-term care (LTC) insurance benefit* is an accelerated death benefit under which the insurer agrees to pay periodic benefits to a policyowner-insured if he requires care in his own home or a qualified facility. The types of care given and the medical condition of the insured required to qualify for the LTC insurance benefit are specified in the LTC policy provision or rider.

Key Terms

supplemental benefit

niche personal life insurance policies

multi-life policy

joint life insurance policy

last survivor life insurance policy

juvenile insurance policy

waiver of premium for payor benefit

direct response distribution system

direct response policy

guaranteed-issue basis

business insurance

business continuation insurance plan

buy-sell agreement

key-person life insurance

key person

employee benefit plan

split-dollar life insurance plan

creditor insurance

business financial supplement

ratio

financial ratio analysis

solvency

debt-to-equity ratio

liquidity

current ratio

current asset

current liability

quick ratio

profitability

return-on-equity (ROE) ratio

sole proprietorship

cross-purchase agreement

entity agreement

internal replacement

external replacement

Section 1035 exchange

cost basis

waiver of premium for disability
  (WP) benefit

accidental death benefit (ADB)

family benefit

guaranteed insurability (GI) benefit

accelerated death benefit

terminal illness (TI) benefit

dread disease (DD) benefit

long-term care (LTC) insurance
  benefit

Endnote

1. Adapted from Sharon B. Allen et al., *Life and Health Insurance Marketing*, 3rd ed. [Atlanta: LOMA (Life Office Management Association, Inc.), © 2003], 349–350. Used with permission; all rights reserved.
2. IRS Final Regulations, September 17, 2003.
3. Adapted from Harriett E. Jones, *Principles of Life, Health, and Annuities*, 3rd ed. [Atlanta: LOMA (Life Office Management Association, Inc.), © 2005], 124–126. Used with permission; all rights reserved.

Chapter 7

Underwriting Group Life Insurance

Objectives:

After studying this chapter, you should be able to

- Describe the group underwriting process and the typical underwriting documents used during this process

- Identify the sources of information for group underwriting

- Explain the enrollment process and compare the process for contributory and noncontributory plans

- List the risk factors pertaining to a group prospect and describe their effect on the risk presented by a group prospect

- Describe how the design of a group plan and the administration of a group plan can affect the group coverage

- Distinguish among manual rating, experience rating, and blended rating and calculate a premium using blended rating

- Describe how an insurer minimizes the risk associated with late enrollees

- Explain renewal underwriting

Outline

Group Underwriting Process

Information Sources for Group Underwriting
- Request for Proposal
- Producer's Letter
- ERISA Documents
- The Master Application

Risk Factors for Group Underwriting
- The Group Prospect
- The Proposed Coverage

Rating Methods for Group Cases
- Manual Rating
- Experience Rating
- Blended Rating
- Rating Approaches for Small Groups

Post-Issue Underwriting for Group Insurance
- Underwriting of Late Enrollees
- Renewal Underwriting

Group life insurance underwriters adhere to many of the same principles as do individual life insurance underwriters. However, some major differences exist between underwriting group and individual products, which we explore in this chapter. Note that we refer to the individuals who are part of a group but are not covered by insurance as *group members*, and we refer to the individuals covered by a group insurance policy as the *group insureds*.

Group Underwriting Process

The group life insurance underwriting process resembles the individual life insurance underwriting process in that group underwriters gather information, assess risk, and decide whether, and on what terms, to approve coverage just as do individual underwriters. Much of the initial information about a group comes from the individual who markets the policy to the group. Most group policies are marketed by *group representatives*, who are salaried insurance company employees specifically trained in the techniques of marketing and servicing group products. Group representatives may work alone or in conjunction with producers. In some cases, the group representative initiates the sale to an organization and is the only contact between the group prospect and the insurer. In other cases, producers initiate contact with the group prospect and then call on the group representative for assistance in selling and implementing the plan.

A group prospect, often with the help of a producer or group representative, develops a *request for proposal (RFP)*, which is a document that provides detailed information about the group and the requested coverage and solicits a bid from an insurer for providing that coverage. The producer or group representative sends the RFP to the underwriter, and the information in the RFP allows the underwriter to make an initial assessment of the risk and determine whether the group meets the insurer's underwriting guidelines for the requested coverage. If the underwriter determines that the insurer cannot offer the requested coverage to the group, he can propose changes in the coverage or decline to respond to the RFP.

If the underwriter decides that the group prospect represents an acceptable risk, he develops a proposal for insurance for the producer or group representative to present to the group prospect for consideration. A *proposal for insurance* is a document that details the specifications of a group insurance plan proposed by an insurer for a group prospect. Although each insurer develops its own format for a proposal for insurance, such a document usually includes the following information:

- A *benefit schedule*, which is a table or schedule that specifies the types and amounts of coverage that will be provided for each class of group insureds. A class is a group of group members categorized according to some nondiscriminatory characteristic for purposes of determining eligibility for coverage and benefit levels.

- A list of the premium rates required for each type of coverage.

- Underwriting principles and assumptions for the proposed coverage.

- Details of plan administration, including the responsibilities of the policyholder and the insurer.

A proposal for insurance enables a group prospect to examine the coverage that the underwriter has approved for the group and compare the cost and benefits of plans offered by several insurers. Because the group insurance market is highly competitive, group underwriters work closely with the producer or group representative to design a group insurance plan that is acceptable to the group prospect and the insurer.

After evaluating the proposals for insurance it has received, the group prospect may accept or reject an insurer's proposal or ask the insurer to modify it in some way. If the underwriter agrees to make modifications to the plan or to the rates, the underwriter makes those changes to the proposal for insurance and provides the revised proposal for insurance to the group prospect.

When a group prospect approves a proposal for insurance, the producer or group representative helps the group prospect complete and submit to the insurer a master application for final underwriting. The *master application* is an application for group insurance that contains the specific provisions of the requested plan of insurance and is signed by an authorized officer of the proposed policyholder. The underwriter examines the master application to ensure that all information is complete and is consistent with the coverage that the group prospect agreed to in the proposal for insurance. The underwriter has the opportunity to investigate any discrepancies or omissions, and the underwriter approves the coverage only after fully evaluating the case and finding the risk to be acceptable.

If the underwriter approves the coverage, information from the master application is used to develop the master group insurance contract, which is typically referred to as the group insurance policy. This legal document certifies the relationship between the insurer and the group policyholder and specifies the benefits provided and the terms of coverage. The group insureds are not parties to the contract.

Figure 7.1 shows the sequence of documents typically exchanged between the insurer and group prospect during group insurance underwriting. Note that some of the terms in the figure will be explained later in the text.

Figure 7.1. Sequence of Typical Group Underwriting Documents

	1 Request for Proposal (RFP)	**2** Proposal for Insurance	**3** Master Application	**4** Master Group Insurance Contract
Person or entity who prepares the document	Group prospect or producer or group representative on behalf of the group prospect	Underwriter	Producer or group representative on behalf of the group prospect	Underwriter
Purpose of the document	To provide general information about the group prospect and to request a bid from the insurer for specified group coverage, including plan benefits and premium rates	To propose a plan for group coverage that may or may not match the coverage or premium rates requested in the RFP	To provide detailed information about the group prospect and the coverage being requested	To certify the relationship between the insurer and the policyholder and specify the benefits provided and the terms of coverage
Information included in or provided with the document	■ Coverage requested ■ Insurance history ■ Current benefits ■ Census ■ Producer's letter ■ List of current open claimants, if applicable	■ Benefit schedule ■ Premium rates	■ Name of the plan administrator ■ Enrollment card for each group member	■ Terms of coverage ■ Benefits

Source: Adapted from Mary C. Bickley et al., *Life and Health Insurance Underwriting*, 2nd ed. [Atlanta: LOMA (Life Office Management Association, Inc.), © 2007], 271. Used with permission; all rights reserved.

Information Sources for Group Underwriting

An underwriter uses various sources to find the information needed to assess the risk represented by a group prospect, including the request for proposal, attachments submitted with the RFP, the producer's letter, ERISA documents, and the master application.

Request for Proposal

An RFP usually includes the following information:

- Name and address of the group

- Characteristics of the group, such as size and industry

- Proposed effective date of coverage

- Types and details of coverage requested

- Administration information for premium billing and claims

- Classes of group members to be covered

- Percentage of the premium that the policyholder will contribute toward the cost of the coverage

- The group's previous insurance history, if any, including premium rates paid, claim experience, and duration of coverage

- The group's current benefits, if different from those being applied for

- Current or expected participation level, which is the percentage of group members who will enroll in the group plan, if the plan is contributory

An RFP for a plan that provides a waiver of premium for disability provision usually includes a list of current *open claimants*, who are group insureds receiving short- or long-term disability income benefits. Closed claim information also is included. The information provided on the open claimant list includes each claimant's name, date of birth, date of the disability, expected date of return to work (if any), and gross and/or net monthly benefit amount. Some lists include the prognosis for each disability. The nature of each disability typically isn't revealed due to privacy regulations. The underwriter uses this information to assess the group's future claim liability. In general, the current insurer retains responsibility for making benefit payments to current open claimants.

Another typical RFP attachment is a *census* that lists demographic information about the group prospect as a unit and about individual members within the group. Figure 7.2 shows a portion of a typical census for an employer-employee group, which we refer to as an *employee census*. An employee census usually includes the following information:

- The total number of individuals in the group.

- Types and amount of coverage requested.

Figure 7.2. Portion of a Typical Employee Census

Date of Birth	M/F	Salary	Classifi-cation	Date of Hire	Depen-dents	Amount of Life Insurance
05/67	F	$33,900	0001	03/1990	Yes	$68,000
01/77	M	$40,000	0001	04/1999	No	$80,000
10/75	M	$43,500	0002	01/2004	Yes	$87,000
09/70	F	$45,000	0001	11/1998	Yes	$90,000
03/60	M	$90,000	0003	09/1995	Yes	$180,000
11/71	M	$55,000	0001	04/2000	No	$110,000
02/68	F	$88,000	0003	03/1993	Yes	$196,000
07/78	M	$39,000	0001	10/1999	No	$79,000

- The total number of group members to be insured by each type of coverage.

- Each group member's date of birth, sex, salary, job classification.

- Whether each group member has dependents for whom coverage is requested. For purposes of dependent coverage, group policies typically define a **dependent** as (1) a spouse, (2) an unmarried child who is under age 19 and who relies on the group member for financial support and maintenance, (3) a child age 19 or older—up to a stated maximum age, often 25—if she is a full-time student, and (4) a disabled child for as long as the disability exists, regardless of the child's age.

Producer's Letter

Along with the RFP, the producer or group representative may submit a letter, which includes observations and recommendations about the appropriateness of the requested coverage. The producer's letter is important to the group underwriter in deciding whether to submit a bid for providing the coverage.

An underwriter typically looks favorably upon recommendations submitted by a producer or group representative who consistently has submitted sound business to the insurer, especially if the producer or group representative has extensive experience selling the type of group product being underwritten. Figure 7.3 contains an example of a recommendation made in a producer's letter for group coverage.

A producer sometimes gives the insurer a letter from the group prospect indicating that the group prospect has authorized the producer to obtain proposals for insurance on its behalf.

Figure 7.3. Producer's Letter for Group Coverage

The ABC company has been in business for 47 years manufacturing and assembling movable windows. Its annual net profit has increased during the past 5 years from $1.3 million to $4.4 million. The current carrier has been underwriting coverage for 7 years; the anniversary date is June 1, 2010. Major claims over $10,000 in the past 24 months have been nonexistent. I feel that the strength of the business and the stability of the group, coupled with its moderate claim experience, make it a prime candidate for coverage under our policy.

ERISA Documents

The U.S. federal Employee Retirement Income Security Act (ERISA) imposes a number of reporting requirements on welfare benefit plans, including employer-sponsored group life insurance plans. Underwriters sometimes find the information contained in documents employers are required to file under ERISA to be helpful in risk assessment. Typically, underwriters evaluate such documents only in cases in which a group is currently self-insured and is requesting coverage under a fully insured group plan. A *self-insured group plan* is a plan for which the group sponsor rather than an insurance company is financially responsible for the claims incurred by group insureds. In contrast, a *fully insured group plan* is a plan for which an insurance company is financially responsible for incurred claims. Plans also may be partially insured and partially self insured.

The Master Application

Typically, the master application provides the group underwriter with the following information about the group prospect and the proposed plan of insurance:

- Identification of the individuals who are eligible for coverage under the plan, including the total number of eligible group members and dependents, if applicable

- Definition of the *probationary period*, also known as a *waiting period*, which is the length of time—typically from one to six months—that a new group member must wait before becoming eligible to enroll in a group insurance plan

- A schedule of benefits, by class if applicable

- The percentage of the premium that the group policyholder will pay for the coverage requested

- The type of plan administration

In addition, the master application includes the name of the *plan administrator*, who is the party responsible for handling the administrative aspects of a group plan. The plan administrator serves as the liaison with the insurer. In employer-employee groups, the plan administrator often is a member of the human resources department.

Along with the master application, the group prospect submits enrollment cards either in hard copy or electronically. An **enrollment card**, also called a *group enrollment card*, an *enrollment application*, or an *employee application*, is a document that must be completed and signed by a group member to enroll in a group insurance plan. In addition to providing the group member's personal data, the enrollment card includes a statement that the group member signs to indicate that he understands the coverage offered and agrees to pay his portion of the premium if the plan is contributory. An employee typically agrees to have his portion of the premium deducted from his salary.

A **contributory plan** is a group insurance plan for which group insureds must pay some or all of the premiums for their coverage. A **noncontributory plan** is a group insurance plan for which the group insureds are not required to pay any part of the premium for the coverage; the premiums are paid entirely by the policyholder and all eligible group members are provided with coverage automatically. A group member who chooses not to participate in a contributory group plan signs a statement to that effect.

Risk Factors for Group Underwriting

Group life insurance underwriters usually do not assess individual group members. However, underwriters may require evidence of insurability from group members in accordance with age and amount requirement charts if the group is small and from those group members who enroll in a plan after the enrollment deadline.

Evidence of insurability also is required when excess coverage is requested. *Excess coverage* is coverage for which the group member is eligible but that exceeds a maximum limit above which the group member must provide evidence of insurability. For example, a group life plan may offer employees coverage in the amount of two times their salary; but if the coverage exceeds $75,000, the group member must provide evidence of insurability. If a group member makes $50,000 a year, she is entitled to only $75,000 without providing evidence of insurability. To obtain the remaining $25,000 in coverage, the group member provides whatever evidence of insurability the insurer requires based on the amount of coverage over the maximum limit and the employee's age.

The factors that a group underwriter considers when assessing the risk presented by a group prospect fall into two major categories: characteristics of the group prospect and characteristics of the proposed coverage. Figure 7.4 lists the factors typically included under each category.

The Group Prospect

In evaluating a group prospect, the underwriter's goal is to accept only those groups that meet the established underwriting guidelines for the product and whose expected claim costs are reasonably predictable. Insurers have identified characteristics of group prospects that most affect the likelihood a group's claim experience will be high.

Figure 7.4. Risk Assessment Factors for Group Insurance

CHARACTERISTICS OF THE GROUP PROSPECT

- Reason for existence
- Type of group
- Size
- Nature of business
- Geographic location(s)
- Age distribution
- Turnover of group membership
- Participation in the plan
- Classes
- Expected persistency
- Prior coverage and claim experience

CHARACTERISTICS OF THE PROPOSED COVERAGE

- Plan of insurance
- Plan administration

Reason for Existence

Most insurance companies in the United States and Canada generally adhere to the principle that an eligible group must have been formed for a purpose other than to purchase insurance coverage. This requirement protects insurance companies from antiselection that would result if a number of people, most of whom are poor insurance risks, joined together for the purpose of obtaining insurance.

Type of Group

Insurers sometimes must comply with regulatory requirements that specify the types of groups that are eligible for group life insurance, and underwriters must ensure that policies are issued only to such groups. Figure 7.5 provides a brief explanation of the typical types of groups that are eligible for group insurance. For each of these types of groups, specific underwriting considerations influence risk assessment.

Figure 7.5. Types of Eligible Groups

SINGLE-EMPLOYER GROUP

A **single-employer group**, commonly referred to as an *employer-employee* group, consists of the employees of one employer. The single-employer group is the most common type of group.

MULTIPLE-EMPLOYER GROUP

A **multiple-employer group** consists of the employees of (1) two or more employers in the same industry, (2) two or more labor unions, or (3) one or more employers and one or more labor unions. The most common types of multiple-employer groups are (1) trade association groups, (2) labor union groups, and (3) multiple-employer welfare arrangements. A *trade association* is a group formed by several employers that are in the same industry and that are members of an association formed for a purpose other than to obtain group insurance. A *labor union group* is a group of workers in a given industry or group of industries who organize a union to improve the terms and conditions under which they work. A *multiple-employer welfare arrangement (MEWA)* is a group formed when two or more small employers—usually in the same industry—band together to provide group insurance benefits for their employees. MEWAs differ from other multiple-employer groups in that each MEWA is sponsored by an insurer or a third party, and the policy is issued to the trustees of a trust established for the purpose of purchasing the coverage.

ASSOCIATION GROUPS

An **association group** consists of the members of an association, which is an organization of employers or individuals formed for a purpose other than to obtain insurance. Two types of association groups are the professional association and the affinity group. A **professional association group** is a group of people who share the same type of occupation and who belong to the association. Professionals such as educators, health care workers, real estate agents, and police officers typically form an association, and often such professional associations purchase group insurance coverage for association members. An **affinity group** is a group of people who share a common bond, background, or interest and who belong to an association or organization. For example, a university alumni association and a fraternal organization are affinity groups, which sometimes purchase group insurance for group members.

DEBTOR-CREDITOR GROUP

A **debtor-creditor group** consists of individuals who have borrowed money from a specific lender or lenders.

Size

Group size is one of the most important factors used to underwrite group life insurance because the size of a group affects an insurer's ability to accurately predict the group's expected claim experience. In general, the smaller the group, the less likely the group's actual claim experience will approximate its expected claim experience. When group insurance was first introduced, only groups with at least 50 or 100 members were approved for coverage. Today, because of increasing information about mortality experience, the minimum group size has been reduced considerably. Some insurers, in fact, underwrite groups with as few as two members.

Each insurer establishes its own standards as to (1) the size of group it is willing to insure and (2) the procedures it will follow for different sizes of groups. Because small-group underwriting for life insurance is similar to individual underwriting for these products, some companies send such small-group cases to an individual underwriter. After assessing the risk, if the case is acceptable, the individual underwriter forwards the case to a group underwriter, who performs the rate calculations.

Underwriting guidelines for small groups typically are more stringent than those used to underwrite large groups. Whereas insurers typically do not require that each large group member provide evidence of insurability, insurers may require that each small group member provide evidence of insurability. The evidence required ranges from a simple health questionnaire completed by each group member to APSs and other medical evidence. An underwriter might require APSs and additional evidence on only those group members whose health questionnaires indicate the possibility of a high risk. Note that even though an underwriter might request evidence of insurability, a group underwriter does not rate or place impairment riders on individual group members. If an individual does not meet the insurability requirements, the underwriter declines coverage for that person.

Nature of Business

The type of work that group members perform affects the degree of risk the group presents to an insurer. Thus, in establishing underwriting guidelines, insurers use claim experience data concerning the likelihood of people in certain jobs to incur covered losses.

The underwriter also considers the economic strength or weakness of the industry in which a group prospect operates. When market trends cause businesses in certain industries to slow production or lay off workers, most insurers closely examine the ability of group prospects in those industries to pay premiums.

The strength and financial condition of a business are also important in underwriting group insurance as indications of the business's ability to pay premiums. Usually, a business or an organization must have been operating on a sound financial basis for at least two years before most insurers will consider the group prospect for insurance coverage because of the high percentage of new businesses that fail.

Geographic Location

The geographic location of a group can affect its mortality rate. For example, certain locations are more susceptible to natural disasters or certain diseases. In addition, economic and living conditions vary, as do the availability and cost of adequate health care. Thus, an underwriter must be aware of the geographic location of a group and the impact it can have on risk.

If a group has members in various locations, an underwriter must consider the environmental, economic, and social conditions of all areas in which group members are living. In assessing groups that operate from multiple locations, an underwriter also must consider all applicable laws and regulations.

Age Distribution

Because mortality rates tend to increase with age, a group composed mostly of older members is likely to present a higher degree of risk than a group composed mostly of younger members.

While underwriters cannot decline a group case based on gender distribution, they do consider the ratio of males to females in a group because it affects the group's expected claim costs and, thus, the group's premium rate. Women as a group tend to have lower mortality rates than men as a group. Thus, all other factors being equal, a predominantly female group will experience fewer life insurance claims than a group with a large proportion of males.

Turnover of Group Membership

Low turnover of group membership results in an increase in the average age of the group members over time. Because a group with low turnover and older employees probably will produce unusually high claim costs, an ideal group from an underwriting perspective has a steady flow of younger, new members to replace or at least balance the gradual aging of older members.

On the other hand, underwriters are wary of unusually high turnover rates because they produce unexpectedly high administrative costs. Unusually high turnover rates also may indicate problems within the organization, such as management issues and low morale.

When the flow of new members into a group is not adequate to compensate for the aging of current members, the underwriter may increase the proposed premium rate to reflect the additional risk or may decline the risk.

A group's turnover rate also affects the length of the probationary period included in the group insurance policy. A probationary period reduces the administrative expenses involved in initiating and terminating coverage on employees who leave employment soon after hire. Typically, the probationary period is shorter if the policy insures a group that experiences low turnover and is longer if the policy insures a group that experiences high turnover.

Participation in the Plan

The more group members who enroll in a group insurance plan, the larger the insured group and the more likely an underwriter can accurately assess the group's mortality risk. Although group insurance policies specify the minimum participation level a group must maintain to keep the coverage in force, an underwriter must factor the likely participation rate into his analysis.

With a noncontributory plan, enrollment is automatic; and insurers typically require a noncontributory plan's level of participation to be 100 percent of all eligible group members. By contrast, with a contributory plan, group members must choose whether to enroll, and some choose not to be insured. Consequently, insurers normally require that between 75 and 100 percent of eligible group members participate in a contributory plan, depending on the size of the group. In general, the larger the group, the lower the minimum participation level can be. The following table illustrates minimum participation requirements established by one insurer for groups of various sizes enrolled in contributory insurance plans:

Number of Eligible Employees	Minimum Participation Requirement
Less than 250	75 percent
250–499	65 percent
500–749	60 percent
750–999	55 percent
1,000 or more	Case-by-case evaluation

Classes

To prevent antiselection, group underwriting guidelines require that the level of benefits provided to each group insured must be determined automatically in accordance with the terms of the group policy. If group members were able to select their own benefit, group members with a higher-than-average degree of risk typically would elect higher benefit levels. Likewise, to ensure that benefit levels are determined fairly for all group insureds, the group policyholder is not permitted to select the benefit levels to be provided to specific individuals.

For purposes of determining eligibility for coverage and benefit levels, insurers usually require group prospects to assign group members to classes according to some nondiscriminatory characteristic. Note that laws in some jurisdictions prohibit classes based on marital status, sex, or age. Figure 7.6 illustrates some typical nondiscriminatory classes established for an employer-employee group.

Expected Persistency

An underwriter evaluates a group prospect's expected persistency because of the effect persistency can have on an insurer's profit. During the first year of a group insurance policy, commissions and administrative costs associated with covering the group greatly reduce—and sometimes eliminate—the insurer's profit. If the policyholder cancels the coverage soon after issuance, the insurer will not be able to recoup the costs of issuing the coverage. The longer a group policy remains in force, the more profitable the business is likely to be for the insurer. Insurers usually decline to cover or charge extra premiums to a group that has a history of poor persistency.

Figure 7.6. Typical Nondiscriminatory Classes for Group Insurance

CLASSES BASED ON SALARY

- All employees earning up to $100,000 per year
- All employees earning more than $100,000 per year

CLASSES BASED ON RANK

- All officers
- All managers who are not officers
- All other employees

CLASSES BASED ON HOURS WORKED

- All employees working 30 hours or more a week
- All employees working less than 30 hours a week

CLASSES BASED ON LENGTH OF SERVICE

- All employees with five or more years of service
- All employees with fewer than five years of service

Prior Coverage and Claims Experience

In analyzing a group prospect's prior coverage, an underwriter generally requires at least three years' documentation of the group's previous benefits, premium rates charged, annual premiums paid, claims incurred, and claims paid. As we mentioned earlier, the underwriter also requests a list of open claimants for disability coverages. In addition, an underwriter may request a copy of the employee handbook or other document that describes the current benefit plan.

The Proposed Coverage

When assessing the coverage requested by a group prospect, an underwriter evaluates certain elements of the plan's design and how the plan is to be administered. Details of these elements vary from one plan to another.

Plan of Insurance

When evaluating the plan's design, the underwriter considers how the plan defines the people who are eligible for coverage and the benefit levels that those people are eligible to receive.

Each group policy identifies which members of the group are eligible for coverage. For example, most employer-employee policies state that an employee must meet the policyholder's definition of a full-time employee to be eligible for coverage. Policies issued to association groups typically provide that only people who are members of the association are eligible for coverage. Policies issued to a creditor provide that certain debtors of the creditor are eligible for coverage.

Group insurance policies often include additional eligibility requirements, including a probationary period. In the case of noncontributory plans, group members who meet other eligibility requirements are automatically enrolled in the plan at the end of the probationary period. In the case of contributory plans, the probationary period is followed by an eligibility period. The *eligibility period*, also known as the *enrollment period*, is the period of time—usually 31 days—during which eligible group members may enroll for contributory group insurance coverage without having to provide evidence of insurability.

Employer-employee group insurance policies also include an *actively at work provision*, which requires that an employee must be actively at work—rather than ill or on leave—on the day the group coverage is to take effect. If the employee is not actively at work on the day coverage is to take effect, then the employee is not covered by the group policy until she returns to work.

Group insurance policies that provide coverage to the dependents of covered group members must define specifically which people qualify for dependent coverage. For example, the definition of group member's child may include an adopted child, stepchild, or foster child. Some policies permit dependent coverage on the partners of covered group members who are in unmarried relationships, including same-sex partners.

Plan Administration

Unlike individual insurance policies, many group plans require the owner of the policy to be actively involved in managing and administering benefits. Effective plan administration is critical to keeping plan costs low and helping ensure the long-term satisfaction of the policyholder—and the group insureds—and, thus, the persistency of the coverage.

A group insurance plan for which the insurer handles most of the administrative aspects of the plan is known as an *insurer-administered plan*, and such a plan for which the group policyholder handles most of the administrative aspects is known as a *self-administered plan*. Alternatively, a group plan may be administered by a *third-party administrator (TPA)*, which is an organization that is not affiliated with an insurer and provides various administrative services to insurers and group policyholders.

As a general rule, the more administrative activities the policyholder performs, the lower the premium rate that will be charged for the coverage. Underwriters evaluate the willingness and ability of the policyholder and its plan administrator to administer the plan. Specifically, a group policyholder and plan administrator should be able to

- Promote the plan and encourage all eligible group members to enroll

- Certify the eligibility of each group member who will be covered by the plan

- Collect and keep accurate records of each group member's contributions to the plan

- Maintain accurate and complete records of costs and claims

- Record additions, terminations, and status changes accurately and promptly (for example, changes in marital status, class, and earnings)

- Assist with claim submissions

Rating Methods for Group Cases

Group insurance premium rates are established on a case-by case basis and typically are recalculated every policy year. The rate needs to be

- Adequate to cover the insurer's costs of paying claims, administering the group insurance plan, and conducting business, including paying commissions

- Equitable so that each insured group pays a premium amount that fairly reflects the group's risk

- Competitive enough to attract group prospects

Although the group premium rate will not change from month to month, the number of group insureds will change from month to month and that will impact the total monthly premium amount. Figure 7.7 gives a simplified example of how an insurer might determine a group's monthly premium amount.

Most insurers now use computer-based rating systems to determine group premium rates. However, an underwriter may have information about a case that is not reflected in the computerized rates. For example, the underwriter may know that the producer or group representative submitting a case has a long history of submitting quality business to the insurer. This knowledge might enable the underwriter to charge the group a lower rate than the rate calculated by the automated system.

In calculating the premium rate to charge for group coverage, insurance companies generally use manual rating, experience rating, or a combination of the two. Other rating approaches may be used for small groups.

Manual Rating

Manual rating is a method of establishing group insurance premium rates under which the insurer establishes rates for very broad classifications of group insureds. The insurer establishes manual rating for a group insurance product using its own experience with the product and information collected by various governmental

Figure 7.7. Example of a Monthly Premium Calculation

Galibila Corporation provides each of its employees with $50,000 of term life insurance coverage at a premium rate of $0.20 per month per $1,000 unit of coverage. In January, Galibila's group policy covered 100 employees. The January monthly premium amount for the coverage is calculated as follows:

$0.20	Premium rate per $1,000 unit of coverage
× 50	Number of units of coverage per employee per month ($50,000 ÷ $1,000)
$ 10	Monthly premium amount per employee
×100	Number of covered employees
$1,000	Total monthly premium amount for all covered employees

and trade associations. Typically, group underwriters use manual rating to determine the initial premium to charge a small group prospect. Group underwriters also use manual rating to calculate the initial premium for a large group prospect that has no recorded or reliable claim experience.

Experience Rating

Experience rating is a method of establishing group insurance premium rates using a group's own claim experience. An important assumption underlying experience rating is that a group's claim experience is likely to remain relatively constant from year to year. Underwriters typically use experience rating to calculate (1) initial premium rates for large groups that have been previously insured and have credible claim experience and (2) renewal premium rates for currently insured groups that have credible experience.

When using experience rating to establish a group life insurance premium rate, the underwriter usually examines the group prospect's claim experience for the past five years, if available. The underwriter also calculates the group prospect's *expected claim experience*, which is the monetary amount of claims that the insurer estimates the group will submit during the upcoming policy year. In addition to the group's claim experience, the following factors affect the calculation of a group's expected claim experience:

■ A change in the number of group insureds

■ Changes in the group's average age or predominant sex

■ Changes in benefit schedules

■ A significant change in the employee mix (for example, shifting from mostly white-collar to mostly blue-collar employees)

■ A reassignment of employees to new job duties that pose significant additional hazards

■ Changes in the group's industry or business segment

■ Economic conditions affecting the financial strength of the group policyholder

The terms of some group life insurance policies provide that a portion of the premiums paid during the year may be refunded to the group policyholder at the end of the policy year. An ***experience refund***, also called a *dividend* or *premium refund*, is the portion of a group insurance premium that is returned to a group policyholder if the group's claim experience during the year was more favorable than expected when the premium was calculated.

All premium refunds are payable to the group policyholder, even if the plan is contributory. If the amount of the refund to the policyholder of a contributory plan is greater than the portion of the group premium that was paid out of the policy-holder's funds, then the excess must be used for the benefit of the group insureds. For example, when an employer receives an experience refund that is larger than the amount the employer paid out of its own funds for the policy year, the employer may apply the excess refund to pay a portion of the employees' contributions during the next year or to pay for additional benefits for group insureds.

Blended Rating

Some groups are too large for an insurer to rely totally on manual rating, but they do not have enough claim experience information for the insurer to rely on experience rating. In such cases, insurers sometimes use ***blended rating***, which is a premium rating method that uses a combination of manual rating and experience rating. In blended rating, the underwriter assigns a credibility factor to the group's experience. A ***credibility factor*** is a percentage that represents the amount of weight given to a group's actual claim experience for premium rate calculation purposes. For example, an underwriter who assigns a 25 percent credibility factor to a group's claim experience assumes that 25 percent of the group's expected claim experience will be based on the group's prior experience. The remaining 75 percent of the group's expected claim experience will be based on the insurer's manual rating of the group.

An underwriter determines the blended rate by (1) multiplying the premium calculated using experience rating by the credibility factor assigned to the rating, (2) multiplying the premium calculated using manual rating by the remaining percentage of the group's expected future claims, and (3) adding the two resulting numbers. For instance, suppose an underwriter arrives at the following information for a group:

■ Premium calculated by experience rating = $250

■ Credibility factor for experience rating = 15%

■ Premium calculated by manual rating = $300

The underwriter calculates the premium using blended rating as follows:

$$(\$250 \times 0.15) + (\$300 \times 0.85) = \$37.50 + \$255.00 = \$292.50$$

Rating Approaches for Small Groups

Developing equitable rates for small groups requires the underwriter to exercise particular caution because each group insured's age, health, and other risk factors increase in importance as group size decreases. In a group of eight people, for example, one person who represents a high level of risk can have a strong effect on the risk represented by the group. However, in a group of 500 people, that same person would have much less effect on the group's level of risk.

Insurers use the following methods to calculate equitable premium rates for small groups:

- Manual rating.

- *Pooling*, which is a rating method by which the insurer combines several small groups into one large group, or pool. The more individuals grouped together in the pool, the better the underwriter's chances of accurately estimating the entire group's expected claim costs.

- *Step rates*, which are group insurance premium rates based on an insurer's experience expressed in age-graded, and sometimes sex-specific, step rate tables. The group policyholder and/or group member generally is charged the actual step rate. On the other hand, manual rating calculates a rate for each group insured and then determines a composite rate for the group. With step rates, a composite group rate is used only in evaluating the group's experience. Step rates are often used when a group insurance policy provides a limited number of benefits and limited amounts of coverage.

Post-Issue Underwriting for Group Insurance

Unlike individual insurance underwriting, group insurance underwriting does not end when a policy is issued. Post-issue group underwriting includes underwriting of late enrollees and renewal underwriting.

Underwriting of Late Enrollees

Under a noncontributory group insurance plan, all group members are enrolled automatically in the plan. Under a contributory plan, however, only those group members who want group coverage and who complete an enrollment card during the eligibility period are covered without having to provide evidence of insurability. Similarly, group members must enroll their eligible dependents during the eligibility period. If a group member acquires a new dependent after the eligibility period, the group member can add that dependent without having to provide evidence of insurability as long as the dependent is added within 31 days of first becoming eligible. For example, an adopted child may be added within 31 days of being adopted without having to provide evidence of insurability.

Group members and eligible dependents who are not enrolled when coverage is first offered and later decide to enroll in the plan are known as *late enrollees* and are required to provide the insurer with evidence of insurability before being allowed to enroll in the plan. In addition, if a group member withdraws from a plan while still employed and then later applies to re-enroll in the plan, the insurer usually requires the group member to provide evidence of insurability. In such cases, the underwriter must be alert to the possibility of antiselection because a group member may be seeking to enroll in the group plan only after discovering that she has a health problem.

The evidence an underwriter requires from late enrollees varies from insurer to insurer and varies depending on the plan of insurance. As a general rule, however, the more extensive the benefits a plan provides, the more detailed the evidence must be. Most insurers require late enrollees to complete a health questionnaire; some also require a medical examination and documentation of medical treatments received by the late enrollees. The insurer has the right to refuse to permit a late enrollee to enroll in a group insurance plan if satisfactory evidence of insurability is not provided.

Renewal Underwriting

Unlike individual policies, group policies must be renewed at the end of the contract term, which typically is every year or two. If premiums have been paid as specified in the group contract and the group policyholder does not specifically request an underwriting review of the group coverage, a group life insurance contract is often renewed without renewal underwriting, as long as the premiums are paid. *Renewal underwriting* is the process by which an underwriter assesses the risk presented by a group that has requested to renew its group insurance contract. However, the insurer can always choose to conduct renewal underwriting if it appears needed. For group life insurance, the underwriter may decline to renew the coverage, increase or decrease the premium rate, or require that the plan design be changed.

In renewal underwriting, the underwriter reviews all the risk assessment factors considered when the group was originally underwritten and determines whether the characteristics of the group have changed in ways that affect the degree of risk the group presents. In addition, the underwriter assesses how efficiently the policyholder has administered the plan during the year. If the underwriter identifies administrative problems, he brings them to the attention of the group policyholder along with suggestions for corrective action.

For most groups, the insurer uses experience rating or a blend of manual rating and experience rating to calculate the renewal premium rate. However, insurers sometimes use manual rating to calculate renewal premium rates for groups that are very small or do not have credible experience.

Generally, if a group's claim experience and administrative costs fall within acceptable limits, the underwriter renews the coverage without changing the premium rate. When a group's claim experience has been very favorable—that is, significantly less than expected—and other factors are equal, the underwriter may approve the renewal and reduce the premium rate required for the coverage. However, demographic changes in the group may lead to a premium rate increase. In addition, if a group's claim experience or administrative costs have exceeded the policy's projected costs, the underwriter likely will increase the premium rate for the coverage as a condition of the renewal. Before proposing a higher rate, however, the underwriter first tries to determine the reasons for the excessive claims or administrative costs and factor these reasons into her decision on the renewal premium rate.

A group policyholder may decide not to renew a group policy if the premium rate increases significantly. In such a case, the underwriter typically suggests ways the group plan can be changed so as to modify or eliminate any proposed premium rate increase. The following are examples of such suggestions:

- Change the benefit design by, for example, reducing the benefit.

- Require a larger premium contribution from group insureds, thus passing part or all of the premium rate increase along to group insureds.

- Pool a small group's experience with other small groups' experience, thereby creating a more acceptable level of risk overall.

- Investigate the cause of the poor experience and take measures to eliminate it.

Key Terms

group member
group representative
request for proposal (RFP)
proposal for insurance
benefit schedule
class
master application
open claimant
census
dependent
self-insured group plan
fully insured group plan
probationary period
plan administrator
enrollment card
contributory plan
noncontributory plan
single-employer group
multiple-employer group

association group
professional association group
affinity group
debtor-creditor group
eligibility period
actively at work provision
insurer-administered plan
self-administered plan
third-party administrator (TPA)
manual rating
experience rating
expected claim experience
experience refund
blended rating
credibility factor
pooling
step rates
late enrollee
renewal underwriting

Chapter 8

Overview of Claim Administration

Objectives:

After studying this chapter, you should be able to

- Explain the importance of an insurer's claim philosophy in guiding its claim practices

- Describe the steps in the claim evaluation process

- Describe the typical staffing, authority levels, and organization of a claim department

- Distinguish between compensatory and punitive damages

- Recognize actions that qualify as unfair claim practices according to the NAIC Unfair Claims Settlement Practices Act

- Describe requirements imposed on insurers by the NAIC Unfair Life, Accident and Health Claims Settlement Practices Model Regulation

- Identify claim administration legal issues associated with privacy and terrorism

- Define insurance fraud and describe the legal requirements in the NAIC Insurance Fraud Prevention Model Act

- Identify the warning signs of a fraudulent claim

- Discuss legal requirements related to insurance fraud

- Describe quality control methods and types of technology used in the claim administration area

Outline

Claim Philosophy and Claim Practices

Claim Evaluation Process

Claim Staffing and Organization
- Staffing
- Authority Levels
- Organizational Systems
- Relationships with Other Insurer Functions

Legal Issues Affecting Claim Administration
- Unfair Claims Settlement Practices
- Privacy
- Financing Terrorists
- Fraud
- Quality Control

Technology

C laim administration is the process of evaluating each submitted claim to determine whether the claim is eligible for payment, informing the person who submitted the claim of the decision, and authorizing the payment of each eligible claim according to the terms of the policy. Effective claim administration fulfills the insurer's responsibilities to its customers (1) to pay all valid claims promptly and accurately and (2) to deny any claim that is not covered under the terms of the policy or is fraudulent.

Claim Philosophy and Claim Practices

An insurer's *claim philosophy* is a statement of the insurer's objectives for administering claims. An insurer's senior management typically develops the claim philosophy, which is focused on timely, accurate, equitable, and courteous administration of claims. For example, an insurer's claim philosophy may be "To act promptly, equitably, and courteously in paying all eligible claims and denying all ineligible claims."

Using the insurer's claim philosophy as a foundation, claim administration senior management develops *claim practices*, which are statements that guide the day-to-day handling of claims. Most insurers' claim practices include commitments to

- Process claims on a timely basis and notify a claimant if an extended time period is necessary to make a claim determination

- Apply the provisions of policies consistently

- Train claim staff so that they can perform their duties professionally and accurately and can document claim handling appropriately

- Investigate questionable claims

- Obtain medical and legal advice when needed to make a decision on a claim

- Process all claims in compliance with state, provincial, and federal regulations

- Provide claimants with courteous, prompt, and complete explanations of claims for which benefits are not payable or are limited

- Permit claimants to submit additional supporting information on a denied or limited claim

- Provide satisfactory means for appeal of denied claims

The International Claim Association (ICA) has developed and distributed a *Statement of Principles* that companies must adhere to as a condition of membership. Figure 8.1 presents the ICA's *Statement of Principles*.

Figure 8.1. The International Claim Association's *Statement of Principles*

The International Claim Association, in recognition of the need to continue public trust and confidence in the insurance industry, reaffirms the following principles:

- Any individual who has, or believes he has, a claim is entitled to courteous, fair and just treatment; and shall receive with reasonable promptness an acknowledgment of any communications with respect to his claim.

- Every claimant is entitled to prompt investigation of all facts, an objective evaluation and the fair and equitable settlement of his claim as soon as liability has become reasonably clear.

- Claimants are to be treated equally and without considerations other than those dictated by the provisions of their contracts.

- Claimants shall not be compelled to institute unnecessary litigation in order to recover amounts due, nor shall the failure to settle a claim under one policy or one portion of a policy be used to influence settlement under another policy or portion of a policy.

- Recognizing the obligation to pay promptly all just claims, there is an equal obligation to protect the insurance-buying public from increased costs due to fraudulent or nonmeritorious claims.

- Procedures and practices shall be established to prevent misrepresentation of pertinent facts or policy provisions, to avoid unfair advantage by reason of superior knowledge, and to maintain accurate insurance claim records as privileged and confidential.

- Reasonable standards shall be implemented to provide for adequate personnel, systems and procedures to effectively service claims. These standards shall be such as to eliminate unnecessary delays or requirements, overinsistence on technicalities, and excessive appraisals or examinations. Claim personnel shall be encouraged and assisted in further developing their knowledge, expertise, and professionalism in the field of claim administration.

Source: *Statement of Principles*, International Claim Association, www.claim.org (19 April 2010). Reprinted with permission.

Claim Evaluation Process

When an insurer is notified of a loss, the insurer must provide the claimant with a claim form or another means of supplying notification of loss such as electronic filing through an insurer's Web site. A ***claim form***, also called a *claimant's statement*, is a document containing information about a loss under an insurance policy that is submitted to an insurance company to begin the claim evaluation process.

A ***claim analyst***, also known as a *claim examiner* or *claim adjuster*, is an insurance company employee who reviews claims and determines the company's liability for each claim. The claim evaluation process the claim analyst uses for individual and group claims typically is composed of the steps listed in Figure 8.2. Note that a claim analyst does not always take these steps in the order they are presented here, because she may have to wait for information pertaining to some of the steps. Also note that any or all of these steps, which will be discussed further in coming chapters, may be fully automated.

Whether an insurer uses paper or electronic claim files, or a combination of both, the claim analyst is responsible for maintaining a complete record of the progress and disposition of every claim. Particularly when a claim analyst reaches a decision to deny a claim, clear and complete written documentation outlining the claim history and supporting the denial must be made a part of the claim file, because such documentation may be of great value in the event of a legal action on the denial.

Although many claims are received, processed, and completed within a matter of days, other claims—for example, those for long-term disability—can continue for months or years. The claim analyst must update such claim files and ensure that their contents are current. In many such cases, more than one claim analyst works on a case. Claim analysts find automated workflow systems to be particularly helpful in processing ongoing claims in which multiple claim analysts are involved.

Claim Staffing and Organization

Insurers have many different systems for ranking their claim personnel, setting authority levels, and assigning claims to claim personnel. The systems used by a particular insurer typically depend on that insurer's size and the variety of products it offers.

Staffing

The day-to-day operations of claim administration are performed by claim analysts and support staff, who are managed by claim supervisors. A vice president or director of claim administration usually oversees the entire claim administration function.

Claim analysts typically are responsible for performing all of the steps in the claim evaluation process listed in Figure 8.2. In addition, claim analysts may explain claim payments, denials, and contract provisions to claimants, providers, and producers.

Figure 8.2. Steps in the Claim Evaluation Process

Verify that the coverage was in force when the loss occurred. The claim analyst must verify that premiums have been paid. For example, if the policy was issued and delivered but the initial premium was never paid, then the policy was never in force and no benefit is payable.

Verify that the deceased is covered. The claim analyst must determine whether the life insurance policy actually covers the deceased. This step is especially important when benefits are claimed under a policy that covers more than one person, such as a family policy or a group policy. Insureds under such policies occasionally mistakenly submit claims for a person who is not covered by the policy. In addition, the claim analyst must verify the identity of the deceased as the insured.

Verify that the loss occurred. To pay policy benefits, the claim analyst must examine evidence that the reported loss occurred.

Determine whether the policy is contestable. If the policy's contestable period has not expired, the claim analyst generally investigates whether the insured made a material misrepresentation on the application. If so, the claim analyst must determine whether the policy should be considered void.

Determine whether the loss is covered by the policy. As part of this step, the claim analyst must ensure that the loss is not excluded from the policy's coverage. For example, if a person insured under a life insurance policy died as a result of suicide during the policy's suicide exclusion period, then the policy's death benefit is not payable; the insurer generally is obligated only to return the premiums paid for such a policy.

Calculate the amount of the benefit payable. The claim analyst must apply the policy's method of calculating benefits to the claim.

7
▼

Determine who is entitled to receive the benefit. The claim analyst must determine if the person claiming the benefits is the person entitled to the benefits under the policy.

Source: Harriett E. Jones and Monica R. Maxwell, *Regulatory Compliance: Companies, Producers, and Operations*, 2nd ed. [Atlanta: LOMA (Life Office Management Association, Inc.), © 2002], 163–64. Used with permission; all rights reserved.

When claims arrive, most claim departments have support staff who order information needed for a claim decision, establish files, assign case or file numbers to claims, exchange information with other functional areas of the insurance company, and perform other routine actions designed to facilitate the decision-making process. When a claim is approved, the analyst authorizes payment be made to the person or entity who is to receive benefits; support staff may facilitate the payment process. In some insurance companies, support staff also handle some communications with claimants, providers, and producers.

A claim supervisor, also known as a *claim manager*, oversees several claim analysts and support staff. Figure 8.3 lists the typical duties of a claim supervisor. Note that a claim supervisor's duties will vary depending on the size of the company and the sophistication of the claim administration system.

Large companies usually assign several supervisors to handle a particular type of product or line of business. For instance, some insurers appoint supervisors for life claims, medical expense claims, and disability income claims, whereas other insurers establish supervisors for individual claims and group claims. Group insurers might assign each group to a specific supervisor.

Authority Levels

Like underwriters, claim analysts receive increasing amounts of decision-making authority as they gain experience and demonstrate enhanced ability and quality of judgment. A new claim analyst usually handles small-amount, routine claims that present few difficulties or unusual circumstances. A more senior claim analyst or

Figure 8.3. Typical Duties of a Claim Supervisor

- Assigns cases to claim analysts in the absence of or in addition to workflow systems

- Consults with and advises claim analysts on cases with which the analyst needs assistance

- May handle difficult and large amount cases personally

- Monitors the training and performance of each claim analyst

- Responds to or assists in handling any complaints

- Assists with claim audits

- Produces periodic production reports that show the quantity and quality of claims made by claim analysts or reviews such reports if they are produced by the claim administration system

- Serves as liaison with the insurer's medical director and legal staff

a claim supervisor normally reviews the new claim analyst's work. As the claim analyst gains more experience, he is assigned more decision-making authority; handles less routine, more challenging cases that involve higher coverage amounts or more complex policy forms; and performs his work without the review of a more experienced person. Experienced claim analysts and claim supervisors usually process claims that require extensive investigation or consideration.

Organizational Systems

Some insurers have one claim department that handles claims for all lines of business offered by the company, while other insurers establish separate claim units to handle specific types of coverages, such as life, medical expense, and long-term care. Within these units, an insurer might choose to allocate claims to claim analysts according to a case assignment system, a work division system, or a combination of the two systems. These claim organizational systems are similar to underwriting organizational systems we described earlier.

Under a case assignment system, the claims typically are divided among claim analysts by alphabet, region, producer, or amount of coverage.[1] The claims received from group insureds under large group policies can be assigned to one or more claim analysts who specialize in handling only those claims.

Under a work division system, claim analysts might work independently to investigate and make decisions on claims, or they might be organized into teams similar to those used for underwriting. Complicated claims may be referred to a committee composed of a claim supervisor and representatives from other functional areas such as underwriting, legal, and medical. However, the role of representatives from other functional areas is to provide counsel rather than to make decisions.

Some insurers also establish a group of claim analysts who are authorized to approve routine or uncomplicated claims in much the same manner that the jet underwriting unit approves routine applications for insurance.

Some insurers hire a third-party administrator to administer claims. Other insurers establish branch offices whose primary purpose is to administer claims. One of an insurer's branch offices might handle only claims submitted under one line of business, and other branch offices might handle claims submitted under other lines of business. Alternatively, an insurer might send simple claims for small amounts of coverage to branch offices or regional service centers, where the claims can be handled electronically and benefit payments can be sent quickly to claimants.

Relationships with Other Insurer Functions

Claim analysts are occasionally in contact with the insurer's underwriters, especially when the analyst suspects misrepresentation or fraud. Claim analysts utilize the underwriters' risk appraisal expertise to review any information first discovered in a claim evaluation and determine how that information would have affected the risk appraisal process. Claim analysts and underwriters also may interact on complex beneficiary designations to make sure that potential problems can be addressed before a policy is issued. Claim analysts also may consult with underwriting regarding the impact that riders have on coverage.

A firm understanding of the claim administration and underwriting functions improves the accuracy and quality of both underwriting and claim decisions, therefore enhancing the insurer's ability to compete successfully in a highly competitive environment. Recognizing the importance of these functions, insurers foster cooperation between claim administration and underwriting by

- Involving staff from underwriting and claim administration in the development of new insurance products and using data from both functions to evaluate the probable success of new products

- Using staff from both functions to review potential new policy documents, including application forms and claim forms, to check for potential underwriting and claim problems

- Providing cross training so that staff gain a deeper knowledge and better understanding of the work requirements and challenges of both functions

Claim analysts also consult with the insurer's medical and legal staff on problematic claims and with producers or vendors who can help gather or verify information related to a claim. Actuaries use statistical information generated by the claim department in setting premium rates for existing and new products, and the insurer's auditors use claim statistics to see if any improvements can be made not only to the claim process, but also to the underwriting process. The insurer's product development staff also uses claim information in developing new products.

Legal Issues Affecting Claim Administration

Life insurance policies are contracts under which the insurer promises to pay policy benefits when those benefits are due. In carrying out this obligation, the insurer has the right to evaluate thoroughly all policy claims that it receives and to enforce the contract terms that govern which losses are covered by the policy. However, if the insurer fails to pay eligible claims when due, the claimant has the right to file an appeal with the insurer. The policy typically states that the claimant must complete the appeal process, which includes a hearing before an appeals committee, before proceeding to a lawsuit against the insurer for breach of contract. Some insurers mandate arbitration instead of a lawsuit.

Whether the lawsuit goes to court or is settled out of court, insurers must pay attorney's fees and other expenses in defending the case; these fees and expenses can be quite substantial. The insurer also suffers a loss of productivity because of the time employees must dedicate to helping the attorneys with the case.

If an insurer is found to have denied a claim improperly, the court can require the insurer to pay *compensatory damages*, which are monetary awards intended to compensate an injured party for the amount of the monetary losses that resulted from the defendant's improper conduct. In the case of a claim lawsuit, compensatory damages typically consist of the policy benefits and, in some instances, interest.

In addition to compensatory damages, a claimant might receive *punitive damages*, which are awarded in addition to compensatory damages when a defendant's conduct meets the jurisdiction's standards for behavior that is so egregious as to warrant such damages. The purpose of a punitive damage award is to punish the defendant and to deter others from similar conduct.

Some insurers establish a claim committee to review claim denials that potentially may result in legal action. The claim committee generally consists of senior claim analysts, a management representative, and a law department representative. The claim committee also may be responsible for replying to insurance department complaints and monitoring lawsuits filed to obtain benefits.

Unfair Claims Settlement Practices

In the United States, most states have enacted laws based on or similar to the NAIC model *Unfair Claims Settlement Practices Act*, which lists a number of actions that are considered unfair claims practices if committed by an insurer (1) in conscious disregard of the law or (2) so frequently as to indicate a general business practice. Figure 8.4 lists some actions that can qualify as unfair claims settlement practices.

State unfair claims settlement practices laws require insurers to establish reasonable standards for the prompt investigation and settlement of claims and to settle claims promptly and fairly when their liability becomes reasonably clear. Some states have adopted regulations based on the NAIC *Unfair Life, Accident and Health Claims Settlement Practices Model Regulation*, which establishes minimum standards that insurers must meet in handling life and health insurance claims. Many of these standards concern the maximum amount of time an insurer has to take a certain action. For example, under the Unfair Life, Accident and Health Claims Settlement Practices Model Regulation, an insurer has

■ 15 days to provide claim forms after receiving notification of a claim

■ 15 days to begin any necessary investigation of a claim after receiving proof of loss

■ 30 days to pay a claim after determining it is liable

■ 15 days to send the claimant a written notice of the denial after deciding to deny a claim

Note that these time limits may differ among states. Also note that most jurisdictions have regulations requiring the insurer to pay interest on claim benefits if the benefits are not paid in a timely manner.

Privacy

As we discussed in Chapter 3, to protect the privacy of customers and the confidentiality of personal information, most jurisdictions have passed laws regulating how insurers collect, use, and disclose that information. Such laws include

■ U.S. state laws based on the Model Privacy Act

■ U.S. state regulations based on the Model Privacy Regulation

■ U.S. federal Fair Credit Reporting Act (FCRA)

■ U.S. federal Gramm-Leach-Bliley (GLB) Act

Figure 8.4. Actions that Can Qualify as Unfair Claims Settlement Practices

The following actions can be considered unfair claims settlement practices if done (1) in conscious disregard of the law or (2) so frequently as to indicate a general business practice:

- Knowingly misrepresenting to claimants or insureds relevant facts or policy provisions relating to coverages at issue

- Failing to acknowledge with reasonable promptness the receipt of communications that are pertinent to claims

- Failing to adopt and implement reasonable standards for the prompt investigation and settlement of claims

- Not attempting in good faith to settle claims promptly, fairly, and equitably when it is reasonably clear the insurer is liable to pay such claims

- Compelling claimants to institute lawsuits to recover amounts due under policies by offering substantially less than the amounts those claimants ultimately recovered in their lawsuits

- Refusing to pay claims without conducting a reasonable investigation of those claims

- Failing to affirm or deny coverage of claims within a reasonable time after completion of the claim evaluation

- Settling or attempting to settle claims for less than the amount that a reasonable person would believe the claimants were entitled to receive according to the terms of advertising material that accompanied or was part of the application for insurance

- Settling or attempting to settle claims on the basis of an application that was materially altered without notice to, or the knowledge or consent of, the policyowner

- Making claims payments without indicating the coverage under which each payment is being made

- Unreasonably delaying the investigation or payment of claims by requiring both a formal proof of loss form and subsequent verification that would result in duplication of information and verification appearing in the formal proof of loss form

- In the case of a claim denial or an offer of a compromise settlement, failing to promptly provide a reasonable and accurate explanation of the reason for such actions

- Failing to provide forms necessary to present claims within 15 calendar days of a request for such forms with reasonable explanations regarding their use

Source: Adapted from NAIC, *Unfair Claims Settlement Practices Act*, Section 4, 1997. Reprinted with permission from the National Association of Insurance Commissioners.

- Canadian federal Personal Information Protection and Electronics Document Act (PIPEDA)

- Various Canadian provincial laws

When conducting a claim investigation, claim analysts must comply with the privacy provisions of all of these laws that apply to a particular jurisdiction. In addition, companies that are members of the Canadian Life and Health Insurance Association must adopt and abide by the CLHIA's Right to Privacy Guidelines unless they have developed their own guidelines that are stricter than the CLHIA's.

In the United States, the Model Privacy Act's general prohibition of pretext interviews directly affects how a claim analyst conducts a claim evaluation. Recall from Chapter 3 that a pretext interview is an interview in which one person attempts to gain information from another person by (1) pretending to be someone he is not, (2) pretending to represent someone he does not represent, (3) refusing to identify himself, or (4) misrepresenting the purpose of the interview. An insurer may conduct a pretext interview during a claim investigation only if the insurer has a reasonable basis to suspect criminal activity, fraud, material misrepresentation, or material nondisclosure in connection with the claim. The insurer may not conduct a pretext interview with any person who has a protected relationship with the person who is the subject of the interview. Such protected relationships include husband and wife, lawyer and client, and doctor and patient.

Financing Terrorists

Recall that the U.S. Treasury's Office of Foreign Assets Control (OFAC) maintains a list of countries, individuals, and organizations that participate in or sponsor terrorism or other illegal acts. Claim analysts must be on guard against making any payments to anyone on the OFAC list. Typically the claim administration system will run such a check.

Fraud

Generally, fraud is an act by which someone intentionally deceives another party and induces that other party to part with something of value. *Insurance fraud* is any fraud that involves an insurance company, whether committed by consumers, insurance company employees, producers, health care providers, or anyone else connected with an insurance transaction.

Many perpetrators of insurance fraud view it as a victimless crime, but that is far from the case. In fact, the cost of insurance fraud is borne by all of an insurer's policyowners in the form of increased premiums. Those who submit fraudulent claims drive up the costs for insurance companies and thus the cost of insurance for everyone.

Insurance fraud is a crime in many jurisdictions, and the governments in such jurisdictions can prosecute those who commit fraud. In addition, victims of insurance fraud can file civil lawsuits against the perpetrator of the fraud in an attempt to recover any financial losses that resulted from the fraudulent acts.

In the United States, the NAIC has adopted the ***Insurance Fraud Prevention Model Act***, which is designed to permit the state insurance departments to

- Investigate and discover fraudulent insurance acts more effectively

- Halt fraudulent insurance acts

- Receive assistance from state, local, and federal law enforcement and regulatory agencies in enforcing laws that prohibit fraudulent insurance acts

Almost all states have enacted either a law based on the Insurance Fraud Prevention Model Act or a law with similar provisions designed to prevent and prosecute insurance fraud.

The Insurance Fraud Prevention Model Act requires insurers to undertake measures to prevent and detect insurance fraud. Some states require each insurer licensed to sell insurance in the state to develop and maintain an antifraud plan that establishes procedures to

- Prevent insurance fraud

- Review claims to detect insurance fraud and investigate claims where fraud is suspected

- Report fraud to appropriate law enforcement authorities and cooperate with such authorities in prosecuting cases of insurance fraud

- Pursue civil actions against persons who commit insurance fraud

- Train employees and producers to detect and prevent fraud

The Insurance Fraud Prevention Model Act also requires persons engaged in the business of insurance who know or reasonably believe that insurance fraud is being committed to report the fraud to the state insurance department. Some states impose a time limit within which the report must be made after the individual discovers insurance fraud, while other states require that the report be made "immediately" or "promptly" after the discovery. Failure to report fraudulent activities to the insurance department can subject such an individual to civil and, in some cases, criminal penalties.

Some people are reluctant to report suspected insurance fraud to the state insurance department for fear that the accused might file a lawsuit saying that by filing the report, the accuser has engaged in defamation or invasion of privacy. ***Defamation*** is a civil wrong that occurs when a person makes false statements that tend to damage the reputation of another. ***Invasion of privacy*** is a civil wrong that occurs when a person (1) appropriates someone's name or personality, (2) publicizes someone's private affairs, (3) intrudes into someone's private affairs and the wrong causes mental suffering, shame, or humiliation, or (4) places someone in a false light in the public eye. To encourage the reporting of suspected insurance fraud, most states have laws that protect from civil liability anyone who in good faith reports such information to the insurance department.

Claim fraud—a subset of insurance fraud—is an action by which a person intentionally uses false information in an unfair or unlawful attempt to collect benefits under an insurance policy. Claim fraud can be committed by any person who is in a position to influence a claim decision or benefit from a claim payment, including an insured, a beneficiary, a medical care provider, a caregiver, a producer, or an employee of an insurance company.

In an effort to prevent claim fraud specifically, the Insurance Fraud Prevention Model Act requires insurers to include a fraud warning statement on all applications for insurance and claim forms. This statement notifies the applicant or claimant that knowingly presenting false information in an application or presenting a fraudulent claim is a crime.

Most people who submit insurance claims are honest. Claimants occasionally make mistakes in providing information on claims, but generally their intent is to submit eligible claims and to receive only benefits to which they are legitimately entitled. Unfortunately, some people try to manipulate the claim system to obtain benefits to which they are not entitled. From false billings and bribes to unnecessary and overpriced medical services, the varieties of fraud are limited only by the ingenuity of those who intend to take advantage of insurance companies. Figure 8.5 provides some of the warning signs of a potentially fraudulent claim.

Figure 8.5. Warning Signs of a Potential Fraudulent Claim

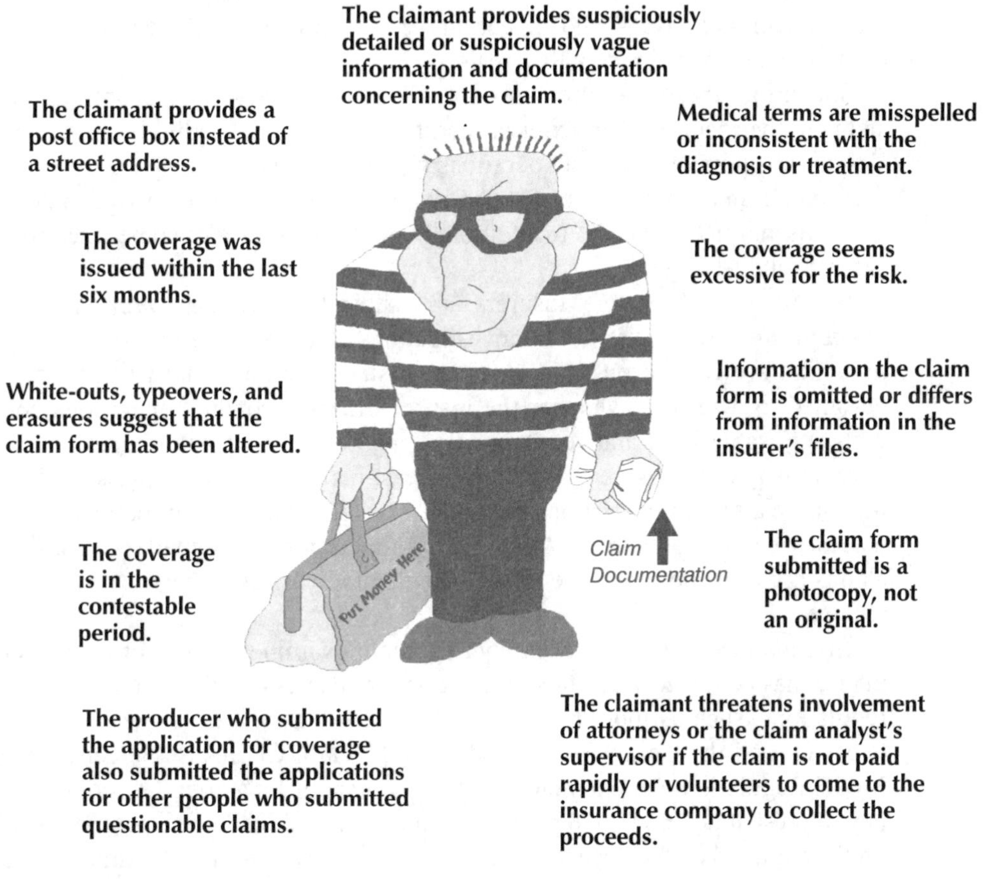
The claimant provides suspiciously detailed or suspiciously vague information and documentation concerning the claim.
The claimant provides a post office box instead of a street address.
Medical terms are misspelled or inconsistent with the diagnosis or treatment.
The coverage was issued within the last six months.
The coverage seems excessive for the risk.
White-outs, typeovers, and erasures suggest that the claim form has been altered.
Information on the claim form is omitted or differs from information in the insurer's files.
The coverage is in the contestable period.
Put Money Here
Claim Documentation
The claim form submitted is a photocopy, not an original.
The producer who submitted the application for coverage also submitted the applications for other people who submitted questionable claims.
The claimant threatens involvement of attorneys or the claim analyst's supervisor if the claim is not paid rapidly or volunteers to come to the insurance company to collect the proceeds.

Source: Adapted from Jane Lightcap Brown and Jennifer W. Herrod, *Reinsurance Administration* [Atlanta: LOMA (Life Office Management Association, Inc.), © 2000], 211. Used with permission; all rights reserved.

Some states require insurers to establish a department to investigate suspected cases of insurance fraud. A *special investigative unit (SIU)* is a group of individuals who are employed by an insurance company and are responsible for detecting, investigating, and resolving cases involving insurance fraud. When a claim analyst suspects fraud of any kind, she contacts the SIU and works with this unit in investigating the case.

MIB's Claims Activity Index (CAI) can assist in detecting fraud and overinsurance. The CAI is a shared, industry-wide data exchange from which claim analysts can learn whether other claims have been filed for the same insured with other insurers. The CAI is available to all life, disability, long-term care, and credit life insurers on a subscription basis.

Quality Control

Insurers judge the quality of their claim function using performance measurements and performance standards, which we defined in Chapter 1. Most companies review a percentage of claims every week or month to confirm that employees are maintaining turnaround time objectives and accuracy standards. Management reviews these reports, as well as reports of "old" pending claims, large dollar claims, names of payees who appear on the government OFAC or money-laundering lists, and any claim denial appeals.

Sometimes these measurements are taken and reviewed as part of an internal audit by the insurer or an external audit by reinsurers. Audits by reinsurers of claims and claim department operations typically focus on reinsurance agreement compliance and procedures and processes for reviewing and investigating claims, as we discuss in Chapter 11. In addition, regulatory authorities sometimes conduct external audits.

In the United States, insurers are subject to regular *market conduct examinations*, which are formal investigations of an insurer's nonfinancial operations that are carried out by one or more state insurance departments and are designed to determine whether the insurer's market conduct operations comply with applicable laws and regulations. A market conduct examination typically covers many of an insurer's functional areas, including new business, underwriting, and claim administration. However, market conduct examinations typically place a great deal of emphasis on the claim function because matters pertaining to claims are near the top of the list of complaints that state insurance departments receive.

In a market conduct examination, the state examiners determine whether the insurer has complied with standards for doing business found in state statutes and regulations, such as those based on the NAIC's Unfair Claims Settlement Practices Act and the Unfair Life, Accident and Health Claims Settlement Practices Model Regulation. For example, a life claim standard may be "The company will pay interest at no less than 8 percent from the date of death until payment is made on the claim when the decedent is a resident of Washington at the time of death."[2] Of course, many companies already have adopted these regulatory standards as their own internal performance measurements. Thus, insurers have experience in complying with such standards.

Market conduct examiners also verify that an insurer has processed claims in compliance with policy terms and claim procedures manuals. They select a sample of claim files and review them to evaluate

- The length of time required to investigate and settle claims

- Whether files contain adequate and accurate documentation

- Whether the amounts of claim payments made are accurately calculated

- Whether claims are paid to the correct payee

Examiners also review claim files that have resulted in lawsuits to determine whether the insurer has improperly denied claims. Examiners also determine whether the insurer conducts its own meaningful internal audits.

Technology

Recall that information systems are important in enhancing the activities involved in insurance administration. Information systems are used to great advantage in the claims area, and particularly with medical expense claims. Many medical expense claims are submitted to insurers via electronic data interchange (EDI). Claims that fit certain parameters specified for electronic handling then can be processed by *auto-adjudication*, which is an electronic claim processing system. Such a system not only can verify information about the coverage and the insured, but also can make claim decisions, calculate benefit amounts, authorize payment of benefits, produce checks or transfer funds electronically to pay benefits, and generate printed explanations of benefits so that each policyowner receives specific information about the amount of benefits paid for each claim—all without human intervention.

Even if a claim is submitted on paper, as life insurance claims typically are, an insurer may use imaging technology to convert it to an EDI format and then process the claim via the auto-adjudication system. Claims that do not fit the parameters specified for electronic handling are assigned to claim analysts for processing. Note that in this text when we refer to the claim analyst processing the claim, the information system actually may be doing so.

Insurers also use technology to detect and deter fraud. Rules-based systems and predictive modeling are particularly effective in determining whether fraud has occurred, especially when a pattern can be detected.

Key Terms

claim philosophy

claim practices

claim form

claim analyst

compensatory damages

punitive damages

Unfair Claims Settlement
    Practices Act

Unfair Life, Accident and Health
    Claims Settlement Practices
    Model Regulation

insurance fraud

Insurance Fraud Prevention Model
    Act

defamation

invasion of privacy

claim fraud

special investigative unit (SIU)

market conduct examination

auto-adjudication

Endnote

1. Joy Horrocks, *Claim Center Organization*, ICA Life Reports 2004, www.claim.org/pdf/2005_life.pdf (8 March 2007).
2. RCW 48.23.300 as quoted in Leslie A. Krier, "Life, Health & Disability Claims Under the Microscope: A State Market Conduct Examiner's Perspective," ICA Annual Conference 2006.

Chapter 9

Administering Life Insurance Claims

Objectives:

After studying this chapter, you should be able to

- ■ Describe the claim administration process for evaluating whether life insurance coverage was in force at the time of death and whether the deceased is the insured

- ■ Identify the typical proof of death for a life insurance claim and describe situations that may complicate the process for verifying that a death has occurred

- ■ Explain how policy exclusions and a change of health statement may affect the coverage under an individual life insurance policy

- ■ Calculate the amount of the policy proceeds payable for a given life insurance policy

- ■ Describe the various settlement options available to the policyowner and beneficiary

- ■ Explain how claim analysts determine the proper payee for life insurance policy proceeds and describe situations involving the beneficiary, policy assignments, adverse claimants, community property laws, divorce, and simultaneous deaths that can complicate the payment process

- ■ Describe how claim analysts evaluate claims for waiver of premium for disability benefits, accidental death benefits, family benefits, and accelerated benefits

Outline

Evaluating Life Insurance Claims

- Verifying the Coverage Was in Force
- Verifying that the Deceased Is Covered
- Verifying the Death Occurred
- Determining Whether the Policy Is Contestable
- Determining Whether the Death Is Covered
- Calculating the Amount of the Policy Proceeds and How They Are Payable
- Determining Who Is Entitled to Receive the Policy Proceeds

Handling Supplemental Benefits

- Waiver of Premium for Disability Benefit
- Accidental Death Benefit
- Family Benefit
- Accelerated Death Benefit

As we mentioned in Chapter 8, claim analysts go through the same basic steps in handling all types of claims. In this chapter, we explain how claim analysts handle each of the steps in the life insurance claim evaluation process. Group and individual life insurance claims are handled in basically the same manner, but we note where the group procedures differ from individual procedures.

Evaluating Life Insurance Claims

In the case of individual life insurance, the beneficiary, an heir, or the producer usually notifies an insurer of the insured's death. In the case of group life insurance, the employer usually notifies the insurer or third-party administrator of the group insured's death. The insurer then provides a claim form to the claimant to complete and asks the claimant to submit proof of loss, which in the case of life insurance is referred to as *proof of death*. A life insurance claim form asks for information about the deceased insured, including the date and place of birth, as well as the date, place, cause, and circumstances of death. The claim form also asks for information concerning the claimant, including her relationship to the insured, date of birth, contact information, and Social Security or taxpayer identification number.

Some companies' claim forms also ask for the names and contact information of all physicians or other health care providers who attended to the deceased insured within the past five years if death occurred during the contestable period. A HIPAA authorization must be obtained if information is to be obtained from these sources. This document typically is signed by the next of kin or an authorized representative of the deceased insured or his estate. Figure 9.1 shows a typical claim form for individual life insurance.

When a claim analyst receives a completed claim form, the analyst can have difficulty acquiring detailed information from some sources. Concerns about patient privacy and confidentiality cause some health care providers to delete information from the medical records before releasing the information to the insurer. In some situations, attorneys or claimants request that all information be sent to them before it is sent to the insurer. If the claim analyst becomes aware of this request, she challenges it to maintain the chain of custody of the medical records.

Figure 9.1. Typical Claim Form for Life Insurance

**VERY IMPORTANT: BEFORE COMPLETING THIS FORM,
PLEASE READ ALL INSTRUCTIONS ON THE INSTRUCTION PAGE**

NOTE: Any person who knowingly and with intent to defraud any insurance company or other person a) files a claim form containing any materially false information or b) conceals information concerning any fact material thereto for the purpose of misleading, commits a fradulent insurance act, which is a crime. Such person may be subject to fines and/or confinement in prison.

PART ONE—To be completed in full

Name of Deceased (Print in Full)		Policy Number(s)
Date and Place of Birth	Date and Place of Death	Cause of Death

If your proceeds exceed the current applicable minimum set by the Company (currently $15,000), an interest bearing checking account will be opened for you, and you will promptly receive your personalized checks. You may immediately utilize all or a portion of those funds by writing checks against that account. The funds in the account, meanwhile, will earn interest at a competitive variable rate.

I certify, under penalty of perjury, the following is my correct Taxpayer Identification Number.

Beneficiary's Social Security Number	Taxpayer Identification Number **if the beneficiary is an Employer/Corporation/Trust/Estate**	
Name of Beneficiary* (Print in full)	Date of Birth (MM/DD/YY) / /	Your Relationship to Deceased
Address (Street, City, State, Zip)		Telephone Number ( ) –
Beneficiary/Payee Signature (Required)		Date

***If there is more than one beneficiary, <u>each</u> must complete his or her own claim form.
Copies of the form are acceptable.**

continued on next page...

Figure 9.1. Typical Claim Form for Life Insurance *continued*

PART TWO—To be completed only IF: **Death has occurred within two (2) years of original issue or reinstatement of the policy**

          1. **Please fully complete claim authorization form XYZ and submit with this claim form.**

          2. **Fully complete information below and on the following page with signature and date**

Deceased driver's license number	Deceased driver's license state of issue	Date deceased first consulted a physician for last illlness / /
Date deceased last worked at his/her regular occupation / /	Did the deceased **ever** use tobacco in any form? ☐ Yes ☐ No If **Yes**, date last used from_____ to _____	

Name and addresses of **all** physicians (include personal physician) who attended to deceased and hospitals where treated for past **(5) five** years.

Name	Address (Street, City, State, Zip) & Telephone Number	Dates	Disease or Condition

List **all** Life and Health insurance of the Deceased

Company	Policy Number(s) and Amount(s)	Policy Issue Date(s)

SIGNATURES

Signature of Next of Kin/Authorized Representative	Date
Address (Street, City, State Zip)	Witness Signature

Claim analysts attempt to obtain all information necessary to evaluate a claim as soon as possible because they are required legally to process claims promptly. In addition, in many U.S. states, interest continues to accrue on the policy proceeds until the claim is resolved. Furthermore, many U.S. states have regulations specifying that the insurer must take follow-up action according to a specified timetable, which may be every 30, 45, or 90 days. ERISA requires that such a timetable be followed for group claims. Compliance with such regulations becomes more difficult and costly the longer a claim is pending.

During the course of evaluating the claim, the claim analyst sends the claimant letters about the status of the evaluation. If the claim analyst denies the claim, he sends the claimant a denial letter explaining why the claim was denied. Many states and ERISA require the denial letter to include information on how a claimant can appeal a denial. Typically, the letter also states that if the claimant can provide additional information that might refute the information on which the denial was based, the insurer will consider such information in reexamining the claim. In some companies, the claim analyst sends such a letter prior to making a final decision to deny a claim so that the claimant may provide input prior to the final decision. In many companies, the claim supervisor—and sometimes the law department—must review and approve of each denial. A special investigative unit also may review the claim if fraud is suspected.

Verifying the Coverage Was in Force

The claim analyst usually can verify that coverage was in force when the death occurred by checking the administration system's record of the policy's premium payments made to date. However, if the policy has been applied for but not yet issued, the claim analyst must investigate whether coverage nonetheless was effective on the date of death. If the deceased paid a premium, then the insurer most likely issued a premium receipt. The claim analyst then may need to refer the claim to the law department to evaluate the terms of the premium receipt, applicable state and federal regulations, and applicable case law governing such matters.

The question of whether coverage was in force on the date of death also may arise if the policy was in the grace period or in the process of being reinstated. During the grace period, the loss typically will be covered even if the renewal premium had not yet been received. If death occurred during the reinstatement process, generally the loss will be covered only if the policyowner had completed all requirements for the reinstatement and the company had approved the application for reinstatement.

When a claim is submitted under a group life insurance policy, the claim analyst verifies that premiums have been paid for the group insured. If the deceased is a dependent under a group policy, the claim analyst verifies that the group insured was paying premiums for the dependent's coverage.

Verifying That the Deceased Is Covered

The life insurance claim analyst must verify that the policy actually covered the deceased at the time of death, which is especially important under multi-life, family, and group policies when claims may be submitted for individuals who actually were not covered. When a claim is submitted under a group life insurance policy, the insurer requires the employer to verify the insured's status as a covered member of the group. If the claim analyst determines she needs more proof of the deceased group member's status, the claim analyst examines payroll records and the employee's enrollment card. If the deceased is a dependent under a group policy, the claim analyst verifies that the dependent is on the group insured's enrollment form.

With life insurance, a claim analyst also must be careful to verify the identity of the deceased as the insured. To do so, the claim analyst compares the deceased's name and other vital information, such as date and place of birth, found on the claim form and documentation submitted as proof of death with the insured's name and information found in the insurer's records. However, difficulties may arise if the deceased is a woman who has changed her name along with her marital status. In such a case, the claim analyst typically would examine the marriage certificate.

Identifying the deceased as the insured may be complicated if the death occurred in a foreign country, the insured is missing and presumed dead, or the insured's body was badly deformed in the event causing the death. In such cases, autopsy reports, police reports, and interviews with those involved may give clues to the identity of the insured.

Verifying the Death Occurred

A typical proof of death for life insurance is a *death certificate*, which is a document that attests to the death of a person and bears the signature—and sometimes the seal—of an official authorized to issue such a certificate. Because of concerns about protecting the privacy of individuals and ensuring the confidentiality of sensitive information, death certificates in some jurisdictions list only "natural causes" rather than specifying the cause of death as being from a particular disease.

Most insurers in the United States accept either an original or a certified copy of the official death certificate as proof of death. Most Canadian insurers accept an official death certificate, a coroner's certificate of death, or a hospital's certificate of death as proof of the death of an insured.

Certain jurisdictions have held that an insurer must accept as proof of death a document that attests to the death of an insured and that is signed by a person with knowledge of the insured's death. Nonetheless, in such circumstances, the insurer generally tries to obtain official death records, if any are available, to corroborate information in the unofficial document.

Death Outside North America

Typically when a death of a U.S. citizen occurs outside the United States, the local authorities issue a death certificate in the local language. The U.S. Consular Officer then usually issues a "Report of Death of an American Citizen Abroad" based on the death certificate. Most insurers require this report as proof of death instead of the death certificate. In addition, most insurers ask the claimant or next of kin to complete and sign a foreign death questionnaire.

Claim analysts sometimes have difficulty establishing how, or even if, a death occurred when the insured died outside North America. Because formalities and procedures for registration of death in other countries are not always as rigorous as those in the United States and Canada, situations in which the insured dies abroad introduce the possibility of fraud. Therefore, additional investigation and care usually are required to verify the validity of the claim. For example, the claim analyst may check to see if the insured's passport or return airline tickets were cancelled.

Disappearance of the Insured

Occasionally, a claim analyst must presume that an insured is dead because the insured has disappeared and the body has not been found. If an insured was exposed to a specific peril that can account for the insured's disappearance, and if no other suspicious circumstances exist, the claim analyst generally approves the claim after an appropriate investigation into the circumstances of the case if a death certificate is provided. For example, if a troop of Boy Scouts on a hike sees their leader swept away in a torrent during a thunderstorm but the troop leader's body is never found, the claim analyst more than likely would approve the claim after a reasonable period if no evidence of fraud was found.

If an insured disappears without exposure to a specific peril or any presentation of other definite proof of death, the insurer may determine that the burden of proof of death has not been met and may conclude that it is unable to pay the policy benefits. However, if an insured has been absent from her home continuously for a specified period—seven years in most jurisdictions—an insurer or a claimant can apply to a court for an order presuming death. If the court evaluates the evidence and is satisfied that the insured is more than likely deceased, the court issues a ***presumptive death certificate***, which is a court-issued document stating that a person is presumed to be dead. Figure 9.2 lists the four elements that the court considers before issuing a presumptive death certificate. When a claim analyst receives a presumptive death certificate, he calculates the policy proceeds as of the date of death shown on the court order.

If the claim analyst locates an insured person who does not want to have her location revealed, the claim analyst respects the insured's wishes. However, the claim analyst can justify nonpayment of insurance benefits only by obtaining a signed, dated, and notarized statement from the insured attesting to identifying information, such as date of birth, place of birth, and the names of such people as the insured's parents, spouse, and children.

Figure 9.2. Considerations for Issuing a Presumptive Death Certificate

Before issuing a presumptive death certificate, a court will consider whether

1. The insured has been missing from his home or usual residence for the period of time required in the jurisdiction

2. The insured's absence has been continuous and whether any factors such as large debts, marital problems, or criminal indictments exist that would give cause for the disappearance

3. A diligent search for the insured has been conducted

4. The people most likely to hear from the insured have not heard from her

Reappearance of the Insured

If an insured reappears after being declared dead by a court and after the insurer has paid the policy proceeds in full, the insurer usually has the right to recover the money because it was paid under a mistake of fact. If the insurer paid less than the full amount of benefits in a compromise settlement, however, the insurer generally cannot recover the benefits because courts will not disturb a compromise settlement.

Determining Whether the Policy is Contestable

If an individual life insurance claim is submitted during a policy's contestable period, the claim analyst investigates whether the application contains a material misrepresentation. Typically, the claim analyst refers the claim to the underwriting department if he suspects that material misrepresentation has occurred. Information on the insured's medical and personal risk factors is obtained and anything that predates the application is compared to the application to ensure the risk factor was disclosed during the underwriting process. If any medical or personal risk factor was not disclosed and if it would have been considered material to the issuance of the policy because the underwriter would not have issued the policy as written had he been fully informed, the claim analyst then may refer the claim to the law department or the special investigative unit to determine the validity of the policy and/or whether the company is required to report a fraud to the state in which the policy was issued.

Determining Whether the Death Is Covered

In deciding whether the loss is covered under the terms of an individual life insurance policy, the claim analyst examines all policy exclusions, including those for aviation, avocations, and suicide. The claim analyst also verifies that no changes in the insured's health or other material information submitted at the time of application have occurred between the time of application and policy delivery.

Aviation, Avocation, and Suicide Exclusions

Aviation and avocation exclusions typically are found in riders, whereas the suicide exclusion is part of the basic policy. Benefits payable under an aviation or avocation exclusion rider differ in accordance with the terms of the rider, which may provide that the insurer will

■ Pay no benefit if death is a result of the activity excluded

■ Return the premiums paid

■ Pay the cash surrender value

If an insured person dies as a result of suicide, the claim analyst checks the policy's suicide exclusion provision. Insurance companies try to protect themselves against the possibility of antiselection by excluding suicide as a covered risk for a specified period—usually two years—following the date the policy is issued. If the policy lapses and is reinstated, the period still is considered to have begun on the date when the original policy was issued in most jurisdictions. In Canada, if a policy has been reinstated, the suicide exclusion period typically begins again on the date the policy is reinstated. The length of the new suicide exclusion period is the same as the length of the original period.

If the claim analyst determines that an insured died by suicide within the exclusion period, the insurer returns the premiums paid and does not pay full policy benefits. Returning the premiums paid is considered to be payment of the limited benefit agreed upon when the application for insurance was submitted and when the insurer accepted the risk. Returning the premiums is not considered to be a refund, and the insurer is not considered to have rescinded the coverage. By invoking the suicide exclusion, the insurer is not contesting the policy or attempting to rescind it, but instead is affirming the validity of the contract by applying the limited-benefit-for-death-by-suicide provision in the contract.

To determine what action to take if a proposed insured commits suicide during underwriting, most insurers rely on the language of the premium receipt. The receipt should state clearly that coverage under the receipt will be effective subject to the limitations contained in the policy applied for—and such a policy would contain the suicide exclusion provision.

If an insurer denies a claim for basic death benefits under a life insurance policy based on the suicide exclusion and is sued, most jurisdictions require that the insurer bear the burden of showing that the insured committed suicide. Most jurisdictions have a legal presumption that the insured did not commit suicide, and the insurer must overcome this presumption.

Change in Health Statement

Most individual life insurance applications and premium receipts contain a *change in health statement* that requires a proposed insured to notify the insurer in writing if his health or any material information in the application changes before the policy is delivered. Some insurers require the producer and/or the policyowner-insured to sign another change in health statement at the time the policy is delivered. A typical change in health statement as it appears in an application is shown in Figure 9.3.

Figure 9.3. Typical Change in Health Statement

I understand that no policy based on this application will be effective unless all of my statements and answers in the application continue to be true as of the date I receive the policy. I understand that if my health changes or any of my answers or statements change prior to delivery of the policy, I must so inform the insurer in writing.

If the insured does not notify the insurer of a change in health prior to delivery of the policy and a policy is issued, the insurer may deny a subsequent claim if it occurs during the contestable period. In most jurisdictions, to deny payment of policy proceeds because of a change in the insured's health between application for and delivery of the policy, the insurer must show that (1) the change in health directly affected the degree of risk for the case, (2) the proposed insured knew of the change in health, and (3) the change in health statement was unambiguous. On the other hand, if a proposed insured dies as a result of a sudden event, such as an accident or an acute condition about which the proposed insured had no prior knowledge, benefits may be payable under the policy depending on the terms of any premium receipt.

Calculating the Amount of the Policy Proceeds and How They Are Payable

In calculating the total amount of individual life insurance policy proceeds due the beneficiary, the claim analyst reviews the policy and policy records to determine (1) the basic death benefit, (2) any additions to the basic death benefit, and (3) any deductions from the basic death benefit. A group insured's death benefit is defined in the group master policy's benefit schedule. When the claim analyst has calculated the total amount of the policy proceeds, he then must determine how the proceeds are to be paid.

Basic Death Benefit

The amount of the basic death benefit due upon the insured's death is based on the face amount of the policy. However, most policies specify that the death benefit will be adjusted if the claim examiner finds that the policy application contained a misstatement of age or sex.

The claim analyst verifies the age and sex of the deceased insured to be certain that the premiums paid have reflected accurately the amount of risk borne by the insurer. If the age of a deceased insured is in question—for example, if the age on the death certificate is different from the insured's age according to the application—the claim analyst asks the claimant for acceptable proof of age. Proof of an insured's age can be established by various documents, including the insured's birth certificate or a document that establishes the insured's age at the time of a ceremony, such as a certificate of baptism, bar or bat mitzvah, or other religious ceremony.

If the claim analyst determines that the age or sex of the insured was misstated on the application and if a different age or sex on the application would have resulted in a different premium being charged, then the analyst adjusts the amount of the basic death benefit appropriately. Such an adjustment is permitted throughout the life of the policy and is not affected by the incontestability clause.

Generally, an adjustment for misstatement of age or sex results in a death benefit amount equal to the death benefit that the premiums paid would have purchased at the correct age or sex, according to the insurer's published premium rates at the time of policy issue. Figure 9.4 provides an example that illustrates how an insurer typically calculates the death benefit if an insured's age was misstated.

Figure 9.4. Calculating the Death Benefit with a Misstatement of Age

Rena Salazar mistakenly stated her age as 34 when she applied for $150,000 of whole life insurance. She was charged an annual premium of $1.42 per thousand, or $213 ($1.42 × 150).

When Rena died and her beneficiary submitted a claim, the claim analyst discovered a discrepancy between Rena's age according to the application and her age at time of death. The insured actually was 43 years old when she applied for coverage. According to the insurer's published premium rates at the time of policy issue, the paid premium of $213 a year would have purchased $136,000 of whole life insurance. Therefore, the amount of the basic death benefit is $136,000.

If Rena actually had been less than 34 years old at the time of application, the premiums she paid while the policy was in force would have purchased more than $150,000 of coverage. In that situation, the claim analyst would adjust the amount of the basic death benefit upward accordingly.

If a claim analyst discovers that an insured's age was misstated on the application, he must bring this to the claimant's attention. The burden of showing a misstatement of age or sex that results in a lower basic death benefit than the stated face amount rests with the insurer. The burden of showing a misstatement of age or sex that results in a higher basic death benefit than the stated face amount rests with the claimant.

In addition to increasing or decreasing the basic death benefit payable, an adjustment for age sometimes causes an insured to be ineligible to receive certain supplementary benefits. For example, if the accidental death benefit is payable only until an insured reaches a specified age, usually 65 or 70, then an insured whose age at death exceeds the limit probably will not be eligible for the accidental death benefit.

Additions to the Basic Death Benefit

After determining the basic death benefit payable, the claim analyst may add certain amounts, if applicable. Examples of such amounts are listed in Figure 9.5.

Deductions from the Basic Death Benefit

The claim analyst also deducts certain amounts from the basic death benefit, if applicable, including

- Premiums due but unpaid during the grace period

- Policy loans

- Interest on any policy loans

- Accelerated death benefits that have been paid

Figure 9.5. Possible Additions to the Basic Death Benefit

- Paid-up additional insurance
- Accidental death benefits
- Unearned premiums paid in advance
- Policy dividends declared but not yet paid
- Policy dividends left with the insurer to earn interest, plus the interest
- Interest on delayed claims payment
- Loan interest paid in advance

Figure 9.6 provides an example that illustrates additions to and deductions from a death benefit.

Settlement Option Administration

Life insurance policy proceeds typically are paid to the beneficiary in a lump sum upon the insured's death. The insurer can pay this sum by check, or the insurer can deposit the policy proceeds into an interest-bearing checking or money market account that the insurer establishes in the beneficiary's name. Because the beneficiary has the ability to withdraw the entire amount at one time, depositing the proceeds into such an account constitutes a lump-sum payment.

In addition to lump-sum settlements, insurers provide alternative methods of receiving the proceeds of a life insurance policy, which are known as *settlement options*. Some group policies offer settlement options if the proceeds payable are at least a stated minimum amount.

During the lifetime of the insured, the policyowner can choose one of the settlement options. When the policy proceeds become payable, the beneficiary can select a settlement option if the policyowner has not done so or change the option selected by the policyowner unless the policyowner made the settlement mode irrevocable. The insurance company and the beneficiary then enter into a settlement agreement. The person or entity who is to receive the policy proceeds under a settlement option is referred to as the *payee* rather than a beneficiary. The typical settlement options are listed in Figure 9.7.

Determining Who Is Entitled to Receive the Policy Proceeds

Perhaps one of the most challenging tasks facing the claim analyst is determining the proper payee of the policy proceeds because of the risk of being subjected to making duplicate claim payments. If the insurer mistakenly pays proceeds to someone who is not entitled to them and the proper payee later asserts a valid claim to the proceeds, the insurer is obligated to pay the claim again. The insurer then can seek to recover the proceeds from the original payee.

Figure 9.6. Calculating Additions to and Deductions from a Death Benefit

Sal Donato purchased a nonparticipating life insurance policy in the amount of $200,000, plus a $150,000 accidental death benefit rider. Sal subsequently bought $60,000 of additional coverage. At the time of Sal's death, which resulted from an accident, he had paid $500 in advance premiums and had an outstanding policy loan of $22,000 plus $1,500 of interest on that loan. The claim analyst would calculate the total benefit payable under this policy in the following manner:

	Face value of policy	$200,000
+	ADB rider	+ 150,000
+	Additional coverage	+ 60,000
+	Premium paid in advance	+ 500
Death benefit plus additions		**$410,500**
−	Unpaid policy loan	− 22,000
−	Unpaid interest on policy loan	− 1,500
Total death benefit payable		**$387,000**

In Canada, an insurer must be notified in writing of any person's right to receive policy proceeds. Therefore, when an insurer pays policy proceeds to a person who appears entitled to them according to the insurer's records, the insurer is fully discharged of all liability for payment of the proceeds. A person who claims he is entitled to the proceeds but didn't notify the insurer may seek to recover the proceeds only from the person who received them.

The claim analyst also must verify the payee's identity. In addition, because a payee generally must have attained the age of majority to provide an insurer with a valid discharge of liability, the insurer requires proof of the payee's age.

Usually the payee is the beneficiary—a spouse, a child or children, an estate, a trust, a charity, or almost any other entity that has an insurable interest in the life of the insured—and is designated clearly on the insurance application. However, a number of circumstances can complicate the claim analyst's responsibility to ensure that the benefits are paid to the correct payee.

No Named Beneficiary

If a policyowner does not name a beneficiary, the terms of the policy specify the recipient of the policy proceeds. In such cases, policies typically direct the claim analyst to pay the policy proceeds to the policyowner or to the policyowner's estate if the policyowner is deceased.

Figure 9.7. Typical Settlement Options

- The **interest option** under which the insurance company invests the policy proceeds and periodically pays interest on those proceeds

- The **fixed-period option** under which the insurance company agrees to pay policy proceeds in equal installments to the payee for a specified period of time

- The **fixed-amount option** under which the insurance company pays equal installments of a stated amount until the policy proceeds, plus the interest earned, are exhausted

- The **life income option** under which the insurance company agrees to pay the policy proceeds in periodic installments over the payee's lifetime

Alternatively, some policies—typically group—state that if no beneficiary has been named, the insurer will pay the policy proceeds in a stated order of preference, such as to the spouse of the insured, if living; then to the children of the insured, if living; then to the parents of the insured, if living. If no one on the list is living, then the insurer pays the policy proceeds to the insured's estate.

Death of the Beneficiary

If the beneficiary named in an insurance policy has predeceased the insured, the claim analyst checks its records to determine whether an alternate beneficiary was named. Such a beneficiary, called a **contingent beneficiary** or *secondary beneficiary*, is the person or entity designated to receive the proceeds of a life insurance policy following the insured's death if the primary beneficiary dies before the insured.

Disqualification of the Beneficiary

A beneficiary who intentionally kills the insured without legal justification, such as self defense, is disqualified by law from receiving the policy proceeds. If the beneficiary did not intend to kill the insured when the policy was applied for, the insurer pays the policy benefits to the contingent beneficiary. If the policyowner-beneficiary obtained the policy with the intent of causing the insured's death, then the contract is void from its inception; the insurer is required to return only the amount of premiums paid with interest, less any outstanding policy loans along with unpaid interest on those loans.

The insurer usually delays payment of the proceeds until the investigation into the insured's death is complete. If the investigation continues for a long period, the insurer generally deposits the amount of policy proceeds with the court for disbursement after a legal decision has been reached concerning the beneficiary's guilt or innocence. Note that a criminal court does not have to convict the beneficiary of intentionally killing the insured without legal justification for the beneficiary to be disqualified. If either a criminal or civil court finds that the beneficiary intentionally and wrongfully killed the insured, the beneficiary will not be eligible to receive the policy proceeds.

Disappearance of the Beneficiary

If a beneficiary has disappeared and cannot be located within a reasonable period, the insurer generally follows the laws of the state or province in which the beneficiary last resided. Most states have adopted variations of the NAIC Uniform Disposition of Unclaimed Property Act, which requires an insurer to hold the proceeds for a specified period—typically five to seven years—and then deposit with the state all proceeds that cannot be paid to a missing beneficiary. The state holds the money in trust for such a beneficiary, who may petition the state for the proceeds. After the state has held the money for a specified number of years, the proceeds then escheat to the state—which means the proceeds become the property of the state.

In all the Canadian provinces except Quebec, an insurer deposits unpayable proceeds with a court, which then determines the proper payee. In Quebec, three years after proceeds become payable, insurers are required by law to deposit proceeds payable to untraceable beneficiaries with the *public curator*, a person authorized to handle the affairs of missing people.

Change in Beneficiary

At the time a claim is made, the claim analyst verifies that any change of beneficiary made by the policyowner was done so accurately and that the new beneficiary is eligible to receive the policy proceeds. A policyowner's right to change a revocable beneficiary is greater than his right to change an irrevocable beneficiary. A *revocable beneficiary* is a life insurance policy beneficiary who has no right to the policy proceeds during the insured's lifetime because the policyowner has the unrestricted right to change the beneficiary designation during the insured's lifetime. During the insured's lifetime, a revocable beneficiary's interest in the life insurance policy is said to be a mere expectancy. An *irrevocable beneficiary* is a life insurance policy beneficiary who has a vested interest in the policy proceeds even during the insured's lifetime because the policyowner has the right to change the beneficiary designation only after obtaining the beneficiary's consent or upon the beneficiary's death.

In Canada, claim analysts must be aware that policyowners of in-force policies issued prior to July 1, 1962 in common law jurisdictions have limitations on their ability to change the beneficiary designations of *preferred beneficiaries*—certain family members of the insured. The policyowner cannot change the beneficiary to anyone outside this group of family members. In addition, the policyowner cannot obtain a policy loan, surrender the policy for its cash surrender value, or assign the policy benefits if doing so would diminish the rights of the preferred beneficiary, unless the preferred beneficiary consents in writing. The rights of a preferred beneficiary continue until that beneficiary dies, is divorced from the spouse-insured, or signs a release.

In both the United States and Canada, if the claim analyst determines that a policyowner was mentally incompetent when he made a beneficiary change, then the change is legally ineffective, and the original beneficiary receives the policy proceeds. If a former beneficiary wishes to challenge a change of beneficiary, the burden is upon the former beneficiary to prove the incompetence of the policyowner to make the change. The claim analyst is not legally bound, however, to question the competence of every policyowner who changes a beneficiary. If an insurer pays the policy proceeds to a new beneficiary and then discovers later that the policyowner was incompetent when he made the beneficiary change, the insurer usually is not required by law to pay the proceeds a second time to the original beneficiary.

Assigned Policy

The claim analyst checks whether an individual life insurance policy has been assigned. An *assignment* is an agreement under which a policyowner—the assignor—transfers some or all of her ownership rights in a particular policy to another party—the assignee. Most individual life insurance policies include an assignment provision stating that the insurer accepts no responsibility for determining the validity of an assignment and that the policyowner must notify the insurer of an assignment. If the insured dies without the insurer receiving notice of the assignment, the insurer may pay the policy proceeds to the designated beneficiary; the assignee will not be able to enforce a claim against the insurer.

An *absolute assignment* is an irrevocable transfer of all of a policyowner's ownership rights in a life insurance policy to the assignee. A *collateral assignment* is the transfer of some of a policyowner's rights in a life insurance policy to provide security for a debt. A collateral assignment gives the assignee the right to share in the policy proceeds to the extent of the policyowner's outstanding debt at the insured's death.

A claim analyst handling a claim involving an assigned policy must be aware that the rights of the policy beneficiary vary when a life insurance policy is assigned depending on the type of assignment, whether the beneficiary is revocable or irrevocable, and the laws of the applicable jurisdiction.

An absolute assignee has the right to change a revocable beneficiary designation; and when he does so, proceeds are payable to the new beneficiary. If an absolute assignee does not change the beneficiary designation and the policy is silent on this matter, some insurers pay the assignee the proceeds in accordance with court decisions that hold that the absolute assignment of a policy revokes the revocable beneficiary designation automatically. Other insurers, in keeping with contrary court decisions, pay the original beneficiary the policy proceeds.

The collateral assignee's rights in the policy are superior to the revocable beneficiary's rights regardless of whether the revocable beneficiary consents to the collateral assignment. Thus, the collateral assignee is entitled to be repaid from the policy proceeds.

According to the terms of most policies, the policyowner cannot assign ownership of the policy without obtaining the irrevocable beneficiary's consent. If the irrevocable beneficiary consents to an absolute assignment, he remains the beneficiary unless he consents to a change of beneficiary.

If the irrevocable beneficiary consents to a collateral assignment, the collateral assignee may be paid his appropriate share of the policy proceeds upon the death of the insured. However, if the irrevocable beneficiary does not consent to a collateral assignment, he generally has a superior right to the policy proceeds than does the assignee.

Adverse Claimants

When a claim analyst receives two or more conflicting claims on the proceeds of a policy, the analyst (1) conducts a thorough claim investigation according to the insurer's established procedures for handling adverse claimants and (2) consults with the insurer's legal department. During the investigation, the claim analyst notifies the adverse claimants of the conflicting claims. If the claimants can resolve the conflict between themselves, the claim analyst should obtain written notice of their decision and pay the policy proceeds in accordance with that decision. If the claimants cannot resolve the matter and the insurer pays the proceeds to one claimant but the other claimant later proves to have a superior claim, the insurer may have to pay the proceeds a second time.

When faced with adverse claimants who cannot agree on the disposition of the policy proceeds, the insurer typically initiates a legal process known in the United States as interpleader. *Interpleader* is a procedure by which the insurer pays the policy proceeds to a court, advises the court that the insurer cannot determine the correct recipient of the proceeds, and asks the court to determine the proper recipient or recipients. The insurer initiates an interpleader action only when the insurer acknowledges that it is liable for paying benefits, not when it is contesting a claim. By using interpleader, the insurer can avoid the risk of having to pay the policy proceeds more than once. In Canada, a procedure similar to interpleader is known as *payment into court*.

Community Property Laws

In some U.S. states, property ownership between spouses is governed by *community property laws* that provide that a spouse is entitled to receive an equal share of earned income and an equal share of property acquired by the other spouse during a marriage. However, some property is considered separate property and belongs solely to one spouse. Separate property includes property acquired by one spouse

- Before marriage

- During marriage with separate property. For example, if a spouse put money in a savings account prior to marriage and uses that money to make a purchase during her marriage, the acquisition is her separate property

- During marriage as a gift or inheritance

As a general rule, both spouses must agree before ownership of community property may be transferred to a third party. When one spouse dies, the surviving spouse is entitled to half of the community property; the other half generally belongs to the estate of the deceased spouse.

When a spouse applies for and is issued an insurance policy on her life during marriage and pays the premiums with community property funds, the policy is considered to be community property. If the beneficiary is the insured's spouse, the proceeds usually are considered the spouse's separate property on the theory that the deceased spouse made a gift to the surviving spouse. If a third party is the beneficiary, the claim analyst is relieved of determining the rights of the beneficiary versus those of the surviving spouse by statutes passed in the community property states. *Exculpatory statutes* are laws that permit an insurer to pay life insurance proceeds according to the terms of a policy without fear of double liability. Unless the insurer has received prior written notice of a conflicting claim, the insurer may pay the policy proceeds to the named beneficiary and will be excused from making any payment that might have been due to a surviving spouse. To prevent possible conflict resulting from appearing to ignore or avoid a spouse's legal property rights, however, insurers generally obtain a release from a surviving spouse before paying policy proceeds above a certain amount to anyone other than the spouse.

Divorce

Sometimes a policyowner-insured who has named her spouse as the beneficiary fails to change the beneficiary designation after getting a divorce. Under the laws of most jurisdictions, the claim analyst must pay the proceeds to the former spouse. However, some states have divorce statutes that automatically remove a former spouse as beneficiary unless the former spouse is renamed as beneficiary after the divorce or in the divorce decree.

If a divorce decree specifies that a policyowner-insured must continue to pay premiums on the life insurance policy and retain the divorced spouse as beneficiary, no problem exists if the policyowner-insured complies with the decree requirements. However, sometimes the policyowner-insured continues to pay premiums but wants someone other than the former spouse as the beneficiary. If the claim analyst has received no notice of a new beneficiary and pays the policy proceeds to the former spouse as beneficiary according to the insurer's records, the insurer typically is not liable to pay benefits a second time if the new beneficiary later submits a claim. If the claim analyst receives notice of the existence of a rival claimant to the policy benefits before paying the benefits, the insurer typically files an interpleader action.

Simultaneous Deaths

If an insured and the beneficiary die in a common disaster and the claim analyst cannot determine with certainty the order of death, the claim analyst generally will rely on the jurisdiction's **simultaneous death act**, which is a law that says if both the insured and the beneficiary die under circumstances which make it impossible to determine which of them died first, the insurer is to presume that the insured survived the beneficiary, unless the policy provides otherwise. Thus, the claim analyst is to pay the policy proceeds to a contingent beneficiary.

A simultaneous death act does not affect how the insurer pays policy proceeds when proof exists that a beneficiary survived the insured, even if only for a few minutes. In such a case, the insurer would pay the proceeds to the beneficiary's estate. Because this outcome may not be what the policyowner desires, some policies include a **survivorship clause** that states that the beneficiary must survive the insured by a specified period, usually 30 or 60 days, to be entitled to receive the policy proceeds. If the beneficiary does not survive for the stated period of time, the proceeds are paid as if the insured survived the beneficiary.

Handling Supplemental Benefits

As we explained in Chapter 6, the insurance protection provided by most individual life insurance policies can be expanded by supplemental benefits, including a waiver of premium for disability (WP) benefit, an accidental death benefit (ADB), a family benefit, and an accelerated death benefit. If such supplemental benefits are involved in a claim, the claim analyst goes through the claim evaluation process for the supplemental benefit in the same manner as he does for the policy's benefit. If a policy has a guaranteed insurability benefit and the policyowner has exercised options to purchase additional insurance, the claim analyst will include the additional benefits in the calculation of the policy proceeds.

Waiver of Premium for Disability Benefit

If a person becomes totally disabled and is insured under a life insurance policy that includes a waiver of premium for disability (WP) benefit, the claim analyst first verifies that the claimant has satisfied the waiting period, if any is required, and then verifies that the claimant is in fact disabled according to the WP benefit's definition. To make this determination, the claim analyst typically uses such tools as the claim form, disability information form, medical records—including the attending physician's statement—financial records, and information from the claimant's employer. In addition, the claim analyst verifies that the cause of the disability is not excluded from coverage.

The disability information form submitted by the claimant includes such information as

- The initial date of disability

- The cause of the disability and the medical diagnosis

- The claimant's occupation and job duties

- Additional sources, if any, of disability income, including names and addresses of providers of such benefits

- The expected return-to-work date

Most insurers review each active waiver of premium case at least annually to determine whether the claimant is still eligible for the waiver of premium. For example, some group WP benefits will terminate or be reduced when the group insured reaches a certain age.

Claim analysts typically review claims for disabilities that the insurer's experience has shown are usually short-term every three to six months. A claim analyst may require the claimant to complete a form to document continued disability periodically, and he may require an APS at least annually. In addition, the claim analyst may telephone the claimant to ask about the claimant's medical condition. If a claimant does not supply proof of continued disability, most insurers notify the claimant that she is being removed from waiver status and that she will be responsible for paying future life insurance premiums if she wants the coverage to remain in force.

Accidental Death Benefit

The purpose of the accidental death benefit (ADB) is to provide a death benefit in addition to the policy's basic death benefit if the insured dies as the result of an accident. A claim analyst must verify that the accidental death benefit was still in force when the insured died, as most such benefits expire when the insured reaches age 65 or 70.

An ADB is payable if the insured's death was caused, directly and independently of all other causes, by an accidental bodily injury. The claim analyst may find it difficult at times to determine the precise cause of an insured's death. For example, an insured might have suffered a heart attack that resulted in a fatal vehicle accident or other mishap. In such a case, the claim analyst may examine the autopsy report and medical records to ascertain the immediate cause of death. If the death resulted from the heart attack, no accidental death benefits would be payable.

Some ADBs specify that the insured's death must occur within a stated time—such as 90 days—after the accident for the benefit to be payable. However, some states now prohibit insurers from including such a time span limitation in ADBs.

An ADB claim may be quite complex due not only to the facts, but also to varying regulations and case law. Claim analysts may consult with the law department on such claims.

Family Benefit

An individual life insurance policy with a family benefit insures the lives of the insured's spouse and children. When a life insurance claim is submitted under a family benefit, the claim analyst verifies that the deceased meets the definition of a spouse or child and that the deceased meets the age requirements specified in the benefit provision or rider. The documents that the claim analyst typically uses for such verification include a marriage certificate, a birth certificate, or an adoption certificate.

Accelerated Death Benefit

An accelerated death benefit give a policyowner-insured the right to receive all or part of the basic policy's death benefit before her death if certain conditions are met.[1] When the policyowner-insured dies, the amount of the death benefit payable under the policy to the named beneficiary is reduced by the amount of the accelerated death benefit that was paid out to the policyowner-insured. Thus, before paying an accelerated death benefit, claim analysts may require the irrevocable beneficiary and any assignee to sign a release acknowledging that the policy's death benefit will be reduced by the amount paid to the policyowner-insured under the accelerated death benefit provision. Because only a portion of the death benefit is accelerated, the policy continues to provide some degree of protection for beneficiaries and assignees.

In administering claims for an accelerated death benefit, the claim analyst must establish the policyowner-insured's eligibility to receive benefits by determining if the policyowner-insured meets the insurer's definition for having a terminal illness, dread disease, or condition requiring long-term care, depending on the type of accelerated death benefit involved. The claim analyst also must be wary of fraudulent claims if a policyowner-insured wants to receive accelerated death benefits during a policy's contestable period.

The amount of the terminal illness (TI) benefit that is payable varies from insurer to insurer. Some TI benefits permit payment of the full face amount prior to the insured's death. Generally, however, the maximum TI benefit payable is a stated percentage—usually between 25 and 75 percent—of the policy's face amount up to a specified maximum dollar limit such as $250,000. The benefit usually is paid in a lump sum to the policyowner, and the remainder is paid to the beneficiary following the insured's death.

Dread disease benefits usually are paid in a lump sum, but some insurers pay the benefit in monthly installments over a period of 6 to 12 months. Some insurers do not make payments for multiple or recurring events.

The amount of each monthly LTC benefit payment generally is equal to a stated percentage of the policy's death benefit. For example, the benefit may state that 2 percent of the policy's death benefit will be paid each month if the insured requires nursing home care and 1 percent of the death benefit will be paid each month if the insured requires home health care. The insurer usually pays monthly benefits until a specified percentage of the policy's basic death benefit has been paid out. This percentage typically falls between 50 and 100 percent of the policy's face amount. Any remaining death benefit is paid to the beneficiary after the insured's death.

Most LTC benefits impose a 90-day waiting period before accelerated death benefits are payable; no benefits are payable until 90 days following the date on which the insured becomes eligible for benefits. According to the terms of some LTC benefits, however, coverage must be in force for a given period of time, usually one year or more, before the insured will qualify for LTC benefits.

Key Terms

death certificate

presumptive death certificate

change in health statement

settlement option

payee

interest option

fixed-period option

fixed-amount option

life income option

contingent beneficiary

public curator

revocable beneficiary

irrevocable beneficiary

preferred beneficiary

assignment

absolute assignment

collateral assignment

interpleader

community property laws

exculpatory statute

simultaneous death act

survivorship clause

Endnote

1. Adapted in part from Harriett E. Jones, *Principles of Life, Health, and Annuities*, 3rd ed. [Atlanta: LOMA (Life Office Management Association, Inc.), © 2005], 124-126. Used with permission; all rights reserved.

Chapter 10

Reinsurance Overview

Objectives:

After studying this chapter, you should be able to

- Identify the roles that insurance companies can take in a reinsurance transaction

- Describe the characteristics of assumption reinsurance and indemnity reinsurance

- Describe several purposes—in addition to spreading the risk—that reinsurance can serve for direct writers

- Identify the rights and obligations of the direct writer and the reinsurer when reinsurance is ceded on an automatic, facultative, or facultative-obligatory basis

- Describe how risk is shared under a nonproportional reinsurance arrangement such as catastrophe coverage

- Describe how risk is shared under a proportional reinsurance arrangement such as the excess-of-retention and quota share methods

- Identify basic reinsurance plans, including coinsurance, funds withheld coinsurance, modified coinsurance (modco), and yearly renewable term (YRT) reinsurance

- Describe the general characteristics of a reinsurance agreement and the provisions that address the scope of the agreement, the termination of the agreement, and the reinsurance coverage

- List the provisions in a reinsurance agreement that govern the administration of reinsured business and describe provisions for making changes to reinsured policies and claim provisions

- Describe the provisions in a reinsurance agreement that address errors and omissions, arbitration, and insolvency

Outline

Roles of Insurance Companies in Reinsurance Arrangements

Indemnity Reinsurance
- Assumption Reinsurance and Indemnity Reinsurance
- Basic Financial Aspects of Indemnity Reinsurance
- Purposes of Indemnity Reinsurance for the Direct Writer

Cession Arrangements in Reinsurance
- Automatic Reinsurance
- Facultative Reinsurance
- Facultative-Obligatory Reinsurance

Risk-Sharing Arrangements
- Nonproportional Reinsurance and Proportional Reinsurance
- Cession Amounts in Proportional Reinsurance

Plans of Reinsurance
- Coinsurance
- Modified Coinsurance
- Yearly Renewable Term Reinsurance

Reinsurance Agreements
- Defining the Reinsurance Coverage
- Reinsurance Administration Procedures
- Potential Problems between a Direct Writer and a Reinsurer
- Reinsurance Rates and Payments

Reinsurance is a primary tool insurers use to manage the financial risks they assume.[1] Recall from Chapter 1 that *reinsurance* is insurance that one insurance company obtains from another insurance company on risks associated with insurance policies issued by the first company. The term ***reinsurance arrangement*** generally refers to the business deal that the two companies make for the transfer of risk from one company to the other.

The business of reinsurance involves vast amounts of money, many insurance companies, and countries around the globe. Reinsurance is available for virtually every line of life, health, property, and liability insurance. Our focus is on reinsurance for individual life and group life policies. The same basic concepts of reinsurance generally apply to individual and group life reinsurance. However, the exact structure and operation of each reinsurance arrangement depend in great part on the type of insurance—individual or group—involved.

A reinsurance arrangement may involve one policy, a group of policies, a block of business, a line of business, or any combination of policies, policy groups, or blocks or lines of business. A ***block of business*** is a number of similar insurance policies. The term *case*, in a reinsurance context, can refer to a single policy or a group of policies.

Roles of Insurance Companies in Reinsurance Arrangements

An insurer can act as a buyer of reinsurance in one transaction and a seller of reinsurance in another transaction. With respect to any given reinsurance arrangement, each company takes on one of the following specific roles:

■ A ***direct writer***, also called a *ceding company*, is an insurer that sells insurance coverage to the public. A direct writer can transfer—or cede—its insurance risks by obtaining reinsurance on those insurance risks. In this text, a reference to a direct writer in a reinsurance transaction means the company that cedes the risk.

■ A ***reinsurer***, also called a *reinsurance company* or an *assuming company*, is an insurer that provides reinsurance coverage by accepting, or assuming, insurance risk from a direct writer or another reinsurance company.

Under some circumstances, a reinsurer can be the ceding company. In other words, a reinsurer can transfer some of the risks it has assumed from a direct writer by obtaining reinsurance from a third insurance company. In such a situation, the third insurer is a ***retrocessionaire***, which is an insurance company that accepts risks from—and provides reinsurance to—a reinsurer. A reinsurer that transfers insurance risk to a retrocessionaire is called a *retrocedent*. Figure 10.1 shows the roles of reinsurance buyers and sellers.

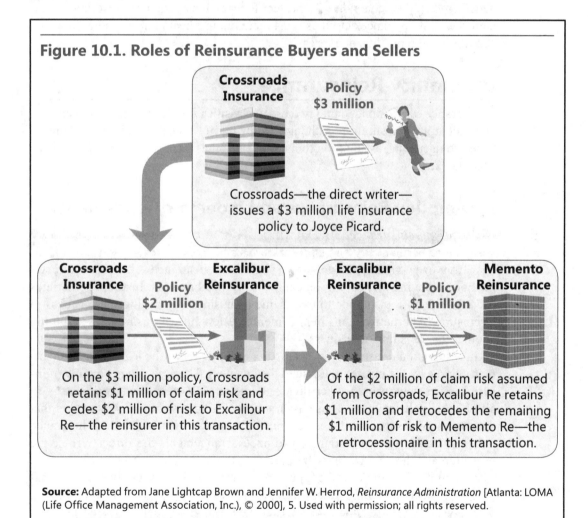

Figure 10.1. Roles of Reinsurance Buyers and Sellers

Crossroads Insurance — **Policy $3 million**

Crossroads—the direct writer—issues a $3 million life insurance policy to Joyce Picard.

Crossroads Insurance — **Policy $2 million** — **Excalibur Reinsurance**

On the $3 million policy, Crossroads retains $1 million of claim risk and cedes $2 million of risk to Excalibur Re—the reinsurer in this transaction.

Excalibur Reinsurance — **Policy $1 million** — **Memento Reinsurance**

Of the $2 million of claim risk assumed from Crossroads, Excalibur Re retains $1 million and retrocedes the remaining $1 million of risk to Memento Re—the retrocessionaire in this transaction.

Source: Adapted from Jane Lightcap Brown and Jennifer W. Herrod, *Reinsurance Administration* [Atlanta: LOMA (Life Office Management Association, Inc.), © 2000], 5. Used with permission; all rights reserved.

Reinsurance is a global business activity. Generally, any direct writer can enter into arrangements and do business with any properly licensed or authorized reinsurer, regardless of where each company is located. Major reinsurers maintain offices on multiple continents and actively seek to disperse risk geographically.

Whether operating in the role of direct writers or reinsurers, insurance companies with reinsurance activities are regulated by the laws that govern all other insurance companies. Additionally, specific regulations apply to their reinsurance activities. Because the parties to a reinsurance arrangement are business entities that are expected to be able to protect themselves legally, reinsurance regulation is less extensive and less detailed than is the regulation governing insurance transactions in which an individual or group is a party to the insurance contract.

The regulation of reinsurance primarily focuses on solvency issues. Recall that solvency is a business organization's ability to meet its financial obligations on time. *Insolvency*, the opposite of solvency, is an organization's inability to pay its financial obligations as they come due. *Solvency laws* are designed to ensure that insurance companies are financially able to meet their debts and to pay policy benefits when they come due. To protect their financial stability, insurance companies with reinsurance activities must meet requirements for licensing, financial condition and reporting, and reserves.

Indemnity Reinsurance

Reinsurance can be divided into two broad classifications: assumption reinsurance and indemnity reinsurance. Although we primarily focus on indemnity reinsurance arrangements, assumption reinsurance also has important roles in the insurance industry.

Assumption Reinsurance and Indemnity Reinsurance

Assumption reinsurance, also known as *portfolio reinsurance*, is reinsurance designed to permanently and entirely transfer blocks of existing insurance business from one company to another. Assumption reinsurance is the most common method of buying and selling blocks of insurance business. Insurers sometimes use assumption reinsurance to exit a line of business by ceding the business to a reinsurer. Alternatively, insurers can enter a new line of business by assuming another insurer's line of business.

In assumption reinsurance, the reinsurer assumes the entire legal obligation formerly borne by the insurer that issued the business. The assuming company (reinsurer) issues new insurance certificates—known as *assumption certificates*—to all affected policyowners. These assumption certificates show policyowners that the assuming insurer has taken responsibility for all risk under their insurance policies. Under an assumption reinsurance arrangement, the direct writer, the reinsurer, and the policyowners are parties to the reinsurance transaction.

Indemnity reinsurance is the type of reinsurance most commonly used to transfer risk. Under *indemnity reinsurance*, a reinsurer is obligated to reimburse a direct writer only after the direct writer pays benefits under reinsured policies. Indemnity reinsurance includes traditional indemnity reinsurance and finite reinsurance; however, a discussion of finite reinsurance is beyond the scope of this text. *Traditional indemnity reinsurance* is a reinsurance arrangement that is used to transfer a portion of a direct writer's accepted risk on an ongoing basis and that is intended to be a permanent transfer. The parties to a traditional indemnity reinsurance arrangement—the direct writer (ceding company) and the reinsurer—negotiate the terms of the arrangement to meet the specific needs of both parties. Direct writers sometimes cede blocks of business using traditional indemnity reinsurance. However, traditional indemnity reinsurance arrangements typically create an ongoing contractual relationship between the parties to the arrangement.

Although the parties to a traditional indemnity reinsurance arrangement intend for the risk transfer to be permanent, traditional indemnity reinsurance arrangements generally include a means for the direct writer and reinsurer to end or otherwise modify the reinsurance arrangement. For example, traditional indemnity reinsurance arrangements usually allow the direct writer to *recapture*—take back—specified reinsurance risks. Traditional indemnity reinsurance arrangements also allow for termination of the entire arrangement either through mutual agreement or automatically due to the inability of one of the parties to the arrangement to meet its financial obligations on time.

Unlike assumption reinsurance transactions, a traditional indemnity reinsurance arrangement is not disclosed to the direct writer's policyowners, because they are not parties to the agreement. Under traditional indemnity reinsurance, the direct writer retains the entire legal liability to its customers whose policies are reinsured.

Figure 10.2 summarizes the primary characteristics of assumption and traditional indemnity reinsurance arrangements. The remainder of this chapter and the next chapter focus on traditional indemnity reinsurance. Unless specified otherwise, the term *indemnity reinsurance* or simply *reinsurance* refers to traditional indemnity reinsurance.

Figure 10.2. Characteristics of Assumption and Traditional Indemnity Reinsurance

	Assumption Reinsurance	Traditional Indemnity Reinsurance
Is the arrangement intended to be temporary or permanent?	Permanent	Permanent
Is recapture permitted?	No	Yes
Does the reinsurer become a party to the underlying reinsured policies?	Yes	No
Is the arrangement primarily used to reinsure new business or in-force business?	In-force	New (typically)
What are the primary purposes of the reinsurance arrangement?	Transfer the risk	Share or transfer risks
Who administers the reinsured insurance policies?	Reinsurer	Reinsurer or direct writer or both

Source: Adapted from Susan Conant, *Capital Management for Insurance Companies* [Atlanta: LOMA (Life Office Management Association, Inc.), © 2001], 149. Used with permission. All rights reserved.

Basic Financial Aspects of Indemnity Reinsurance

In indemnity reinsurance, the direct writer makes periodic payments, known as **reinsurance premiums**, to the reinsurer as compensation for the reinsurance coverage. In return, the reinsurer agrees to reimburse the direct writer for a stated amount or portion of policy benefits the direct writer pays to customers under the reinsured policies. Under many reinsurance arrangements, the reinsurer agrees to establish policy reserves for the reinsured portion of the risk similar to the reserves the direct writer establishes for its portion of the business. **Policy reserves** are a liability amount that, together with future premiums and investment income, the insurer estimates it will need to pay contractual benefits as they come due under in-force policies.

Some reinsurance arrangements also include an allowance for the direct writer. An **allowance**, also known as an *expense allowance*, a *reinsurance allowance*, a *ceding commission*, or a *reinsurance commission*, is an amount the reinsurer reimburses to the direct writer and that is designed to recognize the direct writer's acquisition, maintenance, and other expenses related to the ceded business.

- **Acquisition expenses** are the costs a direct writer incurs in developing, marketing, and issuing new business. Examples of acquisition expenses covered in the reinsurance allowance are first-year commissions, underwriting costs, new business processing costs, and policy issue costs. In yearly renewable term (YRT) arrangements, the first year reinsurance commission and allowance may be as much as 100 percent of the reinsurance premium.

- **Maintenance expenses**, also known as *renewal expenses* or *administration expenses*, are the direct writer's ongoing expenses for administering and servicing a policy or a block of business after it has been placed in force.

The reinsurance allowance generally is larger in early policy years than in later policy years. The allowance reduces the reinsurance premium that the direct writer must pay to the reinsurer. A *gross reinsurance premium* is the reinsurance premium before the allowance is deducted. A *net reinsurance premium* is the actual cost that the direct writer pays for reinsurance coverage, after allowances. The following formula illustrates these relationships:

Reinsurance Gross Premium − Allowance = Reinsurance Net Premium

Under some reinsurance arrangements, when the actual financial outcome from operations is better than the parties anticipated, the reinsurer shares its profits by reimbursing the direct writer for a portion of the reinsurance premiums. An *experience refund* is an amount the reinsurer credits the direct writer as compensation for favorable risk experience. In Chapter 7, we defined experience refund in the context of a group insurance premium.

The reinsurer also may share the direct writer's expenses for **premium taxes**, which are amounts of tax that governments levy on a direct writer's premium income. The reinsurer typically pays a portion of the direct writer's premium taxes by refunding part of the reinsurance premiums to the direct writer.

Purposes of Indemnity Reinsurance for the Direct Writer

The principal purpose of indemnity reinsurance is to transfer or share the risk represented by insurance policies issued by the direct writer. Generally, the use of reinsurance also serves other purposes for the direct writer such as helping to

- Manage capacity

- Ease surplus strain

- Reduce fluctuations in claim payments

- Obtain product, underwriting, claim, and reinsurance information and expertise

Managing Capacity

Many direct writers use reinsurance to strengthen their financial positions. Every insurance company has a limit on (1) the amount of coverage it can approve or afford to pay on a single risk and (2) the total amount of risk it can accept. Generally, a direct writer's **underwriting capacity** or *risk-taking capability* is the highest monetary amount of risk that the company will accept on an individual insured so that unusual fluctuations in claims will not damage the ongoing solvency of the company. Underwriting capacity includes (1) the amount of risk a direct writer transfers to reinsurers plus (2) the direct writer's retention limit. A **retention limit** is a specified maximum monetary amount of insurance that an insurer is willing to carry at its own risk without transferring some of the risk to a reinsurer. A retention limit can be expressed as an amount per policy or an amount per life or as an overall maximum amount. Both direct writers and reinsurers have retention limits.

An insurer's **financial capacity** is the total monetary amount of risk the company can accept based on the investable funds it has available to write new business. If the marketing efforts of a direct writing company cause the company to sell larger policies or more total insurance coverage than its financial position can support, the direct writing company can transfer the excess risk to a reinsurer.

Easing Surplus Strain

In the early years of an insurance policy, the premium payments often are not adequate to cover the expenses associated with selling and issuing the policy and maintaining the required policy reserves. To establish the required reserves for the policy, the direct writer must use some of its surplus. **Surplus**, for an insurer, is the amount of assets the company has over and above its policy reserves and other financial obligations. Laws in many countries establish minimum surplus standards that insurers must maintain in order to conduct business. The use of surplus to establish policy reserves can cause a direct writer's surplus level to fall close to the minimum level.

This decrease in surplus caused by the high initial costs and reserve requirements associated with issuing new insurance policies is called **surplus strain**, or *new business strain*. The direct writer may be able to reduce surplus strain through the purchase of reinsurance. In some reinsurance arrangements, when the reinsurer assumes a portion of the direct writer's risk, the reinsurer establishes reserves for the reinsured portion of the risk, thus reducing the amount of reserves the direct writer must maintain. A decrease in potential surplus strain—which is known as *surplus relief*—strengthens an insurer's financial position.

Reducing Fluctuations in Claim Payments

The timing and amount of insurance claims received by an insurer can fluctuate greatly. Reinsurance cannot control the frequency of claims, but it can smooth the impact of extreme fluctuations because the reinsurer pays a portion of the policy benefits. Thus, reinsurance protects the direct writer from the financial stress that could result from unexpectedly large or early claims or a larger-than-expected number of claims in a single period.

Obtaining Information and Expertise

Through reinsurance arrangements, reinsurers have exposure to the underwriting, claim, and reinsurance administration policies and practices of many direct writers. Reinsurers are aware of challenges that many direct writers face and of successful responses to those challenges. Reinsurers also develop extensive databases of mortality and morbidity statistics based on the collective experience of their direct writer clients and their own reinsurance cases. As a result, reinsurers typically have a great deal of information and expertise to share with direct writers.

A reinsurer can provide expertise on establishing sound policies and practices for many areas—notably product development, underwriting, reinsurance administration, and claim administration. Although the need to protect client confidentiality and proprietary information prevents a reinsurer from sharing the specific details of any direct writer's business practices, the reinsurer can offer general advice to a direct writer about administrative systems, workflows, control mechanisms, best practices, and procedures.

Direct writers often obtain a reinsurer's advice in developing underwriting and claim administration manuals, determining premium rates, and wording policy provisions. A reinsurer can assess the strength of a direct writer's proposed new product by evaluating the product's underwriting standards, administration method, system requirements, pricing assumptions, premium rate structure, commission plan, and marketing approach. However, reinsurers cannot share specific financial design information obtained from direct writers with other direct writers.

Reinsurers' statistics on impairments, such as heart disease, hypertension, and diabetes, can help direct writers more accurately underwrite proposed insureds with these impairments. Typically, if the direct writer requests advice on a particular underwriting or claims case, a reinsurer will review the case and give an opinion on the underwriting or claim issue.

Cession Arrangements in Reinsurance

A *cession* is the unit of insurance risk that a direct writer transfers to a reinsurer. Transfers of reinsurance risk are managed through a *cession arrangement*, which identifies the direct writer's obligations and rights to cede risks, and identifies the reinsurer's obligations to accept risk as well as its rights to reject risk. Through a cession arrangement, a direct writer can cede reinsurance risk on an automatic, a facultative, or a facultative-obligatory (fac-ob) basis.

Automatic Reinsurance

Automatic reinsurance is a reinsurance cession arrangement in which the direct writer agrees in advance to cede all risks that meet the specifications in the reinsurance agreement and the reinsurer agrees in advance to assume these risks. For a risk that meets all agreement specifications, automatic reinsurance allows a direct writer to automatically bind a reinsurer to a risk without first providing the reinsurer with underwriting evidence for the risk and without asking the reinsurer's approval in advance. An automatic cession is the only cession arrangement in which the direct writer must cede and the reinsurer must assume a qualifying risk based only on the direct writer's underwriting evaluation. If a risk meets the requirements for automatic cession, then the direct writer generally must reinsure the risk and the reinsurer must accept the risk, without question.

Automatic reinsurance arrangements may limit cessions based on factors such as the plan of insurance, the age of the insured, the policy issue date, and the underwriting class (standard or substandard). Direct writers and reinsurers also have financial limits for automatic cessions. Figure 10.3 lists several types of financial limits on risk amounts transferred that may apply to an automatic reinsurance arrangement.

Facultative Reinsurance

Facultative reinsurance is a reinsurance cession arrangement in which a direct writer chooses whether to cede a risk and the reinsurer chooses whether to accept that risk. Facultative reinsurance is the only cession basis in which the reinsurer performs an independent underwriting evaluation and has the option to reject risks on the basis of its underwriting. For a facultative case, a reinsurer underwrites the case, assigns the case a risk classification, and can quote a reinsurance price based on its own underwriting guidelines and terms. A reinsurer has no obligation to submit a quote for a risk submitted on a facultative basis. Also, a direct writer is under no obligation to accept a quote from a reinsurer on a facultative case.

Many direct writers choose facultative reinsurance because facultative reinsurance allows them to obtain the benefit of the reinsurer's underwriting judgment before the direct writer issues the policy. Automatic reinsurance agreements often include provisions that allow the direct writer to submit certain applications—such as applications that do not comply with automatic reinsurance limitations—on a facultative or facultative-obligatory basis to its reinsurance partner and to other reinsurers.

Facultative-Obligatory Reinsurance

Facultative-obligatory (fac-ob) reinsurance is a reinsurance cession arrangement in which (1) the direct writer may choose to submit specific cases to the reinsurer and (2) the reinsurer must accept the cases based on the direct writer's underwriting, up to a stated maximum amount, if the reinsurer has available financial capacity. Under a fac-ob arrangement, the reinsurer determines whether the requested coverage exceeds the reinsurer's capacity. If the reinsurer lacks financial capacity and therefore cannot accept the risk, it immediately notifies the direct writer. If the reinsurer fails to notify the direct writer within a specified period, the reinsurer is automatically bound to the risk within the agreed-upon acceptance limits. If the reinsurer lacks capacity to cover the case, the reinsurer may be able to cede the excess risk to other reinsurers.

Figure 10.3. Limits on Risk Amounts Transferred under Automatic Reinsurance Agreements

- A *retention limit* is a specified maximum monetary amount of insurance that an insurer is willing to carry at its own risk without transferring some of the risk to a reinsurer.

- An **automatic binding limit** represents the maximum monetary amount of risk the reinsurer will accept automatically on a given policy or case without making an independent underwriting assessment. The reinsurer must accept the entire ceded risk on all policies when that risk does not exceed the automatic binding limit.

- A **minimum cession** is the smallest monetary amount of risk a direct writer will cede or that a reinsurer will accept in an automatic cession. Having a minimum cession allows a direct writer to avoid the obligation to cede and a reinsurer to avoid the obligation to accept amounts of risk that are relatively small in comparison to the administrative costs associated with the risk amounts. An example of a commonly used minimum cession is $25,000.

- A **jumbo limit** is the maximum allowable monetary amount of total insurance—in force and yet-to-be-placed—with all companies on any one life that a reinsurer will accept for automatic cession. Many companies vary the basic definition of a jumbo limit by specifying whether the allowable amount includes replacement of existing coverage. A jumbo limit on life reinsurance protects a reinsurer from excessive risk resulting from the accumulation of several policies on the same life. Only automatic reinsurance arrangements for life insurance or critical illness coverage are subject to jumbo limits.

Source: Adapted from Susan Conant and Miriam A. Orsina, *Principles of Reinsurance* [Atlanta: LOMA (Life Office Management Association, Inc.), © 2006], 42. Used with permission; all rights reserved.

The following table summarizes the typical options or requirements for the direct writer and the reinsurer under the various cession arrangements we have discussed:

	Direct Writer	Reinsurer
Automatic	Must cede all qualifying cases	Must assume all qualifying cases Does not perform any underwriting evaluation before its assumption of risk
Facultative	Has the option to cede or retain qualifying cases	Has the option to reject cases Performs an underwriting evaluation before accepting a risk
Fac-Ob	Has the option to cede or retain qualifying cases	Must assume all qualifying cases if financial capacity is available May reject qualifying cases if financial capacity is not available

Risk-Sharing Arrangements

In addition to the various cession arrangements just described, reinsurance arrangements also can vary depending on how the sharing of risk is structured between the direct writer and the reinsurer. Reinsurance arrangements generally can be classified as either nonproportional or proportional, depending on the risk-sharing structure of the arrangement.

Nonproportional Reinsurance and Proportional Reinsurance

Nonproportional reinsurance is a type of reinsurance in which neither the reinsurer nor the direct writer knows in advance what share of a risk the reinsurer ultimately will assume. Under nonproportional reinsurance, the reinsurer's liability depends on the actual claims the direct writer pays. Thus, the amount of the reinsurer's liability is not precisely known in advance.

Although nonproportional reinsurance typically is used when reinsuring non-life types of insurance coverage, one common type of nonproportional reinsurance that can apply to life insurance coverage is catastrophe coverage. *Catastrophe coverage*, commonly known as *cat cover*, is a type of nonproportional reinsurance designed to partially protect direct writers from (1) a single catastrophic event resulting in multiple claims or (2) a total amount of claims within a specified period that exceeds a stated amount. Cat cover, therefore, usually requires the reinsurer to reimburse the direct writer for claims when the direct writer's total claims exceed a stated amount, subject to (1) a minimum number of qualified claims or minimum amount of claim benefits and (2) a maximum total reinsurance payout. Catastrophe coverage can be used for life insurance, medical expense insurance, disability income insurance, critical illness insurance, and long-term care insurance. Examples of such single catastrophic events involving multiple life claims are building fires, earthquakes, volcanic eruptions, commercial airplane crashes, environmental accidents, epidemics, and tsunamis.

Proportional reinsurance is a type of reinsurance under which the direct writer and reinsurer agree to share premiums and claim obligations according to a specified amount or percentage. A key characteristic of proportional reinsurance is that the reinsurer's portion of the premiums and claim liability is known in advance of any claims. In proportional business, the direct writer and reinsurer share the policy reserve proportionately. The proportional arrangement may express the reinsurer's share of the claim risk and the direct writer's share of premiums as a percentage or ratio of the face amount of life insurance issued.

For example, a proportional reinsurance agreement states that the reinsurer will accept the risk for 60 percent of the face amount of each of the direct writer's whole life claims. The direct writer, then, will accept the risk for 40 percent of the face amount of each whole life claim. For a claim on a $1 million policy, we can calculate the direct writer's and reinsurer's proportionate claim responsibilities, as follows:

	Proportionate Share	×	Face Amount	=	Liability
Direct Writer	0.40	×	$1,000,000	=	$400,000
Reinsurer	0.60	×	$1,000,000	=	$600,000

A proportional reinsurance arrangement generally specifies a method for determining the amount of risk, or the cession amount, the direct writer will cede.

Cession Amounts in Proportional Reinsurance

Two common methods for determining the cession amount of proportional reinsurance are excess-of-retention arrangements and quota share arrangements.

Excess-of-Retention Arrangements

An *excess-of-retention arrangement* is a method for assigning risk in proportional reinsurance in which the direct writer establishes a monetary amount as its retention limit and the reinsurer agrees to assume monetary amounts greater than the direct writer's specified retention limit, up to the reinsurer's automatic binding limit. The excess-of-retention arrangement is used with automatic reinsurance cessions, as shown in the following example.

Company	Retention Limit and Excess of Retention on $1.5 million policy
Ranier	$ 500,000 retention limit
Yang Re	$ 1,000,000 excess of retention

The *excess of retention* is the monetary amount of risk remaining after the direct writer's retention limit is subtracted from the net amount at risk on a case. Generally, the *net amount at risk (NAR)* is the difference between the face amount of a life insurance policy—other than a universal life policy—and the policy reserve at the end of any given policy year. Thus, the excess of retention for a case is the amount of risk the direct writer cedes and the reinsurer assumes. Suppose the face amount is $100,000 and the NAR is $90,000 for a particular life insurance policy. If the direct writer's retention limit for this type of policy is $25,000, then the direct writer's excess of retention for the case is $65,000, as follows:

Direct Writer's Net Amount at Risk	–	Direct Writer's Retention Limit	=	Direct Writer's Excess of Retention
$90,000	–	$25,000	=	$65,000

Quota Share Arrangements

A *quota share arrangement* is a method for assigning risk in proportional reinsurance in which the direct writer retains a specified amount or percentage of the risk on a case and cedes the remaining risk to one or more reinsurers. Quota share arrangements usually are used with automatic cessions, but they can be used with facultative cessions. Two types of quota share arrangements are excess quota share and the more popular first-dollar quota share.

An *excess quota share arrangement* is a method for assigning risk in proportional reinsurance in which the direct writer keeps its full retention limit and cedes the remaining risk to two or more reinsurers on a percentage basis. For example, the Redfern Insurance Company has a $200,000 retention limit on its whole life insurance policies. Redfern has reinsurance agreements with excess quota share arrangements on these products. The Seascape Reinsurance Company agrees to assume 40 percent of specified risks in excess of Redfern's retention limit and the Bountiful Reinsurance Company agrees to assume 60 percent of specified risks in excess of Redfern's retention limit. The following table shows the amount of excess quota share arrangement for a whole life insurance policy with a face amount of $500,000.

Redfern	Seascape Re	Bountiful Re
$200,000 retention limit $300,000 ceded to reinsurers	$120,000 (0.40 × $300,000) assumed	$180,000 (0.60 × $300,000) assumed

A *first-dollar quota share (FDQS) arrangement* is a method for assigning risk in proportional reinsurance in which the direct writer retains a stated percentage of the risk for each policy in a given block of business, up to its retention limit, and cedes the remaining risk to one or more reinsurers. In FDQS arrangements, the direct writer generally cedes coverage from the "first dollar" on all policies. However, some FDQS arrangements have a minimum cession requirement. The FDQS arrangement usually states a maximum monetary amount of risk that the reinsurer is willing to accept.

For example, the Terranova Insurance Company has a FDQS arrangement with the Sanibella Reinsurance Company and the Mainline Reinsurance Company. In this arrangement, Terranova agrees to retain 20 percent of each risk (thus ceding 80 percent of each risk), Sanibella Re agrees to assume 35 percent of each risk, and Mainline Re agrees to assume 45 percent of each risk. The following table shows the division of risk among the three companies for a policy with a face amount of $500,000.

Terranova	Sanibella Re	Mainline Re
$100,000 (0.20 × $500,000) retention limit $400,000 ceded to reinsurers	$175,000 (0.35 × $500,000) assumed	$225,000 (0.45 × $500,000) assumed

Compared to excess quota share arrangements, FDQS arrangements give the reinsurer greater participation in the direct writer's risks. Under FDQS, the direct writer cedes a fixed percentage—such as 80 percent in the above example—of the risk on each policy, assuming that the resulting amount meets any minimum cession requirements in the reinsurance arrangement as well as any maximum monetary amount or risk that the reinsurer is willing to accept.

Plans of Reinsurance

We've described variations in cession arrangements (automatic, facultative, and fac-ob) and variations in risk-sharing structures (excess-of-retention and quota share arrangements). Now we'll examine several standard plans of reinsurance and variations of those standard plans typically offered by reinsurers. Coinsurance, funds withheld coinsurance (a type of coinsurance), and modified coinsurances (modco) are plans of proportional reinsurance. Industry opinion is divided as to whether yearly renewable term (YRT) reinsurance is a plan of proportional reinsurance.

Coinsurance

Coinsurance is a plan of proportional reinsurance under which the direct writer and reinsurer proportionately share monetary responsibility for almost every aspect of each policy covered under the arrangement. The basic coinsurance agreement may specify each party's proportion of the monetary responsibility as either (1) a percentage of risk, such as 45 percent, or (2) a monetary amount of risk, such as the first $50,000 of a risk. Coinsurance transfers to the reinsurer the surplus strain of the ceded risk of newly issued policies.

Both parties—the direct writer and the reinsurer—are responsible for holding their share of the premiums and the various obligations of the primary coverage, including any death benefit, other policy benefits, nonforfeiture values, and policy reserves. The reinsurer, however, very rarely shares in the direct writer's responsibility for the amounts of outstanding policy loans. In addition, the reinsurer proportionately shares in the direct writer's expenses—for commissions, administration, and sometimes premium taxes—in the form of a specific type of allowance called a *coinsurance allowance*. The reinsurer receives a proportionate share of the direct writer's gross premiums, less the coinsurance allowance withheld by the direct writer.

Funds withheld coinsurance is a variation on basic coinsurance and, thus, is similar to basic coinsurance in many ways. *Funds withheld coinsurance* is a plan of proportional reinsurance under which the direct writer and reinsurer proportionately share responsibility for almost all aspects of a reinsured policy, but the direct writer retains the initial gross reinsurance premium and the reinsurer retains the initial coinsurance allowance. This plan allows the direct writer and reinsurer to limit cash flows between them over the life of the reinsurance arrangement. Both parties maintain accounting records and, thus, track changes in the net balance of the withheld funds. The net balance is the difference between the amounts the direct writer and the reinsurer owe each other.

Modified Coinsurance

Modified coinsurance (modco) is a plan of proportional reinsurance under which the direct writer and reinsurer share proportionately in the policy reserve obligation, the direct writer's gross premiums, and the risks of loss from expenses for death, surrender, or other benefits or from lapse; however, the direct writer holds the entire reserve for each reinsured policy. The reinsurer deposits its proportionate share of the policy reserves with the direct writer and the direct writer pays the reinsurer its share of interest earnings on the reserves. Modco requires a periodic adjustment to the policy reserves to reconcile changes in the reserve amount due to earnings or losses on the assets underlying the reserves.

For any given period, the value of a modco reserve adjustment may be positive or negative. A positive modco reserve adjustment value indicates that the reinsurer owes funds to the direct writer. A negative modco reserve adjustment value indicates that the direct writer owes funds to the reinsurer. When a claim is made on a policy, the reinsurer reimburses the direct writer for the benefit on the reinsured portion of the policy, minus the amount of the reinsurer's reserve deposit for that policy. Modco typically is used for cash value life insurance and annuity products. It is particularly appropriate for interest-sensitive products such as variable life insurance and variable annuities.

For all coinsurance plans, the direct writer and the reinsurer have responsibility for their portion of the policy reserves. However, in funds withheld coinsurance and modified coinsurance, the direct writer holds the reserves, invests the corresponding assets, and credits the reinsurer's reserve fund with the reinsurer's portion of the investment earnings.

Yearly Renewable Term Reinsurance

Yearly renewable term reinsurance, commonly known as *YRT reinsurance*, is a plan of reinsurance that is used to reinsure only the mortality portion of a life insurance risk. For YRT reinsurance, the direct writer pays a one-year term insurance premium to the reinsurer on the anniversary date of each reinsured policy. The direct writer remains responsible for paying policy dividends and cash values and for holding most reserves on the reinsured business. Thus, YRT reinsurance does not significantly reduce the direct writer's surplus strain.

Under YRT reinsurance, the reinsurance liability amount equals the net amount at risk (NAR) on the reinsured portion of a policy. For a term life insurance policy, the NAR is equal to the death benefit. The NAR for a cash value life insurance policy is calculated as

$$\text{Policy's Death Benefit} - \text{Cash Value} = \text{Cash Value Life Insurance Policy's NAR}$$

For cash value life insurance, reinsurers often use the amount of policy reserves as a convenient estimate for the policy's cash value. Thus, insurers can obtain a reasonable estimate for the net amount at risk by using the following formula:

$$\text{Policy's Death Benefit} - \text{Policy Reserves} = \text{Cash Value Life Insurance Policy's NAR}$$

Because the reserves and cash value on a cash value policy typically increase over time, the NAR, and thus the amount of the YRT reinsurance coverage a direct writer needs, typically decrease each policy year. When a whole life insurance policy reaches maturity, the direct writer's accumulated reserves equal the entire mortality risk, leaving no NAR, and the YRT reinsurance terminates.

Under proportional reinsurance, the direct writer and the reinsurer share premiums, claim obligations, and policy reserves according to a specified amount or percentage. Under YRT reinsurance, the direct writer cedes only the life insurance policy's mortality risk to the reinsurer. The YRT mortality cost—and thus, the reinsurance premium—for a cash value life insurance policy increases every year because the mortality risk increases every year as the insured ages. For

YRT reinsurance arrangements, these important elements change in the following directions as time passes:

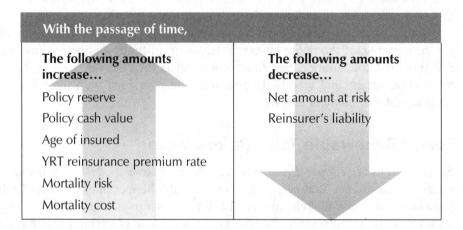

With the passage of time,

The following amounts increase...	**The following amounts decrease...**
Policy reserve	Net amount at risk
Policy cash value	Reinsurer's liability
Age of insured	
YRT reinsurance premium rate	
Mortality risk	
Mortality cost	

Reinsurance Agreements

A *reinsurance agreement*, also historically called a *reinsurance treaty*, documents the terms of the business to be conducted, including the nature of the risk transfer, reinsurance administration procedures, information exchanges, and the rights and duties of each party under the reinsurance arrangement. A reinsurance agreement is a contract that is binding on the parties to the agreement.

An indemnity reinsurance agreement addresses many different aspects of the business conducted between the reinsurance parties during the effective period of the agreement and even after the termination of the agreement. Although oral reinsurance agreements can be valid and binding on the parties, the parties to a reinsurance agreement typically create a written document that specifies the terms of the arrangement. The principal reason for having a written reinsurance agreement is to document the terms of the arrangement. Because reinsurance may remain in effect for many years, a written agreement allows not only the current but also the next generation of reinsurance analysts to understand how to handle a reinsured policy.

Ideally, the reinsurance partners establish a written reinsurance agreement before any reinsurance cessions occur under the reinsurance agreement. In practice, however, the formal agreement can take effect before, during, or after the initial transfer of risk from the direct writer to the reinsurer.

Either the direct writer or reinsurer may develop the written reinsurance agreement. The party that does not draft the agreement must review and approve the document. Some jurisdictions require the reinsurance parties to file reinsurance agreements with insurance regulators before implementing the agreements. Most jurisdictions do not require approval of reinsurance agreements by insurance regulators.

Because a direct writer and a reinsurer negotiate each agreement to meet their specific needs, no two reinsurance agreements are exactly alike. Reinsurance agreements can vary greatly in terms of length, level of detail, and the scope of risks covered. However, reinsurance agreements have become more detailed and more carefully crafted over time. This is the natural effect of a more litigious society and more complex products. A reinsurance agreement was once known as a "Gentleman's Agreement" but no longer.

Regardless of the amount of detail expressed in an agreement, every reinsurance agreement contains certain provisions that protect the interests of the parties. These provisions have become increasingly standardized as a result of guidelines generated by the National Association of Insurance Commissioners (NAIC) and the Society of Actuaries. Provisions protect the interests of the parties to the agreement and they generally define the reinsurance coverage, describe the administration procedures, and define the rates and payments associated with the agreement.

Defining the Reinsurance Coverage

Reinsurance agreement provisions that define the reinsurance coverage describe the (1) scope of the agreement, (2) termination of the agreement, and (3) specific insurance to be ceded and the reinsurance coverage to be provided.

Scope of the Agreement

The following table shows the provisions that describe the scope of the reinsurance agreement, including the parties to the agreement provision, the entire agreement provision, the duration of the agreement provision, and the recapture provision.

Parties to the agreement provision	Typically states that the reinsurance agreement exists solely between the direct writer and the reinsurer. The reinsurance agreement does not create any legal relationship between the reinsurer and the insured, the policyowner, any beneficiary, any assignee, or any party other than the direct writer.
Entire agreement provision	States that the written agreement represents the whole agreement between the parties, and that they have no further agreement than that stated in the written document. Only the reinsurance arrangements that are specifically stated in the written document and its amendments are binding on the parties. In other words, arrangements that are not stated in the written document, even though they may be typical in the industry, are not binding on the parties.
Duration of the agreement provision	Addresses when the reinsurance agreement becomes effective and when it ends. Most reinsurance agreements provide that the agreement takes effect on an agreed-upon date, known as the agreement effective date. Each reinsurance agreement also specifies the **reinsurance effective date**, which is the date on which the reinsurance coverage for a specific risk takes effect. Most agreements specify that, when the agreement has taken effect, it continues to be effective for an unlimited period of time unless canceled by one or both parties.

Recapture provision	Addresses the terms under which a direct writer can recapture some or all of its reinsured risk. *Recapture* is the process by which a direct writer takes back some or all ceded business from a reinsurer. The reinsurance agreement generally permits the direct writer to increase its retention limit. If a direct writer chooses to increase its retention limits, the agreement usually allows the company to recapture some of the reinsured risk so that the company retains full retention on the reinsured policies. Generally, the agreement does not allow the direct writer to cede the recaptured business to another reinsurer.

Termination of the Reinsurance Agreement

The section of the reinsurance agreement that discusses termination of the agreement identifies the terms and conditions under which the agreement may end, describes the procedures for notification of termination, and describes the handling of the reinsurance in force under the agreement at the time of termination. Most reinsurance agreements—particularly those that cover life insurance—stay in effect indefinitely until the agreement is canceled by one or both parties to the contract.

The complete cancellation of a reinsurance agreement for both new business and in-force business is called a *termination*. The parties mutually can agree to cancel the agreement at any time. If one of the parties to a reinsurance agreement notifies the other party of a *termination for new business*, the parties no longer cede or assume new business under that agreement, but reinsurance coverage continues on business already in place. Generally, an in-force life insurance policy remains reinsured until the policy terminates due to lapse, surrender, payment of a claim, or—for term insurance—until the term of coverage has ended.

Reinsurance Coverages

A reinsurance agreement describes the plans of insurance to be reinsured and the reinsurance coverage to be provided. This information includes

- The reinsurance cession arrangement(s)—for example, automatic, facultative, or automatic and facultative

- The method for determining the amount of risk the direct writer will cede—for example, excess of retention or a quota share arrangement

- The type of reinsurance plan—for example, YRT or coinsurance

Generally, an automatic reinsurance agreement is more specific and restrictive than is a facultative agreement. Because the reinsurer must accept policies that are automatically reinsured, an automatic reinsurance agreement specifies the conditions under which the direct writer can submit a risk to the reinsurer. For example, the agreement may specify that only "individual life insurance policies issued to standard or preferred risks" may be submitted for automatic reinsurance. In contrast, a facultative reinsurance agreement can contain more general parameters because the reinsurer has the opportunity to underwrite each policy individually before accepting or declining each risk.

An automatic reinsurance agreement specifies the lower and upper issue ages and the acceptable risk level for each type of coverage. For example, a reinsurance agreement for term life insurance may state that no one under the age of 6 or above the age of 70 and no one with a mortality rate greater than a specified level can be reinsured under the agreement.

The reinsurance agreement specifies other elements of the reinsurance coverage, such as

- The method to be used to calculate the reinsured policy's net amount at risk (NAR)

- The direct writer's retention limits

- The reinsurer's binding limits, including jumbo limits

- A minimum cession (for most automatic reinsurance agreements)

Reinsurance Administration Procedures

Reinsurance agreements also contain provisions that govern the administration procedures for reinsured business. The following sections describe common administration provisions. Legislation in many countries requires certain forms of financial reporting and well-documented procedures.

Procedures for Beginning Reinsurance Coverage

Reinsurance agreements generally include a provision describing the procedures that the direct writer should use to notify the reinsurer of automatic or fac-ob reinsurance liability or to request facultative reinsurance. The provision specifies information the direct writer must send to the reinsurer and the form this information should take. The reinsurance parties typically use one of several methods to administer their reinsurance records.

Reporting Requirements

The reinsurance agreement specifies the method of reinsurance record administration and a number of requirements concerning reports, such as the types of periodic reports to be submitted, the party responsible for submitting the reports, the timing for each report, and the consequences of submitting reports late. The reports serve as a basis for reinsurance premium and allowance payments, retention management, and financial reporting. The reports required depend on the method of record administration specified in the agreement and the requirements of the financial statements that the companies must file with regulatory authorities.

Records Inspection

The *records inspection provision* states the rights of each party to inspect the other party's records and documents relating to the reinsurance provided under the agreement. This provision typically limits the right of record inspection by allowing inspection at any reasonable time for any reasonable purpose and at the respective parties' offices during normal business hours.

Changes to Reinsurance Coverage

Because reinsurance arrangements may remain in force for years, the reinsurance agreement provides specific instructions for handling changes to reinsured policies. Some of these changes include continuations, conversions, reinstatements, and terminations of reinsured policies. The following table shows typical provisions that address changes in reinsurance coverage.

Continuation provision	Addresses which reinsurer(s) should provide the reinsurance, the amount of reinsurance, and the effective date of reinsurance for continued policies. A **continuation** of an insurance policy occurs either when (1) the provisions of an in-force policy are significantly modified or (2) a policy replaces an existing policy from the same direct writer, but differs from a new insurance policy in a specific way. The latter condition occurs when the new policy is not subject to the direct writer's new business underwriting requirements, the direct writer does not pay full first-year commissions to the insurance producer, or the policy does not introduce a new suicide exclusion period or a new contestable period.
Conversion provision	Concerns a new policy that is issued on the basis of the policyowner's contractual right to change the policy form, such as the right to convert a term policy to a whole life policy. In Chapter 3, we defined this provision in the context of a group insurance policy. The conversion provision in a reinsurance agreement typically states (1) that the direct writer must continue the reinsurance on converted policies with the original reinsurer unless the reinsurer releases its right to reinsure the policies and (2) any conditions under which the direct writer or the reinsurer can cancel the reinsurance on conversions. Generally, conversions are considered a less desirable risk for the reinsurer. Thus, tracking conversions is essential if a direct writer changes reinsurers for new business.
Reinstatement provision	Typically specifies that when a reinsured policy lapses for nonpayment of premium, the reinsurance can be reinstated if certain conditions regarding the timing of the request for reinstatement and the payment of reinsurance premiums due are met.
Termination of reinsurance	Describes the process by which a direct writer cancels the reinsurance covering a policy issued by the company. A termination of reinsurance on a life insurance policy can occur because a reinsured policy expires, matures, is surrendered, lapses due to nonpayment of premiums, or because the insured dies. The reinsurance agreement typically states that the reinsurer's liability ends when the reinsured policy is no longer in effect.

An automatic reinsurance agreement addresses most of these changes. As a result, the direct writer is allowed to make changes to a reinsured policy without obtaining the reinsurer's consent, as long as the changes fall within the parameters of the agreement. Under facultative reinsurance agreements, however, the direct writer is required to obtain prior approval from the reinsurer before making policy changes that affect coverage or underwriting ratings.

Increasing and reducing death benefits are other changes that can be made to reinsurance coverage. Increases in death benefit amounts can be contractual—that is, payable in accordance with the terms of a life insurance policy—or noncontractual—that is, requested by the policyowner, although not required under the terms of the policy.

Under automatic reinsurance, the reinsurer generally must accept contractual increases up to the amount of the reinsurer's automatic binding limits. Noncontractual increases generally require new evidence of insurability. The reinsurance agreement typically requires the reinsurance partners to handle the increased amount like new business, and all the requirements for reinsuring new business apply.

When a life insurance policyowner reduces a reinsured policy's face amount or exercises a nonforfeiture option that decreases the value of the policy, the direct writer must reduce the reinsurance on that policy or on other policies covering the insured life, according to the provisions of the applicable reinsurance agreement. A *reduction of reinsurance* is the process of reducing the amount of reinsurance covering an insurance policy.

Claims

A *claim provision* typically states the terms and conditions of the reinsurer's liability for claims submitted under reinsured policies. This provision also describes how the reinsurance parties will handle claim expenses in various situations and discusses contests of claim denials. For life reinsurance, the reinsurance claim provision typically states that, within a specified time period after receiving notice that the direct writer has paid a death claim under a reinsured policy, the reinsurer will pay the reinsurance benefits in a lump sum, even if the reinsured policy calls for the benefit to be paid to the beneficiary in installments. However, for disability income reinsurance or long-term care reinsurance, the reinsurer periodically disburses reinsurance benefit payments to the direct writer throughout the benefit payment period in proportion to the benefit amounts paid by the direct writer.

Under some circumstances, a facultative reinsurance agreement requires the direct writer to obtain an opinion from the reinsurer before settling a claim, or else the reinsurer may not be bound to participate in paying the claim. The claim provision in an automatic or fac-ob reinsurance agreement typically states that the direct writer has the authority to make decisions on claims and that the reinsurer is bound by the direct writer's decisions. However, an automatic reinsurance agreement also usually requires the direct writer to consult with the reinsurer before settling a claim in some or all of the following situations:

■ A claim occurs during the reinsured life insurance policy's contestable period

■ The reinsurer has assumed more than 50 percent of the risk covered by a reinsured policy

■ The total amount of a claim or the amount of risk ceded to the reinsurer exceeds the limits stated in the reinsurance agreement

■ The direct writer has retained less than its published retention limit on a reinsured policy

■ A claim involves an insured's death in a foreign country

■ The direct writer suspects that a claim involves fraud, which is an act by which someone intentionally deceives another party and induces that other party to part with something of value

The reinsurance agreement claim provision usually requires the direct writer to provide the reinsurer the opportunity to review the claim file of any claim that the direct writer plans to deny. This provision also addresses the rights and responsibilities of the direct writer and the reinsurer regarding claim contests. A *contest* of an insurance claim is a court action to determine the validity of the claim. A claim contest generally occurs when an insurer denies liability to pay a claim, and the beneficiary or policyowner files a lawsuit seeking to force the insurer to pay the claim.

Rescissions

The *rescission provision* describes the notification and administrative procedures required when a direct writer rescinds a reinsured policy. This provision generally requires the direct writer to make decisions regarding rescission in good faith and to inform the reinsurer in a timely manner of any rescission of a reinsured policy. *Good faith* refers to a party's honesty of intention and avoidance of attempts to deceive or take unfair advantage of another party to an agreement.

Potential Problems between a Direct Writer and a Reinsurer

The parties to a reinsurance agreement anticipate the potential for occasional problems by stating in the reinsurance agreement the procedures the parties agree to use to resolve such problems. These procedures typically address how the reinsurance agreement will be administered in case errors and omissions, arbitration, or insolvency arise during administration of the agreement.

Errors and Omissions

Unintentional errors or omissions of information may occur during the administration of a reinsurance agreement. The *errors and omissions provision* of a reinsurance agreement states that, if either party to the agreement fails to comply with the terms of the agreement through unintentional administrative mistake or clerical error, then both parties will be restored to the position they would have occupied if the mistake or error had not occurred. Generally, each party to the agreement is required to report errors as soon as they are discovered. Unintentional administrative errors and omissions will not affect the rights and obligations established by the agreement as long as both parties work to handle errors and omissions appropriately.

Arbitration

Reinsurance agreements usually include an *arbitration provision*, which requires the reinsurance parties to submit disputes that they cannot resolve through negotiation to an arbitration panel rather than to a court of law. *Arbitration* is a method of dispute resolution in which impartial third parties—known as *arbitrators*—evaluate the facts in dispute and render a decision that usually is binding on the parties to the dispute. The reinsurance agreement describes the arbitration process to be used if a dispute arises that the parties to the agreement cannot resolve to their mutual satisfaction.

Insolvency

The insolvency of either party to a reinsurance agreement is unlikely. However, reinsurance agreements typically include an *insolvency provision* that describes the rights and responsibilities of the direct writer and the reinsurer in the event that either party becomes insolvent. The provision also may specify circumstances under which a party to the agreement will be deemed insolvent and the procedures that will be followed if either party becomes unable to meet its financial obligations on time.

Under a typical insolvency provision, if the direct writer becomes insolvent, the reinsurer becomes obligated to pay any amounts owed on reinsured policies immediately upon receiving verification that such amounts are rightfully due. Thus, the reinsurer must pay its reinsurance liability in full, even if the direct writer has failed to pay all or a portion of any claim. The reinsurer pays the amounts due into the trust held by the direct writer's receiver. In an insurance context, a *receiver* is an individual who is appointed by a court to hold and administer an insolvent insurer's assets and liabilities.

Reinsurance Rates and Payments

The reinsurance agreement also describes the calculation of reinsurance premiums, allowances, and other payments and specifies when such payments are due. Financial provisions are designed to ensure the accuracy and timeliness of financial exchanges between a direct writer and a reinsurer. Among the elements addressed by financial provisions are reinsurance premiums, allowances, policy cash values, policy dividends, experience refunds, and premium tax refunds.

Key Terms

reinsurance arrangement
block of business
case
direct writer
reinsurer
retrocessionaire
insolvency
solvency laws
assumption reinsurance
assumption certificate
indemnity reinsurance
traditional indemnity reinsurance
reinsurance premium
policy reserves
allowance
acquisition expenses
maintenance expenses
premium taxes
underwriting capacity
retention limit
financial capacity
surplus
surplus strain
surplus relief
cession
cession arrangement
automatic reinsurance
facultative reinsurance
facultative-obligatory (fac-ob)
   reinsurance
automatic binding limit
minimum cession
jumbo limit
nonproportional reinsurance
catastrophe coverage
proportional reinsurance
excess-of-retention arrangement

excess of retention
net amount at risk (NAR)
quota share arrangement
excess quota share arrangement
first-dollar quota share (FDQS) arrangement
coinsurance
coinsurance allowance
funds withheld coinsurance
modified coinsurance (modco)
yearly renewable term (YRT) reinsurance
reinsurance agreement
parties to the agreement provision
entire agreement provision
duration of the agreement provision
reinsurance effective date
recapture provision
recapture
termination
termination for new business
records inspection provision
continuation provision
continuation
reinstatement provision
termination of reinsurance
reduction of reinsurance
claim provision
contest
rescission provision
good faith
errors and omissions provisions
arbitration provision
arbitration
arbitrators
insolvency provision
receiver

Endnote

1. Portions of this chapter are adapted from Susan Conant and Miriam Orsina, *Principles of Reinsurance* [Atlanta: LOMA (Life Office Management Association, Inc.), © 2006], pp. 5, 9–13, 41–49, 69–104, 109–125, 148–153, 179–225, 232, 235–245. Used with permission; all rights reserved.

Chapter 11

Reinsurance Administration

Objectives:

After studying this chapter, you should be able to

- Explain the role of the reinsurance analyst as well as staff in other functional areas of an insurance company in reinsurance administration

- Explain the preplacement of reinsurance and the process for reserving capacity for requested coverage

- Describe the five types of reinsurance reports that are used for administering in-force business

- Describe the procedures followed to administer changes in reinsurance coverage, reinsurance premiums and other amounts included on a billing statement, and terminations of reinsurance

- Describe the steps a reinsurer takes to examine, approve, and settle a request from a direct writer for claim payment reimbursement

- Describe how reinsurance operations are audited

Outline

Reinsurance Staffing and Systems
- Reinsurance Analysts
- Other Staff Involved in Reinsurance Activities
- Reinsurance Information Systems

Administering New Business
- Preplacement of Reinsurance
- Placement of Reinsurance
- Administering In-Force Business
- Administering Terminations of Reinsurance

Administering Claims under Reinsured Policies
- Establishing the Claim File
- Verifying Claim-Related Information
- Approving the Claim Liability
- Settling the Claim Liability
- Notifying Retrocessionaires of a Claim Liability

Auditing Reinsurance Operations
- Internal Audits
- External Audits by the Reinsurer

From the time a direct writer decides to seek reinsurance to the time that all reinsurance coverage under a reinsurance agreement is ended, employees of the direct writer and the reinsurer perform a wide variety of reinsurance-related activities. These activities include

- Selecting a reinsurance partner

- Negotiating a reinsurance agreement

- Ceding or assuming specific risks

- Administering in-force reinsurance

- Terminating the reinsurance agreement

Many of these activities can be classified as *reinsurance administration*, which includes all of the day-to-day activities conducted by the direct writer and the reinsurer to process and manage each risk that the direct writer cedes automatically or submits for facultative or facultative-obligatory consideration.[1] Under some reinsurance agreements, the direct writer accepts primary responsibility for administration. Under other agreements, the reinsurer accepts primary responsibility or the reinsurance parties share administrative duties. Generally, the company that is primarily responsible for administering the reinsurance carries out the following tasks:

- Determining the amount of reinsurance coverage

- Interpreting and complying with the requirements of existing reinsurance agreements

- Handling reinsurance premiums, billing, and payments

- Administering the effects of policy changes and policy terminations on reinsurance coverage

- Maintaining comprehensive records and developing reports

- Ensuring quality control and timeliness of all reinsurance administration activities

- Administering reinsurance agreement terminations

Reinsurance Staffing and Systems

Most reinsurance companies have designated functional areas that handle reinsurance administration activities. However, the organization of reinsurance operations varies greatly among direct writers. Some direct writers have a reinsurance department, but others do not. Direct writers without reinsurance departments typically assign reinsurance administration responsibilities to staff in underwriting, new business, or customer service. The unit or staff involved in reinsurance administration is typically called the *reinsurance administration unit.*

Reinsurance Analysts

The staff members who administer reinsurance may have various titles, such as reinsurance analyst, client administrator, and reinsurance specialist. In this text, we use the term ***reinsurance analyst*** to refer to any direct writer or reinsurer employee—except the person holding top leadership responsibility—who is involved in any phase of reinsurance administration. Reinsurance analysts are responsible for handling many of the activities required to conduct reinsurance transactions between reinsurers and direct writers. However, a reinsurance analyst's job duties may vary from company to company and depending on the reinsurance analyst's level of experience. Reinsurance analysts typically perform some or all of the activities listed in Figure 11.1.

Other Staff Involved in Reinsurance Activities

In addition to the reinsurance administration unit, other operational units of direct writers and reinsurers perform reinsurance-related activities. Functional areas typically involved in reinsurance-related activities include marketing, actuarial, underwriting, legal and compliance, accounting and treasury, auditing, and claim administration.

Some reinsurers use reinsurance marketing officers to help them establish reinsurance agreements. A ***reinsurance marketing officer***, also known as a *reinsurance account executive*, is a reinsurer's employee who sells reinsurance and coordinates the marketing process for the reinsurer. Such employees visit the home offices of current and potential clients—usually direct writing companies and other reinsurers. Reinsurance marketing officers gather information about new reinsurance arrangements that clients need or adjustments they would like to make to existing arrangements. Although not required to be licensed as insurance producers, most reinsurance marketing officers have extensive experience in the insurance industry. Typically, direct writers consider reinsurance marketing officers to be valuable sources of information and advice concerning developments in the insurance and reinsurance markets.

Actuaries who deal with reinsurance calculate appropriate pricing structures and policy reserves for reinsurance ceded and assumed. They also project future liabilities, such as amounts needed to pay future claims. In addition, actuaries

Figure 11.1. Typical Activities of Reinsurance Analysts

- Verifying that the correct reinsurance agreement is used to guide administration of a specified risk and set the effective date of reinsurance coverage

- Verifying that administrative activities for a given risk meet agreement requirements

- Administering changes to reinsurance agreements and the reinsurance coverage on individual policies or blocks of business

- Ensuring that facultative coverage complies with the reinsurer's underwriting decision

- Calculating the portion of each risk that is retained and the portion that is ceded

- Calculating and generating payments for funds due to or from the reinsurance parties

- Reconciling reinsurance billing statements and payments with company records

- Recordkeeping and preparing detailed reports regarding reinsured policies

- Meeting financial and regulatory reporting requirements

- Collaborating with other company staff and outside organizations as necessary

Source: Adapted from Susan Conant and Miriam A. Orsina, *Principles of Reinsurance* [Atlanta: LOMA (Life Office Management Association, Inc), © 2006] 162–163. Used with permission; all rights reserved.

assist direct writers and reinsurers in setting retention limits. Direct writers' actuaries also submit requests for proposals for new reinsurance agreements, evaluate the proposals that reinsurers submit, and—with input from employees working in other functional areas of the company—select reinsurers and negotiate reinsurance agreements. Actuaries also evaluate new reinsurance products and services.

Underwriting plays an important role in reinsurance for both direct writers and reinsurers. Evaluating the risks associated with policies to be reinsured is the central reinsurance-related task of underwriting. If changes occur to ceded or assumed risks, or if a direct writer wishes to modify ceded coverage, underwriters for either reinsurance partner may need to underwrite the changes in risk. Underwriters also may participate in negotiating reinsurance agreements.

The legal department typically helps develop and interpret reinsurance agreements and provides advice when reinsurance agreement negotiations become particularly complex. Many reinsurers and retrocessionaires have separate departments that develop and negotiate reinsurance agreements.

The compliance unit typically has the following responsibilities with respect to reinsurance:

■ Studies current and proposed laws to determine their effects on the insurer's reinsurance activities

■ Educates company employees about applicable regulatory requirements and company compliance policies for reinsurance activities

■ Monitors the conduct of employees and marketers affiliated with the insurer to verify that they are complying with applicable regulatory requirements and company compliance policies for reinsurance activities

■ Oversees internal control procedures for reinsurance activities

Reinsurance accounting involves (1) maintaining accurate records of the numerous financial transactions associated with administering reinsurance, such as the payment of reinsurance premiums to reinsurers and the receipt of reinsurance claim benefits from reinsurers, and (2) preparing financial statements and summarizing the company's reinsurance-related accounts. Each insurer's accounting unit provides advice to other units within the company about accounting requirements and assists those units in setting up procedures to fulfill the requirements. The accounting requirements may vary by the company's role in a particular reinsurance agreement—direct writer or reinsurer—and by the type of reinsurance arrangement.

During a reinsurance audit, auditors examine the company's reinsurance records and procedures and recommend improvements to those procedures. Reinsurance audits typically focus on underwriting, claim administration, and reinsurance administration.

The direct writer's claim analysts notify the reinsurance administration unit when they receive a claim under a reinsured policy. In some cases, a claim analyst can settle the claim without consulting the reinsurer for an opinion on the claim. The claim analyst then passes the information about the settlement on to a reinsurance analyst. The reinsurance analyst prepares reports of claims submitted and paid and sends the reports to the reinsurer to obtain reimbursement for all or a portion of each paid claim.

In certain circumstances such as anticipated denials of claims or large contestable claims, the direct writer must send the claim documentation to the reinsurer for a claim recommendation or opinion prior to settling a claim. The direct writer's claim analysts may contact the reinsurer's claim department for advice on any large or unusual claims. Reinsurers' claim analysts typically have experience with claims submitted under a wide variety of products and complex circumstances. For this reason, reinsurance claim analysts are good resources for the direct writer's claim analysts.

Reinsurance intermediaries, independent parties who are not employed by the direct writer or the reinsurer, can also be of assistance to the direct writer. Because they typically have significant contacts and much industry experience, reinsurance intermediaries can assist in resolving conflicts between the direct writer and the reinsurer. They also have access to reinsurance information systems that are of benefit to the direct writer.

Reinsurance Information Systems

Due to the current high volume of reinsurance business and the global nature of the reinsurance industry, computer-based information systems are essential to the efficient, effective administration of reinsurance activities. These activities, which demand rapid, accurate information in a form that can be collected, organized, corrected, modified, and communicated to those who need it, include

- Negotiating reinsurance agreements

- Requesting facultative coverage

- Sending underwriting advice and information

- Checking agreements for details of implementation

- Calculating the amount of risk to be ceded or assumed on a particular policy or a group of policies

- Calculating premium and claim amounts due and paid

- Producing innumerable reports on all sorts of administrative transactions

- Checking the quality of every aspect of reinsurance operations

Information system technologies—such as spreadsheet software and database management systems—allow reinsurance analysts to organize, analyze, and report information in almost any configuration desired. Reinsurers in particular need flexible, sophisticated systems to manipulate and report data related to a variety of products provided by a large number of direct writers, each of which has its own information system. Some companies also use computer systems for reinsurance decision making and strategic planning. For example, a reinsurance information system for automatic reinsurance can check the direct writer's retention and cede any excess of retention to the appropriate reinsurer.

Telecommunications plays a major role in reinsurance. Voicemail, e-mail, videoconferencing, and e-commerce all facilitate reinsurance partnerships and transactions. An important application of e-commerce for the reinsurance industry is *business-to-business (B2B) e-commerce*, which is the electronic transmission of data or information between organizations to perform or facilitate business transactions. B2B e-commerce between direct writers and reinsurers facilitates the negotiation and preparation of reinsurance agreements, the submission of underwriting information to reinsurers, the payment of reinsurance premiums, claim administration, and many other administrative procedures. Reinsurance transactions usually involve substantial amounts of money. For this reason, reinsurance transactions are typically processed electronically between the direct writer and the reinsurer.

Administering New Business

Reinsurance administration starts when the direct writer seeks reinsurance for a risk and lasts until the reinsurance is no longer in force. Reinsurance administration can involve three or all four of the following stages:

- Preplacement

- Placement

- In-force

- Termination

All reinsurance cases, regardless of the basis of submission, go through the stages of placement, in-force administration, and termination. Generally, preplacement is required only for facultative and fac-ob cases. Preplacement typically is not necessary for automatic cases because the direct writer and reinsurer have agreed in advance that the direct writer will place certain types of risk with the reinsurer. Thus, administration of automatic reinsurance generally begins at the placement stage.

Because reinsurance administration can vary greatly from one reinsurance agreement to another and from one company to another, the procedures described in this text may be somewhat different from the procedures that your company uses. As we've discussed, direct writers and reinsurers typically use automated administration systems to maintain their reinsurance records and telecommunications systems to exchange information.

Preplacement of Reinsurance

In the preplacement stage, the reinsurer reviews the direct writer's request for facultative or fac-ob reinsurance coverage and either offers to reinsure the risk or declines it. If the reinsurer decides to offer coverage, it establishes a reservation for the capacity needed to reinsure the case. *Preplacement* is the process by which a reinsurer (1) reviews a direct writer's request for coverage, (2) establishes appropriate records and reserves capacity for the case, and (3) as necessary, follows up on reservations for capacity that have been inactive for a specified period of time. *Reserved capacity* is the portion of a reinsurer's financial capacity that the reinsurer sets aside to fund its financial obligations under anticipated new business. Preplacement begins when a direct writer requests coverage, and it continues until either (1) the reinsurance coverage begins, (2) the reinsurer denies the direct writer's request for coverage, or (3) the direct writer withdraws its request for coverage.

Reviewing a Request for Coverage

Under facultative and fac-ob reinsurance agreements, the direct writer requests reinsurance coverage on a particular insured or group of insureds by sending the reinsurer a document known as a *request for coverage* or *facultative application*. Underwriters work closely with reinsurance analysts to identify facultative preplacements so that premiums and claims ultimately are paid promptly and accurately. For each preplaced case, the direct writer maintains a file that includes a copy of the request for coverage, reinsurers' requests for additional information on the case, and any offers received. The direct writer's reinsurance analyst responds to any questions or requests from reinsurers about the request for coverage. Upon receiving a request for coverage, with all of the required information, the reinsurer establishes the appropriate records and reserves the necessary capacity.

For facultative cases, sending a request for coverage to a reinsurer does not guarantee that the direct writer will cede the case to that reinsurer. The direct writer may be shopping—that is, submitting cases facultatively to several reinsurers. Direct writers sometimes shop cases to obtain the best reinsurance coverage for the most competitive price. Thus, sometimes a reinsurer reviews a case that the direct writer eventually places with another reinsurer.

Reinsurance agreements sometimes include time limits to protect a direct writer from the risk resulting from a reinsurer's failure to respond to a request for coverage in a timely manner. Recall that a fac-ob reinsurance agreement may state that, if the reinsurer does not respond to a request for coverage within a specified time limit, then the direct writer can assume that reinsurance on the policy will take effect.

Establishing Records and Reserving Capacity

A reinsurer establishes a case file for each submitted case. Reinsurers use status codes to enable them to track the current status of each case. The status code terminology varies from one reinsurer to another. Some of these status codes—*replaced*, *claim*, *paid*, and *terminated*—apply to in-force business rather than to new business. Figure 11.2 lists several common status codes.

For example, when a reinsurer makes an offer on a facultative case, the reinsurer codes the case's status as pending. If the direct writer subsequently sends a cession, the reinsurer updates the case's status to placed, showing that the reinsurance is in force. Alternatively, if the direct writer places the case with another reinsurer, the reinsurer changes the case file's status from pending to withdrawn.

In the process of establishing case files and reserving capacity, the reinsurer's employees perform the following activities, which may not always occur in the sequence shown:

- *Comparing the request for coverage to the reinsurance agreement.* The reinsurance analyst verifies that the direct writer and reinsurer have a reinsurance agreement for the type of coverage requested and that the agreement is in effect for new business. The reinsurance analyst then determines the types and amounts of reinsurance, if any, it is obligated to provide to the direct writer under that agreement and evaluates whether the request for coverage meets all of the agreement's requirements—for example, age limits and residency requirements for the proposed insured, the amount of coverage to be ceded, and the underwriting classification of the proposed insured—for risks to be reinsured.

- *Verifying the reinsurer's retention and financial capacity.* The reinsurer checks the amount of its current retention on the insured and its financial capacity. The reinsurer's reinsurance analyst then compares the amount of risk already retained on an insured to the retention limits listed in its retention schedules to determine the amount of additional risk it can accept on that insured and, if necessary, the amount of risk to cede to a retrocessionaire. Some reinsurance administration information systems automatically perform these calculations for the reinsurer.

Figure 11.2. Sample Status Codes

Reserved — The reinsurer has set aside reinsurance capacity.

Waiting — The reinsurer has requested additional information from the direct writer. Also known as *pending underwriting* or *outstanding requirements*.

Pending — The reinsurer has made an offer on a facultative case and is waiting for a response from the direct writer.

Placed — The direct writer has ceded the case to the reinsurer. Also known as *active*, *premium paying*, or *in-force*.

Declined — The reinsurer has declined the facultative case.

Withdrawn — The direct writer has not accepted the reinsurer's facultative offer. Also known as *not taken*.

Replaced — The policyowner has replaced the original policy with or converted the original policy to a different policy.

Claim — The direct writer has notified the reinsurer of a claim filed under the reinsured policy.

Paid — The reinsurer has paid a claim liability under the reinsured coverage.

Terminated — The policy has lapsed, been surrendered, or otherwise ceased being reinsured.

Source: Adapted from Jane Lightcap Brown and Jennifer W. Herrod, *Reinsurance Administration* [Atlanta: LOMA (Life Office Management Association, Inc.), © 2000], 167. Used with permission: all rights reserved.

■ *Assessing the risk.* The first step in assessing a reinsurance risk is determining whether the case requires an underwriting decision. Facultative cases typically require underwriting approval from the reinsurer. For each case submitted on a facultative basis, the reinsurer's underwriters evaluate the underwriting documents that the direct writer sends with the request for coverage and decide whether to make an offer, decline the case, or ask the direct writer to provide additional information. This evaluation and decision-making process usually is called *facultative reinsurance underwriting*.

The process for facultative reinsurance underwriting is very similar to primary underwriting, which is the underwriting process performed by a direct writer. However, reinsurance underwriters tend to work more often with unusual or problematic cases—such as those involving very large face amounts, complicated medical factors, unusual avocations, or celebrities—than do primary underwriters.

Also, in primary underwriting, the underwriter's judgment of an insurance producer's integrity traditionally has played a role in the underwriting decision. A reinsurance underwriter is concerned primarily with the quality of the direct writer's underwriting department and is less concerned with the producer.

Although reinsurance analysts do not assess reinsurance risks, a reinsurance analyst may be responsible for collecting the required underwriting documents and information, organizing those documents appropriately in a case file, and referring the file to the reinsurer's underwriters. Typically, a case file includes two types of underwriting-related documents: (1) documents received from the direct writer and (2) documents generated by the reinsurer's information systems.

Figure 11.3 provides a list of underwriting-related documents often included in an individual life reinsurance case file. A reinsurance case file for a group life insurance case includes information about the proposed insured group, such as the group's name, size, location, and industry; the scope of coverage; the basis for determining the amount of coverage for each individual; and each group member's sex, date of birth, and salary.

- *Arranging retrocession as needed.* Most reinsurers have established multiple automatic retrocession agreements with retrocessionaires or other reinsurers. If the amount that the reinsurer needs to retrocede exceeds the amount covered by the reinsurer's established automatic retrocession arrangements, the reinsurer generally has four options:

  1. Pursue retrocession coverage with a retrocessionaire with which the reinsurer currently does not have a reinsurance agreement
  2. Ask retrocessionaires to increase the amount they are willing to accept facultatively
  3. Accept a smaller amount of the risk and notify the direct writer to seek additional reinsurance
  4. Decline to reinsure the case (for facultative and fac-ob cases only)

- *Placing the reservation of capacity.* If the reinsurer offers to reinsure the case, the reinsurer codes the status of the file as reserved. This reserved status holds the required capacity for a specified period of time, such as 30 days. The reinsurer assigns the reservation a ***date of expiry***—the date on which the reinsurer will cancel the reservation of reinsurance capacity if the reinsurer does not receive a cession or other placement information from the direct writer. Typically, the date of expiry falls between 90 and 120 days after the date the reservation was made.

Following Up on Reserved Capacity

A direct writer's reinsurance administration system may track the capacity the company has reserved with reinsurers and contact each reinsurer as appropriate regarding potential offers, cessions, delays in processing cases, or cancellations of reserved capacity. Reinsurers also periodically check for reservations that are near their dates of expiry. Follow-up on reserved capacity helps the reinsurer avoid maintaining reserved capacity that the direct writer does not need.

Most reinsurer's administration systems generate lists of outstanding cases for which (1) the date of expiry is near and (2) the direct writer has not sent a cession, a drop notice, or an extension request. A ***drop notice***, or *close notice*, is a written notification from a direct writer to a reinsurer stating that the direct writer no

Figure 11.3. Underwriting-Related Documents Often Included in a Case File

Documents Provided by the Direct Writer

- Cover page containing information about the insured and the reinsurance applied for, including the insured's name, residence, date of birth, underwriting classification, and amount of reinsurance

- Letter from the direct writer to the reinsurer

- Insurance application

- Nonmedical supplement

- Medical questionnaires, such as questionnaires for asthma and diabetes

- Personal questionnaires, such as questionnaires for aviation and scuba diving

- Medical or paramedical report

- Laboratory and x-ray reports

- Physician and hospital reports

- Results of an electrocardiogram

- Inspection report

- Statements describing the insured's financial position

- Motor vehicle records/driving history

- Correspondence with the proposed insured, applicant, producer, medical personnel, and others with relevant information

- Documentation that the direct writer has confirmed that the insurance applicant, policyowner, insured, and beneficiary are not included on any applicable government lists of suspected terrorists

Documents Generated by the Reinsurer

- Reinsurer's underwriting worksheet

- Documentation of the retention check

- Status code documentation

- The underwriting decision sent to the direct writer and worksheets compiled by reinsurance analysts

- Documentation that the reinsurer has confirmed that the insurance applicant, policyowner, insured, and beneficiary are not included on any applicable government lists of suspected terrorists

Source: Adapted from Jane Lightcap Brown and Jennifer W. Herrod, *Reinsurance Administration* [Atlanta: LOMA (Life Office Management Association, Inc.), © 2000], 177. Used with permission: all rights reserved.

longer needs reinsurance that it previously requested and asking the reinsurer to cancel the reservation. An *extension request* is a request from a direct writer to a reinsurer to extend the direct writer's reservation of capacity for a specified period so that the direct writer can gather all information needed to move the case from reserved to placed status.

To follow up on reserved capacity, the reinsurer sends a notice of expiry to each direct writer that has outstanding cases close to their dates of expiry. A *notice of expiry* is a document the reinsurer uses to notify the direct writer that an offer to reinsure is due to expire and to request additional information, a cession, a drop notice, or an extension request from the direct writer. The direct writer marks on the notice of expiry the status of each case listed and returns the notice to the reinsurer, along with any cessions, drop notices, requests for extensions, or requested information.

Placement of Reinsurance

Placement, sometimes called the *submission stage*, is a process in which the direct writer and reinsurer activate reinsurance coverage for a new automatic, facultative, or fac-ob cession. To begin placement, the direct writer verifies which reinsurer should receive the cession and provides specified information about the risk to the reinsurer. After receiving a new business cession, the reinsurance analyst marks the case as placed, updates the reinsurance administration system, and sends reinsurance certificates as necessary. A *reinsurance certificate* is a document that notifies the direct writer that reinsurance is officially in force. A reinsurance certificate includes information about the insured, the reinsured policy, and the terms of the applicable reinsurance agreement. Reinsurers generally send reinsurance certificates only for individual cession reinsurance. Reinsurers typically do not provide reinsurance certificates on automatic placements.

Administering In-Force Business

In the in-force stage, the direct writer pays the reinsurance premiums to the reinsurer to keep the coverage in force. The reinsurance parties make adjustments to the reinsurance coverage as changes are made to the reinsured policies. The reinsurer receives claim notices from the direct writer, reviews and approves or rejects the requests for claim payment reimbursement, and settles valid claim liabilities. Because the payment of a death claim results in the termination of the policy and the termination of the reinsurance on that policy, some direct writers and reinsurers view claim administration as part of the termination stage.

The party administering the reinsurance records provides the information needed for in-force administration through a variety of reports. For simplicity, we refer to the reinsurance party that administers the reinsurance records and reports as the *reporting party*. The reinsurance parties use the information in reinsurance reports to

- Verify that reinsurance transactions comply with the terms of the applicable reinsurance agreement

- Prepare statements and reports for financial and management accounting

- Produce policy reserve reports for various regulatory and accounting bodies

- Study lapse experience

- Detect unusual trends

- Conduct profitability and mortality studies

- Maintain historical data to use for future pricing

To provide information related to changes in risk, revenue, expenses, and policy reserves, the reporting party typically prepares five types of reports: in-force policy report, policy exhibit, policy change report, billing statement, and reserve listing. Although the format of reinsurance reports varies from agreement to agreement, the information included in such reports generally is the same. Regardless of which party to the reinsurance agreement has the primary responsibility for administration, both parties work to verify the accuracy of all reinsurance reports. Most reinsurance reports are in electronic form.

In-Force Policy Report

An ***in-force policy report*** is a reinsurance report that lists all in-force reinsured policies as of a given date and provides detailed information about each policy. The in-force policy report allows the direct writer and reinsurer to verify that they are keeping accurate, parallel records. Figure 11.4 shows a section of an abbreviated in-force policy report. An actual in-force policy report would include columns for additional information, such as the policy number, underwriting rating or class, tobacco use status, plan of insurance, face amount of the policy, and proportion of risk reinsured.

Figure 11.4. Portion of an In-Force Policy Report

Individual In-Force Report

Agree-ment	Ces-sion	Insured	Effective Date	DOB	Issue Age	Sex	Auto/Fac	Reinsurance NAR ($)
200300	12334	Wellyn, Samuel	05/05/03	11/02/44	53	M	F	200,000
200500	14558	Appel, Frank	12/12/05	03/22/45	55	M	A	75,000
200500	14611	Jenks, Gary	10/01/05	07/10/60	40	M	A	16,161
300200	16199	Torres, Arelia	12/13/06	05/05/55	46	F	A	200,000

Source: Adapted from Jane Lightcap Brown and Jennifer W. Herrod, *Reinsurance Administration* [Atlanta: LOMA (Life Office Management Association, Inc.), © 2000], 190. Used with permission; all rights reserved.

For group life insurance, the in-force policy report includes the policy number; effective date; plan of insurance; information about the group, such as the group name, number of group insureds, and amount of coverage for each class; total insurance coverage provided by the policy; the amount or proportion of risk reinsured; and the amount of reinsurance in force.

Policy Exhibit

A *policy exhibit* is a reinsurance report that summarizes and reconciles the changes that have occurred in reinsured policies during the reporting period. Such changes may include new business, increases and decreases in policy face amounts, conversions, lapses, deaths, terminations, and reinstatements. The policy exhibit usually presents a beginning total policy count and reinsured risk amount, any increases or decreases in the policy count and reinsured risk amount, and a final total policy count and reinsured risk amount for that reporting period. A portion of a policy exhibit is shown in Figure 11.5.

Figure 11.5. Portion of a Policy Exhibit

Reinsurance Policy Exhibit
Ceded to: Valhalla Reinsurance Company
For the Period of: 04/01/10–06/30/10
Agreement #:   24653

	Count	Reinsured Amount ($)	Risk Amount ($)	Reinsurance Premium ($)
Beginning In-Force	15	8,320,000	8,320,000	90,231.38
New Business	2	350,000	350,000	4,885.11
Reinstatements	0	0	0	0
Conversions On	0	0	0	0
Other Increases	0	0	0	0
Deaths	0	0	0	0
Maturities	0	0	0	0
Expiries	0	0	0	0
Surrenders	0	0	0	0
Lapses	1	100,000	100,000	598.50
Conversions Off	1	500,000	500,000	5,120.00
Recaptures	0	0	0	0
Rescissions	0	0	0	0
Other Decreases	0	0	0	0
Ending In-Force	15	8,070,000	8,070,000	89,397.99

Source: Adapted from Jane Lightcap Brown and Jennifer W. Herrod, *Reinsurance Administration* [Atlanta: LOMA (Life Office Management Association, Inc.), © 2000], 191. Used with permission: all rights reserved.

Policy Change Report

A *policy change report*, also known as a *transaction report*, is a reinsurance report that shows details for all policies that, during the reporting period, have changed in a way that affects the amount of the reinsurance coverage, the reinsurance premium, or the allowance. Policy terminations due to death or policy lapse, increases or decreases in the face amount, and reinstatements are examples of changes typically listed on a policy change report. Figure 11.6 shows a portion of a policy change report. A policy change report also may show any changes in reinsurance premiums associated with the policy changes.

Billing Statement

A *billing statement* is a reinsurance report that lists the amounts owed by and due to each party to the reinsurance agreement. Sometimes the policy change report also shows this type of information. If the reporting party owes money to the other reinsurance party, the reporting party usually sends payment of the amount owed along with the billing statement. If the nonreporting party owes money to the reporting party, the billing statement notifies the nonreporting party of the amount that it owes. A portion of a simplified billing statement is shown in Figure

---

Figure 11.6. Portion of a Policy Change Report

Policy Changes for February 1, 2010 to February 28, 2010

Reinstatements

Agreement	YRT/ COI	Insured	DOB	Plan	Cession Number	Auto/ Fac	Policy	Change Date	Amount ($)
100	COI	Aponte, Ana	06/23/62	XX	32334	A	59934	02/11/10	300,000
100	COI	Gould, Ben	01/25/56	XY	32699	A	59887	02/24/10	200,000
200	YRT	Dunn, Ryan	04/30/50	XZ	32788	A	65888	02/17/10	240,000

Lapses

Agreement	YRT/ COI	Insured	DOB	Plan	Cession Number	Auto/ Fac	Policy	Change Date	Amount ($)
200	COI	Jerzy, Lorice	05/22/55	XX	32445	A	01242	02/22/10	280,000
300	COI	Corr, Caria	09/23/48	XY	33699	A	02545	02/02/10	135,000

Terminations

Agreement	YRT/ COI	Insured	DOB	Plan	Cession Number	Auto/ Fac	Policy	Change Date	Amount ($)
300	YRT	Eston, Kay	02/12/57	XF	35799	F	21450	02/08/10	8,000
400	YRT	Amir, Gil	08/02/60	XJ	36002	A	01234	02/05/10	12,000

Source: Adapted from Jane Lightcap Brown and Jennifer W. Herrod, *Reinsurance Administration* [Atlanta: LOMA (Life Office Management Association, Inc.), © 2000], 192. Used with permission; all rights reserved.

11.7. Note that an actual billing statement (1) divides reinsurance premiums and allowances into first-year and renewal amounts and (2) includes information about premium refunds, policy dividends, and cash surrender value reimbursements.

Reserve Listing

A *reserve listing* is a reinsurance report that shows all policies reinsured and the reserve held for each policy. The reserve listing helps the parties determine the appropriate amount of reserves to maintain for the reinsured portion of each policy in force at the end of the reporting period. Figure 11.8 shows a portion of a reserve listing.

Processing Changes in Reinsurance Coverage

Certain changes to a reinsured policy or a block of reinsurance business can increase or decrease the amount of risk assumed by the reinsurer. Examples of such changes include

- New business

- Recapture

- Increases or decreases in a policy's face amount

- Claims

- Surrenders

- Lapses

- Reinstatements

- Conversions

- Maturity

Figure 11.7. Portion of a Billing Statement

Policy	Insured	Date	Cession	Initial Amount ($)	NAR ($)	Reinsurance Premium ($)	Allowances ($)	Net Amount Owed to the Reinsurer ($)
10201	Nomi, Akira	1/08/10	23454	200,000	2,000,000	230.00	46.00	184.00
10324	Bozek, Dana	1/18/10	23535	240,000	240,000	691.20	138.24	552.96
10402	Jamelle, Pierre	1/20/10	25699	400,000	400,000	848.00	135.68	712.32
10498	Hahn, Ian	1/26/10	25780	90,000	90,000	574.20	765.68	(191.48)

Source: Adapted from Jane Lightcap Brown and Jennifer W. Herrod, *Reinsurance Administration* [Atlanta: LOMA (Life Office Management Association, Inc.), © 2000], 193. Used with permission; all rights reserved.

The direct writer must notify the reinsurer promptly of any such changes. Other changes—such as corrections to an insured's name—may not affect the amount at risk under a reinsured policy, but such changes still require administration.

The direct writer's reinsurance analyst generally is responsible for updating reinsurance administration records to reflect changes to a reinsured policy and for notifying the appropriate staff at both the direct writer and the reinsurer of the changes. The direct writer may report changes to reinsured policies on a collective basis as is the case with a policy exhibit. Alternatively, the direct writer may report changes on a policy-by-policy basis, under which the reinsurer receives detailed updates on each policy reinsured and not just a summary of total results.

The reinsurer may require approval from its underwriting department for certain types of risk changes to policies reinsured on a facultative basis. Examples of such changes that may require an underwriter's approval are reinstatements, changes from smoker to nonsmoker status, or reinsurance increases not specified in the reinsurance agreement. The reinsurer's reinsurance analyst also may need to verify that the agreement provides for certain types of changes, such as recaptures, policy reductions, and conversions. For an increase in the face amount of a reinsured policy, the reinsurance analyst checks the reinsurer's retention to determine if the reinsurer needs to retrocede some or all of the additional risk.

Processing Billing Statements

Billing statements usually involve the receipt or payment of funds. The nonreporting party processes the billing statements provided by the reporting party. Because direct writers and reinsurers typically use automated systems to prepare and process billing statements, many or all of the processing activities we attribute to reinsurance analysts actually are performed by computerized reinsurance administration systems.

If a payment accompanies a billing statement, the nonreporting party's reinsurance analyst verifies that the amount due according to the statement matches the amount of the enclosed payment. If the nonreporting party owes money, the analyst verifies that the amount requested by the reporting party is accurate and arranges

---

Figure 11.8. Portion of a Reserve Listing

Statutory Reserves

Policy	Plan Code	Effective Date	Age	Attained Age	Sex	Name	Face Amount ($)	Ceded Amount ($)	NAR ($)	Factor	Amount Reserve ($)
122467	XX	5/15/2006	37	48	F	Beck	100,000	94,242	44,272	4.45	8.21
122678	XZ	8/25/2007	43	53	M	Coleo	500,000	370,555	320,555	9.19	122.75
123566	XX	1/14/2008	31	40	M	Landin	100,000	95,768	45,768	3.42	6.52

Source: Adapted from Jane Lightcap Brown and Jennifer W. Herrod, *Reinsurance Administration* [Atlanta: LOMA (Life Office Management Association, Inc.), © 2000], 193. Used with permission: all rights reserved.

for the payment to the reporting party. For each payment made or received, the reinsurance analyst updates the corresponding record in the reinsurance administration system. Depending on the direct writer's or reinsurer's practices, the reinsurance analyst may enter information for each individual policy or only summarized information for blocks of policies.

Administering Terminations of Reinsurance

In the termination stage, the direct writer notifies the reinsurer of any terminations of reinsured policies, and the reinsurer processes the termination of reinsurance on each case. Reinsurance coverage can be terminated as a result of

- Recapture of the ceded risk by the direct writer

- Lapse, surrender, expiration, or maturity of the reinsured policy

- The death of the insured

    To process a termination due to any of these reasons, the reinsurer's analyst verifies the

- Effective date for the termination of reinsurance

- Policies included in the termination

- Current net amount at risk

- Premium refund that may be applicable

- Expense allowances, policy dividends, or cash value for any case involving coinsurance or modco reinsurance

    For all types of terminations, (1) the direct writer must transfer all reinsurance premiums and information due, (2) the reinsurer must process all statements from the direct writer, and (3) the direct writer's current in-force listing must match the reinsurer's records. The reinsurer then terminates the reinsurance administration records for the affected policies and arranges for the refund of any unearned reinsurance premium to the direct writer.

    Terminating reinsurance coverage due to recapture requires an extra administrative step for the reinsurer, however. If a reinsurer receives notice that a direct writer wishes to recapture part or all of a reinsured risk, the reinsurance analyst first must verify that the reinsurance agreement allows recapture at that time. If the agreement does not allow the recapture, the reinsurance analyst arranges for approval of the request for recapture before terminating the reinsurance on the reinsurance administration records. The analyst also verifies any applicable recapture fees owed by the direct writer.

Administering Claims under Reinsured Policies

The direct writer makes the decisions on whether to pay claims submitted under reinsured policies. The direct writer is usually responsible for identifying claims on which recovery from the reinsurer is appropriate. Typically, the direct writer informs the reinsurer of such claim decisions and requests the reinsurer's payment for its portion of any benefits paid or due to the policy beneficiary. The reinsurer's claim analysts—with assistance from the reinsurer's reinsurance analysts—then decide whether to reimburse the direct writer the requested portion of the claim payment. A reinsurer's claim analysts and reinsurance analysts collaborate to

- Ensure that that the reinsurer pays only valid claims that are reinsured under a valid reinsurance agreement

- Respond to claims promptly, accurately, and professionally by meeting all internal guidelines and all external legal and regulatory requirements

- Ensure that the reinsurer records accurate information for claims and processes claim payments in an accurate and timely manner

At some reinsurers, claim analysts handle some of the responsibilities we assign to reinsurance analysts. However, for most reinsurers, a reinsurance analyst has the following administrative responsibilities for claims:

- Establishing a claim file

- Verifying information related to the reinsured policy and the claim

- Securing approval for the claim

- Settling the claim liability (in some companies)

- Notifying retrocessionaires of a claim liability

Establishing the Claim File

The reinsurance claim administration process begins when the direct writer's reinsurance analyst sends the reinsurer a claim notice with information about the

- Insured

- Loss incurred

- Reinsured policy or policies that the direct writer has in force on the insured

- Reinsurance arrangements for the applicable policy or policies

- Status of the claim—for example, under investigation, approved but not paid, or paid

- Amount of payment requested for the claim

The analyst also sends the reinsurer a copy of the (1) claim submitted to the direct writer by the claimant—usually the beneficiary of a life insurance policy—or a representative of the claimant, such as a producer; (2) proof of loss, which is an official document verifying the insured's death; and (3) a copy of the proof of claim payment if the direct writer has already paid the claim.

The direct writer's reinsurance analyst then monitors the time required for the reinsurer to settle its claim liability for the case. The reinsurer's reinsurance analyst establishes a *claim file*, which is an organized collection of all the information relevant to a claim. For example, an individual life reinsurance claim file typically includes the direct writer's name, contact information, and policy number as well as the insured's name, sex, date of birth, date of death (if known), and the date the reinsurer received the claim. The claim file also includes the copies of the claim submitted to the direct writer, the proof of loss, and, if applicable, the proof of claim payment. The reinsurance analyst makes notes in the claim file about the applicable reinsurance arrangement, the reinsured risk for the policy, and any reinsurance claim activities in progress or completed.

Verifying Claim-Related Information

Next, the reinsurer's reinsurance analyst—or in some cases, a claim analyst—performs a variety of activities to determine if the reinsurer has a liability under the claim and, if so, the amount of that liability. The reinsurance analyst verifies

- That a reinsurance agreement covers the policy under which the claim was submitted

- That the policy and the reinsurance on the policy were in force at the time of the loss

- Whether any policy changes—such as reinstatements and increases—affected the cession

- Whether the policy has any riders that might impact the amount recoverable from the reinsurer

The reinsurance analyst then determines whether the reinsurer has reinsured other policies from any other direct writer on this insured. If the reinsurer is covering other policies for the same insured, the analyst notes these policies and direct writers in the claim file. The reinsurance analyst also checks for any amounts retroceded on the case. If the claim involves retroceded coverage, the reinsurance analyst creates a *retrocession claim file*—that is, a file containing all the information relevant to the claim, plus information about the retrocession—to use when the reinsurer notifies the retrocessionaire of the claim.

The reinsurance analyst confirms that the direct writer has paid the reinsurance premiums on the case and adds the premium-related information to the claim file. The reinsurance analyst also calculates any premium refunds due if the reinsurance coverage terminates as a result of the claim.

The reinsurance analyst—or, at some companies, the claim analyst—confirms that the reinsurer is responsible for paying the requested claim amount to the direct writer, based on the criteria set forth for reinsured claim risks in the applicable reinsurance agreement. Figure 11.9 lists the types of reinsurance agreement specifications for claim liability under a reinsured policy.

The reinsurer's reinsurance analyst also determines whether any special instructions or arrangements govern the policy. For example, the reinsurance analyst notifies the claim analyst if the reinsurer has the right to review the claim and offer its opinion to the direct writer on whether to pay the claim, known as the *right of recommendation*. If any discrepancies exist between the claim and the terms of the reinsurance agreement, the reinsurance analyst refers the case to a claim analyst for further examination.

Figure 11.9. Reinsurance Agreement Specifications for Claim Liability

The claim must comply with the reinsurance agreement's specifications for the

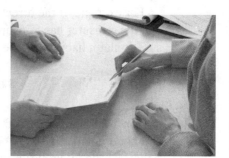

- Type of policy
- Information used to underwrite the policy
- Underwriting classification of the insured
- Age limits for policy issue
- Effective date of the policy
- Allowable coverage
- Maximum amount of risk to be ceded per policy
- Jumbo limit
- Quota share arrangements

Source: Adapted from Mary C. Bickley et al, *Insurance Administration*, 3rd ed. [Atlanta: LOMA (Life Office Management Association, Inc.), © 2008], 309. Used with permission; all rights reserved.

Reviewing the Proof of Loss

The reinsurance analyst or claim analyst verifies that the direct writer has provided a proper proof of loss—such as a death certificate—to the reinsurer. The reinsurance analyst reviews the proof documents and confirms that they apply to the insured and adds the proof documents to the claim file.

Determining Whether the Claim Is Fraudulent or Contestable

Both reinsurance analysts and claim analysts of the reinsurer check claims for signs of fraud. The reinsurance and claim analysts also check each life insurance claim to determine if it is contestable. A *contestable claim* is a claim for life insurance policy proceeds following the death of an insured during the policy's contestable period. If a claim is not contestable, the reinsurance analyst typically refers the claim to the claim analyst for approval. If a claim is contestable, the reinsurance analyst notes the length of time the policy has been in force, checks MIB records if the reinsurer is a member of MIB, and sends the claim to the claim analyst for further investigation.

Determining the Reinsurer's Claim Liability

For coinsurance or modco reinsurance, the reinsurance analyst uses the information found in the reinsurance agreement and reinsurance administration records to determine the reinsurer's claim liability. The reinsurance administration records for a policy reinsured under quota share reinsurance may not provide the reinsurer's claim liability. In this case, the analyst calculates the reinsurer's claim liability by multiplying the direct writer's claim liability by the quota share percentage.

For example, if the direct writer has $200,000 of claim liability under a policy, and the reinsurer has reinsured the policy using a 60 percent quota share, the reinsurer's claim liability on the policy is $120,000, calculated as follows:

$$\$200,000 \times 0.60 = \$120,000$$

For YRT reinsurance, the reinsurer's claim liability is based on the reinsurer's net amount at risk (NAR). For some policies—such as traditional whole life policies—the direct writer generally knows at the time of policy issue the policy reserve amounts for future years. When a policy's future policy reserve amounts are known in advance, the reinsurance administration records for the policy often include a schedule that shows the reinsurer's NAR. However, the direct writer typically cannot predict accurately the future policy reserves and resulting NAR for products with flexible or indeterminate premium rates. When a policy's future policy reserves and NAR are not predictable in advance, the reinsurance analyst generally refers to the most recent billing statement for the reinsurer's current NAR.

If the reinsurer's claim liability calculated by the reinsurance analyst is the same as the reinsurer's claim liability specified on the direct writer's claim notice, the reinsurance analyst updates the claim file to show the reinsurer's claim liability. If the two amounts are not the same, the reinsurance analyst refers the case to the claim analyst for investigation of the discrepancy.

Approving the Claim Liability

Each reinsurer establishes guidelines specifying which staff can approve various amounts and types of reinsurance claim liabilities. In some companies, reinsurance analysts have the authority to approve claim liabilities up to certain amounts under particular circumstances. However, the same reinsurance analyst that verified the information related to a claim generally cannot approve that claim liability. For simplicity, we assume that the person responsible for approving or denying a reinsurance claim liability is a claim analyst.

After approving a reinsurance claim liability, the claim analyst either settles the claim liability or instructs a reinsurance analyst or another claim analyst to settle the liability. After denying a claim, the claim analyst generally notifies the direct writer of the decision and advises the reinsurance analyst who verified the claim-related information how to update the reinsurance administration records.

Settling the Claim Liability

The reinsurance analyst or claim analyst settling the claim liability usually communicates the amount of the payment to the direct writer and arranges for the payment to be made. Some reinsurance arrangements, in which the direct writer is the reporting party and provides only summarized reports to the reinsurer, allow the direct writer to net off claims from billing statements. *Netting off* is a process by which a direct writer subtracts the claim amount owed to it by a reinsurer from the amount that the direct writer owes the reinsurer for premiums. If the reinsurance agreement allows netting off, the direct writer notifies the reinsurer of a claim through the billing statement, which shows claim amounts that the direct writer has netted off.

Notifying Retrocessionaires of a Claim Liability

If the reinsurer retroceded a portion of the reinsured risk to a retrocessionaire, the reinsurer sends the retrocessionaire a copy of the proof of loss, the claim form, and the proof of the claim liability payment to the direct writer, along with a request for payment from the retrocessionaire. The retrocessionaire then examines the claim, secures approval for the claim liability to the reinsurer, and settles the claim liability with the reinsurer.

Auditing Reinsurance Operations

Direct writers and reinsurers undertake quality control activities, including quantitative and qualitative performance measurements, to ensure that employees follow appropriate procedures for reinsurance operations. Auditing is one of the primary methods that direct writers and reinsurers use for quality control. The purpose of an audit is to examine the effectiveness of interrelated objectives, procedures, personnel, records, and process controls. A *process control* is a procedure that allows an organization to monitor the accuracy of its processes on a regular, ongoing basis.

Both direct writers and reinsurers conduct internal audits of their companies' own reinsurance activities. In addition, reinsurance agreements typically grant the reinsurer the right to conduct periodic external audits of the direct writer.

Internal Audits

The purpose of an internal audit of reinsurance activities is to verify that the company's employees are meeting service standards; recording accurate, complete, and current data in the company's records; and following established procedures as defined by the company and its reinsurance agreements. For example, a direct writer's internal audit might include the following questions:

- Do employees transmit information about new cessions and changes to in-force policies to the reinsurer in an accurate and timely manner?

- Do employees adhere to the reinsurance agreement provisions regarding retention limits and recapture?

A reinsurer's internal audit might evaluate how accurately the reinsurer's staff members calculate reinsurance premiums and other financial amounts. Each direct writer's or reinsurer's auditors review the procedural documentation for reinsurance and selected reinsurance cases to determine whether employees followed documented procedures regarding recordkeeping and administrative processes. Internal audits can help to identify any potential shortcomings and opportunities for improvement in a company's process controls. An internal audit may focus on a single aspect of reinsurance, such as claims or underwriting, or it may cover several or all aspects of reinsurance operations. After an internal audit is completed, the company's auditors summarize the audit findings in a report for the company's managers. If the reinsurer is responsible for administering the reinsured business, then the direct writer's internal audit staff might also be involved in verifying the reinsurer's premiums.

External Audits by the Reinsurer

Reinsurance agreements contain an *access to records provision*, which gives the reinsurance company the authority to examine the direct writer's records related to the business conducted between the companies. Typically, this provision also allows the direct writer to audit or access the reinsurer's records when the reinsurer is responsible for administration. Reinsurers typically conduct external audits of a direct writer every two to three years. Both the direct writer and the reinsurer have a right to request additional unscheduled external audits of the direct writer. The direct writer may request an external audit to obtain the reinsurer's objective opinion about any aspect of the direct writer's operations, such as its underwriting processes or its information systems. The reinsurer may request an unscheduled external audit if it discovers irregularities in reinsurance administration by the direct writer. The audits provide information for the reinsurer and the direct writer, and the results are not made public.

In a reinsurer's external audit of a direct writer, the reinsurer's representatives visit the direct writer and examine various aspects of the direct writer's operations, documents, and data. An external audit may include interviews, examination of records, observation of operations, calculations of various values, and review of procedures manuals. The external audit team typically chooses a sample of reinsured cases to examine on site during the audit. Typically, the reinsurer's audit team focuses on the following tasks:

- Understanding the direct writer's operations, workflows, and procedures

- Evaluating the direct writer's administrative processes

- Identifying weaknesses in the direct writer's process control systems

- Evaluating the direct writer's compliance with the reinsurance agreement

- Reviewing cases to verify the accuracy of amounts retained and reinsured, reinsurance premiums charged, policy terminations and lapses, and billing

- Evaluating the timeliness of the direct writer's reporting, particularly for changes to reinsured policies

- Reviewing the direct writer's administration systems

Preparing for an External Audit

Generally, the reinsurer gives the direct writer two to three months' advance notice of an external audit to allow both companies time to prepare for the audit. After negotiating the schedule for the audit, the reinsurer notifies the direct writer about the purposes of the audit, the members of the reinsurance audit team, and the needs of the audit team during the audit. Such needs typically include access to the direct writer's reinsurance computer systems and documentation of processes and process controls for specified administrative activities.

Gathering Information and Reviewing Records

At the beginning of the audit, the direct writer's staff instructs the external audit team on how to use the computer system to access needed files. The direct writer's employees may demonstrate policy administration workflow, their billing process, and controls to monitor timeliness, accuracy, and completeness of data to the external audit team. Next, the external audit team reviews the selected sample files, investigates any special circumstances it encounters, and examines the direct writer's retention management, audit processes, and technology.

The external audit team audits the direct writer's underwriting administration by interviewing the direct writer's staff to determine whether they

- Understand automatic binding limits, jumbo limits, and other constraints, so that cases are assigned to appropriate reinsurers

- Understand retention limits and follow appropriate procedures for determining cession amounts

- Follow appropriate procedures for updating files and other system records

In an audit of a direct writer's claim administration, the external audit team ensures that the direct writer's procedures for administering claims are properly documented and that the direct writer's staff applies claim procedures in a timely and accurate manner. The external audit team also evaluates the expertise of the claim staff. The sample files used for auditing claims generally include files of contestable claims, uncontested but large claims, foreign claims, claims involving errors and omissions, claims involving conversions and reinstatements, and any other unusual claims.

Evaluating and Documenting the Audit Findings

At the end of the audit visit, the audit team meets with the direct writer's staff and presents the audit team's initial findings and recommendations. To document its findings, the audit team prepares a written audit report that includes the following types of documentation:

- An *analysis of problems*. A brief description of the problems uncovered; an assessment of the severity of each problem; whether the problem is a one-time error or a systemic error; the estimated financial impact of the problem; and the proposed resolution for each problem

- An *internal trip report*. A detailed review of the audit, intended for the reinsurer's management team

- The *audit report*. A document created for the direct writer, communicating the audit's significant findings and recommendations

Following Up after the External Audit

After the direct writer receives the report, the direct writer prepares an action plan documenting corrective steps it has agreed to take. Both the direct writer and reinsurer complete actions agreed to during the audit and correct data and processes as needed. As a part of the follow-up, the direct writer and reinsurer collaborate to resolve problems. The external audit team may help the direct writer solve problems or improve its processes, based on recommendations contained in the audit.

Key Terms

reinsurance administration
reinsurance analyst
reinsurance marketing officer
business-to-business (B2B)
   e-commerce
preplacement
reserved capacity
request for coverage
date of expiry
drop notice
extension request
notice of expiry
placement

reinsurance certificate
in-force policy report
policy exhibit
policy change report
billing statement
reserve listing
claim file
retrocession claim file
right of recommendation
contestable claim
netting off
process control
access to records provision

Endnote

1.   Portions of this chapter are adapted from Susan Conant and Miriam Orsina, *Principles of Reinsurance* [Atlanta: LOMA (Life Office Management Association, Inc.), © 2006], 162–175, 179–225, 235–243. Used with permission; all rights reserved.

Chapter 12

Effective Customer Service

Objectives:

After studying this chapter, you should be able to

- List six qualities of effective customer service
- Identify the benefits to insurers of providing effective customer service
- Describe the typical ways that insurers organize customer service departments
- Identify the legal issues affecting customer service
- Describe the tools that insurers use to automate and simplify customer service delivery
- Explain the importance of telephone communication skills and documentation of guidelines and procedures to excellent customer service
- Explain how providing excellent customer service helps conservation and discuss strategies for improving customer loyalty and retaining business

Outline

In earlier sections in this text, we covered the importance of underwriting, reinsurance, and claim administration. We also discussed the many ways in which underwriting, reinsurance, and claim personnel cooperate with one another, with other functional areas of the insurer, and with producers and insurance regulators. Now we turn our attention to customer service. Because effective service to clients is a cornerstone of successful organizations, customer service is an essential insurance administration function. Some insurers use the term *policyowner service* or *member service* to refer to the type of customer service performed for policyowners or groups, respectively.

The term *customer service* refers not only to the activities performed by customer service staff, but also to the functional unit that performs these activities. To simplify the discussion, we use the term *customer service department* to refer to the organizational unit that provides customer service to individual insurance customers. We use the term member services to refer to the organizational unit that provides customer service to group insureds. A customer service staff member typically is known as a ***customer service representative (CSR)***, who is any person, other than a sales person, who provides support to customers face-to-face or through communication media.

Customer service helps maintain important contractual and business connections between the insurer and its customers. Effective customer service also enhances the insurer's reputation for taking good care of its customers and thereby helps increase sales and preserve existing business. Another function of customer service is to compile information for reports to insurance regulatory organizations regarding customer complaints.

In this chapter, we begin by explaining the qualities of effective customer service and discussing the benefits of providing effective customer service. We then examine the organization of a customer service department and the types of service that insurers deliver to various types of customers. We also discuss the legal issues affecting customer service and describe approaches insurers use to deliver effective customer service. After we examine the relationship between customer service and preserving an insurer's existing business, we conclude with a look at how insurers evaluate the effectiveness of the customer service they provide.

Qualities of Effective Customer Service

Generally speaking, effective customer service is prompt, courteous, complete, convenient, accurate, and confidential. An insurer that delivers customer service with these qualities keeps customers satisfied, thus enhancing its strength and competitive position.

Customer service is *prompt* if it is delivered in a timely manner. Ensuring that customers do not experience unnecessary service delays enhances customer service. By contrast, delays can often frustrate customers, leading to reductions in new business, lapses, surrenders, and even legal actions against the insurer. For example, a policyowner who has to wait an unreasonable period of time to obtain a policy loan may become irritated and choose to surrender his policy.

Customer service is *courteous* if the employee delivering the service is polite, tactful, and attentive to the customer's feelings and situations. Courteous CSRs strengthen the bond between an insurer and its customers. Considering the feelings of customers and making every effort to handle transactions politely and professionally can make transactions pleasant experiences for everyone involved and help maintain long-term customer relationships.

Customer service is *complete* when every aspect of the customer's problem or inquiry is resolved to the customer's satisfaction. Providing complete service is sometimes a challenge, especially when requests for service cover a variety of transactions or when transactions are complicated or unusual. Attending to the details of each transaction helps ensure that all parts of a transaction are completed and that the customer will be fully satisfied. Providing complete service saves time for customers and CSRs and reduces the insurer's expense in unnecessary follow-up correspondence and customer contacts.

Customer service is *convenient* if customers have relatively easy access to the services they need. Customers want to obtain service through the communication methods and at the times that work best for them. Virtually all insurance companies have toll-free customer service telephone numbers. Many insurers have customer service staff available from early in the morning until late at night. Also, many insurers have automated phone systems and Internet Web sites that allow customers to perform certain transactions at any time.

Customer service is *accurate* if the insurer provides the customer with correct information or processes transactions without errors. Most insurers enhance accuracy by creating checklists, worksheets, and procedures manuals that guide CSRs through the steps of transactions, particularly those that are complex or have various options. In addition, insurers provide either manual or electronic logs by which CSRs can record every customer transaction processed. Certain transactions also may be audited by a senior CSR.

Customer service is *confidential* when the customer's privacy has been protected by the insurer. Confidentiality is essential in customer service as in all other aspects of insurance administration. Confidentiality in customer service helps the insurer earn the customer's trust and strengthens the bond between the customer and the company. We discuss the legal aspects of confidentiality later in this chapter.

Benefits of Providing Effective Customer Service

The insurance industry is highly competitive, and customers may see little difference between insurers and their products. An insurer with a reputation for effective customer service can differentiate itself from its competitors and increase its ability to attract new customers. In addition, exceptional customer service often encourages customers to maintain their coverage with the insurer. Customers who are satisfied with an insurer's service are more likely to renew and increase their current coverage and to buy new products. They also may recommend the insurer to friends and family members.

Furthermore, retaining customers can greatly increase an insurer's profit margin, because the cost of keeping existing customers is much less than the cost of acquiring customers. Avoiding the time and resources required to replace customers lost due to poor service allows the insurer to direct those resources into building its business.

Not only does exceptional customer service help attract and retain customers and improve profitability, but it also enhances the insurer's work environment. Working for an organization that prides itself on delivering good customer service helps motivate CSRs to excel at their jobs. In contrast, poor customer service can cause the morale of CSRs to drop as they cope with the stressful effects of dealing with unhappy or angry customers. As the quality of a company's customer service improves, CSRs become more productive because they spend less time dealing with problems caused by poor customer service.

Customer Service Organization

As with other administrative areas of insurance companies, customer service areas come in many varieties. Staffing, levels of authority, and organization differ according to the types of services an insurer provides and the preferences of management.

Staffing

A person typically begins her career as a customer service associate, which is an entry-level position based on the candidate's computer skills, core competencies, and pre-employment test scores. Associates may receive training to handle customer requests for various company products and to conduct various service transactions.

An insurer typically promotes a customer service associate to the position of CSR after approximately 18 months of service. Considerations for promotion may include accuracy, communication skills, productivity, completion of continuing insurance education requirements, and attendance. Customer service associates also must demonstrate a proficiency in the company's insurance operations and products. A CSR may be promoted to a senior customer service representative after he has successfully completed training on all the duties performed by CSRs, including complicated service requests. In addition to performing CSR duties, senior CSRs may be responsible for contacting new customers to promote loyalty and answer questions. They also may train and serve as mentors for new CSRs.

Some insurers divide CSRs into separate **work teams** or *work groups*, which are two or more people who work together on a regular basis and coordinate their activities to accomplish common goals. These work groups report to a specified supervisor. The work group supervisor reports to the department manager, who generally reports to a member of senior management. The common types of work teams are listed in Figure 12.1. These types of work teams also may be found in other departments such as underwriting and claims.

In the past, the nature of their work frequently required CSRs to concentrate primarily on administrative tasks, such as processing paperwork. Because administrative services are part of what customers purchase when they buy insurance products, performing such tasks always will be an important part of what CSRs do. Over the years, however, information technology has streamlined many administrative tasks. The reduction in the CSR time needed to perform administrative tasks has led many insurance companies to ask their CSRs to go a step further—to think not only of the customer's specific request, but also to consider the array of

Figure 12.1. Common Types of Work Teams

A **traditional team** is a type of work team in which the manager or supervisor performs most or all of the management tasks, such as organizing, planning, monitoring, and controlling the work; other team members concentrate solely on doing the work—performing the business functions for which the team is responsible.

A **semi-autonomous team** is a type of team in which the manager or supervisor manages the team, while the other team members, in addition to doing their "regular" work, provide input into planning, organizing, and monitoring the work.

A **self-directed team** is a type of team in which the members handle many traditional management responsibilities, such as planning and monitoring work. Self-directed teams are sometimes called *self-managed teams*.

customer needs that the company can fill. Customer service representatives are being trained to understand the full range of a company's products and activities and to recognize marketing opportunities. For example, some insurers encourage CSRs to go beyond the customer's current request and identify life events—such as birth, marriage, or retirement—that would suggest the need for an insurance program review. Typically, however, CSRs do not actually sell products unless they are licensed and trained to do so.

Levels of Authority

Customer service representatives receive increasing amounts of decision-making authority as they gain experience and demonstrate enhanced ability and quality of judgment. Usually, a new customer service associate handles routine inquiries and service requests, such as address changes, that present few difficulties or unusual circumstances. A senior customer service representative or a customer service supervisor normally reviews the associate's work. As the customer service associate gains experience, he handles less routine, more challenging services and performs his work without the review of a more experienced person. Senior customer service representatives and customer service supervisors usually handle service requests that require extensive contract knowledge, investigation, or consideration.

Organization

Some insurers establish one department or area to deal with every kind of customer service activity, while other insurers divide customer service activities by product, territory, distribution system, customer, method of communication, or service request.

Organization by Product

In organizing customer service activities by product, an insurer usually trains CSRs to handle requests concerning one or two products—for example, an individual disability income product or a group life insurance product. A CSR who understands all the details of a product, especially a complex one, is able to provide top quality service to customers.

The biggest challenge to organization by product is making sure that customer interactions do not become fragmented. For example, if a customer has purchased health insurance and life insurance and each is supported by separate customer service units, then coordination of effort is important. Customers calling to make an address change may assume that the change has been made on all policies they own, only to discover the change was implemented for just one product. In Chapter 1, we discussed insurers' technology solutions to this problem.

Organization by Territory

Multinational insurance companies often establish separate customer contact centers in each country where they do business to more effectively address differences in language, culture, products, regulations, and time zones. A *customer contact center* is an organizational unit that provides customers with a variety of channels for communicating with a business entity. Companies that operate in a single country are more likely to establish centralized customer contact centers, often organized into separate units to support different territories. However, if a company supports a number of regions within a country, it may decide to place customer contact centers in several different locations. This geographical dispersion makes it easier to support customers in different time zones, develop expertise in unique regulatory requirements, and become familiar with specific types of customers and their needs, enabling the customer contact center to be "closer to the customer."

Organization by Distribution System

Insurance companies that use multiple methods of product distribution sometimes organize customer service according to the type of distribution systems. For example, an insurer may assign one group of CSRs to provide service on policies sold through insurance producers and another group of CSRs to provide service on policies sold through direct marketing.

Organization by Customer

Another way to organize customer service activities is according to clients served. For instance, some CSRs handle inquiries only from producers, while other CSRs respond to requests from large group clients. Particularly when an insurer provides coverage for a very large group, assigning certain CSRs to handle the service for that group can prove efficient. The CSRs learn the needs and typical requests of the group and can develop response systems that provide prompt, accurate customer service.

Organization by Method of Communication

Face-to-face communication with customers plays an important role in ensuring effective communication. However, most customer service communication is provided through remote customer contacts, such as telephone, paper correspondence, e-mail, and Web sites. As mentioned earlier, a customer contact center is an organizational unit that provides customers with a variety of channels for communicating with a business entity.

- **Telephone.** Despite the availability of new methods of communication, many customers continue to use the telephone to obtain customer service. Consequently, many companies operate *call centers*, which are organizational units that receive and/or place telephone calls to customers.

- **Paper correspondence.** Like the telephone, paper correspondence is a traditional communication channel that still accounts for a substantial number of customer contacts in many companies. Mailed or faxed documents often are used to provide information, handle complaints, and process transactions, such as payments, withdrawals, changes of address, policy loans, and reinstatements. When paper correspondence is received, it is routed to the appropriate CSR for processing.

- **E-mail.** Like mail and faxes, insurers route e-mail correspondence to the appropriate CSRs. Many companies use an automated response system that automatically replies to customers to acknowledge receipt of e-mails and to indicate an expected response time, which is often 24 to 48 hours. For basic, predictable requests, some firms utilize systems that generate automatic responses triggered by certain keywords in the customer's e-mail. Typically, to ensure that these responses are appropriate, automatic e-mails are closely monitored. In some companies, e-mails are routed the same way telephone calls are routed. In other words, e-mail messages go into a queue and are quickly routed to available CSRs, keeping response times to a minimum and sometimes providing customers with a response while still logged into their e-mail systems.

- **Web sites.** Most insurers have Internet Web sites that give customers access to product information and frequently asked questions (FAQs). For example, some Web sites enable customers to check premiums due, change personal information, process transactions such as address changes, and perform other functions. Many Web sites allow customers to send an e-mail through a link on the Web site, request a live internet chat session with a CSR, or request a telephone callback.

Organization by Service Request

Some insurers assign certain CSRs to respond to certain types of service requests, such as address or beneficiary changes and policy loans. In dividing customer service activities by service request, insurers typically establish such divisions as premium billing, loans, and cancellations and surrenders. Keep in mind that a company may change its method of customer organization over time, as illustrated in Figure 12.2.

Legal Issues Affecting Customer Service

An insurance policy is a contract between the policyowner and the insurance company. First and foremost, customer service helps fulfill the insurer's contractual obligations by completing service requests that pertain to customers' rights under their policies. For example, a life insurance policy may give the policyowner the right to take policy loans, change the amount of the death benefit, or add or remove riders.

As we mentioned earlier, protecting the identities of customers is essential to customer service. A contract of insurance between an insurer and a policyowner requires that the insurer protect the customer's privacy. Governmental privacy regulations also determine what type of policy information can be released and to whom that information can be released.

In addition to privacy requirements, CSRs must be aware of the impact of many other types of laws and regulations. Because work practices often vary due to the regulatory requirements of various jurisdictions, CSRs must be knowledgeable of or have access to information about all applicable regulations. Among other things, failure to comply with laws and regulations can result in fines, lawsuits, and negative publicity for the company.

Figure 12.2. Organizing Customer Service Work Teams

In the past, Fountainhead used a service request-based approach to organizing its customer service activities. Each work team specialized in providing a specific type of service for customers. However, if customers needed more than one type of service, they had to contact more than one work group. For instance, a customer who wanted to check account values and make deposits and withdrawals from different accounts had to place multiple telephone calls or ask to be transferred to several areas to obtain the desired services.

Recently, Fountainhead began using a region-based approach to organizing its customer service activities. Now, when customers call the centralized toll-free telephone number, their calls are automatically routed to the appropriate service team: East, Central, or West. The service providers on all three teams are trained to help customers with a variety of inquiries and transactions, such as:

- Requests for account values

- Fund transfers

- Disbursements

- Monthly bank deductions

- Name, address, and telephone number changes

Working on these region-based work teams, service providers are more familiar with their customers and are able to deliver more consistent customer service. Furthermore, the cross-trained team members seldom have to transfer customers to other work teams; they can provide one-stop customer service in most instances.

Source: Adapted from Mark Adel and Barbara Foxenberger Brown, *Foundations of Customer Service* [Atlanta: LOMA (Life Office Management Association, Inc.), © 2003], 287. Used with permission; all rights reserved.

Also, an insurer's customer service function must comply with applicable insurance regulatory requirements by maintaining accurate, complete, and current records of written and significant oral complaints for annual submission to insurance regulatory organizations. State and provincial departments of insurance generally reconcile insurers' annual reports of complaints with records of complaints submitted directly to those departments. In jurisdictions that have established specific standards for handling complaints, state and provincial departments of insurance determine whether each insurer has met such standards and what, if any, actions the insurer has taken to resolve problems involving any standards that were not met. For example, if a jurisdiction has established a time limit within which complaints must be resolved, regulators examine an insurer's resolution time. If the standard is not being met on a consistent basis, the regulator will want to know what steps the insurer is taking to improve the timeliness of its complaint resolutions.

Complaints that could have legal implications usually are referred to the insurer's legal staff. Such complaints might involve customer demands for reinstatement beyond the period allowed, allegations that instructions to the insurer or its producers were not followed, or allegations that the insurer's CSRs or producers behaved in an incompetent, negligent, or dishonest manner.

Furthermore, CSRs must be knowledgeable of work practices designed to reduce the risk of costly errors, lawsuits, unintended liability, and fraud. For example, if a CSR suspects fraud, he may enter the incident into a company-wide tracking system. Then he gives all applicable information and documents to his supervisor, who reviews the file and decides whether or not to forward the incident to the company's law or compliance department for further investigation.

Delivering Effective Customer Service

Every insurer wants to deliver effective service so that all customers are satisfied. Determining specific strategies for providing effective customer service, automating and simplifying customer service delivery procedures, ensuring excellent telephone communication, and documenting customer service guidelines and procedures are some of the approaches insurers use to deliver effective customer service.

Service for Policyowners, Insureds, Beneficiaries, and Producers

An insurer's CSRs provide essential services to customers. In this section, our discussion focuses on the primary activities of customer service; we discuss these activities in more detail in the next chapter. Customer service for individual insurance often involves providing information and processing policy transactions for policyowners, insureds, beneficiaries, and payors. Typical individual insurance customer service activities are listed in Figure 12.3.

Service for Group Policyholders and Group Insureds

The member services department for group insurance provides customer service for both the group policyholder and the group insureds. In addition to assisting the group policyholder with policy installation and member enrollment, CSRs also provide information and process policy transactions for group insureds and beneficiaries.

Service for Producers

Establishing and maintaining productive relationships with producers are important to an insurer's competitive position. Providing exceptional customer service to producers attracts and retains successful producers. To help producers solicit, sell, and conserve business, CSRs may provide information about products and procedures if this function isn't handled by new business analysts, as we discussed in Chapter 1. For instance, CSRs indicate which forms the producer must complete and what additional information the producer must submit with an application. By helping producers submit complete applications, CSRs increase the probability that underwriters can promptly evaluate the application.

Figure 12.3. Typical Individual Insurance Customer Service Activities

- Changing the owner and/or the beneficiary of a policy
- Changing addresses
- Processing coverage changes or adding riders
- Determining cash values, loans, and dividends
- Changing certain policy features such as how dividends are used and nonforfeiture options
- Sending premium due notices and handling premium payments
- Changing billing arrangements and methods of payment
- Answering questions on coverage amounts, policy provisions, and billings
- Providing information about claims submission, status, or settlement
- Processing policy disbursement requests such as loans, partial withdrawals, surrenders, and cancellations
- Changing fund allocations for variable life insurance policies
- Processing reinstatements of lapsed policies

CSRs also provide information and service to help producers provide top-quality service directly to policyowners. Many policyowners consider the producer to be their link to the insurance company, and they communicate directly with the producer when they have questions or problems.

Promptly addressing customer concerns is vital to a continuing relationship between the policyowner, the producer, and the insurer. The producer typically bears the burden of a policyowner's irritation if the insurer makes errors in transactions, is unresponsive to requests for information, or otherwise fails to meet policyowner expectations.

Some CSRs also calculate and pay commissions to producers. If an insurer enables producers, at a policyowner's request, to make certain contractually permitted changes to policies and to submit the changes to the insurer, CSRs usually oversee and maintain records of the changes.

Determining Strategies for Effective Customer Service

Insurers implement various customer service strategies according to the types of coverage involved and the type, frequency, and complexity of the service transactions required. Each insurer adopts strategies that reflect its attitude toward customer service, and these strategies serve as a guide for CSRs in their interactions with customers.

Customer service strategies generally focus on all types of customer interactions, including written and spoken communications and face-to-face meetings. Figure 12.4 illustrates such strategies.

Automating and Simplifying Customer Service Delivery

Insurance companies have long used technology to make customer service more efficient and effective. For example, replacing traditional paper document and file systems with computerized systems that provide instant access to a customer's records enables insurers to provide faster, more accurate customer service.

Computer Networks

CSRs may use the company's intranet, extranet, an external network, or any combination to route a customer's inquiry or request, access the records and information necessary to handle the inquiry or request, and document the actions taken. For example, an insurer with multiple service locations may use an intranet to automatically route, complete, and document service requests. When a service request is received, it is input into the administrative system, where it can be accessed by a CSR in any service location. Networking allows customer service locations to share work, and it allows service requests to be handled by multiple personnel in multiple locations if necessary.

Figure 12.4. Examples of Customer Service Strategies

- Treat all customers as valuable individuals

- Approach every customer contact with empathy for the customer's situation

- Treat each customer contact as an opportunity to build a relationship, not just to process a transaction

- Ensure that customers receive accurate and timely responses

- Improve written communication by using personalized letters

- Improve verbal communication by returning all telephone calls within a timely manner, asking permission before placing any customer on hold, and informing the customer first of the anticipated hold time

- Implement technologies and processes to make conducting business easier for customers

Knowledge Management Systems

CSRs rely upon certain technical resources, such as procedure manuals and internal memos, to provide the information needed to assist customers. In the past, such technical resources were available only in paper format, but today a growing number of insurers provide the information from these technical resources on desktop computers, giving CSRs quick and easy access to the information they need. Such information is part of an insurer's *knowledge management system*, which represents the strategies, resources, and processes that organizations use to apply institutional knowledge to business activities. By using electronic knowledge management systems, an insurer can take information about products and procedures—which once may have been hard to find in volumes of paper manuals—and make this information easily and rapidly accessible throughout a department or an entire organization. Knowledge management systems facilitate the addition or modification of customer service procedures and the immediate distribution of such changes to all CSRs.

Databases

Much of the information found in knowledge management systems comes from databases. Some databases are separately maintained for specific functions. For example, a call center might maintain its own database requiring CSRs to input information into a customer contact system after each transaction. A *customer contact system* is a customer database and work tracking tool that combines a variety of features—such as data entry and retrieval, history of previous customer contacts, document management, scripted presentations, and follow-up tools—to provide a framework for handling and documenting customer contacts.

Document Management Systems and Automated Workflow Systems

Document management systems provide CSRs with computer access to a variety of company-specific forms, such as completed applications, explanations of benefits, account statements, and signature cards. In addition, these systems can provide computer access to correspondence and other documents—such as medical, financial, or other records—from outside the company.

Increasingly, document management systems play an important role in automated workflow systems. The automated workflow system shows the type of transaction, the person to whom it was assigned, when it was received, questions that arose, actions taken, documents created, completion dates and times, and so on. By storing this information electronically, CSRs have immediate access to the information, allowing them to provide a quicker, more complete response to customer requests or inquiries. Such immediate access can be invaluable in handling lengthy or complex transactions on which more than one CSR has worked or that have to be transferred temporarily to a manager for consideration and advice.

Self-Service Options

Advances in technology have led to a variety of self-service options for customers and their intermediaries. One of the most common self-service options is an *interactive voice response (IVR) system*, which is a computer-based technology that answers telephone calls, greets callers with a recorded or digitized message, and prompts them to enter information or make requests by voice or telephone keypad. An IVR also may be called a *voice response unit*. Using an IVR system, customers may pay premiums, check on the status of applications and claims, and order forms.

Many insurers also allow customers to perform transactions through the Internet. For Web-enabled self-service options to be of value to users, the Web site must provide accurate information and reliable service in an easy-to-use format.

A few of the many self-service options available on insurers' Web sites allow customers to

- Complete and submit paperless applications and claims and to check on the status of these transactions

- Make policy changes

- Determine their financial needs and get assistance in implementing an appropriate strategy

Similarly, self-service options allow CSRs to obtain information and conduct transactions over the Internet. For example, some insurers' Web sites allow customers visiting the sites to click a button and immediately be connected to a CSR via real-time online chat. The CSR's computer automatically identifies the customer and provides the customer's records for the CSR. In addition, many insurers offer self-service options to producers, who can visit a Web site to obtain information about products; print copies of marketing materials; download interactive software that enables them to prepare sales presentations for customers; view information about sales commissions and the status of transactions they have submitted; view policyowner correspondence and information regarding claims and policy transactions processed on policies belonging to their customers; and obtain information, complete forms, and submit changes on behalf of their customers.

While some customers view self-service as a convenience, others prefer to interact with CSRs. Thus, most insurers offer customers a choice of self-service or human-assisted service.

Ensuring Excellent Telephone Communication

Although other technologies have become increasingly important, the telephone remains the essential link in maintaining communication between an insurer and its customers. CSRs use telephones extensively to explore customer needs and to gather information to fulfill those needs.

To ensure effective communication with customers, CSRs are taught to avoid using technical terms, but instead to use everyday language and to keep their responses simple and specific. Rather than saying, "Your EOB just arrived, and co-payments and deductibles are being accounted for so that our comm center can cut a check," a CSR would be trained to say, "We now have everything we need to handle your claim, and we'll mail your check this afternoon."

Providing customer service by telephone over a long period can lead to employee frustration and burnout. Therefore, most insurers allow CSRs to rotate off this service for certain hours each day or to work in other customer service areas for weeks or months before returning to telephone duties.

Documenting Customer Service Guidelines and Procedures

To ensure consistency and accuracy in the service provided to all customers, insurers document the guidelines and procedures that CSRs are to use. Insurers use many means of documenting such guidelines and procedures, including—as we mentioned earlier—electronic manuals available on each CSR's computer and printed manuals.

One of the most important ways of ensuring consistent service is to inform every employee promptly about changes in guidelines and procedures. If an insurer uses an electronic procedures manual, such changes can be highlighted or presented in a bright color to capture employees' attention. Many companies also use a daily online bulletin board to inform the staff of changes and additions to procedures, and regulations. If an insurer uses a printed manual, employees typically are required to update their manuals regularly and follow the most recent procedures and guidelines. Most insurance companies assign one employee or one team, depending on the size of the department, to be responsible for updating documentation and communicating the changes to all the staff.

Customer Service and Conservation

As we mentioned previously, an important goal of customer service is to preserve the insurer's existing business. *Conservation* is the process of ensuring that policies do not lapse but are retained on an insurer's books for as long as possible. Today, most conservation efforts are computer-generated. The main role of the CSR in these efforts is knowing what material was generated by the computer so the CSR can respond if the policyholder has questions, needs more information, or is looking for more options. Figure 12.5 lists many approaches an insurer may take to conserve policies, some of which we will elaborate upon in this section.

Providing exceptional customer service helps foster customer loyalty, and as customer loyalty increases, so does policy conservation. *Customer loyalty* represents a customer's feeling of attachment to or preference for a company's people, products, or services. A loyal customer is less likely to surrender her policy or allow it to lapse.

An insurer typically earns customer loyalty by cultivating a strong relationship with the customer and being responsive to the customer's needs and wants. Providing customers with easy access to a CSR is important to customer satisfaction. In addition, by monitoring all customer complaints to identify trends, an insurer often can help policyowners who appear concerned about their coverage or who indicate dissatisfaction with the insurance company.

Providing basic satisfaction of a customer's needs does not automatically guarantee customer loyalty. Customers who claim to be satisfied with the service they have received may be willing to defect to another company if they are offered lower prices or more value for the money. To attain customer loyalty, a company must provide outstanding customer service as well as good products. Figure 12.6 provides examples of how exceptional service can turn a satisfied customer into a loyal customer.

In addition to conserving policies through providing exceptional customer service, CSRs help insurers achieve conservation through communication with policyowners, retention of orphan policyowners (which we describe later in this

Figure 12.5. Approaches to Conserving Business

- Giving producers access to information about payments that policyowners make to flexible premium policies so that producers can take action if payments decline or fall below the required level

- Providing annual reports containing projections of values on flexible-premium policies to ensure products are meeting policyowners' current and future needs

- Providing multiple reminders of premiums due

- Sending notices of late premiums to both policyowners and producers

- Conferring with policyowners who make maximum loan requests to ensure that policy values are adequate to keep coverage in force

- Advising policyowners who request a policy surrender about alternatives, such as a policy loan

- Offering insureds who leave a group plan options for continuing their coverage on an individual basis

- Offering a toll-free number and a Web site or e-mail address for policyowners to contact the insurer

- Surveying policyowners about their satisfaction with producers and products to identify problems and devise solutions

- Providing extensive and ongoing training to CSRs

- Testing the effectiveness of notices, letters, and other communication with policyowners to determine the most effective and efficient approaches

- Tracking the relationship between conservation and persistency and publicizing the results to staff and management

chapter), superior claim service, customer feedback, and producer efforts. Keep in mind that insurers' customer service functions typically are automated and that many of the activities we attribute to CSRs actually are performed by administration systems.

Conservation Through Communication with Policyowners

Conservation requires communication with policyowners. For example, insurers conserve business by informing policyowners of upcoming changes in premiums or coverage. For policies that require higher premiums at certain ages, a CSR usually informs each policyowner of the change and asks whether the policyowner is interested in discussing other coverage options with a producer. If a certain type of coverage terminates on a specific birthday of the insured—for instance, the 60th or 70th—most insurers send policyowners a letter stating that the coverage

---

Figure 12.6. Examples of Providing Exceptional Customer Service to Create Customer Loyalty

- During the course of a telephone conversation with a CSR at Solidarity Insurance Company, an elderly customer, Bill Winslett, remarks that he is worried about his health during the coming snowstorm because he cannot afford to pay his heating bill. Recalling a local news report about reduced heating costs for those in need, the CSR, Maya Singh, suggests that Mr. Winslett contact his local utility company to see if it offers a similar service. Now, whenever Mr. Winslett calls Solidarity with a question, he asks to speak to Ms. Singh because he feels this CSR cares about him as a person as well as a customer.

- A customer, Lara Kirsh, calls her insurance company because her last premium payment was not credited to her account, although she mailed it several days ago. The CSR, Jason Montell, politely explains that the process can sometimes take several days. Hearing the concern in Ms. Kirsh's voice, Mr. Montell promises to check her account each day and notify her as soon as the payment is posted. Ms. Kirsh is confident that Mr. Montell will follow through on his commitment. Two days later, she receives confirmation from Mr. Montell that her account has been credited, and because of the special attention she has received, she recommends the company to several friends.

---

will terminate on that date and asking whether they would like to have a producer explain how to continue coverage with the insurer.

Because customers can feel resentful if the only time they hear from an insurer is on the occasion of such a premium change or policy termination, many insurers maintain frequent contact with customers throughout the length of the business relationship. The insurer may mail an annual summary of benefits statement that explains all existing coverages and the benefits paid during the previous year. CSRs also may stay in touch with customers by asking about their satisfaction with the insurer's service, a topic we discuss later in this chapter.

CSRs also contact policyowners who have not paid premiums in a timely manner to indicate the insurer's interest in continuing the business relationship. CSRs may suggest that the policyowner simplify his premium payment method. Premiums that are paid on a monthly basis by check are the most likely to lapse and to experience problems with late payments. Therefore, many insurers encourage policyowners to pay premiums through *electronic funds transfer (EFT)*, a method of transferring funds between financial intermediaries through an electronic computer network. In some cases, insurers accept credit cards for premium payments.

Insurers also acknowledge that customers' needs change and that insurance coverage may no longer be needed. Every insurer hopes that if customers do terminate their coverage, they will purchase other products from the insurer in the future. Surveying customers about the reasons for the termination of their coverage can help insurers determine if their products or procedures can be improved to conserve business and affect customers.

Conservation of Orphan Policyowners

An *orphan policyowner* is a policyowner whose original producer is no longer available to provide service. The producer may have moved from the area, stopped marketing the insurer's products, retired, or died; or the policyowner may have moved to another geographic area that his original producer does not serve. Without regular communication from the producer, a policyowner could cancel or surrender the policy and purchase coverage from another insurer whose producer can provide ongoing service.

To help conserve the business of orphan policyowners, CSRs attempt to recommend to them a producer who is in the same geographic area. Alternatively, a CSR might contact a nearby producer directly and ask the producer to contact the orphan policyowner. Insurers generally offer some financial incentive to producers to encourage them to "adopt" orphan policyowners and provide them with effective service.

Some insurers have established electronic tracking of producer activities to identify producers who are no longer active and may have left orphan policyowners. The sooner an insurer can identify an orphan policyowner, the more likely the insurer can conserve that person's business. In addition, some insurers establish a unit in the home office to work with orphan policyowners by phone or by mail to fulfill policyowner needs for additional insurance products. Some insurers have established a program to communicate regularly with every policyowner so that even if a policyowner becomes an orphan, she will still feel that she has strong ties to the insurer and can obtain answers to questions and solutions to problems.

Conservation Through Superior Claim Service

Customers who purchase insurance generally interact with an insurer or its producers when the coverage is sold and when a claim is submitted. For health insurance, for example, a customer may interact with the insurance company many times. Therefore, insurance companies that provide top-quality service usually encourage their claim analysts to provide rapid, accessible, customer-focused, and simplified claim handling. Customers want their claims processed as rapidly as possible; they want easy ways to get in touch with the insurer to submit a claim; and they want personal treatment and clear explanations while their claims are being handled. Insurers whose claim handling satisfies these customer desires enhance their relationship with customers.

Conservation Through Customer Feedback

Most insurers demonstrate their interest in providing excellent customer service by evaluating customers' needs through telephone surveys and printed questionnaires. Some insurers have established online feedback systems to gather information about customers' needs, preferences, and knowledge of insurance products and services.

In designing an online feedback system, an insurer must take into consideration the need to preserve a customer's privacy and confidentiality. Transmitting contract numbers, personal identification numbers, and other confidential information may inhibit a customer's willingness to use such a system, so most insurers do not require that kind of information from customers who complete an online survey.

Some insurers' online feedback systems permit customers to respond freely about any topic. Typically, such a system invites customers to send an e-mail, using a statement similar to the following:

> *We welcome your questions and invite you to ask our experts questions about life and health insurance 24 hours a day, 7 days a week. We also welcome your thoughts about the way we have treated you as a customer and how we might serve you better. Please write your questions and comments in the space below, and then click on "SEND" to e-mail your questions and comments to us. We will immediately acknowledge receipt of your e-mail, and we will provide you with a prompt answer.*

Other online feedback systems provide surveys to which customers can give responses. Figure 12.7 provides an example of an online feedback survey system.

Conservation Through Producers

Most insurers have found that a principal cause of lapse or transfer of business is lack of producer involvement with policyowners. Thus, insurance companies train producers to provide on-going, top-quality customer service. Insurers often encourage producers to contact their customers at least once a year to review customers' needs and to maintain relationships.

In addition, insurers (1) try to recruit producers who are concerned with selling only coverage that is appropriate for customers' needs; (2) educate producers about how to match coverage to customers' needs; (3) provide producers with information about the insurer's underwriting principles and requirements; and (4) maintain records of the persistency of each producer's business.

Some unethical producers attempt to generate commission income by engaging in twisting and churning when replacing policies, as we discussed in Chapter 3. To help prevent such activities, insurers who receive notice of surrenders and lapses not only contact the producer, but also send a letter to the policyowner with information comparing the coverage and the premiums of the previous policy and the new policy.

Some insurers also structure their commissions to reward producers whose business remains in force for an extended period. For instance, an insurer might pay a producer a ***persistency bonus***, a sum of money paid as compensation to an insurance producer when a policy continues in force beyond an initial period, usually five years.

Figure 12.7. Example of an Online Feedback Survey System

1. How often do you visit www.longterm.com?

   ____ Daily ____ Weekly ____ Monthly ____ Rarely

2. What's the main reason for your visit to www.longterm.com today?

   ____ Look up daily price information for mutual funds and/or annuities

   ____ Read the latest news about Longterm Life

   ____ Contact my area representative

   ____ Learn about products and services from Longterm Life

   ____ Follow-up on a topic I learned about elsewhere

   ____ Other: _____

3. What is the most important function or content you would like to see added to www.longterm.com?

   ____ Access to all of my account information

   ____ More detailed information about products and services

   ____ Downloadable forms (which ones):

   _____

   _____

Thanks for responding to our survey. Now tell us a little about you.

First Name_____ MI _____

Last Name _____

Address 1 _____

Address 2 _____

City _____ State _____

Zip_____

E-mail _____

I would like to receive more information about Longterm Life products, services and offers. ____ Yes ____ No

Key Terms

customer service representative
work team
traditional team
semi-autonomous team
self-directed team
customer contact center
call center
knowledge management system

customer contact system
interactive voice response (IVR)
   system
conservation
customer loyalty
electronic funds transfer (EFT)
orphan policyowner
persistency bonus

Chapter 13

Customer Service Practices

Objectives:

After studying this chapter, you should be able to

- Distinguish between quantitative and qualitative performance measurements and give examples of each type of performance measurement technique
- Describe customer services practices for routine insurance transactions
- Identify different types of beneficiaries and explain the process for changing a beneficiary designation
- Distinguish between an absolute and collateral assignment of a life insurance policy and describe the CSR's role in an assignment
- Describe the processes for administering policy loans, changing dividend options, and making changes to variable life insurance policies

Outline

Customer Service Quality Control
- Quantitative Performance Measurement
- Qualitative Performance Measurement

Customer Service Transactions
- Routine Customer Service Transactions
- More Complex Customer Service Transactions

In Chapter 12, we reviewed general customer service principles and practices, including providing customer service for policyowners and producers and helping to conserve business. In this chapter, we discuss how an insurer's customer service representatives handle specific types of insurance service transactions.

Customer Service Quality Control

Most insurers evaluate their customer service function by using qualitative and quantitative performance measurements, although usually with a greater emphasis on quantitative measurement.

Quantitative Performance Measurement

Insurers use quantitative performance measurements to assess all administrative functions, but these types of measurements are particularly useful in evaluating customer service. ***Quantitative performance measurement*** is a type of performance measurement that uses numerical methods to track and report objective results to determine how quickly, often, accurately, and profitably processes and transactions are completed. Quantitative performance measurements focus on those dimensions of customer service that can be quantified numerically. Figure 13.1 lists various customer service quantitative performance measurements.

Qualitative Performance Measurement

Most insurers use various methods to gather qualitative performance-related information about customer service. ***Qualitative performance measurement*** is a type of performance measurement that focuses on behaviors, attitudes, or opinions to determine how efficiently and effectively processes and transactions are completed. Qualitative performance measurement methods can be used to evaluate interactions with customers. For example, a customer may be asked to complete a survey in which he assesses the company representative's level of courtesy and clarity of communication. Or, randomly selected customers may receive mail surveys or telephone inquiries asking their views on the customer service they have received and inquiring about their level of satisfaction with it. It is important to note that it is the nature of the information obtained from a survey that categorizes it as either a quantitative or a qualitative performance measurement method. If a survey were to ask for objective information about a customer's usage of self-help customer service options, the survey would be a quantitative performance measurement. Other qualitative performance measurement methods

Figure 13.1. Customer Service Quantitative Performance Measurements

SERVICE LEVEL/ACCESSIBILITY TO THE CUSTOMER

- *Service level.* The percentage of inbound customer contacts answered within a specified time frame—for example, 80 percent within 20 seconds.

- *Number of blocked calls.* The number of telephone calls that encounter a busy signal and cannot get through to the customer contract center.

- *Average speed of answer.* The amount of time, on average, that telephone callers are on hold before being connected with a CSR.

- *Abandonment rate.* The percentage of inbound telephone calls that are automatically placed on hold and then terminated by the caller before the call is answered by a CSR.

- *Misdirected calls.* The number or percentage of inbound telephone calls that are transferred to the wrong department.

TIMELINESS

- *Turnaround time*, also known as *average handling time*. The amount of time necessary to complete a particular customer-initiated request or transaction.

- *First contact resolution.* The percentage of inbound customer contacts that are successfully completed at the initial point of contact—that is, without being transferred and without the need for follow-up work.

QUALITY

- *Quality rate.* The accuracy of a particular type of transaction. Quality rate is often expressed as a percentage of the total number of transactions handled or processed, such as 99.5 percent of account transactions having no reported errors.

- *Error rate.* The percentage of transactions that resulted in errors, such as 0.5 percent of account transactions reported errors.

PRODUCTIVITY

- *Processes completed.* The number of transactions that are handled within a specified period of time.

Source: Adapted from Mark Adel and Barbara Foxenberger Brown, *Foundations of Customer Service* [Atlanta: LOMA (Life Office Management Association, Inc.), © 2003], 321. Used with permission; all rights reserved.

include observation and monitoring, mystery shoppers, and complaint monitoring. Because qualitative performance measures typically require a certain amount of subjective judgment, qualitative performance measurement is more difficult to administer and interpret than quantitative measurement.

Customer Satisfaction Surveys

Customer satisfaction surveys are surveys designed to help a company determine whether its products, prices, and services are meeting customer expectations. Although surveys generally are not used to provide feedback on the performance of individual CSRs, customers may be asked to comment on the following elements concerning verbal and written customer service:

- Friendliness and professionalism of customer service staff

- Easily understood communication

- Timeliness of service

- Accuracy in completing a request

- Overall level of service

Observation and Monitoring

To gather information about the quality of service delivered by individual CSRs, many insurers require managers, senior staff, or trainers to observe or monitor a percentage of each employee's transactions. A manager or trainer might examine files of completed cases and those in progress and might listen to live or taped telephone calls between customers and the CSRs. Figure 13.2 illustrates a portion of a checklist used to evaluate the quality of telephone conversations between CSRs and customers.

Generally, a manager looks carefully at cases that are returned to a CSR for additional work as the result of an error in the initial transaction. Sometimes the manager makes follow-up telephone calls to customers to ask how well their transactions were handled and to solicit suggestions for improving service. Insurers also use peer review, by which CSRs monitor and evaluate one another's service delivery. Peer review requires careful training so that the assessments will be consistent.

Mystery Shoppers

Insurers also measure performance through mystery shoppers. A *mystery shopper* is a trained evaluator who approaches or calls customer service and pretends to be a customer. Mystery shoppers may be company employees who are not known to the CSR, or they may be employees of an outside company that specializes in such evaluations. The mystery shopper conducts a transaction with the employee and then evaluates the employee's handling of the transaction. Mystery shoppers provide greater flexibility than monitoring "real" customer interactions because mystery shoppers can manipulate the circumstances to see how CSRs respond to various scenarios.

Figure 13.2. Checklist Used to Evaluate the Quality of Phone Conversations

✓ Identify self and offer assistance

✓ Determine the reason for the call by listening carefully

✓ Express help/regret/acknowledgment appropriately

✓ Request and verify caller information

✓ Use caller's name and "sir" or "ma'am" as appropriate

✓ Accept appropriate responsibility for actions taken or not taken

✓ Provide accurate, complete information in an organized fashion

✓ Inform caller of any risks involved

✓ Summarize action to be taken and verify customer's understanding, giving an expected timeline where appropriate

✓ Offer additional assistance

✓ Offer alternative solutions to problems

✓ Avoid insurance jargon

✓ Use appropriate presentation: pace, inflection, enunciation, courtesy, personalization

✓ Use "please" and "thank you"

✓ Use a proper approach to placing a customer on hold or transferring customer to another department

✓ Avoid short or curt answers

✓ Remain calm and avoid becoming defensive

✓ End call by saying "Thank you for calling" and "Have a nice day"

✓ Accurately record the call

Complaint Monitoring

Studying complaint letters, e-mails, and telephone calls also can be a valuable method of gathering performance-related information. Typically, isolated complaints are not a reliable measure of a customer service system's overall performance, but a study of the source, number, frequency, and nature of complaints can indicate customer service problems or trends.

Customer Service Transactions

Most insurers accept telephone requests from policyowners for most services, including changing personal information and coverage and requesting policy loans. Typically, only policyowners have the legal right to receive information about the policy. To ensure that the individual calling is the policyowner, a CSR requests key personal information—such as the account number or identifier, date of birth, last four or five digits of her Social Security or social insurance number, or password—before providing information or processing requests.

Many insurers also offer policyowners the option to make changes and requests through the insurer's Web site. In addition to being personalized, this information is secure—only authorized individuals can view the information. To ensure this security, policyowners typically are assigned a login and password or personal identification number (PIN) that helps to confirm their identities before proceeding to a "Members Only" area of the Web site to request information or complete transactions. Many common customer service requests—such as changing contact information, changing beneficiaries, requesting coverage changes, and handling premium payments—can be completed through the insurer's Web site without policyowners having to speak to CSRs.

First, we discuss some routine customer service practices, such as providing information, processing requests, and handling complaints. Then, we examine some more complex transactions that CSRs perform specifically for life insurance.

Routine Customer Service Transactions

Many customer services provided by insurers are routine and can be accomplished quickly. Every day, CSRs handle requests for information and they respond to concerns about various aspects of coverage and service. A complete list of the types of requests fielded by an insurer's customer service staff would fill many pages, but some of the most frequently encountered customer requests relate to

■ Providing information and answering questions about the type, amount, and features of the coverage

■ Changing names and addresses

■ Changing coverage

■ Handling premium payments

■ Handling returned mail

■ Handling complaints

■ Fulfilling other policyowner needs such as providing duplicate policies

Insurers use technology and policy administration systems to complete transactions and generate customer correspondence whenever practical. CSRs can request frequently used forms and correspondence to be automatically generated and sent to policyholders.

In the following discussion, we first distinguish between the types of information generally requested for individual and for group insurance. In discussing other types of customer service activities, we do not distinguish between these types of coverage unless such a distinction is necessary because many of the customer service activities are basically the same whether the coverage is individual or group.

The administration of a group insurance plan is primarily a matter of record-keeping. For example, some of the necessary records for a group life insurance plan include the name and amount of insurance on each group insured and dependent and the name of each beneficiary. Whether the coverage is an insurer-administered group plan or a self-administered group plan, the insurer receives monthly reports regarding the composition of the group and any changes in the group.

Installation is a series of activities involved in issuing a master contract and its individual certificates to an insured group. Whether the group plan is insurer-administered or self-administered, member service plays a part in ensuring that a group policy is installed correctly and completely. The role of member service in a group installation generally involves providing information and answering questions about the plan's eligibility requirements, benefits, and provisions, as well as the portion of the premium, if any, that each group insured must pay.

The policyholder typically informs the group insureds about the policy purchase. The insurer provides sample letters, brochures, enrollment forms, and other information that can be distributed to the group insureds. Member service might help prepare these materials.

While a self-administered group policy is in force, a group representative of the insurance company may provide member service by answering questions and assisting the group in administering the coverage effectively. This representative maintains close contact with the insurer's claim staff to identify and help resolve any problems. For instance, if a group insured is having difficulty in providing information required to process a claim, the insurer's group representative may advise the employee or the group plan administrator about the required information and ways to obtain it. To provide adequate assistance to group insureds, the insurer's group representative must be well informed about the coverage, the claim administration process, and the general administration of group products.

In addition to providing information as requested, the insurer's group representative also enhances communication by making periodic calls on each insured group. During these calls, the group representative checks the activities of the group plan administrator in administering the plan, informs the administrator of changes in laws and insurance practices that affect the group plan, and provides guidance if the plan administration fails to meet the insurer's standards.

The group representative also helps conserve the business by discussing the group's evolving needs for coverage and suggesting changes to the coverage. By evaluating the group's claim history, the group representative helps prepare the group for the next year's rates, which often depend on the level of claims made by the group during the preceding year.

Providing Information and Answering Questions

From the time a policy is sold until the relationship between the policyowner and the insurer comes to an end, a policyowner can have questions about any topic related to his coverage. For example, life changes such as marriage, the birth or adoption of a child, divorce, death of a spouse, or a debilitating illness or injury often cause policyowners to question the effect on their coverage.

CSRs provide valuable information and assistance by knowing the answers to the most commonly asked questions and being familiar with the information sources needed to readily answer the uncommon questions. CSRs often explain policy language and answer questions about policy benefits. For example, an individual insured calls the insurer to find out if he qualifies for the waiver of premium for disability benefit in a life insurance policy. A CSR lets the insured know if and under what conditions he qualifies for this benefit.

Changing Names and Addresses

The name of a policyowner, beneficiary, or insured may need to be changed for several reasons. Sometimes a name has been misspelled, and correction is needed to ensure that the individual's records don't get confused with another person's. More commonly, a name change results from marriage, divorce, adoption, or court order. Most insurers require an individual to complete and sign a form requesting the name change, and many insurers also require a copy of a marriage license, divorce decree, or other legal documentation verifying the name change. When a name change is requested because of naturalization of citizenship, many insurers require as proof a notarized sworn *affidavit*, which is a written statement made before an official who is authorized to administer oaths. After a name change has been made, a CSR sends the policyowner a copy of the face page of the policy or an endorsement to the policy to verify that the insurer has made the requested change.

Figure 13.3 illustrates a form that an insured, a policyowner, or a beneficiary uses to request a name change. Note that this form would be used only for name changes, not to change the policyowner or beneficiary of the policy; however, some companies may include several transactions on one form rather than using separate forms for each request.

Changing the name of a policyowner, a beneficiary, or an insured requires that the insurer modify many different insurance records. The master policy file, the billing file, the producer's file, and other records should all be in accord with one another. If an insurer's administration systems are integrated, a name is changed in all locations when it is changed in any location. Therefore, if a policyowner requests a change in his name, that change will be reflected throughout the insurer's records. As we mentioned in Chapter 1, some insurers' systems are not integrated, in which case the insurer may use middleware or a centralized data repository to effect a name change in all the insurer's records.

Another of the most common changes requested is a change of address for an individual policyowner, beneficiary, or insured. Because the insurer often sends premium notices, correspondence, and checks to the policyowner, beneficiary, or insured by mail, having correct addresses is imperative for continuing communication without delays due to returned or lost mail. Like changing a name, changing an address requires that all of an insurer's records reflect the change. To prevent

---

Figure 13.3. Name Change Form

Current name of the   _____ Insured _____

                         _____ Owner _____

                         _____ Beneficiary_____

Social Security Number _____

Change the name of the _____ Insured to _____

                         _____ Owner to _____

                         _____ Beneficiary to_____

Because of   _____ Marriage

                         _____ Divorce

                         _____ Other

(If the name has been changed for any reason other than marriage, divorce or adoption, a certified copy of the legal document authorizing the change must be submitted.)

_____   _____
Signature of Owner or Officer with Title   Date   Signature of Joint Owner (If any)   Date

_____
Signature of Witness (Disinterested Party), if required   Date

---

fraudulent changes, some companies mail a letter to the policyowner's old and new addresses verifying the changes that were made.

For a self-administered group policy, the policyholder typically maintains records of names and addresses. The insurer needs to verify names and addresses only at the point of a claim submission.

Administering Policy Changes

Often, a policyowner's financial situation, insurability status, or insurance need make it necessary or desirable for the policyowner to request a policy change. Policyowners may want to increase or decrease the amount of coverage, add or delete people from coverage, change the plan of insurance, or add or delete riders.

Policy changes to group insurance occur frequently as employees join or leave an organization. Member service handles the ongoing changes in group insurance coverage by enrolling new insureds and terminating coverage for those who leave the group. In self-administered group plans, the policyholder keeps these records.

Policy changes that involve an increased risk to the insurer often require CSRs to work with underwriting. The underwriter's primary concern is to evaluate the increased risk represented by the requested change in coverage. In considering requested policy changes, the underwriter considers (1) whether a proposed change increases a policy's net amount at risk and/or (2) whether the insured's original insurability status has changed. CSRs and underwriters work closely to ensure that each requested change is promptly evaluated and that those involved—principally the policyowner and, sometimes, the producer—are kept informed of progress on the case.

A policyowner who wants to make a policy change must complete a policy change form specifying the requested changes. Figure 13.4 illustrates part of a typical form used to request a change of coverage.

Increasing the Amount of Coverage

Policyowners often want to increase the amount of coverage provided by a policy. For example, a universal life insurance policyowner may want to increase the face amount of his policy.

Depending on the type of coverage, increasing the amount of coverage can be accomplished by

- Increasing the face amount of the policy

- Adding a new type of benefit or rider not included under the existing coverage

Such requests to increase the amount of coverage usually are handled in a routine manner by customer service, but, because increasing the amount of coverage may increase the risk for the insurer, granting a policyowner an increase in coverage may require additional underwriting. Each insurer establishes its own procedures to define those benefits and levels of coverage that do and do not require the involvement of underwriting.

Decreasing the Amount of Coverage

Just as policyowners may wish to increase the amount of coverage, they also may wish to decrease the amount of coverage provided by a policy.

Depending on the type of coverage, decreasing the amount of coverage can be accomplished by

- Reducing the face amount of insurance

- Removing one or more benefits or riders offered by the existing coverage

Because requests to decrease the amount of coverage entail reducing rather than increasing risk, CSRs can handle such requests without referring them to underwriting.

Change in Type of Insurance

For a policyowner who wants to make a change in the type of insurance, the underwriter considers several factors, among them the reason for the requested change. A policyowner might want to change the insurance program into a higher-premium plan with a greater investment in the policy. This type of change usually

Figure 13.4. Portion of a Typical Change of Coverage Request Form

For Contract/Policy Number_____

Subject to the terms of this policy, I hereby apply for change(s) checked below:

1. (a) Change: ___ Entire Policy ___ Continue Balance ___ Term Rider ___ Rollover Cash Value ___ Refund Cash Value

   Amount _____
   Policy Date _____
   Plan _____
   Premium/How Payable _____
   Auto Premium Loan ___ yes ___ no

   (b) Complete if changing existing Universal or Variable Life
   ____ Increase in Specified Amount of $ _____
   ____ Decrease in Specified Amount of $ _____
   ____ Change Death Benefit Option to
       ___ Increasing, as defined in the policy (check one)
           ____ Reduce the Specified Amount to equal the death benefit minus the cash value, as of the effective date of this change
           ____ Do not change the Specified Amount (satisfactory evidence of insurability may be required)
       ____ Level, as defined in the policy
   ___ Change my Premium to $_____ effective on the _____ mode

   (c) Additional Benefits (include benefits being continued)

   Include Cancel
   ____   ____   Disability Waiver Benefit on Insured
   ____   ____   Waiver of Specified Premium $ _____ on Insured
   ____   ____   Guaranteed Insurability Rider $ _____ Option Amount
   ____   ____   Accelerated Benefit Rider

poses no problem for the underwriter because the insurer's net amount at risk will decrease more rapidly under the higher-premium plan than under the original plan. An underwriting problem may result, however, if a waiver of premium benefit is included in the contract because the high premium for the new plan will increase the amount at risk for the waiver of premium benefit. Thus, a premium increase above a certain dollar amount may require additional evidence of insurability.

Some policyowner requests for a change to a lower-premium plan result in only a moderate increase in the insurer's net amount at risk. Underwriting for such a request may be more liberal than the original underwriting because the first-year acquisition costs, such as the producer's commission, probably already have been paid. In many insurance companies, therefore, policy changes involving only moderate increases in the amount at risk are approved by customer service without referral to an underwriter, but only under the following conditions:

- The insured has no history of impairment or rating

- The height and weight of the insured are within current standard limits

- All answers on the health declaration of the policy change form are acceptable

In addition to the previous conditions, some insurers allow customer service to approve such changes only if no MIB codes are listed for the insured.

Figure 13.5 shows a sample health declaration section of a policy change request form.

Adding or Deleting Riders

When a policyowner makes a request to add a rider, the CSR first evaluates if the product allows for the requested change and, if so, sends the customer the appropriate forms to sign. Because increasing the amount of coverage may increase the risk for the insurer, granting a policyowner an increase in coverage often requires additional underwriting and possibly an increase in premium.

Removing or canceling a rider requires no underwriting action because the risk to the insurer is decreased when the coverage is changed. Instead, the insurer calculates the new premium and, if necessary, sends a premium refund to the policyowner.

Handling Premium Payments

In some insurance companies, customer service sends premium due notices and handles premium payments. Many insurers use automated systems to generate these notices, record the payments, and update the status of the policy. For fixed premium insurance, to continue a policy in force, a policyowner must send premium payments to the insurer according to an established schedule, which may be monthly, quarterly, semiannually, or annually. For flexible premium insurance, such as universal life coverage, the automated systems send reminder notices to encourage policyowners to pay premiums even if additional premiums are not necessary to keep the policy in force.

For group insurance, the policyholder pays premiums to the insurer whether the group plan is contributory or noncontributory. If the group plan is contributory, the policyholder collects the premium amount due from the group insureds, usually by payroll deduction, and submits them to the insurer.

Figure 13.5. Sample Health Declaration Section

SUPPLEMENTAL APPLICATION

The undersigned hereby amends Contract/Policy Number _____ dated _____ .

All the following questions apply to the proposed insured and any additional proposed insureds.

Since the date of the application, have you	Proposed Insured		Additional Insureds		If the answer of any of these questions is "YES", give complete details for each insured including date of last treatment and name/address of attending physicians.
	Yes	No	Yes	No	
a. Started racing of any kind; skin or scuba diving; parachuting, sky-diving, or hang gliding; mountain, rock, or technical climbing; or participating in private aviation?					
b. Applied for life or health insurance to any other insurance company or had any life or health insurance reinstated, declined, postponed, or modified?					
c. Been paid or made claim for any benefits for injuries or sickness?					
d. Had any surgical operation or been advised to have any surgical operation which has not been performed?					
e. Been admitted to a hospital or other medical facility or been treated at any hospital, clinic, or any other medical facility?					
f. Consulted or had an appointment to consult a doctor, surgeon, or other medical practitioner?					

I agree that this Supplemental Application will be considered an amendment and supplement to my original application. I have read the completed Supplemental Application before signing below. All statements and answers in this application are correctly recorded, and are full, complete and true. I understand that any false statements or material misrepresentations may result in the loss of coverage issued in reliance on this application.

_____
Signature of Proposed Insured

_____
Signature of Additional Insured, if applicable

_____
Signature of Agent

_____
Signature of Owner/Trustee (if other than Proposed Insured)

If a premium payment is late, most insurance companies send the policyowner a *policy grace notice*, also called a *lapse notice*, which is a written notification that the policy's grace period is about to expire. If a premium is paid during the grace period, the premium is considered to have been paid on time. Figure 13.6 shows one version of wording used in a policy grace notice.

Some policyowners choose to increase or decrease the frequency of premium payments. For example, a policyowner who previously has paid monthly premiums for health insurance may decide to change to a semiannual or annual premium payment mode because the premium charged for less frequent payments is usually somewhat lower than for more frequent payments.

Generally, when a policyowner submits a request for a change of premium payment frequency, a CSR can approve the change if the request meets the insurer's premium payment requirements. However, insurers sometimes do not permit changes in premium payment frequency because of complications resulting from due dates that are inconsistent with a policy's anniversary. In addition, if a policy has a waiver of premium provision and the premiums currently are being waived, an insurer generally does not allow a change to a more frequent premium payment mode.

CSRs also assist policyowners who may wish to change the method of premium payment. For example, rather than using the direct billing method, where a policyowner would mail a check to pay for the premium, the policyowner may want to authorize an electronic funds transfer (EFT) and have her bank automatically pay the premium on its due date. A group insured may authorize payroll deduction, which allows her employer to deduct the payment from her paycheck.

If insurance coverage provides for a change of premium when an insured reaches a specified age, customer service sends the policyowner a premium bill or a notice that reflects the new premium. In addition, customer service notifies the staff responsible for paying producers' commissions to modify the premium-based commission amount due to a producer, if applicable.

Customer service also handles various other age-related changes to certain coverages. For example, some types of coverage terminate when an insured reaches a specified age, and other types of coverage provide that an insured becomes eligible

---

Figure 13.6. Sample Policy Grace Notice

There is no longer sufficient surrender value in your policy to prevent termination or lapse of the policy. Accordingly, your policy has entered a grace period and will lapse if a sufficient premium payment to continue your policy is not received before the end of the grace period.

To continue your coverage in force, you must pay the minimum premium, which is $ _____ . This premium must be received on or before the grace period expiration date, which is _____ .

We appreciate your business and hope that you will remit your premium promptly.

for alternative coverage at a stated age. For these and other types of changes, customer service is responsible for notifying policyowners of coverage changes and premium rates and arranging premium payment according to policy provisions.

To conserve business, most insurers send producers a list of policyowners whose premium payments have become 20 to 90 days overdue or send producers a copy of the payment notice. Thus, producers have an opportunity to contact policyowners who have not paid their premiums in a timely manner and encourage them to retain the coverage or to modify it so that the coverage and the premium amount more nearly match their current needs.

Handling Returned Mail

Many departments of insurance companies designate staff to handle mail that has been returned. Claims and underwriting, for example, carefully investigate returned mail and send it to its intended recipients, if possible. Customer service also is concerned with handling returned mail because of the need to communicate with the customer and ensure that requested changes and other transactions are completed promptly and accurately.

For most insurers, the first step in attempting to resend mail to its intended recipients involves checking whether a more current address has been received. An insurer's administration system may contain updated address information. If, after checking the system, a CSR discovers that no current address has been entered, a note or code is put into the system to show that mail was returned and that no further mail should be sent to that address.

Many insurance companies subscribe to a national database that allows CSRs to search for a more current address by entering a recipient's name, Social Security or social insurance number, date of birth, and last known address. Insurers usually pay only for successful searches—that is, searches that result in identification of a usable address.

For mail related to variable insurance and other regulated products, CSRs usually intensify the search by calling directory assistance in the city of the last known address and attempting to seek a new address. In many instances, CSRs call a producer to inquire about the location of the addressee.

At the completion of a search, if a CSR has been unable to find a viable address, another note or code is usually entered into the information system to indicate that the insurer not only received returned mail, but also could not locate a mailing address. Having made a good faith attempt to find the addressee, the CSR files the undelivered mail in the event that the client later contacts the insurer.

Handling Complaints

Handling complaints takes priority over many other customer service tasks.[1] The procedures for handling customer complaints are designed to comply with regulatory requirements, minimize the risk of lawsuits, and improve customer service. As mentioned earlier, insurers can identify customer service problems by studying the source, number, frequency, and nature of complaints. Customer complaints can be related to virtually any product or activity and can vary in intensity from minor irritation to extreme frustration and anger. Most insurers establish different policies and procedures for dealing with complaints based on the subject matter and the way the caller presents the complaint.

A complaint that pertains to the timeliness, accuracy, courtesy, or professionalism of the company's interactions with its customers is known as a *service complaint*. Service complaints can be related to customer contacts as well as other types of customer service, such as record-keeping and billing. Upon the receipt of a service complaint, some firms institute service recovery, which are the efforts an organization makes to fully resolve the problem that caused a customer's dissatisfaction and win back the customer's goodwill. In addition to service complaints, an insurer may receive complaints about its products, advertising, sales activities, and compliance with regulatory or legal requirements.

Most insurers establish *escalation processes*, which are procedures that specify how an issue or complaint is to be handled in situations where the CSR is not able or authorized to address a particular request or demand. An escalation process can be as simple as transferring a call to a manager on duty or providing the customer with an address so he may mail in a letter of complaint.

Complaint handling involves many of the same issues associated with any other type of customer contact. Some of the strategies that insurers use to enable CSRs to successfully handle complaints include

- Empowering CSRs to work with dissatisfied customers and to resolve problems

- Empowering CSRs to provide first contact problem resolution

- Training CSRs to acknowledge the customer's feelings and concerns and provide empathy

- Training CSRs to interact with customers and not to take customer complaints personally

- Establishing documentation processes

- Establishing and encouraging CSRs to use escalation processes

By repeating and summarizing the customer's concerns, the CSR can validate those concerns and help the customer understand that the CSR is eager to help. Rather than indulge in blaming, denying fault, or making excuses, the CSR asks questions to help control the dialogue and obtain information needed to resolve problems.

Recognizing the importance and difficulty of complaint handling, some organizations establish work groups called *complaint teams*, also known as *customer relationship teams* or *problem resolution teams*, dedicated solely to resolving customer complaints. When a complaint arrives anywhere in the company, it is forwarded immediately to the complaint team, where it is logged in and assigned for response. A critical role of the complaint team is to identify trends in complaints and determine what might be done to prevent similar problems from occurring in the future. The complaint team is usually comprised of experienced CSRs and/or staff from the law and compliance department.

Fulfilling Other Customer Needs

In addition to performing the functions already discussed, customer service responds to other policyowner needs, including providing a duplicate copy of a policy. A policyowner may need to obtain a duplicate copy of a policy when the original policy has been lost or destroyed or is otherwise unavailable. Most insurers require a written statement signed by the policyowner stating that the policy has been lost or destroyed. A duplicate copy of a policy is stamped to indicate that it is a duplicate, and the insurer's file contains a record of the duplicate issuance.

Before issuing a duplicate copy of a policy, the CSR helps to avoid potential legal problems by verifying that the duplicate copy is needed and that the original copy is lost or destroyed. If a problem arises in verifying the loss of the original policy, the CSR usually issues a certificate of coverage rather than a duplicate policy. The *certificate of coverage* verifies that coverage exists, but does not contain all the provisions and riders that the original policy may have contained. Figure 13.7 illustrates a typical lost policy request form.

More Complex Customer Service Transactions

Although most common customer service practices can be accomplished fairly quickly and easily, some transactions require investigation and sometimes consultation with other areas such as underwriting or legal. Such transactions include converting, terminating, or reinstating a policy; changing a beneficiary; assigning policy ownership; administering loans and dividends; and handling variable life insurance products.

Figure 13.7. Typical Lost Policy Request Form

Insured _____

Contract/Policy Number _____

Choose one:

____ Full Duplicate Policy ($30.00 Administrative Fee)

____ Lost Policy Certificate (no charge)

____ Life ____ Health ____ Annuity

The undersigned hereby represents that each policy, contract, and any attached amendment or endorsements specified on this form has been lost or destroyed, and requests a duplicate copy of each such policy, contract and amendment, or a lost policy certificate as evidence of the coverage. Each of the undersigned agrees that if the lost policy, contract and amendment is later found, the duplicate policy, contract and amendment or lost policy certificate will be surrendered to the insurance company for cancellation.

Each of the undersigned further attests that this policy is not now assigned, nor has it otherwise been transferred or encumbered in any manner.

_____   _____
Date   Signature of Owner, if other than Insured

_____   _____
Signature of Insured   Other Required Signature, if any

Converting a Policy

In Chapter 3, we discussed conversion provisions in group insurance policies. Some individual life policies also contain a conversion provision that permits a policyowner to change coverage from one type of policy to another—for instance, to change from an individual term insurance policy to an individual whole life insurance policy.

A CSR checks several items in handling a request for policy conversion. First, the CSR makes sure that the conversion occurs during the conversion period if one is specified in the policy. In addition, most insurers require that the first premium payment for the new, or converted, policy be remitted when the conversion request is made. After verifying that the conversion is valid and that any required paperwork and the correct premium have been submitted, the CSR instructs the policy issue department to prepare a new policy and updates the policyowner's records to reflect the converted coverage.

Terminating a Policy

If a policyowner does not renew a policy, or if premiums have not been paid on a policy and the policyowner does not respond to a series of premium due notices, then the policy is terminated in accordance with the insurer's established procedures. The insurer sends a letter or notice to the policyowner stating that the coverage has been lapsed. Most insurers also notify the producer when coverage has been terminated so that the producer can determine the cause for the termination.

A policyowner of most types of cash value life insurance, such as whole life and universal life, might decide to terminate—or surrender—a policy by requesting that coverage cease and that the insurer send the policyowner the net cash surrender value of the policy. The *net cash surrender value* is the actual cash value available to a policyowner upon policy surrender or lapse; it equals the cash value shown in the policy increased by any cash values of paid-up additions, policy dividend accumulations, and advance premium payments and decreased by outstanding policy loans and any charges imposed on the surrender.

When a CSR receives a surrender request, she first makes certain that the person who submitted the request is legally entitled to surrender the policy. If a policyowner has assigned some or all of the rights to the policy, then the policyowner is not allowed to surrender it without the assignee's authorization. Figure 13.8 illustrates a typical cash surrender request form.

Before processing a request to surrender a policy, the CSR usually attempts to conserve the business by contacting the policyowner to ask whether an alternative action might fulfill the policyowner's needs. For instance, the CSR might suggest that the policyowner use accumulated policy dividends to pay premiums, request a policy loan for the same purpose, or reduce the amount of coverage if the original amount is no longer needed or is too expensive.

Some insurers also require the policyowner to submit the policy to the insurer before the surrender is completed and the net cash surrender value is disbursed to the policyowner. Usually, the signature of the policyowner is required to surrender the contract.

Reinstating a Policy

Reinstatement—the process by which an insurer puts back in force a policy that lapsed because of nonpayment of renewal premiums—provides advantages for both the insurer and the insured. The insurer is able to keep business on its books without incurring the high first-year expenses normally associated with acquiring new business. The insured continues to have insurance protection that might no longer be offered to new applicants or for which the insured might not qualify

---

Figure 13.8. Typical Cash Surrender Request Form

General Information

Policy/Certificate No_____

Owner's Name _____

Owner's Date of Birth_____

Owner's Social Security Number _____

Declaration of Lost Policy

We do not require the policy be returned to us. However, we do ask that the policy be destroyed once payment is received.

Income Tax Withholding Election

Federal law requires 10 percent tax to be withheld from the taxable portion of certain life insurance payments, unless you request not to have tax withheld. Even if you decide not to have federal tax withheld, you are still liable for payment of the income tax on the taxable portion of this payment. You may be subject to tax penalties under the Estimated Tax Payment Rules if your payment of estimated tax and withholding, if any, are not sufficient.

This section must be completed. If no selection is made and your surrender is considered taxable, taxes will be withheld.

I request payment of the cash surrender value in exchange for surrender of the attached policy.

Check ONE BOX:

____ I do NOT want to have Federal Income Tax withheld.

____ I DO want to have Federal Income Tax withheld.

_____   _____
Date   Signature of Owner, if other than Insured

_____   _____
Signature of Insured   Other Required Signature, if any

---

because of advanced age. In addition, a reinstated policy usually maintains the original, usually lower premium and typically can be reinstated with more liberal underwriting standards than would apply to an application for new coverage. Figure 13.9 shows a typical application for reinstatement of coverage.

When a policyowner applies for reinstatement of a lapsed policy, the CSR determines whether the policy contains a reinstatement provision. Recall that a reinstatement provision describes the conditions a policyowner must meet for an insurer to reinstate a policy within a specified time after lapse. In Chapter 10, we

---

Figure 13.9. Typical Application for Reinstatement of Coverage

Policy # _____

Insured_____

Owner _____

APPLICATION FOR REINSTATEMENT OF POLICY DESCRIBED ABOVE

1. Your present occupation _____

2. Have you for any reason received medical attention or advice since the date you became covered by the policy in question? If so, give the nature of the illness, date, and name of the physician.

_____

_____

_____

3. Do you declare that you are of sound constitution and that you are now in good health?_____

4. In the past 3 years, have you smoked a cigarette, cigar or pipe, chewed tobacco, or used tobacco or nicotine in any form? _____
   If yes, last used (form) _____ on Month, Year_____

5. Name and address of family physician

_____

_____

_____

I hereby certify that the above declarations are complete and true, and I agree that no reinstatement shall take effect until this application is approved by the insurer at its home office.

Date _____ Insured's Signature _____

Date _____ Owner's Signature _____

---

discussed the reinstatement provision in the context of reinsurance. The right to reinstate a policy is generally not available if the policyowner has surrendered the policy for its net cash surrender value, nor does the reinstatement provision obligate the insurer to reinstate the policy.

Most insurers require applicants for reinstatement to pay back premiums. Some insurers, however, allow policies that meet certain strict criteria to be reinstated without payment of back premiums in order to encourage reinstatement of policies that may have lapsed because of temporary financial hardship, as explained in Figure 13.10.

If a policyowner applies for reinstatement, most insurers also require the insured to present evidence of insurability in the form of a completed medical questionnaire. If no significant changes in the insured's health have occurred since the original policy was issued, the CSR reinstates the policy without further investigation. However, if evidence shows the possibility of a significant change in health, the CSR usually refers the reinstatement request to the underwriting staff. After reviewing evidence of insurability, the underwriter can take one of the following three actions:

1. Grant reinstatement as requested
2. Decline reinstatement if the risk has increased so much that the underwriter cannot justify allowing the person to remain insured
3. Offer to reissue the policy at a higher premium rate

Figure 13.10. Reinstatement by Redating

Some insurance companies attempt to conserve canceled business, especially small amount policies, by permitting lapsed policies to be reinstated without requiring the payment of back premiums. Policies that have lapsed but that meet certain criteria can be reinstated by *redating*—advancing the policy date and the paid-to date (the date to which premiums were paid up) by the number of months that the policy has been lapsed.

A policy reinstated in this manner generally must meet the following criteria:

- The policy must be less than two years old and have no cash surrender value.

- The policy must have been lapsed for more than 60 days, but not more than six months beyond the paid-to date.

- The face amount plus any supplementary term coverage cannot exceed a specified amount, usually $20,000 to $30,000.

- Redating can occur only once during the life of the policy.

Changing a Beneficiary

CSRs must be familiar with the numerous and often complex ways in which beneficiaries may be designated. Many different people and entities can be named as the beneficiary of a life insurance policy. These include the spouse and children of an insured person, other people who may be unrelated to the insured, trustees under trust agreements or wills, and the estate of the insured. Moreover, a policyowner can specify contingent, concurrent, or irrevocable beneficiaries and can further specify distribution of proceeds per stirpes or per capita. These beneficiary designation terms are defined in Figure 13.11.

Many insurers establish guidelines for submitting beneficiary changes. The guidelines are designed to prevent mistakes in recording a policyowner's beneficiary designation and avoid delays in the event of a claim. The following beneficiary change guidelines are the most common:

■ The full name—given name and surname—of the beneficiary is required; initials are not acceptable. For example, while "John and Louise Jones" is acceptable, "Mr. and Mrs. John Jones" is not.

■ The relationship of the beneficiary to the policyowner must be specified.

■ Dates of birth for minors must be provided.

■ Use of the words "or," "either/or," "and/or" makes the intent unclear; therefore, the use of these words in a designation is unacceptable.

■ Names that are scratched out or marked over or that contain correction fluid marks are not acceptable.

■ Information about the beneficiary that would allow the insurer to locate him at the time of a claim should be provided. Such information includes the beneficiary's social insurance or Social Security number, address, or date of birth.

■ Dollar amounts cannot be specified for any or all beneficiaries because the final death benefit payable may vary if there are any outstanding loans on the policy or if the policy is in the grace period. In instances of an outstanding policy loan or a policy in the grace period, the loan amount or premium due will be deducted from the death benefit. Also, some policies provide a death benefit that varies with the cash value of the policy at the time of death. Fractions (such as one-fourth or two-thirds) and percentages (such as 30 percent or 70 percent) can be used to specify shares.

■ The beneficiary form must be signed and dated by the policyowner.

■ If a trust is designated, the exact date, legal name of the trust, and the trustee's name must be provided. Some insurers request a copy of the trust. Because some trust documents are difficult to interpret, some insurers attach a disclaimer noting that the insurer is not obligated to inquire into the terms of the trust agreement and will not be liable to other claimants after the policy proceeds have been paid.

Beneficiary changes can be made through the insurer's Web site because the policyowner's identity has been verified by the login and password or PIN. Beneficiary changes cannot be made by telephone, but a policyowner may request a

---

Figure 13.11. Beneficiary Designation Terms

- **Contingent beneficiary.** The party designated to receive the proceeds of a life insurance policy following the insured's death if the primary beneficiary predeceases the insured.

- **Concurrent beneficiaries.** Two or more life insurance beneficiaries who share the policy proceeds on the death of the insured. The shares are distributed equally unless otherwise provided.

- **Irrevocable beneficiary.** A life insurance policy beneficiary who has a vested interest in the policy proceeds even during the insured's lifetime because the policyowner has the right to change the beneficiary designation only after obtaining the beneficiary's consent or upon the beneficiary's death.

- **Class designation.** A life insurance beneficiary designation that identifies a certain group of people rather than naming each person individually. Class designations can be either per stirpes designations or per capita designations.

- **Per stirpes beneficiary designation.** A type of life insurance policy beneficiary class designation in which the descendants of a deceased class member take the deceased class member's share of the policy proceeds by representation. For example, a policyowner-insured who has three children—Roger, Samuel, and Tina—might provide that each child would receive an equal share of the policy proceeds, per stirpes. If Samuel died before the insured died, then at the insured's death Roger and Tina would each receive one-third of the proceeds, and the heirs of Samuel would receive equal shares of the remaining one-third of the proceeds. If Samuel died without heirs, however, Roger and Tina would each inherit one-half of the policy proceeds. Many insurers prohibit the use of some classes, such as "nieces and nephews of the insured" or "children of the insured's brother," in per stirpes beneficiary designations because such classes are not specific in naming the persons who are to be included in the division of the proceeds.

- **Per capita beneficiary designation.** A type of life insurance policy beneficiary class designation in which the class members all stand in the same relationship to the policyowner and the class members who survive the insured share the policy proceeds equally. For example, a policyowner-insured who has three children—Roger, Samuel, and Tina—might provide that each child would receive equal shares of the policy proceeds, per capita. If Samuel died before the insured died, then at the insured's death Roger and Tina would each receive one-half of the proceeds, whether or not Samuel had heirs.

---

change form by phone. CSRs then mail, e-mail, or fax a change of beneficiary form; when it is returned, the signature is compared to the policyowner's signature on file. No matter how the request was made, if the original beneficiary was designated as irrevocable, that person also is required to sign the change of beneficiary form before the change can be made.

Assigning Policy Ownership

As we noted in Chapter 9, assignment of a life insurance policy is a transfer of some or all of the policyowner's rights in the life insurance policy. The insurance company is not a party to the assignment, which involves only the assignor—the person or entity that transfers ownership rights—and the assignee—the person or entity that receives ownership rights. Ownership of some or all of the rights to a policy is most often transferred when a policyowner wishes to use the cash surrender value of a life insurance policy as collateral for a loan or when a divorce results in one party's assumption of full ownership of an insurance policy. As we mentioned in Chapter 9, the irrevocable transfer of all the ownership rights in a life insurance policy is known as an absolute assignment, whereas the transfer of some of the policyowner's rights in a life insurance policy to provide security for a debt is known as a collateral assignment. Figure 13.12 illustrates a portion of an absolute assignment form.

In an absolute assignment, the assignee, in effect, becomes the owner of the policy, and the assignor may no longer change the beneficiary or exercise any other policy rights. However, in a collateral assignment, the rights assigned revert to the assignor when specified requirements—such as repayment of a loan—have been satisfied. When such requirements have been fulfilled, the assignee notifies the insurer that the assigned rights of ownership are being returned to the assignor.

Because the insurer is not a party to the assignment, the insurer rarely asks the reason for the assignment. The role of a CSR in an assignment is to record the change of ownership so that rights of ownership are granted to the proper party and so that, in the event of a claim, benefits can be disbursed to the appropriate party.

Before recording an assignment, the CSR checks whether the policy has an irrevocable beneficiary. If so, that beneficiary must sign the request for assignment. If the irrevocable beneficiary does not sign the request, no assignment can be made. The CSR also reviews the policy provisions to determine whether any provisions exist that would prevent an assignment.

Administering Loans and Dividends

Policy loans made on individual cash value life insurance coverage are actually cash advances issued to policyowners. The policyowner is not legally obligated to repay the policy loan, but may do so at any time. If the loan is not fully repaid, the amount of the outstanding policy loan, plus interest, is deducted from the amount of death benefits paid under the policy at the time of a claim.

The requirements for policy loan requests vary among different insurers. Many insurers will accept telephone requests for loans under a certain monetary amount and require written requests only for amounts over that limit. Other insurers require a written request for all policy loans. For written loan requests, some insurers require the policyowner to complete a policy loan request form and other insurers will accept a signed letter from the policyowner.

If the policy loan request is written, the CSR verifies that the person or people requesting the loan are entitled to do so by comparing the signatures on the loan form to the signatures on the insurer's records. If the signatures do not match, the CSR typically sends a letter with a loan form to the policyowner and instructs the policyowner to return a loan request form with a notarized signature.

Figure 13.12. Portion of an Absolute Assignment Form

ABSOLUTE ASSIGNMENT

Policy # _____ Life of _____

The undersigned hereby assigns and transfers without any exception, limitation, or reservation whatsoever to

_____
[Name and address of each assignee]

all (his, her, its, their) assignable benefits, interest, property, and rights in the policy described above.

The nature and effect of this assignment shall be as indicated in the following expressions of intent and purpose, namely

■ This assignment is_____ for a valuable consideration. _____ without a valuable consideration.

■ If two or more assignees are named above, their interests under this assignment shall be as indicated in the line before which an "X" is inserted below.

___ Joint owners with right of survivorship between them

___ Common owners with no right of survivorship between them

___ Life interest, use, and enjoyment in _____
with absolute control and power of disposition in such assignee during his or her lifetime; remainder interest in other assignee(s). If there are two or more assignees entitled to receive remainder interests, such interests shall be of the nature indicated in the line before which an "X" is inserted below:

____ Joint owners with right of survivorship between them

____ Common owners with no right of survivorship between them

■ This assignment cancels and rescinds any reversionary provision in favor of the assignor or his estate, whether contained in the policy or in any writing or provision pertaining to the policy.

■ This assignment does not affect or change the beneficiary designation or settlement presently contained in the policy assigned. Proceeds payable on death will be paid in accordance with such designation or settlement unless same be hereafter changed by the assignee(s), when the right to make such change exists under the policy.

Upon receiving a request for a policy loan, the CSR examines the policy record to ensure that the request has been made by an eligible person and that, if the policy has been assigned or has an irrevocable beneficiary, the necessary signatures of the assignee or beneficiary (or a spouse in a community property jurisdiction) are provided.

Although the policy loan does not have to be repaid, most insurers offer policyowners a choice of one of the following loan repayment plans:

- *Dividend plan*. The insurer applies available dividends plus future dividends against the loan amount.

- *Coupon plan*. The insurer supplies the policyowner with coupons to return with periodic payments against the loan amount.

- *Automatic deduction plan*. The policyowner authorizes the insurer to automatically deduct a set amount from the policyowner's bank account each month until the loan is repaid.

- *Lump sum plan*. The policyowner submits a check or money order for the entire loan plus the loan interest due.

- *Partial loan repayment plan*. The policyowner submits a check or money order for a partial loan payment.

After calculating the cash value of the policy and verifying that it is adequate to fulfill the requested loan, the CSR then issues a check in that amount. If the cash value is inadequate to fulfill the requested loan, most insurers issue a check for the greatest amount available and notify the policyowner of the reason for not granting the full amount requested.

Most insurers offer individual policyowners the option of obtaining an automatic premium loan to cover unpaid premiums. An *automatic premium loan (APL) provision* in a policy allows an insurer to automatically pay an overdue premium for the policyowner by making a loan against the policy's cash value as long as the cash value equals or exceeds the amount of the premium due. In most jurisdictions, such an option is available only if the policyowner requests it. If a policyowner who has chosen an APL option fails to pay a premium on a timely basis, the insurer automatically grants a loan if the policy's loan value is sufficient to cover the amount of the premium plus interest. A policyowner's use of the automatic premium loan option can signal a potential lapse or surrender of the policy. The insurer, therefore, attempts to conserve the business by notifying the policyowner and the producer that the loan provision has taken effect.

Life insurance policies can be classified as either participating or nonparticipating. All mutual insurers and many stock insurers issue participating life insurance policies. A *participating policy*, also known as a *par policy* or a *with-profits policy*, is an insurance policy under which the policyowner shares in the insurance company's surplus. The portion of the insurance company's earnings that is available for distribution to policyowners is called the *divisible surplus*. A policyowner's share of the divisible surplus is a *policy dividend* and is payable to owners of participating policies at the end of the policy year or on the policy anniversary. Policy dividends are considered a return of the part of the premiums that these policyowners paid to keep their policies in force for that year. Policy dividend amounts are not known in advance, and the policyowner is not guaranteed that policy dividends will be paid.

A person who owns a participating life insurance policy elects a dividend option at the time of policy application. The policyowner is usually free to change the selected option at any time while the policy is in force. The available options usually include

- Receiving cash payment of dividends on a periodic basis, usually quarterly or annually

- Applying dividends to pay some or all of the premiums on the policy

- Applying dividends to pay some or all of the loan on the policy, if any

- Allowing dividends to accumulate at interest, adding to the policy's cash value

- Using dividends to buy additional insurance

The customer service department is responsible for making appropriate changes to the insurer's records when a policyowner changes the dividend option. If the policyowner chooses to receive cash payment of dividends or to withdraw some or all of the dividends that have been left to accumulate with interest, the CSR enters this information into the policy administration system and makes appropriate disbursements to the policyowner.

Although dividend earnings are not taxable in the United States, any interest earned on accumulations is taxable. Typically, automated systems in customer service calculate any amount of taxes due. If a policyowner chooses to apply existing dividends to buy additional insurance, the CSR verifies that the additional coverage is allowable without further evidence of insurability. Elements the insurer generally considers include the amount of insurance already in force, the amount of coverage that dividends would purchase, and the insured's risk classification. If additional evidence of insurability is necessary, the CSR usually notifies both the policyowner and the insurer's underwriters of the required evidence and turns the case over to the underwriters for further processing.

Handling Variable Life Insurance Products

Variable life insurance is a form of cash value life insurance in which premiums are fixed, but the death benefit and other values may vary, reflecting the performance of the investment subaccounts selected by the policyowner. Most variable life insurance products permit a policyowner to choose from several separate subaccounts and to change the selection at least annually and sometimes more often.

Most insurers allow policyowners to make reallocation choices by telephone or through the insurers' Web sites, although some insurers require written notification of the policyowner's desire to reallocate funds. Therefore, in addition to processing other customer service requests, CSRs help policyowners of variable life products (1) reallocate money from one investment subaccount to another— for example, from a money market or bond account to a growth and income stock account—and (2) designate the allocation of future premium payments by specifying the investment subaccounts into which future premiums will be placed. Depending on the jurisdiction, CSRs who assist policyowners with variable life products may be required to obtain special licenses.

Key Terms

quantitative performance measurement	complaint team
qualitative performance measurement	certificate of coverage
service level	net cash surrender value
number of blocked calls	concurrent beneficiary
average speed of answer	class designation
abandonment rate	per stirpes beneficiary designation
misdirected calls	per capita beneficiary designation
turnaround time	dividend plan
first contact resolution	coupon plan
quality rate	automatic deduction plan
error rate	lump sum plan
processes completed	partial loan repayment plan
mystery shopper	automatic premium loan (APL)
affidavit	provision
policy grace notice	participating policy
service complaint	divisible surplus
service recovery	policy dividend
escalation process	variable life insurance

Endnotes

1. This section is adapted from Mark Adel and Barbara Foxenberger Brown, *Foundations of Customer Service* [Atlanta: LOMA (Life Office Management Association, Inc.), © 2003], 306-307. Used with permission; all rights reserved.

Glossary

abandonment rate. The percentage of inbound telephone calls that are automatically placed on hold and then terminated by the caller before the call is answered by a CSR. [13]

absolute assignment. An irrevocable transfer of all of a policyowner's ownership rights in a life insurance policy to the assignee. [9]

accelerated death benefit. A supplemental benefit that gives a policyowner-insured the right to receive all or part of the policy's death benefit before her death if certain conditions are met. Also called a *living benefit* in the United States. [6]

access to records provision. A reinsurance agreement policy provision that gives the reinsurer the authority to examine the direct writer's records related to the business conducted between the companies. [11]

accidental death benefit (ADB). A supplemental benefit that provides a death benefit above the face amount of the basic policy if an insured's death occurs as the result of an accident. [6]

accounting. The functional area of an insurance company that collects, records, summarizes, analyzes, and reports data about a company's financial condition. [1]

acid-test ratio. *See* **quick ratio**.

acquisition expenses. The costs a direct writer incurs in developing, marketing, and issuing new business. [10]

actively at work provision. A provision which requires that an employee must be actively at work—rather than ill or on leave—on the day the group coverage is to take effect. [7]

actuary. A technical expert in insurance, annuities, and financial instruments who applies mathematical knowledge to industry and company statistics to calculate various financial values. [1]

ADA. *See* **Americans with Disabilities Act (ADA)**.

ADB. *See* **accidental death benefit (ADB)**.

ADEA. *See* **Age Discrimination in Employment Act (ADEA)**.

administration expenses. *See* **maintenance expenses**.

administration system. An information system that an insurer uses to manage information about insurance policies. [1]

adverse action. A denial or revocation of insurance coverage, a change in the terms of existing insurance coverage, or a refusal to grant insurance in substantially the amount or on substantially the terms requested. [3]

affidavit. A written statement made before an official who is authorized to administer oaths. [13]

affinity group. A group of people who share a common bond, background, or interest and who belong to an association or organization. [7]

age and amount requirements chart. A chart, typically included in field underwriting manuals, that specifies the kinds of information the underwriter must obtain and review in assessing the insurability of a proposed insured. Also called *table of underwriting requirements*. [2]

Age Discrimination in Employment Act (ADEA). A U.S. federal law that protects workers who are age 40 and older from being discriminated against because of their age. [3]

agent's statement. A section included in most individual life insurance applications in which the producer can comment on any factors relevant to the case and the risk it involves. [2]

allowance. An amount the reinsurer reimburses to the direct writer and that is designed to recognize the direct writer's acquisition, maintenance, and other expenses related to the ceded business. Also called *expense allowance, reinsurance allowance, ceding commission*, or *reinsurance commission*. [10]

Americans with Disabilities Act (ADA). A U.S. federal law that protects disabled individuals against all types of discrimination, including employment discrimination. [3]

annual report. A financial document that a corporation issues to its stockholders to report the business's activities and financial status for a specified period, which is usually the preceding year. [5]

antiselection. The tendency of people who believe they have a greater-than-average likelihood of loss to seek insurance protection to a greater extent than do those who believe they have an average or a less-than-average likelihood of loss. [2]

antivirus software. A software application that detects viruses and prevents them from infecting a computer and/or helps an infected computer recover. [1]

APL provision. See automatic premium loan (APL) provision.

applicant. The person or entity that submits an application for individual insurance and seeks to purchase the insurance coverage. [1]

application. *See* **application software**.

application software. Software used to perform specific tasks or solve particular types of problems. Also called a *software application or simply an application*. [1]

approval premium receipt. A conditional premium receipt that provides temporary insurance coverage only when the insurer approves the proposed insured as a standard or better-than-average risk. [3]

APS. *See* **attending physician's statement (APS)**.

arbitration. A method of dispute resolution in which impartial third parties called arbitrators evaluate the facts in dispute and render a decision that usually is binding on the parties to the dispute. [10]

arbitration provision. A reinsurance agreement policy provision which requires the reinsurance parties to submit disputes that they cannot resolve through negotiation to an arbitration panel rather than to a court of law. [10]

arbitrators. Impartial third parties that evaluate the facts in dispute and render a decision that is binding on the parties to the dispute. [10]

assignment. An agreement under which a policyowner—the *assignor*—transfers some or all of her ownership rights in a particular policy to another party—the *assignee.* [9]

association group. Consists of the members of an association, which is an organization of employers or individuals formed for a purpose other than to obtain insurance. [7]

assuming company. *See* **reinsurer**.

assumption certificate. A new insurance certificate issues by a reinsurer to all affected policyowners. [10]

assumption reinsurance. Reinsurance designed to permanently and entirely transfer blocks of existing insurance business from one company to another. Also called *portfolio reinsurance.* [10]

assured. *See* **insured**.

attending physician. A physician, whether he is a primary care physician or a specialist, who has provided medical care for a proposed insured. [4]

attending physician's statement (APS). A report by a physician who has treated or is currently treating the proposed insured. [4]

audit. An evaluation of a company's records and operations to ensure the accuracy of the records and the effectiveness of operational policies and procedures. [2]

audit log. A record of the work that has been completed on a case. [1]

authentication. A combination of technology and procedures designed to verify a user's identity before giving the user access to a system or database. [1]

auto-adjudication. An electronic claim processing system for processing claims that fit certain parameters specified for electronic handling. [8]

automated workflow system. A technology used to create computer-based records pertaining to the status and processing of specific transactions. Also called a *workflow application.* [1]

automatic binding limit. Represents the maximum monetary amount of risk the reinsurer will accept automatically on a given policy or case without making an independent underwriting assessment. [10]

automatic deduction plan. A policy loan repayment plan in which the policyowner authorizes the insurer to automatically deduct a set amount from the policyowner's bank account each month until the loan is repaid. [13]

automatic premium loan (APL) provision. A policy provision that allows an insurer to automatically pay an overdue premium for the policyowner by making a loan against the policy's cash value as long as the cash value equals or exceeds the amount of the premium due. [13]

automatic reinsurance. A reinsurance cession arrangement in which the direct writer agrees in advance to cede all risks that meet the specifications in the reinsurance agreement and the reinsurer agrees in advance to assume these risks. [10]

average handling time. *See* **turnaround time**.

average speed of answer. The amount of time, on average, that telephone callers are on hold before being connected with CSR. [13]

B2B e-commerce. *See* **business-to-business (B2B) e-commerce**.

balance sheet. A financial statement that shows the business's financial position on a certain date. [5]

benchmark. A performance standard, often based on standards achieved by leading companies, that represents a company's goals for performance. [1]

beneficiary. The person or party that the owner of an individual policy or the group insured named to receive the policy benefit. [1]

benefit schedule. A table or schedule that specifies the types and amounts of coverage that will be provided for each class of group insureds. [7]

billing statement. A reinsurance report that lists the amounts owed by and due to each party to the reinsurance agreement. [11]

binding premium receipt. A premium receipt that provides temporary insurance coverage that becomes effective on the date specified in the receipt. [3]

biometric authentication. Technology that identifies users by "reading" a physical trait that is unique to each user, such as the user's fingerprint or retina. [1]

blended rating. A premium rating method that uses a combination of manual rating and experience rating. [7]

block of business. A number of similar insurance policies. [10]

blood chemistry profile. A group of laboratory tests that analyze a sample of blood to identify factors that point to possible chronic and acute diseases. [4]

BPM. *See* **business process management**.

BRE. *See* **business rules engine**.

build. The shape or form of the body, including the relationships among height, weight, and distribution of the weight. [4]

build chart. A chart that indicates average weights for various heights, along with the mortality debits associated with increases in weight. [4]

business continuation insurance plan. An insurance plan designed to enable a business to continue operations upon the death or disability of an owner or other person important to the business. [6]

business financial supplement. A document that requests information about the type of business, the current financial condition of the business, and the purpose for which the insurance is being requested. [6]

business insurance. Insurance that serves the needs of a business organization rather than those of a person. [6]

business process management (BPM). A strategy for optimizing business processes or adapting them to meet changing needs. [1]

business rules engine (BRE). Application software that automates the decision-making process by creating and applying rules to all available information. [1]

business-to-business (B2B) e-commerce. The electronic transmission of data or information between organizations to perform or facilitate business transactions. [11]

buy-sell agreement. An agreement in which one party agrees to purchase a second party's financial interest in a business following the second party's death, and the second party agrees to direct his estate to sell his interest in the business to the purchasing party. [6]

call center. An organizational unit that receives and/or places telephone calls to customers. [12]

Canada Pension Plan (CPP). A Canadian federal program that provides a pension for wage earners who have contributed money into the plan during their working years. *See also* **Quebec Pension Plan (QPP)**. [3]

case. In a reinsurance context, a single policy or a group of policies. [10]

case assignment system. A method of assigning cases to underwriters based on the characteristics of the case. [2]

cat cover. See catastrophe coverage.

catastrophe coverage. A type of nonproportional reinsurance designed to partially protect direct writers from (1) a single catastrophic event resulting in multiple claims or (2) an annual total of claims in a catastrophic amount. Also called *cat cover*. [10]

ceding commission. *See* **allowance**.

ceding company. *See* **direct writer**.

census. Lists demographic information about the group prospect as a unit and about individual members within the group. [7]

centralized data repository. A database that houses all the relevant data contained in an insurer's separate administration systems. [1]

certificate holder. *See* **group insured**.

certificate of coverage. Issued in the event an original policy is lost or destroyed to verify that coverage exists, but does not contain all the provisions and riders that the original policy may have contained. [13]

certificate of insurance. A document that is provided to each group insured and that describes (1) the coverage that the master group insurance contract provides and (2) the group insured's rights under the contract. [1]

cession. The unit of insurance risk that a direct writer transfers to a reinsurer. [10]

cession arrangement. Identifies the direct writer's obligations and rights to cede risks, and identifies the reinsurer's obligations to accept risk as well as its rights to reject risk. [10]

change in health statement. A document, contained in most individual life insurance applications and premium receipts, that requires a proposed insured to notify the insurer in writing if his health or any material information in the application changes before the policy is delivered. [9]

churning. Occurs when a producer induces a customer to replace one policy after another so that the producer can earn a series of first-year commissions on the replacements. [3]

Civil Rights Act of 1964. A U.S. federal law that prohibits employment discrimination on the basis of race, color, sex, religion, or national origin. [3]

claim adjuster. *See* **claim analyst**.

claim administration. The process of evaluating each submitted claim, deciding whether or not the claim is eligible, informing the person who submitted the claim of the decision, and authorizing the payment of each eligible claim according to the terms of the policy. [1]

claim analyst. An insurance company employee who reviews claims and determines the company's liability for each claim. Also called a *claim examiner* or *claim adjuster*. [8]

claim examiner. *See* **claim analyst**.

claim file. An organized collection of all the information relevant to a claim. [11]

claim form. A document containing information about a loss under an insurance policy that is submitted to an insurance company to begin the claim evaluation process. Also called a *claimant's statement*. [8]

claim fraud. A subset of insurance fraud by which a person intentionally uses false information in an unfair or unlawful attempt to collect benefits under an insurance policy. [8]

claim philosophy. A statement of the insurer's objectives for administering claims. [8]

claim practices. Statements that guide the day-to-day handling of claims. [8]

claim provision. A reinsurance agreement policy provision that typically states the terms and conditions of the reinsurer's liability for claims submitted under reinsured policies. [10]

claimant's statement. *See* **claim form**.

class. A group of group members categorized according to some nondiscriminatory characteristic for purposes of determining eligibility for coverage and benefit levels. [7]

class designation. A life insurance beneficiary designation that identifies a certain group of people rather than naming each person individually. *See also* **per stirpes beneficiary designation** and **per capita beneficiary designation**. [13]

close notice. *See* **drop notice**.

coinsurance. A plan of proportional reinsurance under which the direct writer and the reinsurer proportionately share monetary responsibility for almost every aspect of each policy covered under the arrangement. [10]

coinsurance allowance. A type of reinsurance allowance shared proportionally between the direct writer and the reinsurer for the direct writer's expenses such as commissions, administration, and sometimes premium taxes. [10]

collateral assignment. The transfer of some of a policyowner's rights in a life insurance policy to provide security for a debt. [9]

committee underwriting. A work division approach in which a committee of highly qualified people from inside and outside the underwriting function is called together for case assessment. [2]

community property laws. Laws that provide that a spouse is entitled to receive an equal share of earned income and an equal share of property acquired by the other spouse during a marriage. [9]

comorbidity. The simultaneous appearance of two or more unrelated illnesses or conditions that may act in conjunction with one another. [2]

compensatory damages. Monetary awards intended to compensate an injured party for the amount of the monetary losses that resulted from the defendant's improper conduct. [8]

complaint team. A work group dedicated solely to resolving customer complaints. Also called *customer relationship team* or *problem resolution team*. [13]

compliance department. The functional area of an insurance company that is responsible for ensuring that the insurer adheres to all applicable laws and regulations in each jurisdiction in which the company does business. [1]

concurrent beneficiary. Two or more life insurance beneficiaries who share the policy proceeds on the death of the insured; shares are distributed evenly unless otherwise provided. [13]

conditional premium receipt. A premium receipt that specifies certain conditions that must be met before the temporary insurance coverage provided by the receipt becomes effective. [3]

conservation. The process of ensuring that policies do not lapse but are retained on an insurer's books for as long as possible. [12]

consumer report. Under the Fair Credit Reporting Act (FCRA), any communication of information by a consumer reporting agency that (1) bears on an individual consumer's creditworthiness, credit standing, credit capacity, character, general reputation, personal characteristics, or mode of living and (2) is used or collected as a private business that assembles or evaluates information on consumers and furnishes consumer reports to third parties in exchange for a fee. [3]

consumer reporting agency. A private business that assembles or evaluates information on consumers and furnishes consumer reports to third parties in exchange for a fee. [3]

contest. A court action to determine the validity of an insurance claim. [10]

contestable claim. A claim for life insurance policy proceeds following the death of an insured during the policy's contestable period. [11]

contestable period. The time period within which the insurer has the right to avoid a life insurance policy on the grounds of a material misrepresentation. [3]

contingent beneficiary. The person or entity designated to receive the proceeds of a life insurance policy following the insured's death if the primary beneficiary dies before the insured. Also called *secondary beneficiary.* [9]

continuation. Occurs either when (1) the provisions of an in-force policy are significantly modified or (2) a policy replaces an existing policy from the same direct writer, but differs from a new insurance policy in a specific way. [10]

continuation provision. A reinsurance agreement policy provision that addresses which reinsurer(s) should provide the reinsurance, the amount of reinsurance, and the effective date of reinsurance for continued policies. [10]

contributory plan. A group insurance plan for which group insureds must pay some or all of the premiums for their coverage. [7]

conversion provision. A group policy provision that gives a group insured who meets specific conditions the right to obtain an individual life insurance policy without providing evidence of insurability. [3]

cookie. A file that a server—a computer that contains shared resources—places on a user's personal computer that enables the server to recognize the personal computer. [1]

cost basis. Equal to the total premiums paid minus the total accumulated policy dividends. [6]

coupon plan. A policy loan repayment plan in which the insurer supplies the policyowner with coupons to return with periodic payments against the loan amount. [13]

covered person. *See* **group insured**.

CPP. *See* **Canada Pension Plan (CPP)**.

credibility factor. A percentage that represents the amount of weight given to a group's actual claim experience for premium rate calculation purposes. [7]

creditor insurance. Coverage designed to pay for the economic loss suffered by a creditor when a key person of a debtor business dies before the debt is paid. Also called *loan coverage* or *debt coverage.* [6]

credits. A proposed insured's medical and personal risk factors that have a favorable effect on mortality are assigned "minus" values (such as –25). *See also* **debits**. [5]

critical illness benefit. *See* **dread disease (DD) benefit**.

cross-purchase agreement. A type of buy-sell agreement in which each partner agrees to purchase a share of a deceased partner's interest in the partnership by funding the agreement with an insurance policy on the life of each of the other partners. [6]

CSR. *See* **customer service representative (CSR)**.

current assets. Items that a company presently has or owns that can be readily converted to cash at a close approximation of their true value. [6]

current liabilities. All company debts and obligations due and payable within the next accounting period. [6]

current ratio. A financial ratio calculated by dividing current assets by current liabilities. [6]

customer contact center. An organizational unit that provides customers with a variety of channels for communicating with a business entity. [12]

customer contact system. A customer database and work tracking tool that combines a variety of features—such as data entry and retrieval, history of previous customer contacts, document management, scripted presentations, and follow-up tools—to provide a framework for handling and documenting customer contacts. [12]

customer loyalty. Represents a customer's feeling of attachment to or preference for a company's people, products, or services. [12]

customer relationship team. *See* **complaint team**.

customer service. The broad range of activities that a company and its employees perform to keep customers satisfied so they will continue doing business with the company and speak positively about it to other potential customers. [1]

customer service representative (CSR). Any person, other than a sales person, who provides support to customers face-to-face or through communication media. [12]

data. Unprocessed facts. *Contrast with* **information**. [1]

data backup software. The systems companies use to back up data to the Internet or to intranets while the data is being created and then to store the back-up copies offsite. [1]

data mining. The analysis of large amounts of data to discover previously unknown trends, patterns, and relationships. [1]

data warehouse. A type of database management system that collects data from the company's existing databases and possibly from sources outside the company, screens and edits the data, puts the data in a standard format, and then stores the data in a centralized data repository. [1]

database. An organized collection of data and information. [1]

database management system (DBMS). A group of computer programs that organizes data in a database and allows users to obtain the information they need. [1]

date of expiry. The date on which the reinsurer will cancel the reservation of reinsurance capacity if the reinsurer does not receive a cession or other placement information from the direct writer. [11]

DBMS. *See* **database management system**.

DD benefit. *See* **dread disease (DD) benefit**.

death certificate. A document that attests to the death of a person and bears the signature—and sometimes the seal—of an official authorized to issue such a certificate. [9]

debits. A proposed insured's medical and personal risk factors that have an unfavorable effect on mortality are assigned "plus" values (such as +25). *See also* **credits**. [5]

debt coverage. *See* **creditor insurance**.

debt ratio. *See* **debt-to-equity ratio**.

debtor-creditor group. Consists of individuals who have borrowed money from a specific lender or lenders. [7]

debt-to-equity ratio. A financial ratio which is calculated by dividing a company's total debt by its owners' equity. Also called a *debt ratio*. [6]

declined class. A risk class composed of proposed insureds whose anticipated mortality rates are so great that the insurer cannot provide coverage at an affordable cost or whose mortality risk cannot be predicted because of recent or unusual medical conditions or other risk factors. [2]

defamation. A civil wrong that occurs when a person makes false statements that tend to damage the reputation of another. [8]

dependent. A (1) spouse, (2) an unmarried child who is under age 19 and who relies on the group member for financial support and maintenance, (3) a child age 19 or older—up to a stated maximum age, often 25—if she is a full-time student, and (4) a disabled child for as long as the disability exists, regardless of the child's age. [7]

direct response distribution system. A type of distribution channel in which customers purchase products directly from a company by responding to advertisements, Internet Web sites, or telephone solicitations. [6]

direct response policy. A policy, distributed through a direct response system, which may be fully underwritten, underwritten on a nonmedical basis, or underwritten on a guaranteed-issue basis. [6]

direct writer. In a reinsurance arrangement, an insurer that sells insurance coverage to the public. Also called a *ceding company* [10]

disaster recovery software. Software applications that can aid insurers in developing disaster recovery plans. [1]

dividend. *See* **experience refund**.

dividend plan. A policy loan repayment plan in which the insurer applies available dividends plus future dividends against the loan amount. [13]

divisible surplus. The portion of an insurance company's earnings that is available for distribution to policyowners. [13]

document imaging. A process of converting printed characters or graphics into digital images on a computer by inserting paper documents in a type of hardware called a scanner. Also called *scanning*. [1]

document management system. A type of technology that stores, organizes, and retrieves documents that have been converted to digital images. [1]

dread disease (DD) benefit. An accelerated death benefit under which the insurer agrees to pay a portion of the policy's death benefit to a policyowner-insured if he suffers from one of a number of specified diseases. Also called a *critical illness benefit*. [6]

drop notice. A written explanation from a direct writer to a reinsurer stating that the direct writer no longer needs reinsurance that it previously requested and asking the reinsurer to cancel the reservation. Also called *close notice*. [11]

duration of the agreement provision. A reinsurance agreement policy provision that addresses when the reinsurance agreement becomes effective and when it ends. [10]

e-commerce. *See* **electronic commerce**.

e-mail. *See* **electronic mail (e-mail)**.

ECG. *See* **electrocardiogram (ECG)**.

EDI. *See* **electronic data interchange**.

EFT. *See* **electronic funds transfer (EFT)**.

electrocardiogram (ECG). A graphic record of the electrical forces produced by the heart and a diagnostic tool for detecting a disease or an abnormality of the heart. [4]

electronic application system. A technology that allows producers or applicants to enter application information into a computer, rather than on paper, and transmit the information to the insurer over a computer network. [2]

electronic commerce (e-commerce). The use of the Internet and other networks to deliver commercial information and to facilitate business transactions and the delivery of products and services. [1]

electronic data interchange (EDI). The computer-to-computer exchange of data between organizations using a data format agreed upon by the sending and receiving parties. [1]

electronic funds transfer (EFT). A method of transferring funds between financial intermediaries through an electronic computer network. [12]

electronic mail (e-mail). A form of telecommunication that allows a user to type a message into a computer and then send the message to other computers connected to a network. [1]

electronic signature. A unique personal identifier that makes a legally binding contract using electronic communications media like the Internet. [2]

eligibility period. The period of time—usually 31 days—during which eligible group members may enroll for contributory group insurance coverage without having to provide evidence of insurability. Also called the *enrollment period*. [7]

employee application. *See* **enrollment card**.

employee benefit plan. A program under which an employer provides its employees with various benefits in addition to their wages. [6]

Employee Retirement Income Security Act (ERISA). A U.S. federal law that regulates employee retirement plans and specifies minimum requirements that employee welfare benefit plans must meet. [3]

employee-employer group. *See* **single-employer group**.

encryption. Technology that encodes data so that only an authorized person, who possesses the required hardware and/or software that contains the decryption key, can decode the data. [1]

enrollment application. *See* **enrollment card**.

enrollment card. A document that must be completed and signed by a group member to enroll in a group insurance plan. Also called a *group enrollment card*, an *enrollment application*, or an *employee application*. [7]

enrollment period. *See* **eligibility period**.

entire agreement provision. A reinsurance agreement policy provision that states that the reinsurance agreement represents the whole agreement between the parties, and that they have no further agreement than that stated in the written document. [10]

entity agreement. A type of buy-sell agreement under which the partnership—rather than the individual partners—agrees to purchase the share of any partner who dies. [6]

equity. The amount of the business owned—and not financed—by the owners. [5]

ERISA. *See* **Employee Retirement Income Security Act (ERISA)**.

error rate. The percentage of transactions that resulted in errors, such as 0.5 percent of account transactions reported errors. [13]

errors and omissions provision. A reinsurance agreement policy provision that states that, if either party to the agreement fails to comply with the terms of the agreement through unintentional administrative mistake or clerical error, then both parties will be restored to the position they would have occupied if the mistake or error had not occurred. [10]

escalation process. Procedures that specify how an issue or complaint is to be handled in situations where the customer service representative (CSR) is not able or authorized to address a particular request or demand. [13]

ethics. A system of accepted standards of conduct and moral judgment that combines the elements of honesty, integrity, and fair treatment. [1]

examining physician. A physician who performs an examination of a proposed insured at the request of the insurance company. [4]

excess of retention. The monetary amount of risk remaining after the direct writer's retention limit is subtracted from the net amount at risk on a case. [10]

excess quota share arrangement. A method for assigning risk in proportional reinsurance in which the direct writer keeps its full retention limit and cedes the remaining risk to two or more reinsurers on a percentage basis. [10]

excess-of-retention arrangement. A method for assigning risk in proportional reinsurance in which the direct writer establishes a dollar amount as its retention limit and the reinsurer agrees to assume monetary amounts greater than the direct writer's specified retention limit, up to the reinsurer's automatic binding limit. [10]

exclusion. A policy amendment stating that benefits will not be paid for any loss that results from the condition specified in the rider. [2]

exculpatory statute. A law that permits an insurer to pay life insurance proceeds according to the terms of a policy without fear of double liability. [9]

expected claim experience. The monetary amount of claims that the insurer estimates the group will submit during the upcoming policy year. [7]

expense allowance. *See* **allowance**.

experience rating. A method of establishing group insurance premium rates using a group's own claim experience. [7]

experience refund. The portion of a group insurance premium that is returned to a group policyholder if the group's claim experience during the year was more favorable than expected when the premium was calculated. Also called a *dividend* or *premium refund*. [7]

extension request. A request from a direct writer to a reinsurer to extend the direct writer's reservation of capacity for a specified period so that the direct writer can gather all information needed to move the case from reserved to placed status. [11]

external audit. An audit conducted by a third party who is not employed by the company being audited. [2]

external replacement. A situation in which a new policy is purchased from an insurer other than the insurer that issued the original policy. [6]

extranet. A portion of an organization's intranet that is accessible to people within the organization and to selected external parties. [1]

extra-percentage table. A document that presents the total mortality for each substandard group and that lists all the tables used in the table rating method. [5]

fac-ob reinsurance. *See* **facultative-obligatory (fac-ob) reinsurance**.

factor table. A chart that shows the maximum amount of insurance—expressed in multiples of a person's salary or current gross earned income—that an insurer typically will approve in each of several age ranges. [5]

facultative application. *See* **request for coverage**.

facultative reinsurance. A reinsurance cession arrangement in which a direct writer chooses whether to cede a risk and the reinsurer chooses whether to accept that risk. [10]

facultative-obligatory (fac-ob) reinsurance. A reinsurance cession arrangement in which (1) the direct writer may choose to submit specific cases to the reinsurer and (2) the reinsurer must accept the cases based on the direct writer's underwriting, up to a stated maximum amount, if the reinsurer has available financial capacity. [10]

Fair Credit Reporting Act (FCRA). A U.S. federal law that regulates the reporting and use of consumer information and that seeks to ensure that consumer reports contain only accurate, relevant, and recent information. [3]

family benefit. A supplemental benefit that insures the lives of the insured's spouse and children. [6]

FCRA. *See* **Fair Credit Reporting Act (FCRA)**.

FDQS arrangement. *See* **first-dollar quota share (FDQS) arrangement**.

field underwriting. The practice of gathering initial information about applicants and proposed insureds and screening proposed insureds to determine if they are likely to be approved for a specific type of coverage. [2]

field underwriting manual. A document that (1) presents specific guidance for a producer's assessment of the risk represented by a proposed insured and (2) guides the producer in assembling and submitting the application and any other information needed for the underwriter to evaluate the risk. [2]

financial capacity. The total monetary amount of risk the company can accept based on the investable funds it has available to write new business. [10]

financial ratio analysis. The process of calculating the relationships between various pairs of financial values for the purpose of assessing a company's financial condition. [6]

financial risk factor. Financial information that an underwriter considers to determine whether a person is applying for more insurance than he reasonably needs or can afford. [2]

financial status. A person's (1) current income expressed in terms of amount, sources, and permanency and (2) net worth. [5]

financial underwriting. The assessment of the proposed insured's financial condition, conducted by an individual life insurance underwriter, to determine whether (1) the proposed insured needs the coverage, (2) a reasonable relationship exists between the need for the coverage and the amount of coverage applied for, and (3) the premiums are affordable. [5]

financial worksheet. A document that enables an underwriter to organize financial information and develop a clear picture of a person's financial situation. [6]

firewall. A combination of hardware and software that creates an electronic barrier between the public and private areas of a company's systems. [1]

first contact resolution. The percentage of inbound customer contacts that are successfully completed at the initial point of contact—that is, without being transferred and without the need for follow-up work. [13]

first-dollar quota share (FDQS) arrangement. A method for assigning risk in proportional reinsurance in which the direct writer retains a stated percentage of the risk for each policy in a given block of business, up to its retention limits, and cedes the remaining risk to one or more reinsurers. [10]

first-to-die life insurance policy. *See* **joint life insurance policy**.

fixed-amount option. A settlement option under which the insurance company pays equal installments of a stated amount until the policy proceeds, plus the interest earned, are exhausted. [9]

fixed-period option. A settlement option under which the insurance company agrees to pay policy proceeds in equal installments to the payee for a specified period of time. [9]

flat extra premium method. A method of charging for substandard individual life insurance in which the insurer adds to the standard premium a specified extra dollar amount for every $1,000 of insurance. [5]

fully insured group plan. A plan for which an insurance company is financially responsible for incurred claims. [7]

funds withheld coinsurance. A plan of proportional reinsurance under which the direct writer and reinsurer proportionately share responsibility for almost all aspects of a reinsured policy, but the direct writer retains the gross reinsurance premium and the reinsurer retains the initial coinsurance allowance. [10]

genetic test. A series of human DNA used to indicate a person's predisposition to a certain illness or disease. [3]

GI benefit. *See* **guaranteed insurability (GI) benefit**.

GLB Act. *See* **Gramm-Leach-Bliley (GLB) Act**.

good faith. A party's honesty of intention and avoidance of attempts to deceive or take unfair advantage of another party to a reinsurance agreement. [10]

Gramm-Leach-Bliley (GLB) Act. A U.S. federal law that removed may of the barriers to affiliations among institutions in the various segments of the financial services industry. [3]

group enrollment card. *See* **enrollment card**.

group insurance policy. *See* **master group insurance contract**.

group insured. An individual covered by a master group insurance contract. Also called a *covered person* or a *certificate holder.* [1]

Group Life Insurance Definition and Group Life Insurance Standard Provisions Model Act (Group Life Insurance Model Act). A National Association of Insurance Commissioners (NAIC) model law that defines the types of groups eligible for group life insurance and sets forth provisions that group policies must contain. [3]

Group Life Insurance Model Act. *See* **Group Life Insurance Definition and Group Life Insurance Standard Provisions Model Act (Group Life Insurance Model Act)**.

group member. The individuals who are part of a group but are not covered by insurance. [7]

group prospect. A group that has applied, but has not yet been approved, for group coverage from an insurance company. Also called the *proposed group.* [1]

group representative. Salaried insurance company employees specifically trained in the techniques of marketing and servicing group products. [7]

guaranteed insurability (GI) benefit. A supplemental benefit that gives the policyowner the right to purchase additional insurance of the same type as the basic life insurance policy—for an additional premium amount—on specified option dates during the life of the policy without supplying evidence of the insured's insurability. [6]

guaranteed-issue basis. Insurance products issued with no individual underwriting, so that every eligible proposed insured who applies and meets specified conditions is automatically issued a policy. [6]

hardware. In the context of a technology platform, the types of computers an insurer uses. [1]

human resources. The functional area of an insurance company that recruits and screens job applicants; helps select qualified employees; plans and presents appropriate orientation, training, and development for each employee; administers employee benefit programs; and maintains employee records. [1]

impairment. A physical or psychological abnormality or loss of function. [2]

impairment guide. A list of common impairments and the probable underwriting decision for proposed insureds who have each type of impairment. [2]

income statement. A financial document that reports the business's revenues and expenses during a specified period and indicates whether the business experienced net income or a net loss during the period. Also called a *profit and loss statement.* [5]

indemnity reinsurance. A common type of reinsurance under which a reinsurer is obligated to reimburse a direct writer only after the direct writer pays benefits under reinsured policies. [10]

independent underwriting. A work division system in which underwriters work alone to assess each risk. [2]

industry experience. The collective data about insurance claim experience generated by industry-wide studies. [2]

in-force policy report. A reinsurance report that lists all in-force reinsured policies as of a given date and provides detailed information about each policy. [11]

information. A collection of data that has been converted into a form that is meaningful or useful for the accomplishment of some objective, such as performing a transaction, drawing a conclusion, or solving a problem. *Contrast with* **data**. [1]

information management. The use of information systems to provide a company's information users with the information they need to carry out their job responsibilities. [1]

information system. An interactive combination of technology, people, and processes that collects, manipulates, and disseminates information. [1]

information technology (IT). The functional area of an insurance company that develops and maintains the company's information systems and oversees information management throughout the company. [1]

insolvency. The opposite of solvency; an organization's inability to pay its financial obligations as they come due. [10]

insolvency provision. A reinsurance agreement policy provision that typically describes the rights and responsibilities of the direct writer and the reinsurer in the event that either party becomes insolvent. [10]

inspection report. A type of investigative consumer report that a consumer reporting agency prepares about a proposed insured. [4]

instant-issue underwriting. *See* **real-time underwriting**.

insurability premium receipt. A conditional premium receipt that provides temporary insurance coverage on condition that the insurer finds that the proposed insured was insurable at least as a standard risk on a certain date specified in the premium receipt. [3]

insurable interest. Exists when a person is likely to suffer a genuine financial loss or detriment should the event insured against occur. [3]

insurance administration. Those insurance company activities specifically associated with administering insurance policies, such as underwriting, reinsurance, claims, and customer service. [1]

insurance fraud. Any fraud that involves an insurance company, whether committed by consumers, insurance company employees, producers, health care providers, or anyone else connected with an insurance transaction. [8]

Insurance Fraud Prevention Model Act. A state law, based on the National Association of Insurance Commissioners (NAIC) model law, designed to permit the state insurance departments to investigate and discover fraudulent insurance acts more effectively, halt fraudulent insurance acts, and receive assistance from state, local, and federal law enforcement and regulatory agencies in enforcing laws that prohibit fraudulent insurance acts. [8]

Insurance Information and Privacy Protection Model Act (Model Privacy Act). A National Association of Insurance Commissioners (NAIC) model law that establishes standards for the collection, use, and disclosure of information gathered in connection with insurance transactions. [3]

insured. The person whose life, health, property, or income is covered by an insurance policy. Also called the *assured* in some countries. [1]

insurer-administered plan. A group insurance plan for which the insurer handles most of the administrative aspects of the plan. *Compare to* **self-administered plan**. [7]

interactive voice response (IVR) system. A computer-based technology that answers telephone calls, greets callers with a recorded or digitized message, and prompts them to enter information or make requests by voice or telephone keypad. [12]

interest option. A settlement option under which the insurance company invests the policy proceeds and periodically pays interest on those proceeds. [9]

internal audit. An audit conducted by a company's own staff. [2]

internal replacement. A situation in which a new policy is purchased from the same insurer that issued the original policy. [6]

interpleader. A procedure by which the insurer pays the policy proceeds to a court, advised the court that the insurer cannot determine the correct recipient of the proceeds, and asks the court to determine the proper recipient or recipients. Called *payment into court* in Canada. [9]

intranet. An organization's internal computer network that uses Internet technology but is accessible only to people within the organization. [1]

intrusion detection software. Software that monitors system traffic and identifies sequences of commands that indicate an unauthorized user is attempting to access the organization's systems or databases. [1]

invasion of privacy. A civil wrong that occurs when a person (1) appropriates someone's name or personality, (2) publicizes someone's private affairs, (3) intrudes into someone's private affairs and the wrong causes mental suffering, shame, or humiliation, or (4) places someone in a false light in the public eye. [8]

investigative consumer report. A consumer report that contains information obtained through personal interviews with an individual's neighbors, friends, associates, or others who may have information about the individual. [3]

irrevocable beneficiary. A life insurance policy beneficiary who has a vested interest in the policy proceeds even during the insured's lifetime because the policyowner has the right to change the beneficiary designation only after obtaining the beneficiary's consent or upon the beneficiary's death. [9]

IT. *See* **information technology**.

IVR system. *See* **interactive voice response (IVR) system**.

jet issue electronic system. An information system that uses business rules engines to determine that (1) certain criteria are met and an application for insurance is approved for issue or (2) the criteria are not met, and an application for insurance is either declined or sent to an underwriter. [2]

jet unit underwriting. A work division approach in which a separate group of employees are authorized to approve certain types of individual insurance applications for immediate policy issue. [2]

joint life insurance policy. A multi-life policy under which proceeds will be paid when the first of two (or more) insureds covered by the policy dies. Also called a *first-to-die life insurance policy*. [6]

jumbo limit. The maximum allowable monetary amount of total insurance—in force and yet-to-be-placed—with all companies on any one life that a reinsurer will accept for automatic cession. [10]

juvenile insurance policy. An insurance policy issued on the life of a child but owned and paid for by an adult—usually the child's parent, grandparent, or legal guardian—who typically is also the beneficiary. [6]

key person. A person—including an owner, a top salesperson, or an employee possessing special skills, knowledge, or abilities—whose continued participation in the business is necessary to its success and whose death would cause substantial financial loss to the business. [6]

key-person life insurance. Individual life insurance that a business purchases on the life of a key person. [6]

knowledge management system. A technical resource that represents the strategies, resources, and processes that organizations use to apply institutional knowledge to business activities. [12]

lapse notice. *See* **policy grace notice**.

last survivor life insurance policy. A multi-life policy under which proceeds will be paid when the second (or last) of two (or more) insureds covered by the policy dies. Also called a *second-to-die life insurance policy*. [6]

late enrollee. Group members and eligible dependents who are not enrolled when coverage is first offered and later decide to enroll in the plan. [7]

law department. See legal department.

legal department. The functional area of an insurance company that handles all legal matters for the company. Also called the *law department*. [1]

life income option. A settlement option under which the insurance company agrees to pay the policy proceeds in periodic installments over the payee's lifetime. [9]

life settlement. The sale of a life insurance policy to a third party for a discount from the policy's face amount. [5]

liquidity. A company's ability to readily convert its assets to cash for an approximation of their true value. [6]

living benefit. *See* **accelerated death benefit**.

loan coverage. *See* **creditor insurance**.

long-term care (LTC) insurance benefit. An accelerated death benefit under which the insurer agrees to pay periodic benefits to a policyowner-insured if he requires care in his own home or a qualified facility. [6]

LTC benefit. *See* **long-term care (LTC) insurance benefit**.

lump sum plan. A policy loan repayment plan in which the policyowner submits a check or money order for the entire loan plus the loan interest due. [13]

maintenance expenses. The direct writer's ongoing expense for administering and servicing a policy or a block of business after it has been in force. Also called *renewal expenses or administrative expenses*. [10]

manual rating. A method of establishing group insurance premium rates under which the insurer establishes rates for very broad classifications of group insureds. [7]

market conduct examination. A formal investigation of an insurer's nonfinancial operations that is carried out by one or more state insurance departments and is designed to determine whether the insurer's market conduct operations comply with applicable laws and regulations. [8]

marketing. The functional area of an insurer that has primary responsibility for identifying the insurer's prospective customers and what they want, as well as planning the promotion and distribution of the insurer's products. [1]

master application. An application for group insurance that contains the specific provisions of the requested plan of insurance and is signed by an authorized officer of the proposed policyholder. [7]

master group insurance contract. An insurance contract that insures a number of people. Also called a *group insurance policy.* [1]

material misrepresentation. A misrepresentation that induces the other party—in this case the insurer—to enter into a contract that it would not have entered into had it known the truth. [3]

medical report. A type of the Part II application that contains the proposed insured's answers to medical history questions recorded by a physician and the results of a medical examination conducted by a physician. The results of the medical examination do not become part of the contract. [4]

medical risk factor. A physical or psychological characteristic that may increase the likelihood of loss. [2]

member service. A specific type of customer service that includes all the service activities performed for group insureds. [1]

MIB. *See* **MIB Group, Inc. (MIB).**

MIB Group, Inc. (MIB). A not-for-profit membership corporation established to provide coded information to insurers about impairments that applicants have disclosed or other insurance companies have detected in connection with previous applications for insurance. [4]

middleware. A type of software used to enable two or more systems to work together. [1]

minimum cession. The smallest monetary amount of risk a reinsurer will accept or a direct writer will cede in an automatic cession. [10]

misdirected calls. The number or percentage of inbound telephone calls that are transferred to the wrong department. [13]

misrepresentation. An untrue statement of a fact contained in an application. [3]

modco. *See* **modified coinsurance (modco).**

Model Privacy Act. *See* **Insurance Information and Privacy Protection Model Act (Model Privacy Act).**

Model Privacy Regulation. *See* **Privacy of Consumer Financial and Health Information Regulation (Model Privacy Regulation).**

modified coinsurance (modco). A plan of proportional reinsurance under which the direct writer and the reinsurer share proportionately in the policy reserve obligation, the direct writer's gross premiums, and the risks of loss from expenses for death, surrender, or other benefits or from lapse; however, the direct writer holds the entire reserve for each reinsured policy. [10]

money laundering. The practice of engaging in financial transactions that hide the identity, source, and/or destination of money associated with criminal activity. [3]

moral hazard. A characteristic that exists when the reputation, financial position, or criminal record of an applicant or proposed insured indicates that the person may act dishonestly in the insurance transaction. [2]

mortality. The incidence of death among a specified group of people. [2]

mortality rate. The rate at which death occurs among a specified group of people during a specified period, typically one year. [2]

motor vehicle record (MVR). A report that contains information about a person's driving history, including information about traffic violations, arrests, and convictions. [4]

multi-life policy. A life insurance contract that is written on two or more lives. [6]

multiple-employer group. Consists of the employees of (1) two or more employers in the same industry, (2) two or more labor unions, or (3) one or more employers and one or more labor unions. [7]

MVR. *See* **motor vehicle record (MVR)**.

mystery shopper. A trained evaluator who approaches or calls customer service and pretends to be a customer. [13]

NAR. *See* **net amount at risk**.

net amount at risk (NAR). The difference between the face amount of a life insurance policy—other than a universal life policy—and the policy reserve (or cash value) at the end of any given policy year. [10]

net cash surrender value. The actual cash value available to a policyowner upon policy surrender or lapse; it equals the cash value shown in the policy, increased by any cash values of paid-up additions, policy dividend accumulations, and advance premium payments and decreased by outstanding policy loans and any charges imposed on the surrender. [13]

net worth. The difference between a person's assets and his liabilities. [5]

netting off. A process by which a direct writer subtracts the claim amount owed to it by a reinsurer from the amount that the direct writer owes the reinsurer for reinsurance premiums. [11]

network. A group of interconnected computers and computer devices, including the telecommunications equipment and software that connect them. [1]

new business. The activities an insurer undertakes in receiving applications, underwriting applications, and issuing policies. [1]

new business strain. *See* **surplus strain**.

niche personal life insurance policies. Life insurance policies, including multi-life policies, juvenile insurance policies, and direct response policies, that an insurer designs to fulfill the needs of a specific marketing segment. [6]

noncontributory plan. A group insurance plan for which the group insureds are not required to pay any part of the premium for the coverage; the premiums are paid entirely by the policyholder and all eligible group members are provided with coverage automatically. [7]

nonmedical basis. A circumstance under which the proposed insured is not required to provide medical proof of insurability by undergoing any type of physical examination. [4]

nonmedical limit. The total amount of insurance that the insurer will permit to be issued on a proposed insured without requiring the proposed insured to undergo a physical examination. [4]

nonmedical supplement. A type of Part II application that contains the proposed insured's answers to medical history questions recorded by a producer or tele-underwriter. [4]

nonproportional reinsurance. A type of reinsurance in which neither the reinsurer nor the direct writer knows in advance what share of a risk the reinsurer ultimately will assume. [10]

nonpublic personal information. Under the Gramm-Leach-Bliley (GLB) Act, personally identifiable information about a consumer that is not publicly available. [3]

notice of expiry. A document that the reinsurer uses to notify the direct writer that an offer to reinsure is due to expire and to request additional information, a cession, a drop notice, or an extension request from the direct writer. [11]

number of blocked calls. The number of telephone calls that encounter a busy signal and cannot get through to the customer contact center. [13]

numerical rating system. A risk classification method in which an underwriter calculates a numerical value for the degree of risk a proposed insured presents to the insurer; the underwriter then places the proposed insured in a risk class according to the numerical value. [5]

open claimant. Group insureds receiving short- or long-term disability income benefits. [7]

operating system software. Software that controls the basic operations of a computer including performing common computer tasks, such as saving data to different storage mediums or devices. [1]

oral specimen (saliva) test. A means of screening a proposed insured for habitual use of nicotine or cocaine and the presence of HIV antibodies by testing a specimen of the proposed insured's saliva. [4]

orphan policyowner. A policyowner whose original producer is no longer available to provide service. [12]

overinsurance. An amount of applied-for insurance that, together with in-force insurance, is excessive in relation to the need for which coverage is being purchased. [5]

par policy. *See* **participating policy.**

paramedical report. A type of the Part II application that contains the proposed insured's answers to medical history questions recorded by a paramedical examiner and the results of a paramedical examination conducted by a paramedical examiner. [4]

partial loan repayment plan. A policy loan repayment plan in which the policyowner submits a check or money order for a partial loan repayment. [13]

participating policy. An insurance policy under which the policyowner shares in the insurance company's surplus. Also called *par policy and with profits policy*. [13]

parties to the agreement provision. A reinsurance agreement policy provision that typically states that the reinsurance agreement exists solely between the direct writer and the reinsurer. [10]

payee. The person or entity who is to receive the policy proceeds under a settlement option. [9]

payment into court. *See* **interpleader**.

PBM. *See* **pharmacy benefit manager**.

per capita beneficiary designation. A type of life insurance policy beneficiary class designation in which the class members all stand in the same relationship to the policyowner and the class members who survive the insured share the policy proceeds equally. [13]

per stirpes beneficiary designation. A type of life insurance policy beneficiary class designation in which the descendants of a deceased class member take the deceased class member's share of the policy proceeds by representation. [13]

percentage-of-income rule. The amount of money a proposed insured can afford to spend on insurance annually according to a specified percentage of the proposed insured's current gross earned and unearned annual income. [5]

performance measurement. A process through which a company (1) decides what activities are key to the achievement of the company's goals and objectives, how to measure the performance of those activities, and what performance standards it hopes to achieve; (2) gathers the information; and (3) communicates the results. *See also* **quantitative performance measurement** and **qualitative performance measurement**. [1]

performance standard. An established level of performance against which a company or an individual compares actual performance. [1]

permanent flat extra premium. An amount added to the premium for cases in which a personal risk factor is expected to remain constant throughout the life of the policy. [5]

persistency bonus. A sum of money paid as compensation to an insurance producer when a policy continues in force beyond an initial period, usually five years. [12]

persistency rate. The percentage of a specified group of contracts that remain in force during a specified period, such as a year. [5]

personal history interview (PHI). A conversation between an underwriter or another insurance company employee and the proposed insured in which the underwriter verifies the accuracy of information already received about the proposed insured and obtains any additional information needed for underwriting. [4]

personal information. Information gathered about an individual in connection with an insurance transaction and from which judgments can be made about the individual's personal characteristics such as character, habits, finances, credit, and health. [3]

Personal Information Protection and Electronics Document Act (PIPEDA). A Canadian federal law that governs the collection, use, and disclosure of personal information by organizations in the private sector. [3]

personal risk factor. A lifestyle choice that can significantly affect a person's health or longevity. [2]

pharmacy benefit manager (PBM). A clearinghouse that manages health care prescription benefit programs and maintains pharmaceutical databases containing records of prescriptions filled by the persons enrolled in such benefit programs. [4]

PHI. *See* **personal history interview (PHI)**.

PIPEDA. *See* **Personal Information Protection and Electronics Document Act (PIPEDA)**.

placement. A process in which the direct writer and reinsurer activate reinsurance coverage for a new automatic, facultative, or fac-ob cession. Also called *submission stage*. [11]

plan administrator. The party responsible for handling the administrative aspects of a group plan. [7]

policy change report. A reinsurance report that shows details for all policies that, during the reporting period, have changed in a way that affects the amount of the reinsurance coverage, the reinsurance premium, or the allowance. Also called *transaction report*. [11]

policy dividend. A policyowner's share of divisible surplus, payable to owners of participating policies at the end of the policy year or on the policy anniversary. [13]

policy exhibit. A reinsurance report that summarizes and reconciles the changes that have occurred in reinsured policies during the reporting period. [11]

policy grace notice. A written notification that a policy's grace period is about to expire. Also called *lapse notice*. [13]

policy issue. The insurance company unit that prepares the insurance contract and facilitates the delivery of the policy to the customer. [2]

policy reserves. A liability amount that, together with future premiums and investment income, the insurer estimates it will need to pay contractual benefits as they come due under in-force policies. [10]

policy rider. An amendment to an insurance policy that becomes part of the insurance contract and either expands or limits the benefits payable under the contract. [2]

policyholder. The employer or other organization that decides what kind of insurance coverage to purchase for a group and negotiates the terms of and enters into the master group insurance contract with the insurer. [1]

policyowner. The person or entity that owns an individual insurance policy. [1]

policyowner service. A specific type of customer service that includes all the service activities performed for people or entities that own individual insurance policies. [1]

pooling. A rating method by which the insurer combines several small groups into one large group, or pool. [7]

portfolio reinsurance. *See* **assumption reinsurance**.

predictive modeling. An automated technique for predicting future behavior or events. [1]

preferred beneficiary. In Canada, a certain family member of the insured for whom policyowners of in-force policies issued prior to July 1, 1962, in common law jurisdictions have limitations on their ability to change the beneficiary designation. [9]

preferred class. A risk class composed of proposed insureds whose anticipated mortality rates are lower than average and who represent the lowest degree of mortality risk. [2]

Pregnancy Discrimination Act. A U.S. federal law, part of the Civil Rights Act, that requires employers to treat pregnancy, childbirth, and related medical conditions the same as any other medical condition. [3]

premium refund. *See* **experience refund**.

premium taxes. Amounts of tax that governments levy on a direct writer's premium income [10]

preplacement. The process by which a reinsurer (1) reviews a direct writer's request for coverage, (2) establishes appropriate records and reserves capacity for the case, and (3) as necessary, follows up on reservations for capacity that have been inactive for a specified period of time. [11]

presumptive death certificate. A court-issued document stating that a person is presumed to be dead. [9]

pretext interview. An interview in which one person attempts to gain information from another person by (1) pretending to be someone he is not, (2) pretending to represent someone he does not represent, (3) refusing to identify himself, or (4) misrepresenting the purpose of the interview. [3]

Privacy of Consumer Financial and Health Information Regulation (Model Privacy Regulation). A National Association of Insurance Commissioners (NAIC) model law that includes requirements similar to those contained in the Gramm-Leach-Bliley (GLB) Act, including limits on an insurer's right to disclose nonpublic personal information about a consumer without the consumer's consent. [3]

privileged information. Information that relates to either an insurance claim or a court proceeding. [3]

probationary period. The length of time—typically from one to six months—that a new group member must wait before becoming eligible to enroll in a group insurance plan. Also called a *waiting period*. [7]

problem resolution team. *See* **complaint team**.

Proceeds of Crime (Money Laundering) and Terrorist Financing Act. A Canadian federal law that requires companies, including life insurers, to report every financial transaction that occurs for which there are reasonable grounds to suspect that the transaction is related to money laundering or financing terrorists. [3]

process control. A procedure that allows an organization to monitor the accuracy of its processes on a regular, ongoing basis. [11]

processes completed. A quantitative performance measurement of how many transactions are handled within a specified period of time. [13]

producer. A person or entity that (1) sells insurance, including agents, brokers, financial advisors, and bank personnel or (2) is involved in insurance sales made through direct marketing or the Internet. [1]

professional association group. A group of people who share the same type of occupation and who belong to the association. [7]

profit and loss statement. *See* **income statement**.

profitability. The degree to which a company is successful in consistently generating returns to its owners; measures the productivity of the company's assets and its return on the owners' investment in the company. [6]

proportional reinsurance. A type of reinsurance under which the direct writer and the reinsurer agree to share premiums and claim obligations according to a specified amount or percentage. [10]

proposal for insurance. A document that details the specifications of a group insurance plan proposed by an insurer for a group prospect. [7]

proposed group. *See* **group prospect**.

proposed insured. The term used during the underwriting process to refer to the person whose life, health, property, or income is to be covered by an insurance policy. [1]

public curator. A person authorized to handle the affairs of missing people. [9]

punitive damages. Monetary awards which are in addition to compensatory damages when a defendant's conduct meets the jurisdiction's standards for behavior that is so egregious as to warrant such damages. [8]

QPP. *See* **Quebec Pension Plan (QPP)**.

qualitative performance measurement. A type of performance measurement that focuses on behaviors, attitudes, or opinions to determine how efficiently and effectively processes and transactions are completed. [13]

quality control. The process of ensuring that an organization accomplishes its objectives and follows its standards. [1]

quality rate. A quantitative performance measurement of the accuracy of a particular type of transaction. [13]

quantitative performance measurement. A type of performance measurement that uses numerical methods to track and report results to determine how quickly, often, accurately, and profitably processes and transactions are completed. [13]

Quebec Pension Plan (QPP). A Canadian provincial program that functions in the same manner as the Canada Pension Plan (CPP) except that the QPP applies only to wage earners in Quebec. [3]

quick liquidity ratio. See quick ratio.

quick ratio. A financial ratio calculated by dividing a company's most liquid current assets—consisting of cash, liquid investments, and accounts receivable, which are also called *quick assets*—by the company's current liabilities. Also called a *quick liquidity ratio* or *an acid-test ratio.* [6]

quota share arrangement. A method for assigning risk in proportional reinsurance in which the direct writer retains a specified amount or percentage of the risk on a case and cedes the remaining risk to one or more reinsurers. [10]

rating. Approving a higher-than-average risk by charging a higher-than-usual premium rate for the coverage applied for. [2]

ratio. A comparison of two numeric values that results in a measurement expressed as a percentage or fraction. [6]

real-time underwriting. A straight through processing system that evaluates insurance applications typically submitted over the Internet and that almost instantly provides the applicant or producer with an underwriting decision. Also called *instant-issue underwriting.* [2]

recapture. The process by which a direct writer takes back some or all ceded business from a reinsurer. [10]

recapture provision. A reinsurance agreement policy provision that addresses the terms under which a direct writer can recapture some or all of its reinsured risk. [10]

receiver. An individual who is appointed by a court to hold and administer an insolvent insurer's assets and liabilities. [10]

records inspection provision. A reinsurance agreement policy provision that states the rights of each party to inspect the other party's records and documents relating to the reinsurance provided under the agreement. [10]

reduction of insurance. The process of reducing the amount of reinsurance covering an insurance policy. [10]

reinstatement provision. A reinsurance agreement policy provision that specifies that when a reinsured policy lapses for nonpayment of premium, the reinsurance can be reinstated if certain conditions regarding the timing of the request for reinstatement and the payment or reinsurance premiums dues are met. [10]

reinsurance. Insurance that one insurance company obtains from another insurance company on risks associated with insurance policies issued by the first company. [1]

reinsurance account executive. *See* **reinsurance marketing officer**.

reinsurance administration. All the day-to-day activities conducted by the direct writer and the reinsurer to process and manage each risk that the direct writer cedes automatically or submits for facultative or facultative-obligatory consideration. [11]

reinsurance agreement. A document that contains the terms of the business to be conducted, including the nature of the risk transfer, reinsurance administration procedures, information exchanges, and the rights and duties of each party under the agreement. [10]

reinsurance allowance. *See* **allowance**.

reinsurance analyst. Any direct writer or reinsurer employee—except the person holding top leadership responsibility—who is involved in any phase of reinsurance administration. [11]

reinsurance arrangement. The business deal that two companies—the direct writer and the reinsurer—make for the transfer of risk from one company to the other. [10]

reinsurance certificate. A document that notifies the direct writer that reinsurance is officially in force. [11]

reinsurance commission. *See* **allowance**.

reinsurance company. *See* **reinsurer**.

reinsurance effective date. The date on which the reinsurance coverage for a specific risk takes effect. [10]

reinsurance marketing officer. A reinsurer's employee who sell reinsurance and coordinates the marketing process for the reinsurer. Also called a *reinsurance account executive*. [11]

reinsurance premium. In indemnity reinsurance, the periodic payments made by the direct writer to the reinsurer as compensation for the reinsurance coverage. [10]

reinsurer. An insurer that provides reinsurance coverage by accepting, or *assuming*, insurance risk from a direct writer or another reinsurance company. Also called a *reinsurance company* or an *assuming company*. [10]

renewal expenses. *See* **maintenance expenses**.

renewal underwriting. The process by which an underwriter assesses the risk presented by a group that has requested to renew its group insurance contract. [7]

replacement. The purchase of one life insurance policy or annuity contract to take the place of another. [3]

Replacement of Life Insurance and Annuities Model Regulation. A National Association of Insurance Commissioners (NAIC) model law that states that replacement of policies is generally permissible if the replacing insurer provides full and fair disclosure and no deceptive practices are involved. [3]

request for coverage. Under facultative or fac-ob reinsurance agreements, a document in which the direct writer requests reinsurance coverage on a particular insured or group of insureds. Also called *facultative application*. [11]

request for proposal (RFP). A document that provides detailed information about the group and the requested coverage and solicits a bid from an insurer for providing that coverage. [7]

rescission. A remedy provided by law to an insurer that discovers that it has issued a policy based on material misrepresentation. [3]

rescission provision. A reinsurance agreement policy provision that describes the notification and administrative procedures required when a direct writer rescinds a reinsured policy. [10]

reserve listing. A reinsurance report that shows all policies reinsured and the reserve held for each policy. [11]

reserved capacity. The portion of a reinsurer's financial capacity that the reinsurer sets aside to fund its financial obligations under anticipated new business. [11]

retention limit. A specified maximum monetary amount of insurance that an insurer is willing to carry at its own risk without transferring some of the risk to a reinsurer. [10]

retrocession claim file. A file containing all the information relevant to the claim, plus information about the retrocession. [11]

retrocessionaire. An insurance company that accepts risks from—and provides reinsurance to—a reinsurer. [10]

return-on-equity (ROE) ratio. A financial ratio calculated by dividing net income by owners' equity. [6]

revocable beneficiary. A life insurance policy beneficiary who has no right to the policy proceeds during the insured's lifetime because the policyowner has the unrestricted right to change the beneficiary designation during the insured's lifetime. [9]

RFP. *See* **request for proposal (RFP)**.

right of recommendation. The right of a reinsurer to review the claim and offer its opinion to the direct writer on whether to pay the claim. [11]

risk assessment. The process of determining the degree of risk represented by each proposed insured using a number of factors established when the insurance product was designed and priced. [2]

risk class. A group of insureds who represent a similar level of risk to an insurance company. [2]

risk factor. For individual insurance underwriting purposes, any aspect of a proposed insured's present health, medical history, family history, health habits (such as tobacco use), financial condition, reputation, driving record, criminal record, occupation, or activities that increases the likelihood that the person will suffer a covered loss. [2]

risk-taking capability. *See* **underwriting capacity**.

ROE. *See* **return-on-equity (ROE) ratio**.

saliva test. *See* **oral specimen (saliva) test**.

scanning. *See* **document imaging**.

secondary beneficiary. *See* **contingent beneficiary**.

second-to-die life insurance policy. *See* **last survivor life insurance policy**.

Section 1035 exchange. A tax-free replacement of an insurance policy for another policy insuring the same person and meeting conditions specified in the tax code. [6]

security. The physical, technical, and procedural steps a company takes to prevent the loss, wrongful disclosure (accidental or intentional), or theft of data or information. [1]

self-administered plan. A group insurance plan for which the group policyholder handles most of the administrative aspects of the plan. *Compare to* **insurer-administered plan**. [7]

self-directed team. A type of work team in which the members handles many traditional management responsibilities, such as planning and monitoring work. Also called *self-managed team*.

self-insured group plan. A plan for which the group sponsor rather than an insurance company is financially responsible for the claims incurred by group insureds. [7]

self-managed team. *See* **self-directed team**.

semi-autonomous team. A type of work team in which the manger or supervisor manages the team, while the other team members, in addition to doing their "regular" work, provide input into planning, organizing, and monitoring the work. [12]

service complaint. A complaint that pertains to the timeliness, accuracy, courtesy, or professionalism of the company's interactions with its customers. [13]

service level. A quantitative performance measurement of the percentage of inbound customer contacts answered within a specified time frame. [13]

service recovery. The efforts an organization makes to fully resolve the problem that caused a customer's dissatisfaction and win back the customer's goodwill. [13]

settlement option. An alternative method—other than a lump-sum settlement—of receiving the proceeds of a life insurance policy. [9]

simultaneous death act. A law that says if both the insured and the beneficiary die under circumstances which make it impossible to determine which of them died first, the insurer is to presume that the insured survived the beneficiary, unless the policy provides otherwise. [9]

single-employer group. Consists of the employees of one employer. Also called an *employer-employee group*. [7]

SIU. *See* **special investigative unit (SIU)**.

software. Computer programs that provide the sequences of instructions for a computer and that govern its operation. [1]

software application. *See* **application software**.

sole proprietorship. A business owned by one person (or, in some jurisdictions, by a husband and wife). [6]

solvency. An entity's ability to meet its financial obligations on time. [6]

solvency laws. Laws designed to ensure that insurance companies are financially able to meet their debts and to pay policy benefits when they come due. [10]

special class. *See* **substandard class**.

special investigative unit (SIU). A group of individuals who are employed by an insurance company and are responsible for detecting, investigating, and resolving cases involving insurance fraud. [8]

specialized medical questionnaire. A document that requests detailed information about a specific illness or condition from a proposed insured's attending physician or examining physician. [4]

speculation. The unethical purchase of insurance to make a profit on the proceeds rather than to protect against the risk of financial loss. [5]

split-dollar life insurance plan. Under IRS regulations, any arrangement between an owner of a life insurance contract and a non-owner of the contract under which either party to the arrangement pays all or part of the premiums, and one of the parties paying the premiums is entitled to recover (either conditionally or unconditionally) all or any portion of those premiums and such recovery is to be made from, or is secured by, the proceeds of the contract. [6]

standard class. A risk class composed of proposed insureds whose anticipated mortality rates are average. [2]

statement of cash flows. A financial statement that indicates the amounts of cash received and paid in the operating, investing, and financing activities associated with the business. [5]

statement of changes in owners' equity. *See* **statement of owners' equity**.

statement of owners' equity. A financial statement that shows the changes in owners' equity during a specified period. Also called a *statement of changes in owners' equity*. [5]

step rates. Group insurance premium rates based on an insurer's experience expressed in age-graded, and sometimes sex-specific, step rate tables. [7]

STP. *See* **straight through processing**.

straight through processing (STP). The electronic processing of every step of a transaction without manual intervention. [1]

submission stage. *See* **placement**.

substandard class. A risk class composed of proposed insureds whose anticipated mortality rates are higher than average, but who are still considered to be insurable. Also called a *special class*. [2]

supplemental benefits. Benefits added to the coverage specified in the basic insurance policy. [6]

surplus. The amount of assets a company has over and above its policy reserves and other financial obligations. [10]

surplus relief. A decrease in potential surplus strain that strengthens an insurer's financial position. [10]

surplus strain. The decrease in surplus caused by the high initial costs and reserve requirements associated with issuing new insurance policies. Also called *new business strain*. [10]

survivorship clause. A clause contained in some life insurance policies that states that the beneficiary must survive the insured by a specified period, usually 30 or 60 days, to be entitled to receive the policy proceeds. [9]

table of underwriting requirements. *See* **age and amount requirements chart**.

table rating method. A method for adjusting individual life insurance premium rates to compensate for extra mortality that divides substandard risks into broad groups—or tables—according to their numerical value. [5]

team underwriting. A work division system in which underwriters are divided into small groups. [2]

technology platform. The combination of hardware and operating system software on which an administration system runs. [1]

telecommunications. The electronic transmission of communication signals. [1]

teleunderwriting. A method by which the insurer, rather than a producer, takes responsibility for gathering from the proposed insured most of the information needed for underwriting. [2]

temporary flat extra premium. An amount added to the premium for a risk factor for which the extra mortality risk is expected to decrease and eventually disappear over a limited time period. [5]

temporary insurance agreement (TIA). A contract between an insurer and an applicant that provides temporary coverage on the proposed insured before a policy is issued and delivered; such coverage may be subject to certain conditions. [3]

terminal illness (TI) benefit. An accelerated death benefit under which the insurer pays a portion of the policy's death benefit to a policyowner-insured if he suffers from a terminal illness and has a physician-certified life expectancy of 12 months or less. [6]

termination. The complete cancellation of a reinsurance agreement for both new business and in-force business. [10]

termination for new business. Occurs if one of the parties to a reinsurance agreement notifies the other party that the parties no longer cede or assume business under that agreement, but reinsurance coverage continues on business already in place. [10]

termination of reinsurance. A reinsurance agreement policy provision that describes the process by which a direct writer cancels the reinsurance covering a policy issued by the company. [10]

third-party administrator (TPA). An organization that is not affiliated with an insurer and that provides various administrative services to insurers and group policyholders. [7]

third-party policy. An individual insurance policy purchased by one person to insure the life of another person. [1]

TI benefit. *See* **terminal illness (TI) benefit**.

TIA. *See* **temporary insurance agreement**.

TPA. *See* **third-party administration (TPA)**.

traditional indemnity reinsurance. A reinsurance arrangement that is used to transfer a portion of the direct writer's accepted risk on an ongoing basis and that is intended to be a permanent transfer. [10]

traditional team. A type of work team in which the manager or supervisor performs most or all of the management tasks, such as organizing, monitoring, and controlling the work; other team members concentrate solely on doing the work—performing the business functions for which the team is responsible. [12]

transaction. Any business-related exchange—such as a death benefit paid in exchange for proof of death received or payment of a renewal premium for the continuation of coverage. [1]

transaction processing system. An organized collection of procedures, software, databases, and devices used to perform high-volume, routine, and repetitive business transactions. [1]

transaction report. *See* policy change report.

treasury operations. The functional area of an insurance company that manages cash as it flows through the company. [1]

turnaround time. A quantitative performance measurement of the time it takes to complete a request or transaction, such as processing a loan or responding to a policyowner's or producer's request for information. Also called *average handling time*. [13]

twisting. Occurs when a producer misrepresents the features of a policy to induce a client to purchase a policy. [3]

undeliverable. An insurance policy that the applicant chooses not to accept when a producer attempts to deliver it. [2]

underwriter. An individual who (1) assesses and classifies the degree of risk represented by a proposed insured or group with respect to a specific insurance product and (2) makes a decision to accept or decline that risk. [1]

underwriting. The process of (1) assessing and classifying the degree of risk represented by a proposed insured or group with respect to a specific insurance product and (2) making a decision to accept or decline that risk. [1]

underwriting capacity. The highest monetary amount of risk that a direct writing company will accept on an individual insured so that unusual fluctuations in claims will not damage ongoing company solvency. Also called *risk-taking capability*. [10]

underwriting guidelines. General standards that underwriters follow as they establish the level of risk presented by a proposed insured or group. [2]

underwriting manual. A document that contains a proposed insured's debits and credits and typically provides descriptive information on impairments and serves as a guide to underwriting action. [5]

underwriting objective. *See* **underwriting philosophy**.

underwriting philosophy. A set of objectives that guides all of an insurer's underwriting actions, generally reflects the insurer's strategic business goals, and includes its pricing assumptions for products. Also called an *underwriting objective*. [2]

underwriting worksheet. A document that contains records of telephone calls, letters, and other communications; documentation of requests for reinsurance; lists of reports and other information requested; and other notations that will explain clearly the manner in which the underwriter has handled the case beginning with the submission of the application to the insurer. [3]

Unfair Claims Settlement Practices Act. A state law, based on the National Association of Insurance Commissioners (NAIC) model law, which lists a number of actions that are considered unfair claims practices if committed by an insurer (1) in conscious disregard of the law or (2) so frequently as to indicate a general business practice. [8]

Unfair Life, Accident and Health Claims Settlement Practices Model Regulation. A state law, based on the National Association of Insurance Commissioners (NAIC) model law, which establishes minimum standards that insurers must meet in handling life and health insurance claims. [8]

urinalysis. The analysis, of a urine specimen, which can detect the presence of protein, sugar, blood cells, and hypertension, as well as prescription medication and certain other drugs, in the urine. [4]

USA Patriot Act of 2001. A U.S. federal law designed to strengthen the federal government's ability to investigate, prosecute, and seize the assets of terrorists. [3]

variable life insurance. A form of cash value life insurance in which premiums are fixed, but the death benefit and other values may vary, reflecting the performance of the investment subaccounts selected by the policyowner. [13]

virtual private network (VPN). An organization's network that uses public telecommunications infrastructure such as the Internet to provide authorized individual users or remote offices with secure access. [1]

VPN. *See* **virtual private network**.

wagering agreement. An agreement under which either party may gain or lose depending on the outcome of an uncertain event, such as the timing of an individual's death. [3]

waiting period. *See* **probationary period**.

waiver of premium for disability (WP) benefit. A supplemental insurance benefit that provides that, in the event an insured is totally disabled as defined in the WP benefit, the insurance company will waive the payment of all premiums that become due during the period of disability. [6]

waiver of premium for payor benefit. A supplemental benefit that provides that the insurer will waive payment of the policy's premiums if the payor—the person paying the policy premium—becomes disabled or dies prior to the insured child's attainment of a specified age, usually 21. [6]

with profits policy. *See* **participating policy**.

work division system. A method of assigning cases to underwriters that divides cases according to the person or group that underwrites them. [2]

work group. *See* **work team**.

work team. Two or more people who work together on a regular basis and coordinate their activities to accomplish common goals. Also called *work group*. [12]

workflow application. *See* **automated workflow system**.

WP benefit. *See* **waiver of premium for disability (WP) benefit**.

yearly renewable term (YRT) reinsurance. A plan of reinsurance that is used to reinsure only the mortality portion of a life insurance risk. Also called *YRT reinsurance*.

YRT reinsurance. *See* **yearly renewable term (YRT) reinsurance**.

Numbers in *italics* indicate figures

aviation
> exclusions for, 103, 190
> as underwriting factor, 102–103

avocation
> exclusions for, 190
> as underwriting factor, 100, 142

B

balance sheet, *112*
bankruptcy, as factor in financial underwriting, 114
benchmarks, 37
beneficiary, 23
> change in, 197–198, 297–298
> contingent, 196, *298*
> death of, 196
> disappearance of, 197
> disqualification of, 196–197
> not named, 195–196
> secondary, 196

benefit schedule, 148
billing statement, 243–244
binding premium receipt, *62*
biometric authentication, *36*
blended rating, 163
block of business, 206
blood chemistry profile, *91*
body mass index, 94
BPM. *See* business process management
BPM suites (BPMSs), 31
branch offices, for handling claims, 173
BRE. *See* business rules engine
B2B e-commerce. *See* business-to-business e-commerce
build, as underwriting factor, 94
build chart, 94
business
> financial assessment of, 129–134
> nature of, as group underwriting risk factor, 156

business-to-business (B2B) e-commerce, 234
business continuation insurance plan, *128*
business financial supplement, 129, *130*
business insurance (business life insurance), 127–140
> buy-sell agreements, 135–136
> creditor insurance, 138–140
> key-person life insurance, 136–140
> needs met by, *128*
> split-dollar life insurance plans, 138
> underwriting considerations for, 134–140

business process management (BPM), 31
business rules engine (BRE), 32, 33, 34, 45, 58
business valuation, 131–132
buy-sell agreements, *128*, 135–136

C

CAI. *See* Claims Activity Index
call centers, 261
Canada Pension Plan (CPP), 75
Canada regulatory requirements, group insurance, 75
capacity, managing, with indemnity reinsurance, 211
case, as reinsurance term, 206
case assignment system, 56–57, 173
case file, 46
case managers, 46
cash management, 27
cash surrender request form, *294*
catastrophe coverage (cat cover), 215
CDT (lab test for alcohol use), 101
ceding commission, 210
ceding company, 207
census, 150, *151*
centralized data repository (centralized database), 32, 35
certificate of coverage, 292
certificate holders. *See* group insureds
certificate of insurance, 23
cession, 212
> amounts of, in proportional reinsurance, 216–217
> arrangements for, 212–214

change in health statement, 191–192
charitable contributions, continuing, with life insurance proceeds, 113
chief underwriter, 54, *56*
churning, 70, 140, 273
civilian aviation, as underwriting factor, 102–103
Civil Rights Act of 1964, 74
claim adjusters. *See* claim analysts
claim administration, 25, 26, 168. *See also* claims
> claim evaluation process, 170, *171*, 184–200
> claim philosophy and practices, 168–169
> legal issues affecting, 174–181
> quality control in, 180–181
> staffing and organization, 170–174
> supplemental benefits, 200-203
> technology for, 181

claim analysts, 170, 172–173
> role of, in reinsurance, 233
> working with other functional areas, 173–174

claim committee, 175
claim evaluation process, 170, *171*, 184–200
claim examiners. *See* claim analysts
claim experience, 51
claim file, for reinsurance, 247–248
claim form, 170

R